ROCKY MOUNTAIN FLORA

Rocky Mountain

A field guide for the identification of the Ferns,

Southern Rocky Mountains

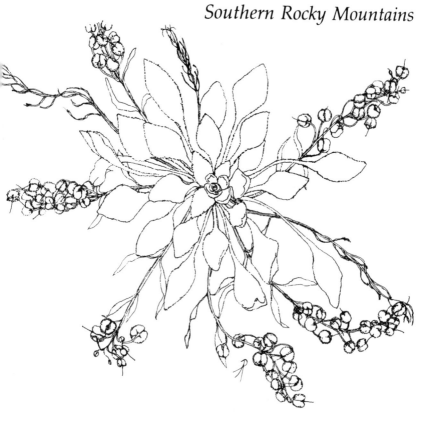

Flora

Conifers, and Flowering Plants of the
from Pikes Peak to Rocky Mountain National
Park and from the Plains to the Continental Divide

William A. Weber

PROFESSOR OF NATURAL HISTORY,
CURATOR OF THE HERBARIUM, UNIVERSITY OF COLORADO MUSEUM

Colorado Associated University Press

BOULDER, COLORADO

Library of Congress Card Number 67-15956
ISBN 87081–068-5

Rocky Mountain Flora is the fifth edition, revised, of the book originally published by the University of Colorado Press in August, 1953, under the title, *Handbook of Plants of the Colorado Front Range*.

Printed in the United States of America
Designed by Dave Comstock

Contents

The Illustrations

The principal illustrator is Dr. Charles F. Yocom, Professor of Wildlife Management at Humboldt State College, Arcata, California and a colleague of the author for many years. Dr. Yocom has illustrated numerous books dealing with the western biota, including his *Shrubs of Crater Lake National Park* (Crater Lake Nat. Hist. Assn.); Baker, Larrison, Yocom and Baxter, *Wildlife of the Northern Rocky Mountains;* and Yocom, Beidleman, Weber and Malick, *Wildlife and Plants of the Southern Rocky Mountains* (Naturegraph, Inc.). Additional illustrations for the present edition have been prepared by Ann Pappageorge of Loveland, Colorado. Mrs. Pappageorge's drawings are identifiable by her signature. Color plates are reproduced from the Kodachrome collection of the University of Colorado Museum. Photographers were the late Harold W. Roberts, Denver attorney, and the author.

Preface to the Fifth Edition

Over the thirty years since this book was first conceived, the Colorado Front Range has changed a great deal. Mountain homes, ski resorts, reclamation and flood-control dams, jeeping and snowmobiling have utterly transformed what once was relative wilderness. The idyllic rural piedmont valleys now constitute an "urban corridor", officially designated and irreversibly changed, stretching from Fort Collins to Colorado Springs. Much of the natural landscape has disappeared and along with it the native vegetation, particularly the natural wetlands and meadows. Highway construction, stripping of topsoil, gravel mining, excavation of mountain peat bogs for garden supplies, the exploitation of native ornamentals such as *Yucca*, cacti, even the lichens on the "moss-rocks," and grubbing of roots, foliage and bulbs by "survival" faddists and "natural food" enthusiasts is virtually raping our environment to an extent that was not dreamed of not long ago. This edition might be dedicated to the flora that I remember.

Urbanization and its attendant disturbance and soil depletion creates habitats for numbers of undesirable introduced weeds which have been latent in very small populations for many years, or have recently arrived with new crops, garden plants, or in pants-cuffs of travelers. As more land is disturbed, these plants often explode over large areas, threatening crops, livestock grazing, lawns and gardens, and producing unsightly botanical junkyards and fire hazards. Draining of the meadows, restriction of stream flow to artificial concrete-lined channels, and damming of natural waterways to form impounded, fluctuating-shoreline reservoirs in the mountain canyons is destroying habitats of many rare moisture-loving plants. The pressure of marching feet, tote-goats and motorcycles compacts the soil along trails and creates deserts even in the scenic parks and tundra. Horses penned on limited acreages without supplemental food supply remove every particle of vegetation on mountain slopes, creating severe erosion problems.

The accessibility of our area has decreased as well. Not long ago one could leave the road anywhere and roam the canyonsides and forests unchallenged. Now every gulch seems to have a house nestled in it, industrial firms have fenced off huge areas of prime botanizing country, and property is fenced and posted with No Trespassing signs. Abuse of the trespass privilege forces this on landowners, but with many it is the desperate search for privacy in a part of the country experiencing an extraordinary population growth. I deeply regret, for myself and for future amateur botanists, that this has happened here.

At the same time I am gratified to find that, because of the availability of this book, a fair group of knowledgeable amateur botanists has developed in Colorado who were conspicuous by their absence thirty years ago. Mountain home-owners are interested in the vegetation on their properties, there is much interest in re-establishing natural vegetation on disturbed land, and botany has become a legitimate leisure-time avocation along with ornithology and rock-collecting. And I am convinced that we now have enough botanical expertise scattered through the region to guarantee more intelligent use of our natural botanical heritage in the future.

I had not made a full-scale revision of this book since 1953 because the funds available permitted only minor corrections. In the meantime I have learned more about the flora and have come to my own conclusions concerning generic and specific concepts that I accepted at first on authority. The most cogent single observation I can make about our local flora is that it is among the least insular of any in the contiguous United States because the Rocky Mountain Chain connects our region to the American Arctic and Eastern Asia and it undoubtedly has been a migration route for plants since Tertiary times. Therefore the taxonomy of our local flora has to be considered in the light of research involving the related floras of all the northern regions of the world.

When I first assembled this material, the intimate relationship of our flora with that of the larger Holarctic area was only beginning to be appreciated. Since that time I have had the opportunity of doing field work in mountains and tundra in Europe, Australasia and South America, and specialists from these regions have had the opportunity of visiting the Rocky Mountains. We have compared notes extensively. Scientists in the Soviet Union are deeply interested in the relationships between the Rockies and the Altai, for so many of our species are identical or very closely related to theirs. Unfortunately for us, some of our plants will have to be called by the names in use in Eurasia, since they have priority, and because more intensive research is going on in Eurasia on the mountain floras than here in the United States.

To accept the concepts of the Eurasian botanists is often to run counter to deeply ingrained American tradition, particularly as to generic concepts. In this edition I am reflecting many of these new trends. It is interesting to note that more often than not this means returning to generic concepts proposed earlier by Rydberg and Greene, whose narrower generic concepts are being validated by modern biosystematic research.

In this edition I have added species that have been discovered recently, rewritten many of the keys, adjusted my observations on the ecology, and added many new illustrations. To make the text more generally readable I introduce each family with a paragraph of interesting facts, and I indicate some sources for further reading.

I am deeply grateful to my students and colleagues everywhere who have drawn my attention to errors and omissions and who have suggested ways in which the book might be improved.

My deepest gratitude goes to Barry Johnston, Myra Klockenbrink and Peggy Finucane, who during my absence in the Galapagos Islands shepherded the manuscript from galley through page proofs and prepared the index, and to Miriam Colson, for her excellent revision of the treatment of *Carex*.

Introduction

The Front Range of Colorado is one of America's most famous and spectacular summer playgrounds. Thousands of people from all over the nation visit our Rocky Mountains each year to enjoy the scenery and the many types of recreational activities which the region provides. Not among the least of the scenic attractions to be found here are the lavish displays of wild flowers in the mountain meadows and alpine heights, the vast expanses of cool, green forested lands, the brilliant splashes of autumn color of our aspens and sumacs, and the endless rolling grasslands of the eastern plains. There are very few places in the United States where so many types of vegetation are crowded into such a relatively small area, and where in the space of a few minutes time one may alternately bake in the climate of the desert, and shiver in the climate of the far north.

Why learn about a flora? In a modern society, the increase of leisure time suggests an obvious answer—the development of an interesting hobby. If this were the only reason, the study would be justified, but there are more important considerations. In children the study of a flora sharpens the eye, enlarges the horizon, and provides solid training in the use of the mind in making sound decisions based on careful observation. Adults may benefit from this training also. On a higher plane, the development of a conservation-minded public needs to be accompanied by a preparation of the mind adequate to interpret and justify the esthetic groping of the senses. For the preservation of the landscape, beautification of highways, control of grazing and prevention of projects which may tend to destroy more values than they create, the natural landscape must be understood in detail. Forests must be seen as assemblages of timber trees and weed species, grasses as edible forage types or noxious weeds. The average person is too prone to see the forest as a green blur or a weed-patch as a waving field of verdure. Intelligent and effective conservation demands that we develop a body of citizens who know the intimate facts about the living environment. This book attempts to open some windows onto this environment.

Learning to recognize the plants is a first, faltering step toward understanding a flora. Endless vistas of opportunity to study emerge as one becomes aware that we really know little about our flora beyond the identity of the species. Their life histories, uses, migrations, significance to aboriginal cultures, and so on, are largely uncharted. Amateurs can find much satisfaction and may make real contributions to science by delving deeply into some small area of the field. In Great Britain and elsewhere the amateur has always been in the forefront of biological science. Darwin and Mendel were distinguished amateurs. More Americans should join their company.

Rocky Mountain Flora

This book is the spiritual descendant of several, of which there is room here only to mention those dealing specifically with the Front Range area. In 1898, Alice Eastwood, then a teacher of classics in the Denver High Schools, published in paperback, *A Popular Flora of Denver, Colorado,* later (1900) expanding her work into the *Key and Flora, Part II. Rocky Mountain Edition of Bergen's Botany.* Alice Eastwood went on to become the director of the herbarium of California Academy of Sciences and the most renowned woman botanist of her generation.

It is fitting, in a book especially designed for the amateur botanist, to be able to record the fact that the first comprehensive flora of the Front Range was written by an amateur. Francis Potter Daniels, Professor of the Romance Languages, Wabash College, in 1911 published *The Flora of Boulder, Colorado, and Vicinity.* Although it contained no keys, it is extremely important for its careful documentation of the collections then available.

Another important amateur contribution to our flora was Ruth Ashton Nelson's *Plants of Rocky Mountain National Park,* first published in 1933. This has had subsequent reprintings and is very useful in the Park area. Walter Pesman, still another amateur, produced several editions of *Meet The Natives* in which he used different colored pages for easy reference to the respective flowers. Harold D. Roberts, an esteemed Denver attorney, provided the remarkable color slides which went into three pamphlets on *Rocky Mountain Flowers.* And John D. Long, a prominent Denver ophthalmological surgeon, has recently written *Native Orchids of Colorado.* This is an impressive record of solid botanical contributions on the part of dedicated amateurs. May there be more of them!

On the other hand, probably no other region in America was graced by the visits of such an illustrious number of the great men of American and European botany, although they came to see and collect rather than to write comprehensive manuals for this area. Asa Gray, Sir Joseph Dalton Hooker, John Torrey, George Engelmann, Edward Lee Greene, Ira Clokey, C. C. Parry, Edwin James, Marcus Jones, William Trelease, Alfred Russel Wallace, G. E. du Rietz, and Adolph Engler, visited the region and explored it in depth. Some of our highest peaks commemorate their contributions—James, Gray, Parry, Torrey, and Engelmann. Many fundamental and long-enduring notions of plant geography were gained from excursions in these hills.

THE FRONT RANGE

The term "Front Range" as it will be used in this book applies to the first rugged chain of mountains which the traveller sees when he approaches Denver from the East. Rocky Mountain National Park and Pikes Peak mark the approximate northern and southern limits, respectively; the Continental Divide marks the western limit from Longs Peak to James Peak; and a line connecting the summits of James Peak and Mount Evans, and extending southward toward Pikes Peak, marks the western limit in the southern part. The area covered by this book includes the entire range of altitude, 1,500 to over 4,000 meters, from the western margin of the Great Plains to the Continental Divide. The map of Colorado (Fig. 1) shows in black the area specifically covered by this book. The map also shows, in gray, the other mountainous areas in which the book may be used to good advantage because of a general similarity of the flora. Approximately 1,600 species, or over one half of the total number found in Colorado, occur in the Front Range.

PLANT ZONES IN THE FRONT RANGE

In order to keep this handbook small enough to carried into the field, I have omitted a detailed description of each species. In partial compensation for this omission, however, I have added to the text certain remarks concerning flower color,

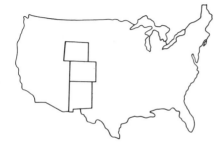

■ Area specifically covered by this book.

▨ Area with generally similar flora.

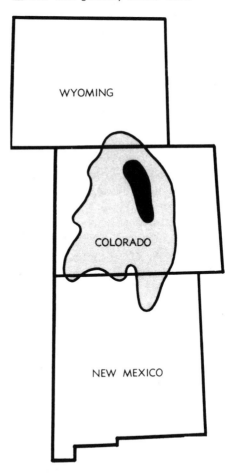

WYOMING

COLORADO

NEW MEXICO

Fig. 1. Map of region

relative abundance, habitat, altitudinal range, and so on. It is fortunate for us that, as a rule, two closely related species seldom are found growing together; therefore if we know which of the two such species is more likely to grow in a particular zone or habitat, our task of identification is that much easier.

The late Professor Francis Ramaley, botanist at the University of Colorado, provided us with a simple and understandable classification of the plant communities of the Front Range as they are related to altitude. With a few modifications, this is outlined below:

Plains—altitude up to 1,750 meters. Level or rolling grassland, except for fringes of trees along the watercourses. Sand hills are frequent but mostly east of our area.

Piedmont Valleys—the irrigated valleys at the base of the mountains, mostly under cultivation, and possessing a varied weedy flora.

Mesas—table-lands or "benches" where the plains meet the foothills. Vegetation is transitional between the plains and foothills, mostly grassland with a scattering of ponderosa pine, and with shrubs on the north slopes.

Foothills—1,800 to 2,500 meters altitude. Scrub oak or mountain mahogany at lower elevations, ponderosa pine above, mixed with grassland; Douglas-fir in the north-facing ravines, and thickets of broad-leaved trees and shrubs along the streams.

Montane—2,500 to 2,700 meters altitude. Lodgepole pine, Engelmann and blue spruce, Douglas-fir, aspen, and some ponderosa pine. This zone is in many ways transitional between the foothills and subalpine.

Subalpine—2,700 to 3,400 meters altitude. Engelmann spruce, subalpine fir, and limber pine forests, interspersed with moist meadows, ponds, and bogs. Very rich in wild flowers.

Alpine Tundra—3,400 to above 4,000 meters altitude. Above timberline; no trees, mostly deep-rooted mat- and cushion-plants, dwarf willows, grasses, and sedges. The grassy slopes are usually referred to as alpine meadows, to distinguish these areas from the more rocky fell-fields or boulder-fields.

The zones listed above overlap and telescope into each other considerably. One zone will often be present on a south slope, and another will be found across the valley on the north slope at the same altitude. The zones merge into each other on the margins, and the plants which are characteristically found in one zone are sometimes found in favorable sites in the neighboring zone above or below. Occasionally, because of peculiarities of slope or exposure, the zones may be found in exactly the reverse position from that expected. These peculiarities make our region an interesting one, always full of surprises.

Plant Geography

Plants have been moving into and out of the Colorado Front Range ever since it was first lifted up, probably in the Pliocene Period. We have good reason to believe that some of the species have persisted in this area without much evolutionary change since the Oligocene Period. The Rocky Mountains have been at once a highway for migration and a barrier to migration. The area is an intricate mosaic of altitudes, slopes, exposures, microclimates and ecological gradients of all sorts and the distribution of plants mirrors this complexity.

Many of our species range all through the Rocky Mountains up into Canada and down the Sierra Nevada–Cascade Ranges as well. A significant number are circumpolar—occurring around the world in northern regions. A smaller but exciting group are Asiatic mountain genera or species, occurring in the Rocky Mountains and cropping up again in the mountains of Central Asia (Altai-Pamir). This group is hard to explain without postulating more or less continuous mountain chains connecting the regions during Tertiary times. A small group of species are evidently survivors of a very ancient Tertiary flora which existed over western North America but was eliminated or restricted to the Mexican highlands in recent times. Because of the similarity of climates, our introduced weeds tend to be natives of southeastern Europe and Asia Minor.

Along the Front Range, one of the most interesting elements in the flora is an Eastern North American group surviving from Pleistocene times when the eastern woodland-prairie flora pressed westward and contacted the Rocky Mountain flora along the river-drainages. In the Black Hills of South Dakota this mixture is still apparent, but in Colorado the eastern species are restricted to a few moist sites on the base of the mountain front. A small group of genera and species are endemic in this area, that is, found nowhere else in the world. This subject is treated in detail in another place (Weber, 1965). A brief list of examples of these distribution types is given below.

Rocky Mountain: *Acer glabrum, Alnus tenuifolia, Holodiscus dumosus, Pedicularis groenlandica, Picea engelmannii, Populus angustifolia, Shepherdia canadensis, Trifolium parryi.*

Asiatic: *Acomastylis, Avenochloa, Bistorta, Ciminalis, Eritrichum, Gentianodes, Helictotrichon, Leucopoa, Ligularia.*

Tertiary relicts: *Asplenium adiantum-nigrum, A. septentrionale, Mahonia repens, Dryopteris filix-mas, Selaginella weatherbiana, Jamesia americana, Humulus lupulus* var. *americanus, Smilax lasioneuron, Pachystima myrsinites, Pinus aristata, Rubus deliciosus.*

Eastern woodland-prairie: *Aralia nudicaulis, Betula papyrifera, Carex sprengelii, Corylus cornuta, Lilium philadelphicum, Aster ptarmicoides, Impatiens capensis, Lactuca canadensis, Lobelia siphilitica, Pedicularis canadensis, Prenanthes racemosa.*

Circumboreal: *Adoxa moschatellina, Koenigia islandica, Phippsia algida, Lloydia serotina, Menyanthes trifoliata, Oxyria digyna, Poa alpina, Polystichum lonchitis.*

SE Europe–Asia Minor weeds: *Alyssum minus, Carduus nutans, Centaurea diffusa, Kochia iranica, Salsola collina, Linaria dalmatica, Onopordum acanthium, Salvia aethiopis, Tamarix pentandra.*

Local endemics: *Aletes anisatus, Aquilegia saximontana, Artemisia pattersonii, Aster porteri, Chionophila jamesii, Cryptantha virgata, Draba crassa, Harbouria trachypleura, Physaria bellii, Penstemon virens, Primula parryi, Ranunculus adoneus.*

THREATENED AND ENDANGERED SPECIES

The Endangered Species Act of 1973 (Public Law 93-205, approved December 28, 1973) directed the Smithsonian Institution to prepare a list of endangered and threatened plant species, to review methods of adequately conserving these species, and to report the Institution's recommendations to the Congress. The Smithsonian report, House Document No. 94–51, Serial No. 94-A, 1975, is available from the U.S. Government Printing Office, Washington, D.C. *Endangered* species are those species of plants in danger of extinction throughout all or a significant portion of their ranges, through destruction of habitat, overexploitation, disease, grazing or even unknown reasons. Species occurring in very limited areas are considered endangered. *Threatened* species are those that are likely to become endangered within the foreseeable future. *Recently extinct* or *possibly extinct* species are listed if they have not been found after repeated search of the known areas of their occurrence.

In this edition I have tried to draw attention to those species that I consider threatened or endangered in Colorado, even if they happen to occur in other parts of the world. Their loss to Colorado should be prevented if at all possible.

The Smithsonian's report correctly emphasizes: "Preservation of rare species of plants requires the preservation and protection of the habitats upon which they depend for growth and reproduction. *In situ* perpetuation of sufficient populations of endangered and threatened plants is required to ensure their survival." Often the preservation of an area of critical habitats cannot be ensured without the protection of an extensive buffer zone around it.

The Rocky Mountain area is full of endangered species, and the pressure of development, grazing, coal, oil shale and other mining, highway-building, urbanization and recreational use of fragile habitats makes the Endangered Species concept one of our urgent legislative priorities. Developers speak of returning a developed area to equal or better productivity, but not in terms of returning the original ecosystem to the land. In the continental climate of the arid west this may never be possible. Yellow sweet-clover, "Foothills mix" and crested wheatgrass may provide a temporary green cover, but the recovery of the ecosystem is not something that can be accomplished by man, or by Nature, within a short time span.

How to Use the Keys

The dichotomous key has become the standard method for the identification of organisms and should need little introduction. It involves the presentation of successive pairs of choices, from which the reader arrives at a decision and then proceeds to the next choice (as indicated by the parenthetical number on the right) and the next until he arrives at the name of the organism. Keys are simply means by which one arrives at a tentative decision, which should be followed up by careful reading of a detailed description and examination of authentically named specimens and illustrations. In a field guide, the so-called "Excursion-flora" of the European, format makes this impossible. As a compromise, the keys are somewhat more detailed and notes are added concerning the habitat, altitudinal range, and special characteristics which serve to confirm the final decision.

Keys are made by fallible men and do not always work. Furthermore, one key-writer of note has pointed out that "if the presence of various small features is useful as a means of identifying some kinds of plants, then the absence of the same features must be equally useful in distinguishing other kinds. Persons using a key for identification seldom have any difficulty in recognizing the presence of a structural feature but often find it difficult to convince themselves of its absence. This is purely a matter of mental attitude and has nothing to do with the size and conspicuousness of the feature in question. Those who use this or any similar work should guard against this tendency." (Gleason 1952, page xxx).

The limitations of the author's experience and his foolhardiness in making statements of range and habitat should be warning to the reader that alpine species might be expected occasionally to occur at lower altitudes and *vice versa*. Plants with blue flowers frequently will throw white-flowered mutants. Low plants growing on a well-manured site may assume giant proportions. In such matters the reader is requested to bear with the author, for a definite statement subject to modification is often preferable to silence.

The keys presented here, save for those few which were completely rewritten for this edition, have been tested over more than twenty-five years and have proved satisfactory and workable for a variety of students ranging from professional botanists to grade-school children. The author will welcome suggestions for improvement in the keys as well as specimens of plants representing extensions of range or species new to the area.

GROWTH FORMS

In order to use the key intelligently, we must become familiar with some of the characteristic growth forms of plants. This takes some practice in keen observation. Take, for instance, the differences between annuals and perennials. It is easy to find a book-definition which states that an Annual is a plant which lives for one season, blossoms, and then dies, or that a Perennial is a plant which lives for an indefinite number of years. It is not so easy to point to a plant and say, "This is a perennial." People who keep gardens learn to do this with experience because the growth form of plants has a great deal to do with their performance in the garden. Here are a few hints about growth forms.

TREES, SHRUBS, AND HERBS

Trees—woody plants, usually over 5 meters tall, with one main stem.

Shrubs—woody plants, usually less than 7 meters tall, with several more or less equal main stems.

Herbs—non-woody plants (plants having slightly woody bases are called "sub-shrubs").

ANNUALS, BIENNIALS, AND PERENNIALS

Annuals—never woody; reproduce by seed each year; develop within a few weeks' or months' time. Annuals usually have rather weak root systems (never have rhizomes, bulbs, or corms) and are easily pulled out of the ground intact.

Biennials—not woody; first year's growth is a cluster (rosette) of leaves at the surface of the ground; no flower stalk the first year; flower and die the second year; usually have a stout, carrot-like taproot. Flowering specimens may be recognized by the remnants of the withered cluster of last year's leaves at the summit of the taproot. Carrots, turnips, and the like are good examples of biennials.

Perennials—either woody or herbaceous; have a well-developed root-system or some means (bulbs, corms, rhizomes) of carrying the plant over the winter; usually hard to pull out of the ground without breaking off some of the roots; easily recognized when remnants of the previous year's growth (old leaves, stems, flower stalks) are present.

FERNS, GYMNOSPERMS, AND ANGIOSPERMS

Many times, members of the carrot family and sunflower family are mistaken for ferns because of the fern-like character of their leaves. Since the first choices in the key (page 25) call for distinguishing between the three great groups of higher plants, a few hints may be in order concerning these misleading individuals.

Ferns—Ferns never have flowers. Thus, any plant that has a flower must never be mistaken for a fern. The flowering plants which are most commonly mistaken for ferns are almost all in the Carrot Family (Umbelliferae) and Sunflower Family (Compositae). Most of these have leaves which give off a strong odor when they are crushed. Ferns sometimes smell faintly like hay but never smell like anise, carrot, or parsley. Most fern leaves arise directly from a horizontal rhizome just below the surface of the ground. Most flowering plants which have fern-like leaves have the leaves arising from an erect stem or from a fleshy taproot.

Gymnosperms and Angiosperms—The seed plants are divided into two main groups, called gymnosperms (meaning "naked seed") and angiosperms (meaning "covered seed"). The gymnosperms include our common evergreen trees such as pines, spruces, firs, and junipers. Only one species in our area, the common juniper, is shrubby. Mormon Tea (*Ephedra*) is also shrubby, but it does not occur in our range.

Gymnosperms produce their seeds on the open faces of scales which make up the cone, and the seeds are shed simply by the separating of the cone scales when the cone becomes mature. In the angiosperms, or flowering plants, the seeds are always confined within an ovary, as in apples, peas, peanuts, and so forth.

FLOWERS

A simple chart of flower parts is shown below (Fig. 2). It presents the minimum knowledge needed in the use of the keys.

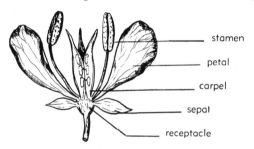

stamen

petal

carpel

sepal

receptacle

FIG. 2. Parts of a flower

Class of organs	Individual name	Collective name
Floral envelope (perianth, or accessory organs)	sepal	calyx
	petal	corolla
Essential organs	stamen	androecium
	carpel	gynoecium
Floral axis	receptacle	————————

The other terms used in this book are explained or illustrated in the Illustrated Glossary, page 449, or at appropriate places in the text.

Here are some simple answers to a few of the questions that come up most often in using the keys.

How Many Carpels Are There?

When the gynoecium consists of more than one separate unit (carpel), all we have to do is count the units. Thus in buttercup (Fig. 3) there are a great number of carpels; in larkspur (Fig. 4) there are usually three. However, when the carpels are

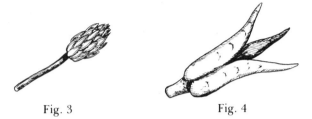

Fig. 3   Fig. 4

fused into a single unit, it is more difficult to decide. Here are a few rules of thumb. None of these are a hundred percent reliable, but they should help in most instances.

1. There are usually as many carpels as there are stigmas or branches of the style (Fig. 5).

2. There are usually as many carpels as there are locules ("cells," or compartments of the ovary). To see this, make a cross-section with a pocket-knife or razor-blade. Try to find a large ovary for this (Fig. 6).

3. There are usually as many carpels as there are *parietal placentae* (if the plant has this type of placentation). Plants with parietal placentation have the ovules attached to the side walls of the ovary (Fig. 7).

Fig. 5

Fig. 6   Fig. 7

Is the Ovary Superior or Inferior? Is There an Hypanthium?

A plant with a superior ovary has the petals, sepals, and stamens attached below the ovary or at the base of it, and not fused to the side of it. The floral parts may surround the ovary in any way, but as long as they are not fused to it, the ovary is superior (Fig. 8).

If the ovary is inferior, the floral parts are fused to it, or the ovary itself is embedded in the floral axis so that the floral parts appear to be attached to the top of the ovary. The ovary cannot be removed in one piece without tearing the tissues in which it is imbedded (Fig. 9).

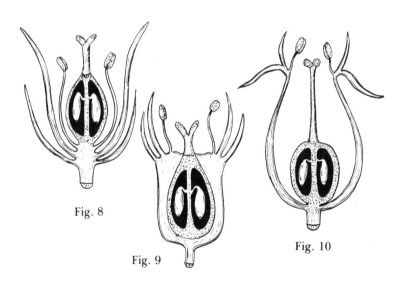

Fig. 8

Fig. 9

Fig. 10

An hypanthium (Fig. 10) is a structure which forms a cup around the gynoecium. It may consist of the fused bases of the stamens, petals, and sepals, but usually looks like a green calyx-cup, with the petals and stamens mounted on the rim. A tubular corolla, with the stamens attached to it, should not be confused with an hypanthium.

LEAVES

When Is a Leaf Simple and When Is It Compound?

A compound leaf is one which is divided into a few or several separate leaflets. Since the leaflets themselves resemble leaves, students sometimes have trouble deciding where a leaf ends and a leaflet begins. Here are some rules of thumb:

1. In most plants a bud is always present where the leaf

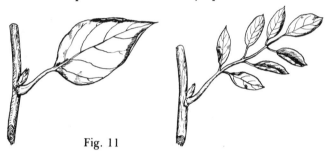

Fig. 11

joins the stem (Fig. 11). There are no buds where the leaflets join the common leaf-stalk (rachis).

2. In woody plants, and in many non-woody plants, the leaf-stalk (petiole) has a different color or texture than that of the stem to which it is attached; there is usually hardly any difference or demarcation between the stalks of leaflets and the main leaf rachis.

How to Make a Plant Collection

An herbarium, or collection of dried and pressed plants, is very useful as an aid to remembering the plants you have already named, and as a reference whereby you can check your "unknowns" against the plants you already know. A collection of carefully named and preserved plants is better for these purposes than the best description or picture you might find.

In order to make a plant collection, there are a few things which everyone should have. These are:

1. Some sort of digging tool (a trowel, prospector's pick, or weed digger) and a good sharp knife for cutting twigs.

2. A good stock of old newspapers, torn along the main fold so as to make single sheets folded once into 12 × 18-inch (30 × 40 cm) folders.

3. At least 100 blotters, 12 × 18 inches. These can be bought at any biological supply house.

4. Two flat frames of wood, either solid or constructed as a lattice from slats, to measure 12 × 18 inches.

5. Two lengths of rope or trunk straps for tying the press together.

The above list includes the minimum equipment. If you forage around in areas where it is inconvenient to carry the press along with you, you may want to invest in a collecting can, or vasculum, which can be carried over your shoulder, and which will keep plants fresh for several hours or days, until you are ready to press them. This and most of the other equipment mentioned here may be obtained at biological supply houses, some of which are listed on page 17. Plastic bags are available at food lockers, and they keep specimens fresh for several days.

The technique of plant collecting is very simple. Quality varies with the fastidiousness of the collector. The plant is picked, cut, or dug, and is placed in a newspaper folder, with care being used to clean off any adhering soil and to arrange the plant in the way you wish it to appear when dry. If you wish to have the best results with delicate flowers, place a few thicknesses of soft absorbent paper between the flower and the newspaper. If the plant is too large to fit in the folder it may be folded or cut in two. A good rule is this: either collect the entire plant, including the root system, or take notes on the size of the plant, the kind of root system, and so on. Any notes that might help in identification later on, such as flower color, habitat, altitude, and so on should be taken when the plant is collected. Do not leave it to memory.

Next, place the newspaper folder, with the plant in it, between two blotters. Put the blotters between the wooden frames and tie the press together, applying as much pressure as you can. Put the press in the sun to dry. After a day in the press, the plants will have given up much of their moisture to the blotters, which will be quite damp. Open the press and remove the wet blotters, replacing them with dry ones. Do not disturb the plants inside the newspapers. Repeat this process every few days until the plants are dry, that is, until the newspapers no longer feel damp, or until a leaf will crack when it is bent. Some of us like to hasten the drying process along by using corrugated cardboard in addition to or in place of the blotters as the plants become dry, or by placing the press over heat. In general, the more rapid the drying, the more natural the plants will appear. When the plants are dry, they are removed from the press, and may be stored indefinitely in the newspaper folders. Care should be taken to prevent careless handling of them.

The pressing does not destroy any of the features of the living plant except that many flowers fade or change color in drying. In other words, plants may be examined for details long after they have been pressed. Flowers and leaves are softened by dipping them for a second or two into boiling water. Thus we can collect and store plants throughout the summer and postpone the job of identification for some long winter evening.

A collection is worth a great deal more when it is carefully labelled. A good rule in labelling is to include enough information on a label to enable a person to return to the same spot at some future date and find the plant again. Thus the minimum should include the state and county in which the plant was found, and the distance and direction from the nearest town. It is very desirable to take notes on certain other things, such as the date, altitude or habitat, and notes as to the features of the plant itself. A sample label is shown below (Fig. 12). It is wise to keep a notebook for this purpose which can be carried along in the field. Each plant should be given a number, written on the newspaper sheet with a china marking pencil, to correspond with a number in the notebook. Only one kind of plant should be pressed in a single newspaper folder. If the notebook is too much bother, a slip of paper, inserted in the folder with the plant, will do. Because of the eventual cracking and tearing of the sheet, it is advisable not to make notes on the margin of the newsprint.

COLORADO, U. S. A.

MENTZELIA MULTICAULIS (Osterh.) Goodman   LOA

SUMMIT CO.: on black shale of Pierre Formation, steep slopes along east side of Green Mountain Reservoir 21 km S of Kremmling, 2,400 m s m ; plants 3-4 dm high, branched from the base; flowers chrome yellow

16 Aug. 1975   W. A. Weber & B. Johnston 15144

Herbarium of the University of Colorado
Boulder

Fig. 12 Sample label

SOURCES FOR HERBARIUM SUPPLIES

Cambosco Scientific Company
    37 Antwerp Street, Brighton Station, Boston, Massachusetts 02135
Carpenter/Offut Paper, Inc.,
    P.O. Box 3333, San Francisco, California 94080
General Biological Supply House
    761-763 Sixty-ninth Place, Chicago, Illinois 60607

How Plants are Named

The scientific name is the one name by which all people, laymen as well as scientists, regardless of their nationality or language, can refer to and talk about a particular kind of plant. Each species, or kind, of plant has one scientific name, and no two species can have the same scientific name. A scientific name is constructed according to the rules of Latin grammar because Latin has been chosen as the international language of biologists.

Every species belongs to a genus (plural, genera), which is a group of closely related species. Every genus belongs to a family. Every family belongs to an order, and every order belongs to a class, every class to a subdivision, every subdivision to a division, and every division to a kingdom. All of these categories, likewise, have Latin names. The complete classification of one of our common wild flowers, for example, the pasque-flower, would read as follows:

> Species: *Pulsatilla patens*
> Genus: *Pulsatilla*
> Family: Ranunculaceae
> Order: Ranales
> Class: Dicotyledoneae
> Subdivision: Angiospermae
> Division: Spermatophyta
> Kingdom: Plantae

Fortunately, it is not necessary to recite this entire classification each time we mention the pasque-flower. We simply say *"Pulsa-*

tilla patens," and the rest is taken for granted. Species are sub-divided further into subspecies or varieties, but for the most part the species is the most readily recognized category within the genus.

Botanists do not consider a scientific name complete unless it includes, in addition to the generic and specific designations, the name of the botanist who is responsible for the specific name as it is used at the present time (Example, *Betula occidentalis* Hooker). Complete information about the rather complicated business of naming plants may be found in some of the textbooks of systematic botany listed on page 466.

ORIGINS OF THE SPECIFIC NAMES

Whenever the meaning of the specific epithet is not self-evident, the approximate meaning or derivation is given in parentheses following the citation. Unfortunately, it is not possible here to give biographical details about the men for whom many of our species were named. Parry, Engelmann, Rydberg, James, Fendler and Hall, for example, were the early collectors of this flora. Other names are those of early explorers, famous botanists or even patrons of the science. Searching out the historical details can be an absorbing study. Fortunately, almost all of the needed information may be found in two books (Ewan, J. *Rocky Mountain Naturalists,* and McKelvey, S.D. *Botanical Exploration of the Trans-Mississippi West, 1790-1850),* cited in full on page 467. For a very interesting account of Linnaeus' reasons for selecting certain generic names, see his *Critica Botanica,* available in English translation.

COMMON NAMES

Common names for the plants listed in the text are given whenever one is available. However, a great many plants of the region do not have any common names. This is partly because the Rocky Mountain West still is a cultural frontier and our people have not lived with the plants long enough to make them topics of everyday conversation. Most of the common names which are used for Rocky Mountain plants did not originate here but were brought in by visitors from the East who recognized in our flora some old friends from their home states. Another reason why some species do not have common names is that several closely related species may be so similar to each other that one common name will suffice for all of them.

Many so-called "common" names are merely translations of the scientific name and have never enjoyed general use; some of them never will. A few names like "kinnikinnik" (for *Arcto-staphylos uva-ursi*) and "yampa" (for *Perideridia gairdneri*) were used by Indians of the region, and these, in my estimation, would be good names to try to preserve. The best common names are those which originate in the imaginations of the people who must use them.

Some acceptable common names originate logically from a translation of the specific name, especially when that name is a descriptive one. In order to help students who are interested in the meanings of the scientific names, I have added the approximate English meaning for almost every species treated in this book.

I would urge wild flower lovers not to worry about the fact that different common names are used for the same plants in different regions, and *vice versa*. "Kinnikinnik," for example, means *Arctostaphylos uva-ursi* in Colorado; in Canada it means *Amelanchier*; the Indians used the name for almost any plant whose leaves were used for pipe-tobacco. On the other hand, *Arctostaphylos uva-ursi,* our "Kinnikinnik," is called "mountain-box," "universe-vine," "rapper-dandies," "barren-myrtle," and "hog-crawberry," depending on the locality. In Europe and Asia, where the same plant is widespread, thousands of other common names doubtless are used. The use of common names for plants is a distinctive part of the human culture of a region, and I believe it is a mistake for us to try to standardize these names in any way. We already have one standard system, the scientific name, by which plants are identified the world over, and this seems to be enough for all practical purposes.

ARRANGEMENT OF THE FAMILIES AND TREATMENT OF SUBSPECIFIC CATEGORIES

This book is arranged alphabetically by families within the larger sections of the flowering plants—the dicots and the monocots. This arrangement is heretical in botanical circles, but it was arrived at by a frank appraisal of the purpose of the book. We are not teaching the reader a system of classification here;

that is the function of the general taxonomy textbook. On the contrary, our intent is to provide the best and most convenient method for identifying the species, and for this the alphabet is the best data-retrieval method yet devised. The alphabetical arrangement allows the taxonomist to keep his notions of relationship fluid, and makes the book more useful to non-specialists of all degrees of sophistication.

The subdivision of species into races follows the descending sequence: *subspecies* (ssp.), *variety* (var.), *forma* (f.). Although the variety should be a subdivision of the subspecies, historically the categories were often interchangeable depending upon the botanist. We see no great value in changing all published varieties to subspecies without proper investigation or simply for the sake of uniformity; therefore, both categories occur in the text. A *forma* is a sporadic mutant occurring in a population of the normal type.

Key To The Families

Plate 1. *Harbouria trachypleura*   Weber
WHISK BROOM PARSLEY

Plate 2. *Pachystima myrsinites*   Weber
MOUNTAIN-LOVER

Plate 3. *Shepherdia canadensis*   Weber
BUFFALO BERRY

Plate 4. *Coryphantha missouriensis*   Weber
NIPPLE CACTUS

Plate 5. *Arceuthobium campylopodum*   Weber
MISTLETOE

Plate 6. *Rumex venosus*   Roberts
WILD "BEGONIA"

Plate 7. *Pulsatilla patens*
PASQUE FLOWER

Roberts

Plate 8. *Lilium philadelphicum*
WOOD LILY

Roberts

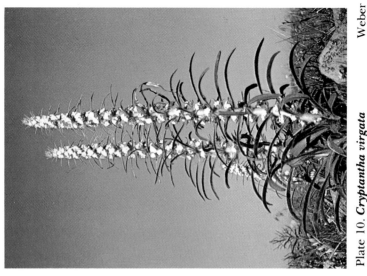

Plate 9. *Eustoma grandiflorum*   Roberts
TULIP GENTIAN

Plate 10. *Cryptantha virgata*   Weber
MINERS CANDLE

Plate 11. *Chimaphila umbellata*   Roberts
PIPSISSEWA

Plate 12. *Gentianopsis thermalis*   Roberts
FRINGED GENTIAN

Plate 14. *Mentzelia decapetala*
EVENING STAR

Roberts

Plate 13. *Frasera speciosa*
MONUMENT PLANT

Roberts

Plate 15. *Leucocrinum montanum*   Weber
SAND LILY

Plate 16. *Toxicodendron rydbergii*   Weber
POISON IVY, fruit

Key to the Families

1a. Plants not producing seeds or true flowers, but reproducing by spores; fern-like, moss-like, rush-like plants. DIVISION PTERID-OPHYTA, FERNS AND FERN ALLIES, page 49.

1b. Plants producing seeds, either by means of flowers or cones; plants of various aspects (DIVISION SPERMATOPHYTA, SEED PLANTS) .... (2)

2a. Leaves needle-like or scale-like, not falling in autumn; evergreen trees and shrubs, never with flowers; ovules and seeds not borne in a closed cavity, but borne instead on the open face of a scale or bract (rarely the cone becomes a fleshy "berry," in *Juniperus*). SUBDIVISION GYMNOSPERMAE. PINE FAMILY, page 64.

2b. Leaves various, but seldom needle-like or scale-like (if so, flowers present), rarely evergreen; ovules and seeds borne in a closed cavity (ovary). (SUBDIVISION ANGIOSPERMAE. FLOWERING PLANTS) .... (3)

3a. Plants either parasitic or saprophytic, often highly colored but not green (mistletoe, in this category, usually has some chlorophyll but is quite yellowish in color), KEY A, page 26.

3b. Plants not parasitic, or at least having green leaves .... (4)

4a. Stems thick and succulent, spiny; true leaves absent or greatly reduced and early deciduous. CACTACEAE, CACTUS FAMILY, page 89.

4b. Plants not as above .... (5)

5a. Submerged aquatics, with or without floating leaves, KEY B, page 26.

5b. Terrestrial or semiaquatic, not wholly submerged nor with floating leaves .... (6)

6a. Vines, climbing or twining among other plants, often possessing suckers or tendrils, not merely creeping along the ground, KEY C, page 28.

6b. Herbaceous or woody plants, not vines .... (7)

25

7a. Leaves usually parallel-veined; flower parts usually in threes; stem hollow or with scattered vascular bundles; herbaceous (except **Yucca**); seeds usually with only one cotyledon. CLASS MONOCOTYLEDONEAE, MONOCOTS, KEY D, page 29.

7b. Leaves usually netted-veined; flower parts in fives, fours, or twos; stems with vascular bundles arranged in a ring around the pith; herbaceous or woody; seeds usually with two cotyledons (CLASS DICOTYLEDONEAE, DICOTS) . . . . (8)

8a. Trees or shrubs, KEY E, page 31.

8b. Herbaceous plants, sometimes woody at the very base, KEY F, page 34.

KEY A (PARASITES)

1a. Plants attached to the bark of trees, or attached by suckers to the aerial stems of herbaceous plants . . . . (2)

1b. Plants without obvious attachments to the aerial parts of their hosts . . . . (3)

2a. Plants attached to the trunks or branches of evergreen trees. VISCACEAE, DWARF MISTLETOE FAMILY, page 357.

2b. Plants thread-like, orange or yellow, attached by suckers to the aerial parts of herbaceous plants. **Cuscuta**, in CONVOLVULACEAE, MORNING-GLORY FAMILY, page 172.

3a. Flowers zygomorphic or irregular . . . . (4)

3b. Flowers actinomorphic or regular, arranged in a long raceme. **Pterospora**, in ERICACEAE, HEATH FAMILY, page 196.

4a. Flowers tubular, the petals united; ovary superior. OROBANCHACEAE, BROOM-RAPE FAMILY, page 248.

4b. Flowers with separate petals; ovary inferior, often spirally twisted. **Corallorhiza**, in ORCHIDACEAE, ORCHID FAMILY, page 437.

KEY B (AQUATICS)

1a. Plants disk-shaped or thallus-like, without true stems and leaves; free-floating or submerged. LEMNACEAE, DUCKWEED FAMILY, page 432.

1b. Plants with stems and leaves, not thallus-like nor free-floating. . . . . (2)

2a. Stems short or lacking, the leaves attached to the bottom, elongate-linear, the tips floating on the surface. SPARGANIACEAE, BUR-REED FAMILY, page 446.

2b. Plants with definite stems . . . . (3)

3a. Leaves simple, entire .... (4)
3b. Leaves distinctly lobed or finely dissected .... (15)

4a. Leaves linear or oblong, arranged in whorls .... (5)
4b. Leaves variously shaped, not in whorls. .... (6)

5a. Leaves translucent, lax, two cell layers thick; flowers, if present, sessile or on long pedicels. HYDROCHARITACEAE, FROG-BIT FAMILY, page 425.
5b. Leaves opaque, rather rigid unless submerged, more than two cell layers thick; flowers in a terminal spike. HIPPURIDACEAE, page 214.

6a. Leaves almost orbicular, deeply cordate, very thick and leathery; flowers large, yellow, solitary. NYMPHAEACEAE, WATER-LILY FAMILY, page 242.
6b. Leaves narrower, not cordate; flowers not as above .... (7)

7a. Leaves linear or filiform .... (8)
7b. Leaves with distinctly broadened blades .... (12)

8a. Flowers in spikes. POTAMOGETONACEAE, PONDWEED FAMILY, page 443.
8b. Flowers sessile in the leaf axils or on slender, often coiled pedicels .... (9)

9a. Fruit minute, blackish, on an elongate, often coiled peduncle; leaves filiform, over 3 cm long. RUPPIACEAE, page 446.
9b. Flowers and fruits sessile in the leaf axils; leaves shorter ..... (10)

10a. Fruits rounded or emarginate, oblong or wider, not beaked. CALLITRICHACEAE, WATER-STARWORT FAMILY, page 91.
10b. Fruits narrowly cylindric, tapered to a beak .... (11)

11a. Fruits flattened, slightly curved, with a stout beak; leaves filiform. ZANNICHELLIACEAE, page 447.
11b. Fruits terete, straight, the beak whitish, not rigid; leaves linear, flat, the margins very finely toothed (under high magnification). NAJADACEAE, page 436.

12a. Leaves alternate, at least 1 cm long; flowers not sessile in the leaf axils .... (13)
12b. Leaves opposite, less than 1 cm long; flowers inconspicuous, sessile in the leaf axils .... (14)

13a. Floating leaves pinnately veined; flowers pink, with showy perianth parts. *Persicaria*, in POLYGONACEAE, BUCKWHEAT FAMILY, page 264.

13b. Floating leaves with parallel veins, or floating leaves absent; flowers greenish, not showy. POTAMOGETONACEAE, PONDWEED FAMILY, page 443.

14a. Stipules lacking; calyx and corolla absent; ovary 4-locular; floating and submerged leaves often strikingly different in shape. CALLITRICHACEAE, WATER-STARWORT FAMILY, page 91.
14b. Stipules present; calyx and corolla often present; ovary 3- or 5-locular; leaves not dimorphic. ELATINACEAE, page 195.

15a. Leaves bearing small bladder-like traps; flowers showy, yellow, spurred, on racemes projecting above water level. LENTIBULARIACEAE, BLADDERWORT FAMILY, page 233.
15b. Leaves not bearing bladders; flowers not spurred .... (16)

16a. Leaves in whorls; flowers greenish, inconspicuous .... (17)
16b. Leaves alternate; flowers with white or yellow petals. *Ranunculus*, in RANUNCULACEAE, BUTTERCUP FAMILY, page 279.

17a. Leaf divisions dichotomous, finely serrate; flowers sessile in the axils of normal leaves. CERATOPHYLLACEAE, HORNWORT FAMILY, page 111.
17b. Leaf divisions pinnate, entire; flowers in an interrupted terminal spike resembling a knotted cord. HALORAGACEAE, WATER MILFOIL FAMILY, page 213.

KEY C (VINES)

1a. Leaves with parallel veins, more or less cordate in outline; floral parts in threes or sixes. SMILACACEAE, SMILAX FAMILY, page 446.
1b. Leaves with netted veins; floral parts not in threes or sixes .... (2)

2a. Leaves simple .... (3)
2b. Leaves compound (*Caution! Poison ivy in this category*) .... (7)

3a. Leaves palmately lobed, sometimes only slightly so .... (4)
3b. Leaves not lobed .... (6)

4a. Plants with tendrils .... (5)
4b. Plants without tendrils. MORACEAE, MULBERRY FAMILY, page 240.

5a. Herbaceous plant; fruit a papery, spiny bur or a gourd. CUCURBITACEAE, CUCUMBER FAMILY, page 190.
5b. Woody plant; fruit a fleshy "grape." VITACEAE, GRAPE FAMILY, page 358.

6a. Flowers 1 cm long or more; petals united. CONVOLVULACEAE, MORNING-GLORY FAMILY, page 172.

6b. Flowers smaller; perianth parts separate. POLYGONACEAE, BUCK-WHEAT FAMILY, page 264.

7a. Leaves pinnately compound; flowers resembling those of sweet-pea. LEGUMINOSAE, PEA FAMILY, page 222.

7b. Leaves trifoliolate, palmately 5-7-foliolate, or ternately compound; flowers not as above .... (8)

8a. Leaves palmately 5-7-foliolate. *Parthenocissus*, in VITACEAE, GRAPE FAMILY, page 359.

8b. Leaves not as above .... (9)

9a. Leaves with three shiny leaflets; flowers greenish; plant short (scarcely a vine in this area), commonly bearing clusters of greenish-white berries. *Toxicodendron*, Poison Ivy, in ANACARDIACEAE, SUMAC FAMILY, page 73.

9b. Leaves twice ternately compound, or if 3-foliolate, the flowers blue or yellow, with conspicuous feathery styles when in fruit. *Clematis*, in RANUNCULACEAE, BUTTERCUP FAMILY, page 276.

KEY D (MONOCOTS)

1a. Woody plants with stiff evergreen dagger-like leaves and racemes or panicles of large white flowers, later large 3-locular pods. *Yucca*, in AGAVACEAE, page 360.

1b. Herbaceous plants .... (2)

2a. Tall fern-like plants, the true leaves minute, triangular, papery, subtending clusters of filiform green cladodes; flowers small, yellowish; fruit a red berry. ASPARAGACEAE, page 363.

2b. Plants not as above .... (3)

3a. Plants with broad cordate leaves, tendrils, and umbellate fruits and flowers. SMILACACEAE, page 446.

3b. Plants not as above .... (4)

4a. Flowers minute, enclosed in chaffy bracts; 3- or 6-parted perianth lacking; flowers arranged in spikes or spikelets (grasses and sedges) .... (5)

4b. Flowers not enclosed in chaffy bracts or scales; perianth usually present, with 3 or 6 parts which may themselves appear papery or chaffy .... (6)

5a. Leaves two-ranked (in two rows on the stem), the edges of their sheaths usually not fused together; stems cylindrical or flattened and almost always hollow; anthers attached to filaments at their middles. GRAMINEAE, GRASS FAMILY, page 385.

5b. Leaves three-ranked (in three rows on the stem), sometimes absent, the edges of their sheaths united; stems almost always triangular and solid (a few cylindrical and hollow); anthers attached at one end. CYPERACEAE, SEDGE FAMILY, page 364.

6a. Flowers with only a rudimentary perianth, sometimes consisting of bristles or scales .... (7)
6b. Flowers with sepals and petals (sometimes the two are similar in shape and texture) .... (9)

7a. Flowers in a thick spike protruding from the side of a 3-angled grass-like stem; stems with a sweet odor when crushed. *Acorus*, in ARACEAE, ARUM FAMILY, page 363.
7b. Flowers not as above; stems not triangular, not aromatic ..... (8)

8a. Flowers in elongate terminal spikes, the staminate flowers in a separate group above the brown carpellate part. TYPHACEAE, CAT-TAIL FAMILY, page 446.
8b. Flowers in spherical clusters. SPARGANIACEAE, BUR-REED FAMILY, page 446.

9a. Carpels numerous (over 6), separate and distinct, in a whorl or ball. ALISMATACEAE, WATER-PLANTAIN FAMILY, page 361.
9b. Carpels 3 or 6 .... (10)

10a. Carpels separate .... (11)
10b. Carpels united .... (12)

11a. Plant arising from a bulb; carpels united at the base but often appearing to be separate; perianth parts 4-10 mm long, petal-like. *Zigadenus*, in LILIACEAE, LILY FAMILY, page 435.
11b. Plant annual, or perennial from a rhizome; carpels separating as units at maturity; perianth parts small, greenish; grass-like plants of alkali flats or mountain bogs. JUNCAGINACEAE, ARROW-GRASS FAMILY, page 432.

12a. Ovary superior, the floral parts attached to the receptacle just below the ovary .... (13)
12b. Ovary inferior, the floral parts attached to the top of the ovary .... (18)

13a. Perianth of 6 chaffy or scale-like similar segments, hardly petal-like; grass-like plants. JUNCACEAE, RUSH FAMILY, page 425.
13b. Perianth segments petal- or sepal-like, not chaffy or scale-like .... (14)

14a. Semiaquatic herbs with fleshy, spatulate leaves; stamens 3, partly attached to the perianth, the 6 perianth parts all much alike. PONTEDERIACEAE, PICKEREL-WEED FAMILY, page 443.

14b. Terrestrial herbs, otherwise not quite as above .... (15)

15a. Outer and inner perianth segments strongly differentiated in color or size. .... (16)
15b. Outer and inner perianth segments similar .... (17)

16a. Sepals green; petals lavender; stamens yellow, the filaments with bead-jointed hairs. COMMELINACEAE, SPIDERWORT FAMILY, page 364.
16b. Sepals brownish; petals white or pinkish, with a basal colored glandular pad. *Calochortus*, in LILIACEAE, LILY FAMILY, page 434.

17a. Foliage with an onion or garlic odor when crushed; flowers in umbels and stem arising from a bulb. ALLIACEAE, ONION FAMILY, page 361.
17b. Foliage lacking a distinctive onion odor; plants otherwise not as above. LILIACEAE, LILY FAMILY, page 434.

18a. Flowers erect, radially symmetrical. IRIDACEAE, IRIS FAMILY, page 425.
18b. Flowers facing sideways, bilaterally symmetrical. ORCHIDACEAE, ORCHID FAMILY, page 437.

KEY E (WOODY DICOTS)

1a. Leaves very minute (less than 5 mm long), scale-like, overlapping and appressed to the stem. TAMARICACEAE, TAMARISK FAMILY, page 339.
1b. Leaves larger and otherwise not as above .... (2)

2a. Leaves opposite .... (3)
2b. Leaves alternate or scattered .... (12)

3a. Leaves palmately lobed or compound (*Acer negundo* sometimes has five leaflets, thus pinnate) .... (4)
3b. Leaves neither palmately lobed nor palmately compound .... (5)

4a. Fruit a samara; terminal bud blunt or merely acute, protected by overlapping scales. ACERACEAE, MAPLE FAMILY, page 70.
4b. Fruit a berry; terminal bud long-pointed, not protected by overlapping scales. *Viburnum*, in CAPRIFOLIACEAE, HONEYSUCKLE FAMILY, page 96.

5a. Leaves evergreen .... (6)
5b. Leaves deciduous .... (8)

6a. Leaves entire, pale on the underside. *Kalmia*, in ERICACEAE, HEATH FAMILY, page 197.

6b. Leaves serrulate or crenate, not noticeably paler beneath .... (7)

7a. Plant definitely woody, with stout spreading branchlets; leaves about twice as long as broad; flowers inconspicuous, sessile in the leaf axils. *Pachistima*, in CELASTRACEAE, page 62.

7b. Plant only slightly woody, very slender, trailing; leaves about as long as broad; flowers in pairs, on an erect stalk, *Linnaea*, in CAPRIFOLIACEAE, page 96.

8a. Leaves pinnately compound. OLEACEAE, OLIVE FAMILY, page 243.

8b. Leaves simple .... (9)

9a. Leaves and buds covered with rusty or silvery scales. ELAEAGNACEAE, OLEASTER FAMILY, page 194.

9b. Leaves and buds not as above .... (10)

10a. Leaves soft-pubescent or felty beneath. HYDRANGEACEAE, HYDRANGEA FAMILY, page 214.

10b. Leaves glabrous or nearly so .... (11)

11a. Young stems bright red; leaves entire, the lateral veins tending to curve toward the leaf-tip. CORNACEAE, DOGWOOD FAMILY, page 175.

11b. Stems not red; leaves serrate or serrulate, or, if not, then the veins definitely pinnate, without a tendency to curve toward the leaf-tip. CAPRIFOLIACEAE, HONEYSUCKLE FAMILY, page 94.

12a. Leaves compound .... (13)

12b. Leaves simple .... (18)

13a. Leaves spiny-margined (resembling holly). BERBERIDACEAE, BARBERRY FAMILY, page 81.

13b. Leaves not as above .... (14)

14a. Leaves with three leaflets *(Caution! Poison ivy in this category)*. ANACARDIACEAE, SUMAC FAMILY, page 73.

14b. Leaves not trifoliolate, usually pinnately compound .... (15)

15a. Flowers zygomorphic; fruit a legume; leaflets more than 9, entire. LEGUMINOSAE, PEA FAMILY, page 222.

15b. Flowers not as above; fruit not a legume; leaflets various, but if numerous, then serrate or with shallow lobes or auricles at the base of the leaflets .... (16)

16a. Leaflets more than 11; branches stout, the pith occupying a major portion of the cross-section .... (17)

16b. Leaflets 11 or fewer; otherwise not as above. ROSACEAE, ROSE FAMILY, page 288.

17a. Leaflets serrate; fruits red, round, with a velvety surface. ANACARDIACEAE, SUMAC FAMILY, page 73.

17b. Leaflets entire except for basal auricles; fruit a flat winged samara. SIMAROUBACEAE, QUASSIA FAMILY, page 336.

18a. Leaves pinnately lobed, leathery, glossy; fruit an acorn. FAGACEAE, OAK FAMILY, page 202.

18b. Leaves not as above; fruit not an acorn .... (19)

19a. Flowers unisexual, produced in catkins (at least the staminate ones) .... (20)

19b. Flowers not produced in catkins .... (21)

20a. Plants monoecious, the carpellate flowers subtended by conspicuous bracts (in *Alnus* they resemble scales of a pine-cone); calyx present in staminate flowers; fruit a dry, indehiscent, one-seeded nutlet. BETULACEAE, BIRCH FAMILY, page 81.

20b. Plants dioecious, the bracts minute; calyx absent; fruit a capsule; seed with a conspicuous tuft of silky hairs. SALICACEAE, WILLOW FAMILY, page 304.

21a. Leaf-blades very unequal at the base. ULMACEAE, ELM FAMILY, page 339.

21b. Leaves not as above .... (22)

22a. Flowers in heads, each flower-cluster surrounded by an involucre of bracts. COMPOSITAE, SUNFLOWER FAMILY, page 119.

22b. Flowers not in heads surrounded by involucres .... (23)

23a. Flowers unisexual; leaves linear or oblong, with a scurfy pubescence; alkaline areas on the plains. CHENOPODIACEAE, GOOSEFOOT FAMILY, page 111.

23b. Flowers perfect .... (24)

24a. Leaves palmately lobed (sometimes obscurely so) .... (25)

24b. Leaves not at all palmately lobed .... (26)

25a. Stamens numerous; carpels 1 to numerous, separate; flowers never tubular. ROSACEAE, ROSE FAMILY, page 288.

25b. Stamens 5 or fewer; carpels 2, united; flowers often tubular. GROSSULARIACEAE, GOOSEBERRY FAMILY, page 211.

26a. Low shrubs (3 dm or less high), often evergreen, the leaves never with three prominent veins; flowers usually vase-shaped, waxy in texture; petals united. ERICACEAE, HEATH FAMILY, page 195.

26b. Not as above .... (27)

27a. Leaves ovate, with 3 prominent veins; stamens opposite the petals. RHAMNACEAE, BUCKTHORN FAMILY, page 287.

27b. Without the above combination of characters. ROSACEAE, ROSE FAMILY, page 288.

KEY F (HERBACEOUS DICOTS)

1a. Flowers several to many, in heads, each flower-cluster surrounded or subtended by an involucre of bracts; ovary inferior
. . . . (2)

1b. Flowers not as above . . . . (3)

2a. Prickles present on the stems, leaves and involucre; leaves opposite; corolla 4-parted; stamens separate. DIPSACACEAE, TEASEL FAMILY, page 191.

2b. Stems not prickly, or leaves alternate if with prickly stems and leaves; corolla 5-parted or strap-shaped or of both types; stamens with united anthers. COMPOSITAE, SUNFLOWER FAMILY, page 119.

3a. Perianth none or of a single set of parts, the parts all much alike in color and texture . . . . (4)

3b. Perianth present, evidently double, the outer segments (sepals) and inner segments (petals) usually conspicuously different in texture, color or both . . . . (23)

4a. Inflorescence a spike of inconspicuous flowers, below which is attached a circle of large white or pink petal-like bracts, producing the effect of a single flower; leaves basal, fleshy; plant stoloniferous, pepper-scented. SAURURACEAE, LIZARD-TAIL FAMILY, page 311.

4b. Plants not as above . . . . (5)

5a. Ovary inferior . . . . (6)

5b. Ovary superior . . . . (10)

6a. Ovary with two locules, one ovule in each locule; fruit 2-seeded
. . . . (7)

6b. Ovary with one locule, the locule with 1-2 ovules (or ovary with 1-3 locules, but only one locule containing an ovule); fruit 1-seeded . . . . (8)

7a. Perianth parts united at the base; leaves opposite or whorled; flowers in cymes, not in umbels. RUBIACEAE, MADDER FAMILY, page 302.

7b. Perianth parts separate; leaves alternate or basal; flowers in umbels. UMBELLIFERAE, CARROT FAMILY, page 339.

8a. Leaves alternate, the flowers greenish-white. SANTALACEAE, SANDALWOOD FAMILY, page 309.

8b. Leaves opposite; flowers white or pink ....(9)

9a. Leaves simple, entire; flowers pink or flesh-colored; fruits hard and bony or with papery wings. NYCTAGINACEAE, FOUR-O'CLOCK FAMILY, page 240.

9b. Leaves pinnately lobed or divided; flowers white; fruits provided with a delicate parachute of feathery bristles. VALERIANACEAE, VALERIAN FAMILY, page 349.

10a. Carpels several to many in a single flower, separate; stamens usually numerous. RANUNCULACEAE, BUTTERCUP FAMILY, page 272.

10b. Carpels one or several united; stamens one to many (usually not over 10 in most families) ....(11)

11a. Ovary with 2 or more locules ....(12)

11b. Ovary with one locule ....(16)

12a. Plants with milky juice. EUPHORBIACEAE, SPURGE FAMILY, page 199.

12b. Plants without milky juice ....(13)

13a. Flowers perfect ....(14)

13b. Flowers unisexual; ovary on a stalk (in this group the flowers are reduced to single stamens or single gynoecia, but the stamens and gynoecia are surrounded by a cup-like involucre which resembles a perianth). EUPHORBIACEAE, SPURGE FAMILY, page 199.

14a. Leaves opposite or whorled, entire; stamens one to many (rarely 2); flowers axillary, solitary or in small clusters. CARY-OPHYLLACEAE, PINK FAMILY, page 97. (Note: if stamens 3, and leaves whorled, see *Mollugo*, in AIZOACEAE, page 72.)

14b. Leaves alternate, or crowded at the base of the stem, usually toothed; stamens 2; flowers in terminal spikes or racemes ....(15)

15a. Perennials; flowers in spikes; fruit several-seeded. SCROPHULA-RIACEAE, FIGWORT FAMILY, page 318.

15b. Annuals; flowers in racemes; fruit 2-seeded (one seed in each locule). CRUCIFERAE, MUSTARD FAMILY, page 176.

16a. Ovary with several to many ovules; fruit a capsule, several- to many-seeded. CARYOPHYLLACEAE, PINK FAMILY, page 97.

16b. Ovary with only one ovule; fruit a one-seeded achene or utricle ....(17)

17a. Leaves with stipules, these united around the stem in a sheath just above the nodes. POLYGONACEAE, BUCKWHEAT FAMILY, page 259.

17b. Leaves without stipules, or these, when present, not sheathing the stem .... (18)

18a. Conspicuous, persistent stipules present; leaves opposite ... (19)
18b. Stipules lacking; leaves usually alternate .... (20)

19a. Stipules papery; plants small with spreading, prostrate, or densely caespitose stems rarely over 30 cm tall; stinging hairs not present. CARYOPHYLLACEAE, PINK FAMILY, page 97.
19b. Stipules not papery; plants with erect stems usually over 30 cm tall; stinging hairs present. URTICACEAE, NETTLE FAMILY, page 349.

20a. Flowers perfect, the flower clusters surrounded by a cup-like involucre; stamens 6 to 9; fruit an achene. POLYGONACEAE, BUCK-WHEAT FAMILY, page 259.
20b. Flowers perfect or unisexual but not surrounded by a cup-like involucre; stamens 1 to 5; fruit an achene or utricle .... (21)

21a. Bracts and perianth more or less papery or membranous. AMARANTHACEAE, AMARANTH FAMILY, page 73.
21b. Bracts and perianth herbaceous to fleshy, not papery or membranous .... (22)

22a. Style and stigma one; leaves alternate and entire; fruit an achene; plants annual; rare, in shaded places on the mesas. *Parietaria*, in URTICACEAE, NETTLE FAMILY, page 349.
22b. Styles and stigmas 1 to 3 (but if one the leaves toothed); fruit a utricle; plants annual or perennial; weedy species, often coarse and scurfy-pubescent. CHENOPODIACEAE, GOOSEFOOT FAMILY, page 111.

23a. Petals separate .... (24)
23b. Petals united (at least at the base) .... (79)

24a. Ovary inferior, at least the lower part fused to the hypanthium or calyx-tube .... (25)
24b. Ovary completely superior (if hypanthium is present the ovary may seem to be inferior but upon dissection it is seen not to be imbedded in the hypanthium tissues, cf. rose hips) .... (32)

25a. Stamens as many as the petals and opposite them. PORTULACA-CEAE, PURSLANE FAMILY, page 267.
25b. Stamens fewer or more numerous than the petals, or, if the same number, then alternate with them .... (26)

26a. Ovules and seeds more than one in each locule; ovary with 1 to 4 locules .... (27)

26b. Ovules and seeds only one to each locule; ovary with 2 to 6 locules .... (29)

27a. Only one style present (stigmas may be lobed) .... (28)
27b. Two or more styles present. SAXIFRAGACEAE, SAXIFRAGE FAMILY, page 311.

28a. Stamens 10 or more; plants rough-pubescent, usually because of barbed hairs. LOASACEAE, LOASA FAMILY, page 234.
28b. Stamens 4 or 8; plants not rough-pubescent. ONAGRACEAE, EVENING-PRIMROSE FAMILY, page 243.

29a. Leaves whorled, entire; ovary usually with two locules and only one style. CORNACEAE, DOGWOOD FAMILY, page 175.
29b. Leaves alternate, opposite, or basal, toothed or entire (never whorled); ovary with 4 locules, or, if with two locules, then two styles present .... (30)

30a. Stamens 2, 4, or 8; petals 2 or 4; style one, locules usually 4 (except in *Circaea*). ONAGRACEAE, EVENING-PRIMROSE FAMILY, page 243.
30b. Stamens 5, rarely 4; petals usually 5; styles 2 or more; locules 2 to 6 .... (31)

31a. Locules 4 to 6; fruit a several-seeded berry. ARALIACEAE, GINSENG FAMILY, page 77.
31b. Locules 2; fruit dry, 2-seeded. UMBELLIFERAE, CARROT FAMILY, page 339.

32a. Corolla distinctly irregular or zygomorphic .... (33)
32b. Corolla regular or nearly so .... (39)

33a. Leaves pinnately or palmately compound .... (34)
33b. Leaves simple, entire, to deeply lobed or pinnatifid, but never truly compound .... (36)

34a. Sepals 2, very minute and scale-like; corolla spurred; leaves greatly dissected. FUMARIACEAE, FUMITORY FAMILY, page 203.
34b. Sepals 4 or 5; corolla not or very inconspicuously spurred; leaves once or twice compound .... (35)

35a. Ovary with one placenta; petals 5 (or rarely one), flowers usually shaped like those of sweet-peas. LEGUMINOSAE, PEA FAMILY, page 222.
35b. Ovary with two placentae on opposite sides of the ovary; petals 4; flowers not at all sweet-pea-shaped. CAPPARIDACEAE, CAPER FAMILY, page 94.

36a. Petals irregularly but conspicuously cleft; stamens usually many inserted on one side of the flower. RESEDACEAE, MIGNONETTE FAMILY, page 286.

36b. Petals entire or only slightly lobed; stamens fewer than 10, or, if many, then not inserted on only one side .... (37)

37a. Stamens many; carpels usually more than one, separate or separating in fruit and becoming follicles; leaves palmately cleft or parted. RANUNCULACEAE, BUTTERCUP FAMILY, page 272.

37b. Stamens 10 or fewer; carpels one, or, if more than one, united into a compound ovary; fruit a capsule or legume; leaves simple or compound, rarely palmately cleft or parted .... (38)

38a. One of the sepals spurred, only 3 present; ovary with 5 locules; flower shaped like a gnome's slipper. BALSAMINACEAE, JEWELWEED FAMILY, page 80.

38b. None of the sepals spurred (petal may be), five sepals present; ovary with one locule and with three parietal placentae. VIOLACEAE, VIOLET FAMILY, page 354.

39a. Stamens of the same number as the petals and opposite them (40)

39b. Stamens fewer or more numerous than the petals, or, if the same number, then alternate with them .... (42)

40a. Sepals, petals, and stamens each 6 in number, 3 of the sepals petal-like; leaf margins spiny· BERBERIDACEAE, BARBERRY FAMILY, page 81.

40b. Sepals, petals, and stamens 2 to 5 (sepals rarely 6); branches and leaves spineless .... (41)

41a. Styles and stigmas one; sepals usually 5. PRIMULACEAE, PRIMROSE FAMILY, page 269.

41b. Styles and stigmas 2 or more; sepals usually 2. PORTULACACEAE, PURSLANE FAMILY, page 267.

42a. Ovary one (a single unit), with one locule .... (43)

42b. Ovaries more than one (several separate units), or, if one, then with 2 or more locules .... (59)

43a. Stamens 13 or more .... (44)

43b. Stamens 12 or fewer .... (50)

44a. Ovary simple (of a single carpel, having one placenta, one style, one stigma; many such ovaries may be present in a single flower). RANUNCULACEAE, BUTTERCUP FAMILY, page 272.

44b. Ovary compound (two or more placentae, styles or stigmas). .... (45)

45a. Placenta free central or basal. PORTULACACEAE, PURSLANE FAMILY, page 267.
45b. Placentae parietal .... (46)

46a. Ovary with 2 parietal placentae; plants usually sticky-hairy and ill-smelling. CAPPARIDACEAE, CAPER FAMILY, page 94.
46b. Ovary with 3 or more placentae; plant not sticky nor ill-smelling
.... (47)

47a. Petals conspicuously cleft; stamens inserted on one side of the flower. RESEDACEAE, MIGNONETTE FAMILY, page 286.
47b. Petals entire or obscurely toothed; stamens not inserted on one side of the flower .... (48)

48a. Leaves opposite, with minute translucent dots (hold up to the light). HYPERICACEAE, ST. JOHNSWORT FAMILY, page 217.
48b. Leaves alternate, without translucent dots .... (49)

49a. Sepals 2 to 3, early deciduous (falling when the petals unfold); leaves toothed or lobed; flowers white or cream-colored, seldom bright yellow. PAPAVERACEAE, POPPY FAMILY, page 250.
49b. Sepals 4 or 5, usually persistent; leaves entire, with slightly revolute margins; petals yellow. CISTACEAE, ROCK-ROSE FAMILY, page 118.

50a. Gynoecium composed of a single carpel (one placenta, style, and stigma) .... (51)
50b. Gynoecium compound (more than one placenta, style, or stigma)
.... (52)

51a. Stamens and petals attached to the calyx-tube. ROSACEAE, ROSE FAMILY, page 288.
51b. Stamens and petals not attached to the calyx-tube. LEGUMINOSAE, PEA FAMILY, page 222.

52a. Petals conspicuously cleft; stamens inserted on one side of the flower. RESEDACEAE, MIGNONETTE FAMILY, page 286.
52b. Petals entire to deeply notched or two-lobed; stamens not inserted on one side of the flower .... (53)

53a. Petals inserted on the throat of a bell-shaped or tubular calyx. LYTHRACEAE, LOOSESTRIFE FAMILY, page 236.
53b. Petals inserted on the receptacle; calyx of separate or united sepals .... (54)

54a. Stamens 5, alternating with 5 clusters of gland-tipped staminodia (abortive stamens); leaves all basal except one. SAXIFRAGACEAE, SAXIFRAGE FAMILY, page 311.

54b. Stamens various but not alternating with staminodia; stem-leaves present or absent .... (55)

55a. Ovule one .... (56)
55b. Ovules more than one .... (57)

56a. Petals 4; stamens 2, 4, 6; stipules absent or inconspicuous. CRUCIFERAE, MUSTARD FAMILY, page 176.
56b. Petals 5; stamens 5; stipules usually conspicuous. CARYOPHYLLACEAE, PINK FAMILY, page 97.

57a. Ovules attached to base of ovary or to a free-central placenta (not parietal). CARYOPHYLLACEAE, PINK FAMILY, page 97.
57b. Ovules attached to two or more pariental placentae .... (58)

58a. Ovary with 2 parietal placentae; sepals and petals 4 each. CAPPARIDACEAE, CAPER FAMILY, page 94.
58b. Ovary with 3 to 5 parietal placentae; sepals and petals usually 3 or 5 (rarely 4). HYPERICACEAE, ST. JOHNSWORT FAMILY, page 217.

59a. Stamens 13 or more .... (60)
59b. Stamens 12 or fewer .... (63)

60a. Stamens united by their filaments into a tube surrounding the style. MALVACEAE, MALLOW FAMILY, page 237.
60b. Stamens separate, or grouped in several sets .... (61)

61a. Leaves opposite, with translucent dots (hold up to light). HYPERICACEAE, ST. JOHNSWORT FAMILY, page 217.
61b. Leaves usually alternate or basal, without translucent dots (62)

62a. Stamens and petals attached to the calyx-tube or hypanthium (i.e., the flower is perigynous). ROSACEAE, ROSE FAMILY, page 288.
62b. Stamens and petals attached to the receptacle; hypanthium not present (i.e., the flower is hypogynous). RANUNCULACEAE, BUTTERCUP FAMILY, page 272.

63a. Carpels or ovaries two, separate for the most part but united above by a fleshy common stigma; anthers united to each other and more or less imbedded in the stigma or style; plants with milky juice. ASCLEPIADACEAE, MILKWEED FAMILY, page 77.
63b. Ovaries one to many, not united in the above manner; anthers not united to each other nor to a fleshy stigma; juice rarely milky .... (64)

64a. Ovaries more than one, wholly separate or united only at the base, each carpel with its own style .... (65)

64b. Ovary only one (this may be lobed, but the carpels do not separate until the fruit is mature); style one (this may branch above) .... (68)

65a. Carpel one-seeded; carpels 2 to many, not at all united ..... (66)
65b. Carpel containing more than one seed; carpels 2 to 5, often united at the base .... (67)

66a. Petals and stamens attached to the calyx-tube or hypanthium. ROSACEAE, ROSE FAMILY, page 288.
66b. Petals and stamens attached to the receptacle; hypanthium absent. RANUNCULACEAE, BUTTERCUP FAMILY, page 272.

67a. Leaves fleshy and entire; carpels 3 to 5; stems leafy. CRASSULACEAE, STONECROP FAMILY, page 176.
67b. Leaves entire, toothed, or lobed, not especially fleshy; carpels 2; stems with chiefly basal leaves. SAXIFRAGACEAE, SAXIFRAGE FAMILY, page 311.

68a. Ovules 1 to 2 in each locule .... (69)
68b. Ovules 3 or more in each locule .... (73)

69a. Flowers unisexual, borne in a calyx-like involucre, with petal-like glandular appendages often present; plants usually with milky juice. EUPHORBIACEAE, SPURGE FAMILY, page 199.
69b. Flowers perfect, not enclosed in a calyx-like involucre; plants without milky juice .... (70)

70a. Sepals and petals 4; stamens 2, 4, or 6. CRUCIFERAE, MUSTARD FAMILY, page 176.
70b. Sepals and petals 5; stamens 5 or 10 .... (71)

71a. Leaves alternate, simple, entire, linear; stamens 5. LINACEAE, FLAX FAMILY, page 233.
71b. Leaves opposite or chiefly basal, compound or palmately lobed or divided; stamens usually more than 5 .... (72)

72a. Carpels separating at maturity, remaining attached by the tip of the style; leaves palmately lobed or cleft, or pinnately cleft with the divisions again toothed or lobed. GERANIACEAE, GERANIUM FAMILY, page 209.
72b. Carpels very spiny, separating at maturity, without conspicuous styles; leaves pinnately compound, the leaflets entire. ZYGOPHYLLACEAE, CALTROP FAMILY, page 359.

73a. Leaves palmately compound with 3 heart-shaped leaflets; ovary with 5 locules; stamens 10, somewhat united at the base; leaves with pleasantly acid taste when chewed. OXALIDACEAE, WOOD-SORREL FAMILY, page 249.

73b. Leaves simple, or if compound, not as above; ovary 2-10-loculed; stamens 2 to 10 (but seldom with 10 stamens and 5 locules) (74)

74a. Petals white or pink, waxy in texture; leaves often evergreen; anthers opening by pores at one end, this end with two more or less prominent horns. ERICACEAE, HEATH FAMILY, page 195.
74b. Petals scarcely waxy in texture; leaves seldom (but sometimes) evergreen; anthers opening longitudinally, not by pores, the anthers not at all 2-horned .... (75)

75a. Styles 2 or 3, distinct .... (76)
75b. Style one (at least at the base; it may be branched above) (78)

76a. Leaves with translucent dots (hold up to the light). HYPERICA-CEAE, ST. JOHNSWORT FAMILY, page 217.
76b. Leaves without translucent dots .... (77)

77a. Leaves opposite, entire; low plants with inconspicuous axillary flowers, occurring on drying mud flats on the plains and piedmont valleys. ELATINACEAE, WATERWORT FAMILY, page 195.
77b. Leaves alternate or basal; plants of the mountains, otherwise not as above. SAXIFRAGACEAE, SAXIFRAGE FAMILY, page 311.

78a. Stamens attached to the receptacle, usually 4 long, 2 short; sepals and petals 4; leaves various, but often toothed or lobed. CRUCIFERAE, MUSTARD FAMILY, page 176.
78b. Petals and stamens attached to the throat of a calyx-tube; stamens rarely 6; leaves simple, entire. LYTHRACEAE, LOOSESTRIFE FAMILY, page 236.

79a. Ovary partly or wholly inferior .... (80)
79b. Ovary superior .... (85)

80a. Flowers sessile in dense heads surrounded by an involucre; calyx greatly modified or absent. COMPOSITAE, SUNFLOWER FAMILY, page 119.
80b. Flowers not in heads (may be in head-like spikes but then not involucrate at base), not closely subtended by an involucre; calyx usually normal .... (81)

81a. Stamens attached to the corolla tube; leaves opposite or whorled .... (82)
81b. Stamens free from the corolla or very nearly so; leaves alternate. CAMPANULACEAE, BELLFLOWER FAMILY, page 91.

82a. Stamens twice as many as the corolla lobes; leaves ternately compound. ADOXACEAE, ADOXA FAMILY, page 70.

82b. Stamens as many as the corolla lobes or fewer; leaves simple and entire to pinnately parted or compound, never ternately compound ....(83)

83a. Stamens 3, always fewer than the corolla lobes; calyx usually reduced to bristles, these elongate and feathery in fruit; ovary with one ovule, fruit one-seeded. VALERIANACEAE, VALERIAN FAMILY, page 349.

83b. Stamens usually 4 or more, but in any case just as many as the corolla lobes; calyx never bristle-like or feathery; ovary usually with more than one ovule; fruit of two nutlets, each either berry-like, capsular, or drupe-like ....(84)

84a. Plants herbaceous, or woody only at the base (and then the flowers not in pairs); leaves usually appearing whorled. RUBIACEAE, MADDER FAMILY, page 302.

84b. Plants woody at the base, creeping, the flowers in pairs on a long peduncle; leaves opposite. CAPRIFOLIACEAE, HONEYSUCKLE FAMILY, page 94.

85a. Stamens more numerous than the corolla lobes, 6 to many .. (86)

85b. Stamens as many as the corolla lobes or fewer ....(89)

86a. Stamens many, united into a tube around the style. MALVACEAE, MALLOW FAMILY, page 237.

86b. Stamens 6 to 10, separate and distinct, or some or all united by their filaments ....(87)

87a. Petals united at apex only, free below; ovary 1-loculed, with 2 parietal placentae. FUMARIACEAE, FUMITORY FAMILY, page 203.

87b. Petals united below apex (free or united at very base); ovary with more than one locule or with one locule and one placenta .. (88)

88a. Ovary with 4 to 10 locules; corolla regular; stamens 10, the anthers commonly opening by terminal pores. ERICACEAE, HEATH FAMILY, page 195.

88b. Ovary with 1 to 2 locules; corolla usually very irregular; stamens 4 to 10, the anthers opening by longitudinal slits. LEGUMINOSAE, PEA FAMILY, page 222.

89a. Ovaries 2, separate below but united above by the common stigma; plants with milky sap ....(90)

89b. Ovary 1 (may be lobed to appear like 2 or 4); plants seldom with milky sap ....(91)

90a. Stamens with anthers united; a "crown" present between the corolla and the stamens. ASCLEPIADACEAE, MILKWEED FAMILY, page 77.

90b. Stamens with free and distinct anthers; no crown present. APOCYNACEAE, DOGBANE FAMILY, page 76.

91a. Either the calyx or corolla spurred .... (92)
91b. Flowers without a spur .... (93)

92a. Ovary with 5 locules; one of the sepals spurred, the orange flowers shaped like a gnome's slipper. BALSAMINACEAE, JEWEL-WEED FAMILY, page 80.
92b. Ovary with 2 locules; corolla spurred. SCROPHULARIACEAE, FIG-WORT FAMILY, page 318.

93a. Stamens of the same number as the corolla lobes and opposite them; ovary with one locule; placenta basal or free-central. PRIMULACEAE, PRIMROSE FAMILY, page 269.
93b. Stamens of the same number as the corolla lobes and alternate to them, or fewer; ovary more than 1-loculed or if 1-loculed then the placenta rarely basal or free-central .... (94)

94a. Stamens 5, all bearing anthers; corolla regular or nearly so . (95)
94b. Anther-bearing stamens 2 or 4 (a rudimentary stamen may be present in addition); corolla regular or irregular .... (104)

95a. Ovary 4-lobed, developing into 4 (or by abortion fewer) one-seeded nutlets. BORAGINACEAE, BORAGE FAMILY, page 83.
95b. Ovary not 4-lobed, not developing as above; fruit a capsule or berry, usually several-seeded .... (96)

96a. Leaves basal, long-petioled, palmately compound with 3 large (over 5 cm long) entire leaflets; semiaquatic. MENYANTHACEAE, BUCKBEAN FAMILY, page 239.
96b. Leaves simple or compound but not as above; usually terrestrial .... (97)

97a. Ovary with one locule .... (98)
97b. Ovary with 2 or more locules .... (99)

98a. Leaves opposite or whorled, entire; styles one or none; plants mostly glabrous; inflorescence not curled in the bud. GENTIANA-CEAE, GENTIAN FAMILY, page 204.
98b. Leaves usually alternate (if opposite, then not entire); styles 2, or single and 2-cleft above; plants mostly hairy; inflorescence commonly curled in the bud. HYDROPHYLLACEAE, WATERLEAF FAMILY, page 214.

99a. Stigma 3-lobed or style 3-branched; ovary with 3 locules. POLE-MONIACEAE, PHLOX FAMILY, page 253.
99b. Stigma entire or 2-lobed, or style 2-cleft; ovary usually with 2 locules .... (100)

100a. Flowers yellow, in dense terminal spikes or spike-like racemes over 20 cm long; flowers only slightly zygomorphic. SCROPHU-LARIACEAE, FIGWORT FAMILY, page 318.
100b. Flowers variously colored, never in spikes or racemes over 20 cm long; flowers usually strictly regular ....(101)

101a. Stems trailing or twining. CONVOLVULACEAE, MORNING-GLORY FAMILY, page 172.
101b. Stems not trailing or twining ....(102)

102a. Styles 2, distinct, each one again 2-cleft; ovules 2 in each locule; flowers solitary and axillary. CONVOLVULACEAE, MORN-ING-GLORY FAMILY, page 172.
102b. Styles 1, or, if 2, rarely separate to the base, never again 2-cleft; ovules usually more than 2 in each locule; inflorescence various (sometimes as above) ....(103)

103a. Style one, the stigma entire or 2-lobed; fruit a capsule or berry. SOLANACEAE, POTATO FAMILY, page 336.
103b. Styles 2 or definitely 2-branched before reaching the stigmas; fruit a capsule. HYDROPHYLLACEAE, WATERLEAF FAMILY, page 214.

104a. Ovary with 1 (or possibly 2) ovules in each locule, the ovary appearing 4-loculed and often 4-lobed (2-lobed in *Phyla*, VERBENACEAE); fruit separating at maturity into 4 (or by abortion fewer) one-seeded nutlets ....(105)
104b. Ovary with more than 1 ovule in each locule, usually not 4-celled or 4-lobed; fruit not separating into one-seeded nutlets ..(106)

105a. Ovary 4-lobed, the style arising in the center between the lobes; corolla usually distinctly zygomorphic; inflorescence various (can be heads or spikes); plants frequently with a minty odor. LABIATAE, MINT FAMILY, page 217.
105b. Ovary entire or longitudinally grooved, the style apical; corolla regular or slightly irregular; inflorescence a spike or head. VERBENACEAE, VERVAIN FAMILY, page 352.

106a. Corolla papery; flowers small, in dense terminal spikes; leaves basal; fruit a circumscissile capsule (dehiscent in the manner one would open a soft-boiled egg). PLANTAGINACEAE, PLANTAIN FAMILY, page 251.
106b. Corolla not papery; flowers, if small, seldom in dense terminal spikes in combination with leaves all basal; fruit not circum-scissile ....(107)

107a. Stigma 3-lobed; ovary with 3 locules. POLEMONIACEAE, PHLOX FAMILY, page 253.

107b. Stigma entire or 2-lobed; ovary with one or two locules .. (108)

108a. Ovary with one locule .... (109)
108b. Ovary with two locules. SCROPHULARIACEAE, FIGWORT FAMILY, page 318.

109a. Stems creeping and rooting; leaves all basal; corolla small, not over 3 mm long; ovary divided at the base into 2 locules. SCROPHULARIACEAE, FIGWORT FAMILY, page 318.
109b. Stems not creeping and rooting; some leaves on the stem, these opposite or whorled; corolla usually large and showy, over 3 mm long; ovary not at all divided at the base into 2 locules. GENTIANACEAE, GENTIAN FAMILY, page 204.

Keys to the Genera and Species

Division Pteridophyta, Ferns and Fern Allies

1a. Stems jointed, hollow, green (except the fertile stems of *Equisetum arvense*, which are yellowish-brown), the nodes covered by toothed sheaths. EQUISETACEAE, HORSETAIL FAMILY, page 50.

1b. Stems not jointed, seldom green; toothed sheaths not present ... (2)

2a. Plants aquatic, inhabiting lake shores or actually submerged in ponds and lakes .... (3)

2b. Plants terrestrial, growing on soil or rocks .... (4)

3a. Leaves grass-like, the bases swollen and bearing sporangia, in a bulb-like cluster; plants submerged in shallow water of mountain lakes and ponds for the greater part of the growing season. ISOËTACEAE, QUILLWORT FAMILY, page 50.

3b. Leaves with distinct petioles and blades, the blades four-parted, resembling a four-leaf clover; spores borne at the base of the plant in round nut-like "sporocarps"; borders of ponds and sandy streamsides on the plains and piedmont valleys. MARSILEACEAE, PEPPERWORT FAMILY, page 53.

4a. Leaves very numerous, lanceolate or linear, sometimes bractlike, sessile, spirally or oppositely arranged in 4 to many ranks upon branched perennial stems .... (5)

4b. Leaves relatively few, broad or more or less dissected (except in *Asplenium septentrionale*, the Grass Fern, which has linear leaves), arising from an underground stem .... (6)

5a. Leaves minute (less than 3 mm long). SELAGINELLACEAE, LITTLE CLUB-MOSS FAMILY, page 61.

5b. Leaves larger (5 mm to 1 cm or more long). LYCOPODIACEAE, CLUB-MOSS FAMILY, page 52.

6a. Fronds (the "leaves" of ferns) linear, undivided except for a few very narrow lobes at the apex. *Asplenium septentrionale*, in POLYPODIACEAE, FERN FAMILY, page 54.

6b. Fronds broader, more or less dissected (fern-like) .... (7)

7a. One entire branch of each frond completely altered in appearance, modified for spore production, the remainder of the frond green and not producing spores. OPHIOGLOSSACEAE, ADDERS-TONGUE FAMILY, page 53.

7b. Fronds without conspicuously altered branches; entire fronds modified for spore production, or spores borne on the undersides of relatively unmodified fronds. POLYPODIACEAE, FERN FAMILY, page 54.

EQUISETACEAE—HORSETAIL FAMILY

1a. Stems bearing numerous branches in whorls at the nodes. *Equisetum arvense* L., FIELD HORSETAIL, Fig. 13. Abundant along wet ditches and floodplains throughout our range. The stems are of two kinds, either green, branched and sterile, or brown, unbranched and bearing a spore producing cone at the tip. The latter are produced in early spring and soon wither.

1b. Stems simple or only occasionally with a few short branches scattered irregularly on the main stem .... (2)

2a. Stems brown, terminated with a blunt cone containing the sporangia. *Equisetum arvense* L. (fertile stems), see above.

2b. Stems green, sometimes but not always terminated by a blunt or sharp-pointed cone; stems living for one or more seasons .... (3)

3a. Stems slender, 5-12-angled and -grooved; sheaths loose, with fine-pointed teeth which are persistent; central cavity of stem usually half the diameter of the stem. *Hippochaete variegata* (Schleich.) Bruhin, SCOURING-RUSH. Infrequent in wet ground, streambeds, montane, piedmont valleys and plains (*Equisetum* of Ed. 4).

3b. Stem stout, 16-48-angled and -grooved; sheaths loose or tight, the teeth persistent or deciduous; central cavity of the stem more than half the stem diameter .... (4)

4a. Sheaths with dark band at base; teeth often deciduous; cone sharp-pointed; stems perennial. *Hippochaete hyemalis* (L.) Bruhin (of winter), TALL SCOURING-RUSH, Fig. 13. Especially abundant along railway embankments but frequent along streams, foothills (*Equisetum* of Ed. 4).

4b. Sheaths without dark band at base; teeth persistent; cone rounded at apex; stems annual. *Hippochaete laevigata* (A. Br.) Farwell (smooth) SCOURING-RUSH, Fig. 13. Common in wet ground of ditches and streamsides. These plants are called scouring-rushes because of the deposits of silica in the stems; they are effective for scouring pots and pans but will scratch aluminum (*Equisetum* of Ed. 4).

ISOËTACEAE—QUILLWORT FAMILY

Identification of the quillworts is a technical business requiring examination of the megaspores with a high-powered dissecting microscope and comparison material of correctly named specimens. Mature plants are needed, which means collecting in late summer or fall, when the spores in the leaf-bases are ripe.

1a. Megaspores with scattered low tubercles becoming joined to form low ridges. *Isoëtes bolanderi* Engelm. (for H. N. Bolander, Californian

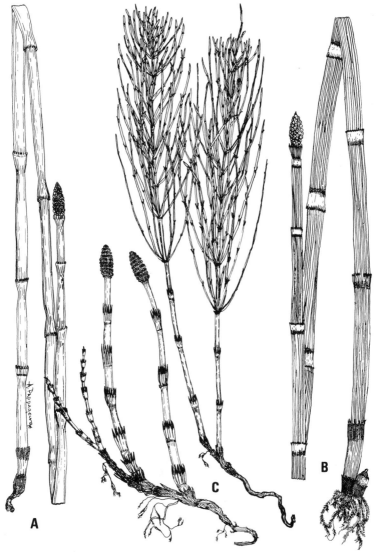

Fig. 13. A, *Hippochaete laevigata*; B, *H. hyemalis*; C, *Equisetum arvense*

botanist). This is frequent in smaller lakes and ponds in the upper montane and subalpine and is the species most commonly collected, Fig. 14.

1b. Megaspores with high, sharp spines and jagged ridges . . . . (2)

2a. Megaspores usually less than 5 mm diam, studded with sharp or forked spines; leaves thin-textured, slenderly acuminate. *Isoëtes setacea* Lam. (bristly). Our only record for Colorado is from Pikes Peak, probably in an alpine tarn (*I. echinospora, muricata, braunii* of manuals).

2b. Megaspores 0.5-0.8 mm diam, with ridges and jagged crests; leaves coarse and tough, broadly acuminate. *Isoëtes lacustris* L. (of lakes). In deep water of larger lakes (Grand Lake, etc.). F. J. Hermann recently found mature plants and scattered leaves washed ashore by wave action at Bierstadt Lake in Rocky Mountain National Park.

LYCOPODIACEAE—CLUB-MOSS FAMILY

The spores of *Lycopodium* were once used as a fine baby powder as well as inflammable powder for flash photography. In Scandinavia, where they are abundant ground cover in forests, lycopods are gathered in enormous quantities for ornamental Christmas wreaths and greens. In Colorado they are so rare as to be considered endangered species.

1a. Stem creeping extensively, the erect branches not tightly bunched; spores produced in an elongate cone. *Lycopodium annotinum* L. (a year old; from the clearly marked separation of each year's growth of the branches), STIFF CLUB-MOSS, Fig. 15. Under thickets of willows or wind timber and in subalpine spruce forests.

1b. Stem not creeping extensively, the erect branches tightly bunched; sporangia in the axils of unmodified leaves, not in cones. *Huperzia selago* (L.) Bernh., FIR CLUB-MOSS. Very rare, on open rocky cirque-basins and on cliffs at or above timberline (*Lycopodium selago*).

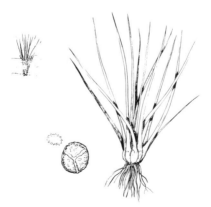

Fig. 14. *Isoëtes bolanderi*

Marsileaceae—Pepperwort Family

One species, **Marsilea mucronata** A. Br., Hairy Pepperwort, Fig. 16. Rare or overlooked, borders of ponds and streams, piedmont valleys and plains, especially in sandy areas. The plants become conspicuous in August and September when ponds begin to dry up. The sporocarps of Nardoo, *M. drummondii* of Central Australia, are edible and gathered by the aborigines, who taught the early explorers to use this wild food as a last resort against starvation in the outback.

Ophioglossaceae—Adders-tongue Family

All of the members of this family are rare and endangered, and should not be collected. Fortunately they are mostly difficult to see in the field; one either stumbles on them or finds them only after much diligent searching. Populations are usually very small.

1a. Plant several dm tall, the green, sterile portion more or less triangular in gross outline, very delicately and finely dissected; fertile branch narrow, consisting of a spike of light brown spore-bearing branches. **Botrychium virginianum** (L.) Sw., Rattlesnake Fern. Extremely rare, in cool ravines in the foothills.

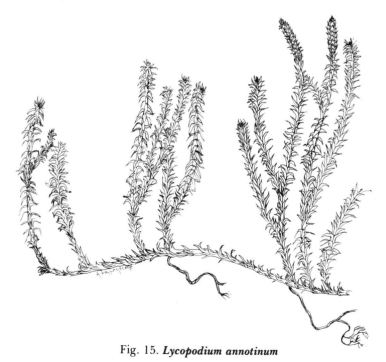

Fig. 15. *Lycopodium annotinum*

1b. Plant small (15 cm or less tall), the green sterile portion unbranched or only pinnatifid; fertile branch short, yellowish-brown, the sporangia in a grape-like or elongate cluster like the rattles of a snake .... (2)

2a. Sterile blade attached near the base of the common stalk, petiolate, ternate-pinnate. **Botrychium simplex** E. Hitchc. This and the next are found on moraines and meadows in the subalpine and alpine zones.
2b. Sterile blade attached near or above the middle of the common stalk .... (3)

3a. Sterile frond pinnately lobed with recurved-fan-shaped divisions, the lowermost pair sometimes shallowly lobed but not ternately divided. **Botrychium lunaria** (L.) Sw. MOONWORT, Fig. 17.
3b. Sterile frond with the branches tending to be ternate, or if pinnate, with some of the lower pinnae divided .... (4)

4a. Sterile frond in general outline longer than wide; fertile portion erect in bud; pinnae rather wide .... (5)
4b. Sterile frond in general outline as wide as or wider than long; pinnae very narrow; fertile portion reflexed in bud. **Botrychium lanceolatum** (Gmelin) Angstrom.

5a. Sterile frond petiolate, the segments usually longer than wide. **Botrychium matricariaefolium** (Doell) A. Br. *ex* Koch.
5b. Sterile frond sessile, the segments as wide as long. **Botrychium boreale** Milde. Very like *B. lunaria* but with non-recurved pinnae.

POLYPODIACEAE—FERN FAMILY

Except for the abundant bracken (*Pteridium*) and brittle fern (*Cystopteris fragilis*) all of our ferns should be treated as rare and endangered species. Their habitats are very specialized and fragile and many species would be eliminated by careless collecting or exploitation for rock gardens. A number of families is represented in this assemblage, but I am treating them as one in the traditional way, merely for convenience.

1a. Fronds linear, undivided except for a few narrow lobes at the tips. **Asplenium septentrionale** (L.) Hoffm. (northern), GRASS FERN, Fig. 18. Crevices of exposed rock outcrops and cliffs in the foothills. The evergreen fronds grow in dense grass-like clumps. Widely disjunct over the Northern Hemisphere (Colorado, North Africa, Northern Europe, The Alps, Caucasus, Central Asia, Siberia and Japan).
1b. Fronds broader, more or less dissected (typically fern-like) .... (2)

2a. Fronds with the lower pair of branches more or less equalling the central branch, creating the illusion of a ternate frond .... (3)
2b. Fronds distinctly pinnate, with one main axis from which the pinnae arise along the sides .... (5)

3a. Fronds tall and very coarse, forming thicket-like stands; sporangia, when present, borne on the inrolled edges of the pinnules. **Pteridium** *aquilinum* (L.) Kuhn (of an eagle; from the wing-like fronds), BRACKEN. Ravines at low or medium altitudes in the foothills. The largest native fern in this area.

3b. Fronds small, delicate; sporangia, when present, borne on the flat undersides of the pinnules .... (4)

4a. Ultimate pinnules broad, coarsely lobed, not deeply dissected, the lobes broadly rounded. *Gymnocarpium dryopteris* (L.) Newm., OAK

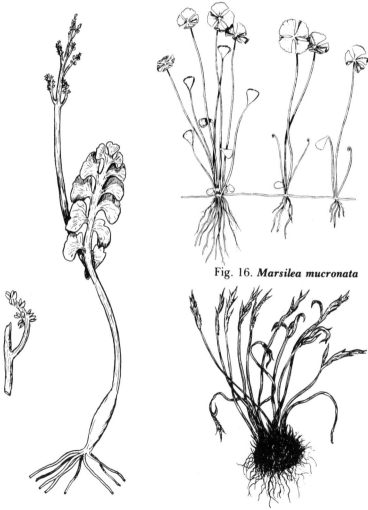

Fig. 16. *Marsilea mucronata*

Fig. 17. *Botrychium lunaria*

Fig. 18. *Asplenium septentrionale*

FERN, Fig. 19. Infrequent in deep, moist forests, upper montane and subalpine.

4b. Ultimate pinnules delicately lobed, finely dissected and narrowed to the base, the lobes with fine teeth. *Cystopteris montana* (L.) Bernh. Extremely rare, in cool, moist spruce forests, mostly west of the Divide, including the Grand County portion of Rocky Mountain National Park.

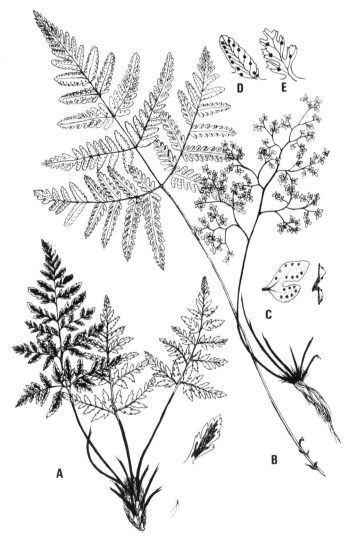

Fig. 19. A, *Asplenium adiantum-nigrum*; B, *Gymnocarpium*; C, *Notholaena fendleri*; D, E, venation of *Cystopteris fragilis* and *bulbifera*

5a. Fronds all alike in general appearance, the spores borne on unmodified vegetative fronds .... (6)
5b. Fronds of two distinct kinds—green sterile ones with broad pinnules, and fertile fronds with smaller pinnae or otherwise different in gross appearance .... (24)

6a. Underside of frond with a dense covering of brown scales, hairs, or a mass of white wax .... (7)
6b. Underside of frond without a covering of scales, hairs or wax, although sometimes covered with crowded sporangia .... (10)

7a. Fronds with a white coating of wax; frond delicately much-branched, the branches naked save for the small terminal pinnules. ***Notholaena fendleri*** Kunze (named for August Fendler), ZIGZAG CLOAK FERN, Fig. 19. Crevices of rock outcrops and talus slopes, foothills, more common south of the Arkansas Divide.
7b. Frond with a dense covering of reddish-brown scales or hairs, or both, on the underside .... (8)

8a. Fronds gray or ashy in color, with mixed scales and hairs beneath. ***Cheilanthes eatonii*** Baker (named for D. C. Eaton), EATONS LIP FERN. Rimrock and overhanging cliffs, chiefly in the Arkansas drainage of southeastern Colorado. Rare in our area.
8b. Fronds green, with either scales or hairs, but not both .... (9)

9a. Fronds reddish-hairy beneath, lacking scales. ***Cheilanthes feei*** Moore (named for A. L. Fée), SLENDER LIP FERN. Common on dry cliffs on the plains and foothills.
9b. Fronds scaly beneath, lacking hairs. ***Cheilanthes fendleri*** Hook. (named for August Fendler), FENDLERS LIP FERN. Infrequent, along horizontal seams in granite outcrops in the foothills.

10a. Fronds broadest at the base, almost triangular; sori elongate, parallel, in two rows on each pinnule; ripe sori forming an irregular brown mass of sporangia. ***Asplenium adiantum-nigrum*** L., Spleenwort, Fig. 19. One of the rarest of American ferns, known only from White Rocks, where it is rigorously protected on private land. Two other localities were once known in the U.S. (Zion National Park and Flagstaff, Arizona) but it has not been found in many years. In 1958 it was reported from a few localities in Mexico. It is a widely disjunct species around the Northern Hemisphere, chiefly in areas with an oceanic climate. Extremely endangered!
10b. Fronds broadest at or near the middle, or not conspicuously broader at the base .... (11)

11a. Frond simple, with a deeply lobed margin, the pinnae not actually separate from the main stem. ***Polypodium hesperium*** Maxon (western), POLYPODY, Fig. 20. Infrequent on boulders in cool ravines, foothills and montane.
11b. Frond compound, the primary pinnae separate from the main stem
.... (12)

12a. Lateral pinnae simple, undivided .... (13)
12b. Lateral pinnae deeply lobed or further subdivided .... (15)

13a. Lateral pinnae less than 5 mm long, not spiny-toothed; frond weak, often trailing .... (14)
13b. Lateral pinnae 1 cm or more long, spiny-toothed; frond stiff, erect. ***Polystichum lonchitis*** (L.) Roth, MOUNTAIN HOLLY FERN, Fig. 21. Rare on cliffs and rock walls on high mountain cirques, subalpine and alpine.
14a. Stipe of frond purple-black. ***Asplenium trichomanes*** L., MAIDENHAIR SPLEENWORT, Fig. 21. Cool cliffs and overhangs, plains to montane. In southeastern Colorado two similar species occur with longer pinnae: *A.platyneuron* (L.) Oakes in Eaton, and *A. resiliens* Kunze, with opposite pinnae.
14b. Stipe of frond green. ***Asplenium viride*** Huds., GREEN SPLEENWORT. Extremely rare in Colorado. We have an old record from near Pikes Peak.

15a. Pinnules evergreen, glaucous, mucronate-tipped, with rolled margins and purple-black stipe. ***Pellaea truncata*** Goodding. Common in canyons flowing into the Arkansas River, from Colorado Springs southward.
15b. Pinnules not evergreen or if so, not glaucous etc. .... (16)

16a. Fronds over 3 dm long, up to 15 cm or more wide .... (17)
16b. Fronds less than 3 dm long, up to about 10 cm wide .... (20)

Fig. 20. ***Polypodium hesperium***

17a. Ultimate divisions of frond blunt; frond bipinnatifid; sori round, in parallel rows on the pinnules; indusium shield-shaped, attached by the middle. ***Dryopteris filix-mas*** (L.) Schott, MALE FERN, Fig. 21. Frequent in deep shade in the outer foothills. Formerly gathered for the oil in the

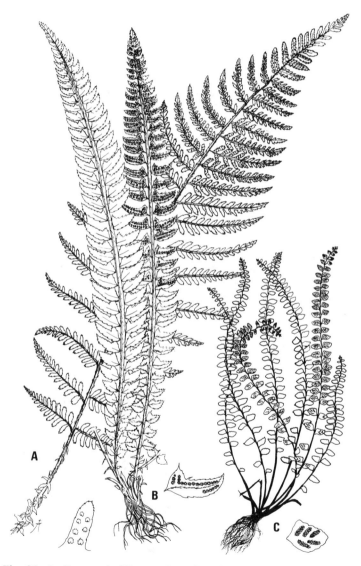

Fig. 21. A, ***Dryopteris filix-mas;*** B, ***Polystichum lonchitis;*** C, ***Asplenium trichomanes***

rhizomes, from which an anthelmintic was prepared, this species was almost exterminated by drug collectors. Fortunately it is no longer gathered commercially, but should be on the endangered list.

17b. Ultimate divisions of frond sharp-pointed; frond bipinnate; sori round, linear, or crescent-shaped; indusium attached by the middle or along one edge .... (18)

18a. Ultimate divisions of pinnules spinulose-tipped; lowest main lateral pinnae broadly ovate to triangular in gross outline (i.e., their basal pinnules very long); rachis of frond very scaly, even up into the pinnule-bearing portion. *Dryopteris assimilis* Walker, MOUNTAIN WOOD FERN. Very rare, deep subalpine forests, found only in Rocky Mountain National Park (*D. spinulosa* of 2nd Ed.)

18b. Ultimate divisions of the pinnules acute, not distinctly spine-tipped; lateral pinnae usually with the middle pinnules longest; scales mostly restricted to the basal, non-pinnule-bearing portion of the stalk ... (19)

19a. Indusium crescent-shaped, usually visible; frond well expanded, the pinnae not appearing crowded or directed sharply toward the apex of the frond; fronds few to a clump. *Athyrium filix-femina* (L.) Roth, LADY FERN. Common in forests of the foothills, never at or above timberline.

19b. Indusium rarely seen, minute, withering early; frond narrow, the pinnae appearing crowded, directed sharply toward the apex of the frond; fronds in dense clumps. *Athyrium distentifolium* Tausch *ex* Opiz var. *americanum* (Butters) Cronquist (with expanded leaves), ALPINE LADY FERN. At or near timberline, on open rock-slides. The fresh foliage is fragrant (*A. alpestre* of 4th Ed.).

20a. Fronds crowded, with remnants of the stalks of the previous season present on the rhizome; indusium splitting into linear segments which remain attached beneath the sporangia .... (22)

20b. Fronds not crowded; stalks brittle, thus those of the previous season are usually lacking or at least are not numerous; indusium a hood-like structure attached at one side .... (21)

21a. Veins of the pinnules ending in the teeth; fronds never with bulblets along the rachis. *Cystopteris fragilis* (L.) Bernh., BRITTLE FERN, Fig. 19. The most abundant fern in our area, in rock crevices from the plains to subalpine.

21b. Veins of the pinnules ending in the sinuses between the teeth; frond often with vegetatively reproductive bulblets along the rachis. *Cystopteris bulbifera* (L.) Bernh., Fig. 19. Never reported from Colorado, but found in adjacent states and probably to be found somewhere in our range, probably southward. It is included here to stimulate the search for it.

22a. Stems and fronds with stiffly spreading hairs. *Woodsia scopulina* D. C. Eaton (of rocks), ROCKY MOUNTAIN WOODSIA. Frequent in rock crevices, foothills.

22b. Stems and fronds not hairy .... (23)

23a. Lower half of the stipe usually reddish-black; cilia of the indusium either obscured by the sorus or just visible beyond it; cells of the epidermis regular in shape. **Woodsia oregana** D. C. Eaton, OREGON WOODSIA. Common on rocky slopes in the foothill canyons.

23b. Lower half of stipe usually brown; cilia of the indusium usually surrounding the sorus, and quite evident; cells of the epidermis with jagged walls. **Woodsia mexicana** Fée, MEXICAN WOODSIA. Found southeast of the Arkansas Divide but not definitely reported from our area.

24a. Sterile fronds short, yellow-green, with much-divided pinnae, the ultimate divisions blunt-tipped; fertile fronds taller, with narrow, pod-shaped pinnules .... (25)

24b. Sterile fronds tall, once-pinnate, the pinnae with wavy margins; fertile fronds brown, stiffly erect, the pinnules converted to little brown spheres; fronds solitary or a few together. **Onoclea sensibilis** L., SENSITIVE FERN. Extremely rare, only collected once, near Sedalia, and now extinct at that site.

25a. Fronds crowded on a short rhizome; in crevices of talus slopes and outcrops. **Cryptogramma crispa** (L.) R. Br. ssp. **acrostichoides** (R. Br.) Hultén, AMERICAN ROCK-BRAKE, Fig. 22. A very common fern on rock outcrops from the foothills to the high alpine cirques.

25b. Fronds small and weak, one or two together; in narrow crevices of steep cliff walls. **Cryptogramma stelleri** (Gmelin) Prantl, STELLERS CLIFF-BRAKE. Extremely rare, but scattered over the mountains of Colorado in the San Juans, Gunnison Basin, and Rabbit Ears Pass. Very likely to be found eventually in our area.

SELAGINELLACEAE—LITTLE CLUB-MOSS FAMILY

This family includes the remarkable "resurrection-plants" of Texas and Mexico, that roll into balls when dry and revive spectacularly under humid conditions. As in the Isoëtaceae, the spores are of two sizes (micro- and megaspores). This difference is evident even with the hand lens or naked eye. The orange-yellow sporangia are in the upper leaf-axils, megasporangia containing no more than four spores, and bulging irregularly by their contours. Microsporangia contain hundreds of very minute spores. The different spores produce female and male gametophytes, respectively.

1a. Leaves blunt, ciliate on the margins but lacking a white hair-point. **Selaginella mutica** D. C. Eaton (blunt). Rocky slopes in the more arid parts of the foothills.

1b. Leaves narrowed to a slender usually white hair-point ...... (2)

2a. Stems creeping along the ground, with rootlets along the main branches .... (3)

2b. Stems erect, densely matted, the main branches not bearing roots except at the base, in the soil. **Selaginella weatherbiana** Tryon (for C. A.

Weatherby, a fern specialist). North-facing cliffs in the foothills, locally abundant and forming huge rounded mounds. Endemic from Fort Collins to Santa Fé. A Tertiary relict closely related to *S. balansae*, of Morocco.

3a. Stems very short, the leaves curved upward, gray-green; fruiting branches erect, elongate, four-angled. **Selaginella densa** Rydb., Rock

Fig. 22 *Cryptogramma crispa*—lower left and right, fertile and sterile fronds

SELAGINELLA, Fig. 23. Common on rocks and soil, foothills to alpine tundra. To the inexperienced, this plant may be mistaken for the common hairy-cap moss, *Polytrichum piliferum*, which has similar hair-pointed leaves, but lacks the branching system and roots.

3b. Stems elongate, the leaves not strongly upcurved, bright green; fruiting branches inconspicuous. **Selaginella *underwoodii*** Hieron. (for L. M. Underwood, fern specialist). Abundant on cliffs in the foothills canyons, mostly on protected north slopes.

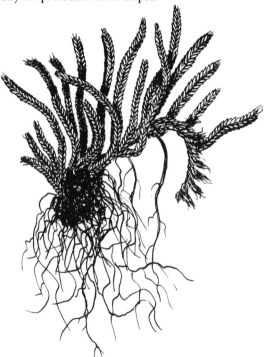

Fig. 23. *Selaginella densa*

Division Spermatophyta. Seed Plants.
Subdivision Gymnospermae.
Gymnosperms

PINACEAE—PINE FAMILY

The first and foremost question in the catechism of Rocky Mountain botany is "Can you recognize the gymnosperms?" These trees form our living scenery, their presence or absence tells us the altitude, the points of the compass, where the rocky ground is found, and what to expect in plant associations. Ecologists categorize a site on the basis of its forest type. One simply must learn to recognize the conifers first; all else follows.

1a. Leaves in the adult state closely imbricate (overlapping), minute, scale-like, or, if not imbricate and scale-like, then the cones berry-like, juicy. *Juniperus*, JUNIPER or RED CEDAR .... (2)
1b. Leaves in the adult state elongate, needle-like, not closely imbricate; cones dry at maturity, composed of overlapping woody scales ... (4)

2a. Shrub, usually less than 1 meter high; branches prostrate or spreading; leaves 5-15 mm long, not thickened or imbricate, the upper surface exposed to view and noticeably whitened. *Juniperus communis* L. ssp. *alpina* Celakovsky, COMMON JUNIPER, Fig. 24. Common in dry forests and on open slopes, from the mesas to alpine. The other species of *Juniperus* have juvenile foliage which is needle-like, but the needles are never as long as in this species, nor are the plants prostrate.
2b. Shrub or small tree, 2-16 meters high; leaves of the ultimate twigs 1-3 mm long, ovate, thickened, closely overlapping as if braided, the upper surface not exposed to view .... (3)

3a. Plants usually gray-green in color; leaves entire, paired; berry with 1 to 3 seeds, usually 2; branchlets usually rather slender, often with very slender terminal growth. *Juniperus scopulorum* Sarg., RED CEDAR, Fig. 25. Common in canyons and moist draws, foothills to montane.
3b. Plant usually dark green in color; leaves minutely denticulate, usually in pairs but often in whorls of 3; seeds 1 or 2, commonly solitary; branchlets usually rather stout. *Juniperus monosperma* (Engelm.) Sarg., ONE-SEED JUNIPER. On open mesas, from Colorado Springs southward.

4a. Leaves sheathed at the base, at least when young, usually in clusters of 2 or more; cone-scales very thick and woody, with swollen tips; bracts of the cone-scales minute, much shorter than the cone-scales; fruit maturing the second year (*Pinus*, Pines) .... (5)

4b. Leaves not sheathed at the base, nor in clusters; cone scales not very thick and woody, not swollen at the tip; bracts relatively large; fruit maturing the first season .... (9)

5a. Fascicles (leaf clusters) containing 5 needles .... (6)

5b. Fascicles containing 2 or 3 needles .... (7)

6a. Leaves commonly less than 5 cm long, usually strongly curved, sticky to the touch; cone-scales bristle-tipped. ***Pinus aristata*** Engelm. (awned), Fox-tail or Bristlecone Pine, Fig. 26. Mountainsides, upper montane and subalpine, from Caribou southward.

6b. Leaves usually more than 5 cm long, straight or only slightly curved, not sticky to the touch; cones lacking bristles. ***Pinus flexilis***

Fig. 24. ***Juniperus communis***   Fig. 25. ***Juniperus scopulorum***

James (flexible), LIMBER PINE, Fig. 27. The common pine of wind-swept summits, foothills to subalpine.

7a. Leaves 10-18 cm long, in three's or two's; cones 7-12 cm long; leaf fascicles crowded at the ends of the branches, at least in older trees. ***Pinus ponderosa*** Laws. var. ***scopulorum*** Engelm., PONDEROSA PINE; BULL PINE or YELLOW PINE, Fig. 28. The dominant tree of mesas, foothills, and south slopes of the montane. The number of needles is often unreliable in separating this from Lodgepole Pine.

7b. Leaves 3-7 cm long, usually in pairs; cones 5 cm long or less; leaves scattered along the branches .... (8)

Fig. 26. *Pinus aristata*

Fig. 27. *Pinus flexilis*

8a. Tall, slender tree; cone-scales bristle-tipped, the cones persistent on the tree for several years after maturity; needle in cross-section showing two vascular bundles. ***Pinus contorta*** Dougl. var. *latifolia* Engelm. (twisted, broad-leaved), LODGEPOLE PINE, Fig. 29. The common pine of burned-over areas, upper montane and subalpine.

8b. Low, bushy tree; cone-scales not bristle-tipped, the cones falling soon after maturity; needle in cross-section showing one vascular bundle. ***Pinus edulis*** Engelm. (edible), PINYON PINE, Fig. 30. Mesas

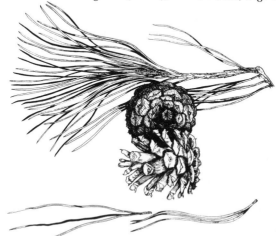

Fig. 28. ***Pinus ponderosa***

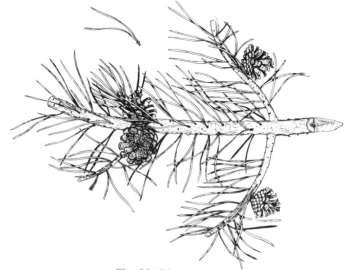

Fig. 29. ***Pinus contorta***

and foothills, from Colorado Springs southward. An isolated colony occurs in Owl Creek Canyon, northwest of Fort Collins. Scattered individuals occur in Rist and Boulder canyons.

9a. Older twigs studded with the persistent stumps of fallen leaves
....(10)
9b. Older twigs smooth ....(11)

10a. Young branches and leaf-bases pubescent; leaves not rigid, acute or acutish at apex; cones about 5 cm long, the scales more or less rounded and distinctly thinner at apex. ***Picea engelmannii*** (Parry) Engelm. (for George Engelmann), ENGELMANN SPRUCE, Fig. 31, right. Most common at high altitudes, upper montane and subalpine. At lower altitudes this species apparently hybridizes and intergrades with *Picea pungens*.
10b. Young branches glabrous; leaves rigid, almost spine-tipped; cones commonly 8 cm long, the scales truncate and not distinctly thinner at the apex. ***Picea pungens*** Engelm. (sharp), COLORADO BLUE SPRUCE, Fig. 31, left. Streamsides in steep canyons of the foothills. The trees vary considerably in the degree of "blueness."

11a. Leaf-scars elliptical; leaves stalked; cones hanging down, the scales persistent at maturity and the cone falling in one piece; bracts of the cone-scales longer than the scales, and 3-cleft. ***Pseudotsuga menziesii*** (Mirb.) Franco (for Archibald Menzies), DOUGLAS-FIR, Fig. 32. Moist canyons in the foothills and montane, mostly on north slopes (*P. taxifolia* of Ed. 2).

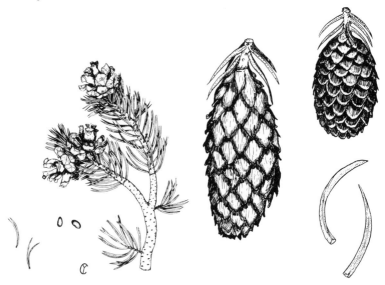

Fig. 30. ***Pinus edulis***

Fig. 31. SPRUCES: left, ***Picea pungens***;
right, ***P. engelmannii***

11b. Leaf-scars round; leaves sessile; cones erect, the scales falling away from the axis at maturity; cone-scales not noticeably exceeded by the bracts .... (12)

12a. Cones grayish-green; bracts of the cone-scales with a short triangular tip; cones 7-12 cm long; resin ducts of the leaves near the lower epidermis. **Abies concolor** (G. & G.) Lindl. (one-colored), WHITE Fir. Canyons near Colorado Springs and southwestward. A very handsome fir of medium elevations in the foothills.

12b. Cones dark brown-purple; bracts of the cone-scales with long subulate tips; cones 5 to 10 cm long; resin ducts of the leaves central. **Abies lasiocarpa** (Hook.) Nutt. (shaggy-fruited), SUBALPINE FIR. Common component of subalpine forests. The leaves of *A. concolor* are usually much longer than those of *A. lasiocarpa*, but this characteristic is not always reliable.

Fig. 32. *Pseudotsuga menziesii*

Division Spermatophyta
Subdivision Angiospermae
Flowering Plants
Class Dicotyledoneae. Dicots

ACERACEAE — MAPLE FAMILY

Maples of our area can always be recognized by the combination of three characters: palmately lobed (rarely pinnately compound) leaves; opposite arrangement; and two-winged fruits (samaras). Several genera of the Rosaceae as well as the genus *Ribes* have "maple leaves" but lack the other features. In Japan there are maples with elm-like leaves, so really the only reliable features are the opposite leaf arrangement and the samara.

1a. Leaves simple and 3- to 5-lobed, or sometimes (in forma *trisectum* Sarg.) palmately 3-parted, both types of leaves often on the same plant; twigs slender, the new growth red. *Acer glabrum* Torr., MOUNTAIN MAPLE, Fig. 33. Streamsides and canyons, foothills to montane. Three-parted leaves are more common on trees in the southern part of the area. In midsummer the leaves develop large bright red blotches. These are masses of minute galls containing Eriophyid mites.

1b. Leaves pinnately compound, with 3 to 5 leaflets; twigs stout, the new growth gray or bluish, often with a waxy covering. *Acer negundo* L. (an aboriginal word), BOX-ELDER, Fig. 34. Common in gulches and along streams, mesas and foothills. Variety *interius* (Britt.) Sarg., the native western race, has the young branchlets covered with short hairs, while the eastern variety *violaceum* Jaeg. & Beissn., introduced as a shade tree, has smooth, pale, glaucous twigs. This species is sometimes considered as a genus in its own right, *Negundo aceroides* Moench.

ADOXACEAE — ADOXA FAMILY

The name of this family comes from the Greek *adoxos*, meaning without glory, alluding to the unprepossessing aspect of our single species, *Adoxa moschatellina* L. (little musk), MOSCHATEL, Fig. 35. Moist, usually shaded sites, upper montane, subalpine and alpine. Rare or infrequent, inconspicuous and growing in such diverse sites as forested streambanks and alpine rockslides. The pale green flowers have a musky smell. With its thrice-ternate leaves and umbel-like flower cluster, the plant suggests a small umbellifer.

AIZOACEAE—CARPETWEED FAMILY

The family name is from the Latin *aizoon*, a succulent evergreen plant, and the family contains a number of *Sedum*-like plants. Our only local species comes closer to resembling a *Spergularia* or related caryophyll.

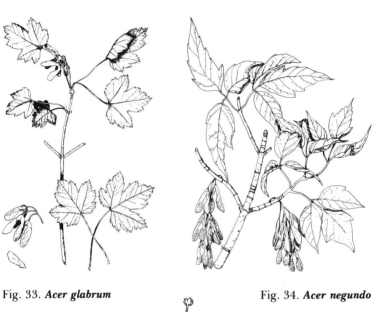

Fig. 33. *Acer glabrum*

Fig. 34. *Acer negundo*

Fig. 35. *Adoxa moschatellina*

One genus and species, ***Mollugo verticillata*** L. (whorled), Carpet-
weed, Fig. 36. Locally abundant introduced weed on sand bars of the
creeks of piedmont valleys and in gardens. The plants are prostrate
annuals, with slightly fleshy, whorled, oblanceolate leaves. The sepals are
white on the inner face, simulating petals. The shiny brown seeds are
beautifully sculptured with parallel, curved ridges.

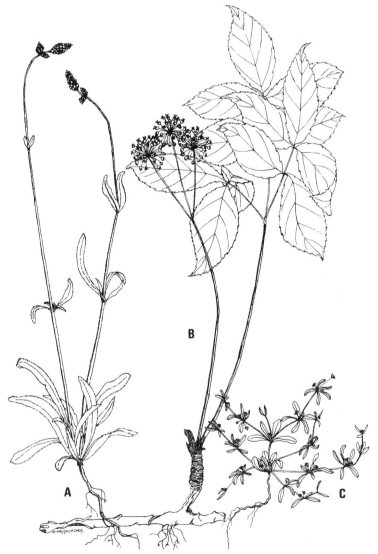

Fig. 36. A, *Froelichia*; B, *Aralia nudicaulis*; C. *Mollugo*

AMARANTHACEAE—AMARANTH FAMILY

The family name comes from a Greek word meaning unfading, alluding to the "everlasting" quality of the papery perianth parts. Many amaranths are cultivated for this quality: the Princes Feather, *Amaranthus hypochondriacus*, with red nodding "melancholy" spikes, and the Cockscomb, *Celosia argentea*. Our local amaranths are weeds of late summer, growing in waste or fallow ground, but in tropical America and Asia "grain amaranths" are important food crops in high elevations. The seeds are popped and made into balls with a syrup binder, or they are ground to meal and baked into cakes or drunk in a slurry.

1a. Leaves opposite; plants woolly-pubescent. ***Froelichia gracilis*** (Hook.) Moq. (slender), FROELICHIA, Fig. 36. Slender weedy annual with short interrupted spikes of small woolly flowers. Sandy soil on the plains and along roadsides of the lower foothills.
1b. Leaves alternate; plants glabrous or nearly so .... (2)

2a. Flowers mostly in terminal and axillary compound spikes ...... (3)
2b. Flowers all in small leafy-bracted axillary clusters .... (4)

3a. Spikes very elongate, narrow, rope-like. ***Amaranthus arenicola*** Johnston (sand-dweller), Fig. 37. Weed in cultivated ground and vacant lots, plains.
3b. Spikes thick, more or less pyramidal. ***Amaranthus retroflexus*** L. (bent backward), ROUGH PIGWEED, Fig. 37. Abundant weed in cultivated ground.

4a. Perianth parts 4 or 5, seeds 1.5 mm in diam; bracts ovate, not bristle-tipped. ***Amaranthus graecizans*** L. (resembling *A. graecus*), PROSTRATE PIGWEED, Fig. 37. Common weed in cultivated ground, sidewalk cracks, and trampled sites.
4b. Perianth parts 3 or fewer; seeds 1 mm or less in diam; bracts subulate, bristle-tipped. ***Amaranthus albus*** L., WHITE PIGWEED, Fig. 37. In similar habitats.

ANACARDIACEAE—SUMAC FAMILY

While a bout with poison ivy will instill certain knowledge of this family, it is nice to know that the anacards contain some of our most delicious fruits and nuts. *Anacardium occidentale* is the Cashew, *Pistacia vera* the Pistachio, and *Mangifera indica* is the Mango, which has to be picked dead ripe from the tree to be appreciated. Under cultivation as an ornamental in local parks is *Cotinus coggygria*, the Smoke Tree, so named for the exceedingly slender plumose sterile branches of the inflorescence that create an illusion of mist. The ubiquitous street tree of Southern California, Pepper Tree (*Schinus molle*) also belongs to this family.

1a. Leaflets 9 or more, regularly serrate; tall shrub with thick twigs; fruits

red, in pyramidal clusters. **Rhus glabra** L., SMOOTH SUMAC, Fig. 38.
Gulches in lower foothills and mesas. The Staghorn Sumac, *R. typhina*
L., is occasionally found as an escape from cultivation. It differs from
the above in having velvety-hairy twigs. *Ailanthus altissima*, in the
Simaroubaceae, looks like a sumac but has entire leaves with a few

Fig. 37. A, *Amaranthus retroflexus*; B, *A. albus*; C, *A. graecizans*; D, *A. arenicola*

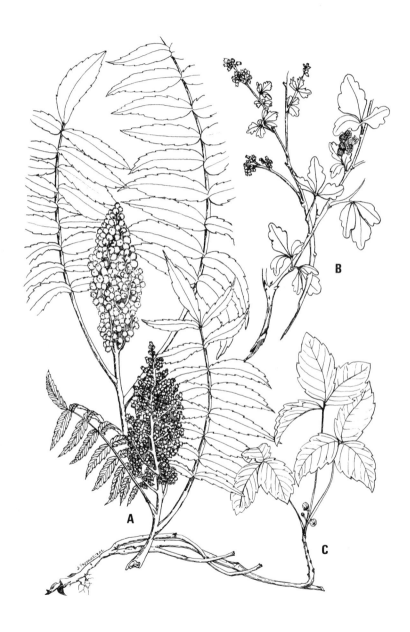

Fig. 38. A, *Rhus glabra*; B, *R. trilobata*; C, *Toxicodendron*

shallow lobes or auricles at the base of the leaflet, and the fruits are papery samaras rather than red velvety berries.

1b. Leaflets 3, irregularly crenate or cleft; low shrub or climber with slender twigs; fruit red or whitish, in small clusters . . . . (2)

2a. Plant erect or semi-erect, sparingly branched; terminal leaflet petiolate; fruits yellowish-white, glabrous or shining, in a loose panicle. ***Toxicodendron rydbergii*** (Small) Greene, Poison Ivy; Poison-oak, Fig. 38, Plate 16. Gulches and hillsides on the mesas and lower foothills, spreading into picnic areas as the result of disturbance and trampling of the ground.

2b. Erect, much-branched shrub; terminal leaflet narrowed to the sessile base; fruits red, pubescent, in dense clusters. ***Rhus trilobata*** Nutt., Skunkbrush, Fig. 38. One of the most abundant shrubs on the open sunny slopes of mesas and foothills, particularly in clay soils; foliage very aromatic.

Apocynaceae—Dogbane Family

The dogbane family is diversified in the tropics, where members are used as fiber plants, sources of India rubber, and arrow poisons. In recent years *Rauwolfia*, a tropical tree, was found to yield a wonder drug for high blood pressure. Most of the well-known genera are ornamentals. In our

Fig. 39. ***Apocynum androsaemifolium***

gardens, *Vinca minor*, Periwinkle, is a standard ground cover in shaded corners, and the Oleander, *Nerium oleander*, separates lanes of divided highways in California and Arizona. *Plumeria* provides the lovely Frangipani flowers of the Hawaiian leis.

1a. Corolla pink, 3 times the length of the calyx; branching mostly alternate, often dichotomous; leaves usually drooping. *Apocynum androsaemifolium* L. (with leaves like *Androsaemum*), SPREADING DOG-BANE, Fig. 39. This and the next species hybridize freely in the wild. Intermediates are known as *Apocynum medium* Greene. Common weedy herb of mesas and foothills.
1b. Corolla greenish-white, 1.5-2.0 times the length of the calyx; branching opposite; leaves erect or spreading, not drooping . . . . (2)

2a. Leaves all petiolate; upper leaves only slightly smaller than the lower leaves. *Apocynum cannabinum* L. (hemp-like), INDIAN HEMP. Roadsides, railroad embankments and similar disturbed areas, mesas and plains.
2b. Leaves (at least the lower ones) sessile, frequently clasping the stem; upper leaves noticeably smaller than lower leaves. *Apocynum sibiricum* Jacq., SIBERIAN DOGBANE. Same habitats as the last and probably the commoner of the two.

ARALIACEAE — GINSENG FAMILY

Rice paper is not made from rice at all but from an aralia, *Tetrapanax papyrifera*. The English Ivy, symbolic of the "ivory tower" is an aralia, *Hedera helix*. The spiny Devil's Club of the rain forests of the Pacific Northwest is an aralia, *Oplopanax horrida*. And Ginseng, one of the most ancient of medicines, is an aralia, *Panax ginseng*. Aralias are very close relatives of the Umbelliferae, differing in their 5-merous flowers.

1a. Stem scapose, the leaves and peduncle arising from the underground rhizome; umbels 1 to 3. *Aralia nudicaulis* L. (naked-stemmed), WILD SARSAPARILLA, Fig. 36. Infrequent in cool ravines, foothills and montane. A plant of the northeastern American forests disjunct in our eastern foothills. Formerly used as a substitute for sarsaparilla.
1b. Stem leafy; umbels very numerous, in a large terminal, compound panicle. *Aralia racemosa* L. This plant occurs rarely in New Mexico and Texas, and widely throughout the northeastern states, but has not been found in Colorado since Edwin James reported seeing it in 1820 somewhere above the Platte River near the present site of Bailey.

ASCLEPIADACEAE — MILKWEED FAMILY

The milkweed flower contains 5 sepals, 5 petals (which are usually reflexed), 5 stamens, and a gynoecium composed of two carpels which are free for most of their length, but which are united at the apex. Each carpel splits down one side at maturity, liberating the seeds, which are equipped with a tuft of silk-like hairs at one end, serving as a parachute.

Milkweed flowers are unique in their possession of what would appear to be a whorl of floral organs between the petals and the stamens. This whorl of 5 petal-like parts is called a corona, and each segment is a hood. On its inner surface, each hood may or may not have a horn-shaped structure protruding. The base of the hood may be expanded into flap-like structures called auricles.

The stamens themselves are united to the style, the two structures together forming a unit in the central part of the flower. The pollen grains formed within the anther sacs are sticky and hang together in masses called pollinia. The pollinia of adjacent anthers are united by a thread-like structure called a translator. The pollinia and connecting translator resemble a tiny pair of water wings. Insects, during visits to flowers, accidently catch their feet on the translators, yanking the pollinia free and carrying the pollen to other flowers.

1a. Lobes of the corolla erect or spreading at anthesis (flowering time). *Asclepias asperula* (Dcne.) Woodson (roughened), CREEPING MILKWEED. Mesas and plains, southern part of our range (*A. capricornu* of Ed. 2).
1b. Lobes of the corolla reflexed at anthesis .... (2)

2a. Entire plant usually not much more than 10 cm high. *Asclepias uncialis* Greene (an inch long, probably referring to the small size), DWARF MILKWEED. Rare or overlooked, mesas and plains.
2b. Plants usually at least 2 dm high .... (3)

3a. Hoods of the corona each bearing an incurved horn; flower clusters terminal and in the axils of only the uppermost leaves .... (6)
3b. Hoods of the corona lacking horns; flower clusters axillary .... (4)

4a. Auricles at the base of the hoods concealed; leaves oval to broadly linear. *Asclepias viridiflora* Raf. (green-flowered), GREEN MILKWEED. Common on dry slopes of mesas and plains.
4b. Auricles at the base of the hoods conspicuously spreading; leaves narrowly linear .... (5)

5a. Hoods 3-lobed at apex; corolla greenish-white. *Asclepias stenophylla* Gray, NARROW-LEAVED MILKWEED. Infrequent on the mesas.
5b. Hoods entire or merely notched in the middle; corolla white. *Asclepias engelmanniana* Woodson (for George Engelmann). Habitat similar to the preceding.

6a. Leaves narrowly linear; flowers white .... (7)
6b. Leaves lanceolate or broader; flowers pink, red, purple, or orange .... (8)

7a. Plant low, usually not more than 2 dm high, the leaves crowded, not very obviously whorled. *Asclepias pumila* (Gray) Vail, LOW MILKWEED. Mesas and plains.
7b. Plant 3 dm high or more, the leaves whorled, the internodes several cm long. *Asclepias subverticillata* (Gray) Vail (almost whorled), WHORLED MILKWEED. Mesas and plains, southern part of our range.

8a. Corolla and corona orange; leaves nearly all alternate. ***Asclepias tuberosa*** L. ssp. ***interior*** Woodson, Butterfly-weed. Canyons and mesas around Colorado Springs.

8b. Corolla greenish, purplish, red, or white .... (9)

9a. Corolla and hoods bright red or purple; lateral veins directed forward, curving to parallel the midrib. ***Asclepias incarnata*** L. (flesh-colored, a misnomer). Sloughs and wet ditches, in the piedmont valleys.

9b. Corolla and hoods varying from pink or dull purplish to white; lateral veins diverging at almost right angles from the midrib of the larger leaves .... (10)

10a. Whole plant, especially the pedicels, tomentose; pod knobby with soft spiny outgrowths. ***Asclepias speciosa*** Torr., Showy Milkweed, Fig. 41. The most abundant milkweed, in fields, along fence-rows, roadsides, etc., on the mesas, piedmont valleys, and plains.

10b. Foliage and pedicels minutely pubescent or almost smooth; pod without knobby outgrowths. ***Asclepias hallii*** Gray (for Elihu Hall). Mesas and plains in the southern part of our range.

Fig. 40. ***Impatiens capensis***

BALSAMINACEAE—JEWEL-WEED FAMILY

If the leaves of jewel-weed are held under water they assume a silvery sheen. Possibly this is where the family gets its name. Everything about the plant is fascinating. The orange flowers are shaped like a Persian slipper, and the pods are elastically dehiscent, needing only a slight touch to explode, scattering the round seeds several feet. Jewel-weed has occurred around Boulder for many years and spreads along irrigation ditches. Whether it is indigenous or was introduced deliberately or accidentally by a nurseryman or gardener from the eastern U.S. we probably will never be certain.

One genus and species, *Impatiens capensis* Meerb. (from Cape of Good Hope, erroneously thought to have come from there), JEWEL-WEED, Fig. 40. Frequent in shade along irrigation ditches and streams, vicinity of Boulder.

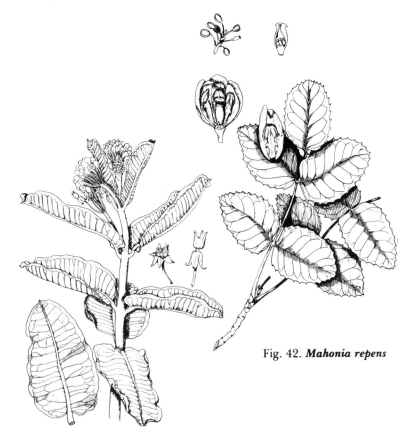

Fig. 42. *Mahonia repens*

Fig. 41. *Asclepias speciosa*

BERBERIDACEAE—BARBERRY FAMILY

The barberries include two very different groups, the evergreen, spiny-margin-leaved *Mahonia*, of which *M. aquifolium* is the erect type commonly cultivated as an ornamental, and *Berberis*, a spiny-stemmed plant with oval deciduous leaves. Of the latter, *Berberis thunbergii* DC. is cultivated as a barrier hedge and for its red berries. *Berberis vulgaris* L., another cultivar, has been nearly exterminated because it is a carrier of the black stem rust of wheat. One plant grew in Bluebell Canyon near Boulder for many years but seems to have disappeared now. *Berberis fendleri* A. Gray is native to the canyonsides of southern Colorado.

One genus and species, **Mahonia repens** (Lindl.) G. Don (creeping), OREGON-GRAPE; HOLLY-GRAPE, Fig. 42. Abundant on dry slopes, mesas and foothills to upper montane. The berries make a good jelly. *Mahonia* is a "living fossil," and several species occur as fossils in the Oligocene beds of Creede and Florissant.

BETULACEAE—BIRCH FAMILY

Boulder boasts the southernmost colony of Paper or Canoe Birch in North America—a small group of trees on Green Mountain, where it has hybridized extensively with the common River Birch. Only a few trees have the characteristic white, peeling bark and many trees are intermediate, with silvery-gray peeling bark. The trees are not very

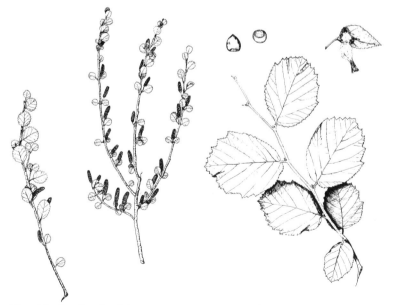

Fig. 43. *Betula glandulosa*

Fig. 44. *Corylus cornuta*

sturdy, and their stems succumb to rot as they attain full size, but they sucker well, and thus survive. This small colony has been analyzed thoroughly and the results published (*Evolution* 6:268-282. 1952) by S. G. Froiland. These plants deserve the utmost protection that our park system can afford.

1a. Low shrub of subalpine bogs; leaves almost round, thick, crenate-serrate; young twigs dotted with warty resinous glands. **Betula glandulosa** Michx., BOG BIRCH, Fig. 43. Common along streams and around ponds, subalpine.
1b. Tall shrubs or small trees; leaves ovate or obovate, sharply serrate; young twigs usually lacking warty resinous glands .... (2)

2a. Only the staminate flowers in catkins, catkin-like or cone-like structures; carpellate flowers sessile on the twig; fruit a nut enclosed in a green or papery brown husk; leaves rough-hairy. **Corylus cornuta** Marsh.(horned), FILBERT; BEAKED HAZELNUT, Fig. 44. Cool ravines in the foothills.
2b. Staminate and carpellate flowers in catkins, catkin-like clusters, or "cones"; leaves smooth or nearly so .... (3)

3a. Scales of the carpellate catkins thin, falling separately from the axis at maturity; leaves flat .... (4)
3b. Scales of the carpellate catkin thick, woody and persistent, resembling a small pine cone; leaves wrinkled. **Alnus tenuifolia** Nutt. (narrow-leaved), ALDER, Fig. 45. Streambanks and pond borders, foothills to subalpine.

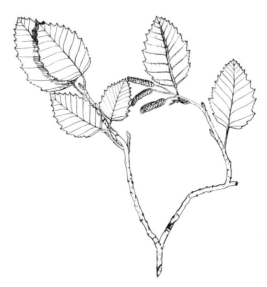

Fig. 45. *Alnus tenuifolia*

4a. Bark dark in color, not peeling; shrub with numerous slender main stems; lenticels elliptical, chalky-white. ***Betula fontinalis*** Sarg., RIVER BIRCH, Fig. 46. The common birch in the Rocky Mountain region, abundant along streams, foothills to subalpine.

4b. Bark gray, naturally peeling into thin layers, the underneath layers pink or white; trees with a few main stems over 10 cm diam; lenticels horizontally elongate. ***Betula papyrifera*** Marsh., PAPER or CANOE BIRCH. Very rare, in a cool, north-facing ravine in the foothills near Boulder. ***Betula X andrewsii*** Nels. is the hybrid between our two species.

BORAGINACEAE—BORAGE FAMILY

The borages share with the mints and verbenas the unique feature of a gynoecium divided into four discrete nutlets. When in doubt as to which family you have, remember that the borages alone have a radially symmetrical corolla and alternate leaves. Most borages, with a few exceptions such as *Mertensia*, characteristically have very stiff and harsh hairs on stems and leaves. The name, borage, comes from a Middle Latin source, *burra*, meaning rough hair or short wool, just as the modern word, bur; in fact the pronunciation of borage used to rhyme with courage.

1a. Flowers yellow or orange .... (2)
1b. Flowers not yellow .... (3)

2a. Individual flowers lacking bracts; weedy annuals with stiffly spreading hirsute pubescence; corolla deep yellow or orange. ***Amsinckia***, page 85.

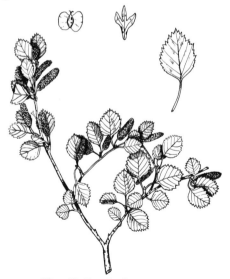

Fig. 46. *Betula fontinalis*

2b. Individual flowers bracteate; native perennials with mostly appressed pubescence; corolla lemon-yellow or bright yellow. *Lithospermum*, Puccoon, page 87.

3a. Very dwarf caespitose matted perennials of tundra; flowers blue or white, with yellow center. *Eritrichum*, Alpine Forget-me-not, page 87.
3b. Taller leafy-stemmed plants, or not strictly tundra species ..... (4)

4a. Margins or surfaces of the nutlets bearing hooked spines ...... (5)
4b. Margins of the nutlets not bearing spines .... (7)

5a. Flowers dull red-purple; nutlets large, the broad, convex outer surface covered by short hooked bristles. *Cynoglossum*, Hounds Tongue, page 86.
5b. Flowers blue or white; nutlets small, only the margins with hooked bristles .... (6)

6a. Plants annual; pedicels erect; in fruit the style surpassing the nutlets. *Lappula*, Stickseed, page 87.
6b. Plants perennial or biennial; pedicels reflexed; in fruit the style surpassed by the nutlets. *Hackelia*, False Forget-me-not, page 87.

7a. Lower stem leaves opposite; small, weak, delicate plants branched from the base, rooted in mud, mostly montane and subalpine; flowers minute, white. *Plagiobothrys*, page 89.
7b. Stem leaves all alternate (or if occasionally opposite, flowers blue); more robust plants .... (8)

8a. Flowers blue, axillary or in terminal bractless clusters .... (9)
8b. Flowers white, in usually bracteate clusters or racemes (bractless only in one species of *Cryptantha*) .... (12)

9a. Flowers sessile in the axils of the upper leaves; calyx enlarged in fruit, veiny, flattened and about 10-toothed; stems weak; leaves rounded-oblanceolate. *Asperugo*, Madwort, page 85.
9b. Flowers in terminal clusters, becoming more or less elongated racemes .... (10)

10a. Corolla tubular, with a slightly wider cylindric or campanulate limb, the ultimate lobes very small and not widely spreading; native plants of the foothills and mountains. *Mertensia,* Chiming Bells; Bluebells, page 88.
10b. Corolla salverform or broadly funnelform, the lobes spreading; escaped garden plants .... (11)

11a. Corolla small, sky-blue with yellow center; annual, with slender stem and elongate raceme. *Myosotis*, Forget-me-not, page 89.
11b. Corolla large, deep blue or purple; perennial with stout stem, harsh pubescence, and flowers in dense clusters. *Anchusa*, Alkanet, page 85.

12a. Leaves ovate-lanceolate, with very prominent parallel veins and a dense, furry pubescence of appressed hairs; corolla-lobes acute, erect, the flower with a closed appearance. **Onosmodium**, FALSE GROMWELL, page 89.

12b. Leaves linear-lanceolate, or oblanceolate, the veins inconspicuous; corolla-lobes rounded, spreading. **Cryptantha**, page 85.

AMSINCKIA

1a. Corolla throat closed by a ring of hairs; stamens attached below the middle of the corolla tube. **A. lycopsoides** Lehm. *ex* Fisch. (resembling the genus *Lycopsis*). This and the following two species are natives of the far West but have weedy tendencies. They have been accidentally introduced in scattered localities in the foothills, where they colonize disturbed ground.

1b. Corolla throat open, glabrous inside; stamens attached above the middle of the corolla tube .... (2)

2a. Stem with two distinct kinds of hairs, the one long, stiff, spreading, the other much more slender, shorter and bent downwards; pubescence of the leaves tending to be appressed and directed forward. **A. retrorsa** Suksdorf.

2b. Stem with coarse, stiff, spreading hairs, basally swollen; hairs of the leaves similar; fine hairs nearly or quite lacking. **A. menziesii** (Lehm.) Nels. & Macbride.

ANCHUSA. ALKANET

1a. Corolla 15-20 mm wide; calyx cleft nearly to the base; nutlets longer than wide, erect. **Anchusa azurea** Miller (*A. italica* of Ed. 4). A handsome ornamental borage commonly escaping from old gardens in and around towns.

1b. Corolla 6-10 mm wide; calyx cleft to about the middle; nutlets wider than long, horizontal. **Anchusa officinalis** L. Similar habitats but probably not as common as the last.

ASPERUGO. MADWORT

One species, **Asperugo procumbens** L. (Fig. 47), a weak, spreading Eurasian weed naturalized near Georgetown. The flowers are small, dark blue, and the calyx becomes enlarged and flattened at maturity, showing up to 15 lobes or teeth.

CRYPTANTHA

1a. Plants biennial or perennial, with a basal rosette of leaves; corolla 0.5 cm wide or more .... (2)

1b. Plants slender, annual; flowers smaller .... (4)

2a. Stem simple, the flower-stalk spike-like; bracts longer than the flowers, standing out at right angles from the stem; leaves linear or narrowly oblanceolate. **Cryptantha virgata** (Porter) Payson (wand-like),

MINERS CANDLE, Plate 10. Abundant on dry slopes, mesas to montane.
2b. Stem branched, or if simple, the inflorescence with several distinctly
   elongated branches .... (3)

3a. Flowers in short-paniculate clusters; nutlets smooth and shining;
   perennial. *Cryptantha jamesii* (Torr.) Payson. Common on mesas and
   plains, flowering in early spring.
3b. Flowers in a bushy-branched panicle, the branches elongate; nutlets
   wrinkled; biennial. *Cryptantha thyrsiflora* (Greene) Payson (with a
   thyrse inflorescence). Mesas and plains, barely entering our area at
   the northern and southern limits.

4a. Nutlets four, all of them smooth and shining; plants becoming very
   much branched and forming hemispherical "bushes"; inflorescence
   branches elongate, slender, with remote flowers. *Cryptantha fendleri*
   (Gray) Greene. Plains, mesas, and foothills.
4b. Nutlets four, but three of these small and tuberculate-roughened,
   the fourth larger and smooth; plants little-branched, the inflorescence
   stout, stiff, with two distinct rows of flowers. *Cryptantha minima* Rydb.
   Plains, mesas, and foothills; a very abundant weed in dry disturbed
   ground.

CYNOGLOSSUM. HOUNDS TONGUE
   One species, *Cynoglossum officinale* L., Fig. 47. A Eurasian weed
occurring in forest clearings in the mountains, often appearing after
logging operations.

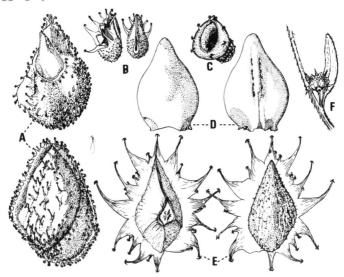

Fig. 47. Fruits of borages. A, *Cynoglossum*; B, *Lappula redowskii*; C, *L. diploloma*; D, *Lithospermum*; E, *Hackelia*; F, *Asperugo*

ERITRICHUM. Alpine Forget-me-not

One species, **Eritrichum aretioides** (Cham.) DC. (resembling *Aretia*, a genus of Old World primroses), Fig. 48. Dry stony alpine and subalpine mountainsides. White-flowered mutants are not uncommon. The spelling *Eritrichium* has to be replaced by the original given above. The genus represents a distinct Asiatic element in our alpine flora.

HACKELIA. False Forget-me-not

1a. Flowers 2.5 mm long; nutlets about 2.5 mm long, the prickles free to their bases. **Hackelia besseyi** (Rydb.) J. Gentry. Only known from canyons near Colorado Springs.
1b. Flowers 4-6 mm long; nutlets 3-4 mm long, the prickles usually somewhat merging at the base. **Hackelia floribunda** (Lehm.) Johnston, Fig. 47. Mountain meadows, roadsides and aspen groves, upper montane and subalpine. The blue flowers, with a yellow center, resemble those of the true Forget-me-not (*Myosotis*).

LAPPULA. Beggars-tick

1a. Nutlets with a double row of hooked prickles along the margin. **Lappula echinata** Gilib. Until now this has been found only west of the Divide but it is spreading rapidly and probably already occurs in our area. Introduced weed from Eurasia.
1b. Nutlets with a single row of prickles along the margin .... (2)

2a. Some or all of the nutlets with an inflated rim formed of the swollen bases of the marginal prickles; plants branched mostly from the base, the branches mostly simple. **Lappula diploloma** (F. & M.) Guerke (*L. redowskii* var. *cupulata* of Ed. 4), Fig. 47. A common weed in dry silty soils on the plains and lower valleys. Also found in Siberia. The inflated rim resembles a horse collar.
2b. Nutlets not conspicuously swollen at the base into an inflated rim; plants usually unbranched below, then with a whorl of branches above. **Lappula redowskii** (Hornem.) Greene, Fig. 47. An extremely common weed from the plains to montane. This may hybridize with the former, but the two certainly appear to represent distinct species.

LITHOSPERMUM. Puccoon

1a. Corolla bright yellow .... (2)
1b. Corolla very pale yellow, almost greenish-white. **Lithospermum ruderale** Dougl. in Lehm. Abundant in the intermountain parks and valleys of the western slope but only represented by an old record from the Denver area. A robust species with many stout leafy stems from a single base; flowers inconspicuous, almost hidden in the upper leaves.

2a. Corolla-tube 3-4 times as long as the calyx, the lobes fringed; corolla with prominent crests in the throat. **Lithospermum incisum** Lehm. (sharply cleft), Narrow-leaved Puccoon. Very common spring flower on the plains and mesas.

2b. Corolla-tube about twice as long as the calyx, the lobes rounded; crests of the corolla-throat inconspicuous. ***Lithospermum multiflorum*** Torr., MANY-FLOWERED PUCCOON. Later-flowering (June-July) than the preceding, and ranging to higher altitudes, mesas to subalpine.

The puccoons are biologically interesting. *L. incisum*, later in the season, produces cleistogamous flowers that produce seed without ever opening. *L. multiflorum* exhibits floral dimorphism, some plants having flowers with long styles ("pin" flowers) and others with short styles and stamens attached high in the corolla tube ("thrum" flowers). This is a device that helps to ensure cross-pollination. Read Charles Darwin, *The Different Forms of Flowers on Plants of the Same Species.*

MERTENSIA. CHIMING BELLS; BLUEBELLS

1a. Plants with several pairs of prominent lateral veins in the stem leaves; stem usually 4 dm or more tall; plants of moist sites, flowering in late spring and summer. ***Mertensia ciliata*** (James) G. Don, TALL MERTENSIA, Fig. 49. Abundant along subalpine rivulets.

1b. Plants without lateral veins in the stem leaves or with only one or two pairs; stems usually less than 4 dm high; plants of fairly dry, open habitats, flowering in early spring, or later at much higher altitudes
. . . . (2)

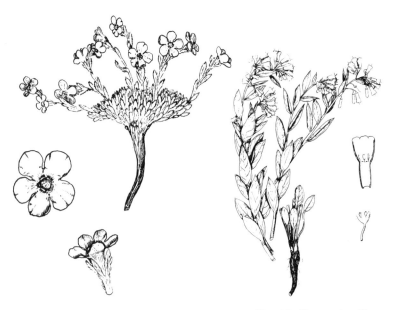

Fig. 48. *Eritrichum aretioides* Fig. 49. *Mertensia ciliata*

2a. Filaments attached in the corolla tube, the anthers not projecting beyond the junction of the tube and the expanded limb; alpine only. **Mertensia alpina** (Torr.) G. Don, ALPINE MERTENSIA. Rare, on high tundra, Pikes Peak.

2b. Filaments attached near the throat of the corolla, the anthers projecting beyond the junction of the tube and the expanded limb ... (3)

3a. Calyx divided to the very base; filaments shorter than the anthers; style usually not reaching the anthers; anthers straight; alpine or subalpine. **Mertensia viridis** Nels., GREEN MERTENSIA. The common species of high altitude grassland. In the alpine tundra it appears to be excessively variable in pubescence and flower shape, suggesting that it has hybridized in the past with *M. alpina*, which no longer grows over most of the region.

3b. Calyx not divided quite to the base; filaments longer than anthers; style usually surpassing anthers; anthers usually curved; plants usually not alpine nor subalpine. **Mertensia lanceolata** (Pursh) A. DC., NARROW-LEAVED MERTENSIA. Abundant on the mesas and foothills in early spring. Replaced at higher altitudes by the preceding.

MYOSOTIS. FORGET-ME-NOT

1a. Slender annuals established in moist shaded places; inflorescence elongate. **Myosotis scorpioides** L. Occasionally escaped around mountain cabins near Nederland.

1b. Low perennials with mostly basal leaves; inflorescence compact and not elongating. **Myosotis alpestris** Schmidt ssp. **asiatica** Vestergren. Although this has only been collected on the White River Plateau there is no reason why it should not occur in our area and I include it in the hope that it may be discovered.

ONOSMODIUM. FALSE GROMWELL

One species, **Onosmodium molle** Michx. var. **occidentale** (Mack.) Johnston. Common on the plains and mesas. The corolla is very odd, since the lobes are infolded to form a cone through which the long style protrudes. The nutlets, hard as ivory and of the same color, attract attention late in the season, while the leaves, with their parallel veins and stiff hairs laid in one direction, are very elegant.

PLAGIOBOTHRYS

One species, **Plagiobothrys scopulorum** (Greene) Johnston (of the Rockies). A weak little spreading annual growing in muddy depressions from the mesas to the subalpine. Flowers minute, white.

CACTACEAE—CACTUS FAMILY

Except for the prickly-pears (*Opuntia* spp.) we should consider our cacti as rare and endangered plants and refrain from collecting them in the wild. They are rapidly disappearing because of exploitation from the rock garden trade. In Arizona the collecting of cacti is prohibited by state law, a precedent that should be followed by Colorado.

1a. Stems jointed, bearing short-lived leaves on the young joints ... (2)
1b. Stems not jointed, but frequently in clusters, branched at the base; leaves absent .... (6)

2a. Stems cylindrical, branching like a tree; spines hooked at the end. *Opuntia imbricata* (Haw.) DC., CANDELABRA CACTUS. Barely entering the area from the south, around Colorado Springs. Flowers purple (*O. arborescens* Engelm.).
2b. Stems not as above .... (3)

3a. Stem segments round or only slightly flattened in cross-section; segments brittle, easily detached. *Opuntia fragilis* (Nutt.) Haw., BRITTLE CACTUS. Open ponderosa pine forests on the mesas.
3b. Stem segments strongly flattened in cross-section; segments neither brittle nor easily detached .... (4)

4a. Joints 15-30 cm long, the distance between areoles (clusters of spines) 3-4 cm. *Opuntia phaeacantha* Engelm. (brown-spined), NEW MEXICAN PRICKLY-PEAR. Southeastern Colorado north to Canyon City, but also in gulches on the mesas north of Boulder. The very large, bluish stems and long stout brown-tipped spines, plus the fleshy red fruit, are diagnostic.
4b. Joints 10-15 cm long; distance between areoles 1.5-2.5 cm ...... (5)

5a. Joints with rather sparse spines, the flat surface wrinkled transversely; fruits fleshy, edible. *Opuntia compressa* (Salisb.) Macbr., PRICKLY-PEAR. Common on the plains and mesas. Flowers yellow.
5b. Joints usually very spiny, not wrinkled; fruits dry, withering. *Opuntia polyacantha* Haw., STARVATION CACTUS. Abundant on the plains. Flowers yellow, pink, or copper-colored.

6a. Plants with parallel longitudinal ridges; flowers greenish-yellow. *Echinocereus viridiflorus* Engelm. (green-flowered), HEN-AND-CHICKENS. Common on rocky ground of mesas. Plant commonly reddish-tinged.
6b. Plants with nipple-like tubercles, these not united to form parallel longitudinal ridges .... (7)

7a. Tubercle with a narrow groove or line running along the upper side; flower not arising from spine-bearing tubercles but between them .. (8)
7b. Tubercles not grooved; flowers arising from spine-bearing tubercles. *Pediocactus simpsonii* (Engelm.) Britt. & Rose (for James H. Simpson), MOUNTAIN BALL CACTUS. Grassy openings in pine forests in the foothills. Flowers pink with a heavy rose fragrance.

8a. Flowers pink; fruit green or brown. *Coryphantha vivipara* (Nutt.) Britt. & Rose (sprouting on the parent plant), BALL CACTUS. Frequent on the plains (*Mammillaria vivipara* of manuals).

8b. Flowers green or yellow; fruit red, maturing the following year. **Coryphantha missouriensis** (Sweet) Britt. & Rose (of Missouri), Nipple Cactus, Plate 4. Very inconspicuous, but fairly common on the mesas.

Callitrichaceae — Water-starwort Family

While the water-starworts are easily recognized as a genus through their slender stems, opposite linear or oblong leaves and sessile fruits in the leaf-axils, the species are very difficult to identify partly because of their environmental plasticity. Stem length, leaf shape and succulence vary with the degree of submergence. They are very complex genetically, most of the species being partially apomictic.

1a. Flowers without bracts at the base; leaves uniform, submerged. **Callitriche hermaphroditica** L.
1b. Flowers 2-bracted at base; floating leaves usually broad, submerged leaves linear .... (2)

2a. Fruit definitely longer than wide, narrowed to the base, the sides keeled. **Callitriche palustris** L. (of marshes), Fig. 50. Floating or submerged in irrigation ditches and slow streams, plains to subalpine.
2b. Fruit as broad as long, rounded at the base, the sides with rounded edges. **Callitriche heterophylla** Pursh (various-leaved). Similar habitats.

Campanulaceae—Bellflower Family

This family contains some choice rock-garden plants, many of them originally native to the meadows and tundra of Eurasia. Most species of *Campanula* are known by the deep bell-shape of the usually blue to purple corolla, and the species differ in the ways the flowers are grouped

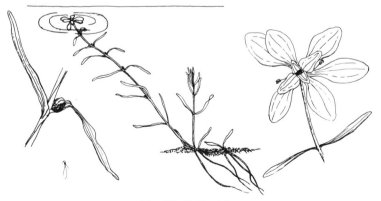

Fig. 50. *Callitriche*

together as well as by their sizes and shapes. The family also contains a group of plants differing from the bluebells in having a bilaterally symmetrical corolla reminiscent of a *Penstemon* but belonging here by virtue of the three style branches and inferior ovary. These are the lobelias, of which we have only one. Lobelias are commonly cultivated as flowering border plants. A firecracker-red lobelia, the Cardinal Flower, occurs in moist gulches in southeastern Colorado.

1a. Corolla bilaterally symmetrical, tubular, 2-lipped; anthers united. *Lobelia siphilitica* L. (for its supposed curative properties), GREAT LOBELIA. Rare or only locally abundant in wet meadows and ditches in the piedmont valleys, a prairie disjunct here.

1b. Corolla radially symmetrical, flat open or bell-shaped, with 5 equal lobes . . . . (2)

2a. Corolla bell-shaped (campanulate) . . . . (3)
2b. Corolla flat open (rotate) . . . . (7)

3a. Tall coarse herb with ovate, coarsely serrate basal and stem leaves and purple flowers in a long raceme. *Campanula rapunculoides* L. Formerly cultivated in old-fashioned gardens, but escaped and now a difficult weed to eradicate where it is not wanted. It spreads by deep underground rhizomes and, although attractive, crowds out other desirable plants. Weeds do have their saving graces, nevertheless. Recently it was reported that a chemical found in the leaves of this species is effective in reducing cancer tumors implanted in laboratory rats and studies are under way to isolate the substance.

3b. Tall or low herbs with linear or narrow stem leaves, only the basal leaves sometimes ovate . . . . (4)

4a. Stem tall, very leafy; flowers small (about 5 mm diam), pale purple or white; stem and leaves retrorse-scabrous (like a bedstraw). *Campanula aparinoides* Pursh. Extremely rare, collected only once, probably in the north end of South Park in 1861.

4b. Stem tall or low, not very leafy; flowers very variable in size, highly colored (except for occasional mutants); stem smooth . . . . (5)

5a. Anthers 1.5-2.5 mm long; corolla usually deeply and narrowly lobed; plant usually less than 8 cm tall; leaves oblanceolate, more or less crenulate; plants of alpine tundra only. *Campanula uniflora* L., ALPINE HAREBELL. Rare, easily distinguished from dwarfed alpine forms of the next two species by the distinctive shape of the corolla. The fruit is elongate, club-shaped, in contrast to the short cup-shaped fruits of the next species. Circumpolar.

5b. Anthers 4.0-6.5 mm long; corolla usually shallowly and broadly lobed; plant usually over 10 cm tall; leaves commonly linear, the lower and basal sometimes ovate or cordate, obscurely if at all crenulate; foothills to alpine . . . . (6)

6a. Bases of lower stem leaves ciliate with white hairs up to 0.7 mm long, the plants otherwise glabrous; flower usually solitary, the corolla lobed halfway, the lobes widely spreading and the bell shallow; capsule erect, opening by pores near the summit. ***Campanula parryi*** Gray (for C. C. Parry), Harebell. Subalpine to near timberline, and at lower altitudes on the Arkansas Divide near Palmer Lake.

6b. Leaf bases never long-ciliate; flowers usually numerous except in high altitude populations; corolla lobed about one-third, the lobes not flaring and the bell deep; capsule nodding, opening by pores near the base. ***Campanula rotundifolia*** L. (round leaves—which the plants only rarely exhibit), Common Harebell, Fig. 51. Abundant on dry mountainsides from foothills to alpine tundra. At high altitudes the plants are small, with very large often solitary flowers; these may represent a good subspecies.

7a. Leaves broadly ovate-cordate, clasping the stem. ***Triodanis perfoliata*** (L.) Nieuwl. (clasping-leaved), Venus Looking-glass. Frequent on the outer mesa slopes, in grassland. The flowers are sessile in the cups formed by the clasping leaf-bases.

7b. Leaves lanceolate or linear, not clasping the stem. ***Triodanis leptocarpa*** (Nutt.) Nieuwl. Habitat similar to the preceding. In fruit the elongate narrow capsule crowned by the stiffly-spreading needle-like calyx-lobes is distinctive. The flowers of *Triodanis* are short-lived.

Fig. 51. ***Campanula rotundifolia***   Fig. 52. ***Cleome serrulata***

CAPPARIDACEAE—CAPER FAMILY

Capers are the pickled flower buds of *Capparis spinosa* and are essential to the preparation of the German meatball dish called "Königsberger Klops." The plant is a usually spiny shrub of the Mediterranean region. The giant "Spider-flower" of gardens, so called because of its stalked slender petals and long-exserted stamens, is *Cleome spinosa*, a giant relative of our common Rocky Mountain Bee Plant. Many capparids have sticky and unpleasant smelling foliage and pods. "Cutting capers" has nothing to do with this name but with the Greek word *caper* meaning billy-goat.

1a. Plant glabrous; stamens 6; capsule long-stalked; flowers purplish, rarely white. *Cleome serrulata* Pursh, ROCKY MOUNTAIN BEE PLANT, Fig. 52. Abundant in midsummer along roadsides on the plains. In western Colorado a more dwarf species with yellow flowers, *C. lutea* Hook., is common on barren clay flats.
1b. Plant sticky-glandular-pubescent; stamens 8 or more; capsule almost sessile; flowers pale pink or white, rarely deeply colored. *Polanisia dodecandra* (L.) DC. (with 8 stamens), CLAMMY-WEED, Plate 27. Frequent as a weed along roadsides on the plains, mesas and foothill canyons. A dwarf relative of this, with minute cream-colored flowers, is abundant on sand hills east of our area. *Polanisia jamesii* (T. & G.) Iltis could well occur within our range in sandy places.

CAPRIFOLIACEAE—HONEYSUCKLE FAMILY

Every gardener is familiar with Elderberry, Viburnum, Honeysuckle and Snowberry. Fewer know the most famous plant of the family—the Twinflower, *Linnaea*, which covers forest floors across the Northern Hemisphere. Linnaeus was so proud of this little plant that most of his portraits show him holding a sprig of it. He perhaps deliberately overmodestly wrote that "*Linnaea* was named by the celebrated Gronovius and is a plant of Lapland, lowly, insignificant, disregarded, flowering but for a brief space, after Linnaeus who resembles it."

1a. Leaves pinnately compound (*Sambucus*, ELDERBERRY) . . . . (2)
1b. Leaves simple . . . . (3)

2a. Inflorescence broadly short-pyramidal, with the main axis extended beyond the lowermost floral branches; berries red, rarely darker. *Sambucus racemosa* L. ssp. *pubens* (Michx.) House (hairy), RED-BERRIED ELDER, Fig. 53. The common wild elderberry of the region, from foothills to subalpine.
2b. Inflorescence flat-topped, the axis not or seldom extended beyond the lowermost branches; berries black. *Sambucus canadensis* L., ELDERBERRY, Fig. 53, upper right. Frequent along the mesa-plain irrigated fringe, in most or possibly all instances escaped from cultivation.

3a. Plant low, only slightly woody, with prostrate creeping stems; flowers

Fig. 53. **Sambucus racemosa**. Upper right, **S. canadensis**

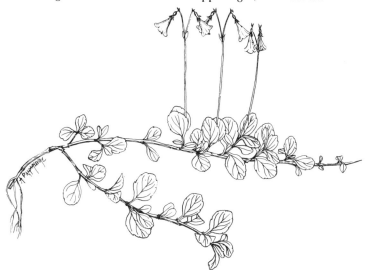

Fig. 54. **Linnaea borealis**

in pairs on an elongate, erect peduncle. **Linnaea borealis** L. ssp.
americana (Forbes) Hultén, Twin-flower, Fig. 54. Spruce-fir forests,
subalpine.
3b. Plant shrubby, with erect stems .... (4)

4a. Flowers numerous, in open, flat-topped clusters (genus *Viburnum*)
.... (5)
4b. Flowers solitary in the leaf-axils, or in pairs or short spikes .... (7)

5a. Leaves ovate, finely serrate, not lobed .... (6)
5b. Leaves 3-lobed, coarsely serrate or dentate. **Viburnum edule** (Michx.)
Raf. (edible), High-bush-cranberry. Infrequent in moist forests,
upper montane and subalpine. A close relative of the Snowball-tree,
Viburnum opulus L., a common cultivar in this region, but in that the
leaves are more deeply lobed, they have stipules, and the marginal
flowers of the cluster are greatly enlarged and neuter.

6a. Leaves covered on both sides by a velvet nap of stellate hairs; leaves
strongly veined, merely acute at the apex. **Viburnum lantana** L.,
Wayfaring-tree. Naturalized in the foothills gulches, the seeds
probably carried there from gardens in town by jays.
6b. Leaves glabrous, not strongly veined, shortly acuminate at the apex.
Viburnum lentago L., Nannyberry. Rare, in a mesa gulch near Boulder,
probably originally planted by the early settlers. Native in eastern
North America.

7a. Corolla two-lipped .... (8)
7b. Corolla radially symmetrical .... (9)

8a. Flowers pale to deep pink, not changing to yellowish. **Lonicera
tatarica** L., Tartarian Honeysuckle. A common escape from gardens
and locally established in the foothill gulches with the next.
8b. Flowers yellow or white changing to yellow. **Lonicera morrowii**
Gray. Commonly escaped from gardens and naturalized in wild areas.
Said to commonly hybridize with *L. tatarica*.

9a. Flowers yellow, in pairs on long axillary peduncles; berry black or
purplish. **Lonicera involucrata** (Rich.) Banks *ex* Spreng. (with an involucre), Bush Honeysuckle, Fig. 55. Very common shrub along
streams, foothills to subalpine.
9b. Flowers pink or white, almost sessile or in short spikes; berry white,
juicy (*Symphoricarpos*) .... (10)

10a. Corolla bell-shaped, the lobes about as long as or slightly longer
than the tube .... (11)
10b. Corolla tubular or funnel-shaped, the lobes much shorter than the
tube. **Symphoricarpos oreophilus** Gray (mountain-loving), Snowberry;
Buckbrush. Mesas to montane. (incl. *S. vaccinioides* Rydb.)

11a. Style and stamens shorter than or only equalling the corolla, not
exserted. **Symphoricarpos albus** (L.) Blake (white), Snowberry; Buckbrush. Frequent in the foothill canyons.

11b. Style and stamens exserted. ***Symphoricarpos occidentalis*** Hook.
(western), SNOWBERRY; BUCKBRUSH, Fig. 56. Common low shrub,
plains, mesas, and foothills. A close relation of the garden species.

CARYOPHYLLACEAE—PINK FAMILY

This is a very easily recognized family containing some handsome
cultivated plants such as Carnations, Garden Pinks, Baby's-breath and the
showy rock-garden "Snow-in-summer," *Cerastium tomentosum.* A good
vegetative character rarely mentioned in the keys is the distinctly swollen
node at which each pair of leaves arises.

1a. Sepals united for most of their length, 5-toothed at the apex; petals
with long stalks (claws) .... (2)
1b. Sepals separate, 5 in number; petals, when present, not stalked (8)

2a. Calyx closely invested at the base by two short bracts. ***Dianthus***, PINK,
page 101.
2b. Calyx without two bracts at the base .... (3)

3a. Styles 5; capsule opening by 5 or 10 teeth. ***Melandrium***, CAMPION,
page 101.
3b. Styles 2 or 3; capsule splitting into 3, 4 or 6 parts .... (4)

Fig. 55. *Lonicera involucrata*

4a. Calyx 10-nerved; styles 3; capsule 3- or 6-valved. **Silene**, CATCHFLY; CAMPION, page 105.
4b. Calyx 5-nerved or 5-angled, or terete and only obscurely nerved; styles 2; capsule 4-valved .... (5)

5a. Flowers less than 4 mm long, very numerous, in much-branched cymes. **Gypsophila**, BABY'S BREATH, page 101.
5b. Flowers over 5 mm long, relatively few in number .... (6)

6a. Calyx terete; flowers white or pink; plant annual or perennial .... (7)
6b. Calyx 5-angled; flowers deep pink; plant annual. **Vaccaria**, COW COCKLE, page 109.

7a. Flowers deep pink; plant annual, leaves linear. **Agrostemma**, CORN COCKLE, page 99.
7b. Flowers white or pale pink; plant perennial; leaves broadly oblong-ovate. **Saponaria**, BOUNCING BET; SOAPWORT, page 105.

8a. Leaves with colorless, papery stipules .... (9)
8b. Leaves without stipules .... (10)

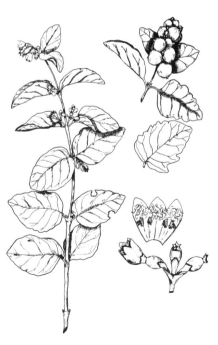

Fig. 56. *Symphoricarpos occidentalis*

9a. Annual; glandular-pubescent, somewhat fleshy low herb of alkaline areas on the plains. ***Spergularia***, SAND SPURRY, page 107. See Addenda.
9b. Perennial, somewhat woody at the base; variously pubescent or glabrous, but seldom glandular; plants of foothills, mesas and high mountains. ***Paronychia***, NAILWORT, page 105.

10a. Plants minute (2 cm or less high) from a slender taproot; leaves mostly basal, linear; stems one-flowered; plant of muddy or moist sites in the subalpine and alpine zones . . . . (11)
10b. Plants larger, rarely less than 5 cm high, or if low, then perennial and forming mats . . . . (12)

11a. Styles 3; flower buds oblong. ***Minuartia stricta***, page 104.
11b. Styles 4-5; flower buds spheroidal. ***Sagina***, PEARLWORT, page 105.

12a. Styles 5; capsule cylindric, often curved, dehiscent at the apex; tip of ovary splitting into 10 teeth. ***Cerastium***, MOUSE-EAR, page 100.
12b. Styles 3; capsule short, ovoid or oblong, straight, splitting into 3 or 6 segments . . . . (13)

13a. Petals deeply 2-lobed. ***Stellaria***, CHICKWEED, page 107.
13b. Petals entire or only shallowly notched . . . . (14)

14a. Leaves elliptic, rounded at the ends, 5 pairs or more on slender, relatively unbranched stems; flowers a few in a cyme. ***Moehringia***, page 104.
14b. Leaves linear, mostly basal; flowers solitary or in many-flowered cymes or clusters . . . . (15)

15a. Leaves narrowly linear or filiform, grasslike, over 3 cm long; ovary splitting at maturity into 3 valves which are again partly split to form 6 teeth. ***Arenaria***, SANDWORT, page 99.
15b. Leaves linear but very short and often thickish, less than 1 cm long; ovary splitting at maturity into 3 entire valves. ***Minuartia***, SANDWORT, page 104.

AGROSTEMMA. CORN COCKLE

One species, ***Agrostemma gracilis*** Boiss., a native of Asia Minor and Greece, recently has turned up as a weed in gardens and neglected land around Boulder. It evidently has not been reported previously in North America, although a related species, *A. githago*, is common in grain fields in the eastern U.S., where its poisonous seeds are an unwanted contaminant in grain. In *A. githago* the petals are not as long as the calyx lobes, while *A. gracilis* has handsome flowers with petals twice as long as the calyx lobes and with lines of dark purple spots running down the basal parts of the petal limb.

ARENARIA. SANDWORT

1a. Flowers crowded into dense clusters . . . . (2)

1b. Flowers in open cymes. **Arenaria fendleri** Gray (for August Fendler, collector of New Mexico's flora), SANDWORT, Fig. 57. Common on dry mountainsides, foothills to alpine. The alpine race is smaller and very sticky-glandular, var. *tweedyi* (Rydb.) Maguire.

2a. Sepals about 3 mm long; flowering stems usually over 15 cm tall. **Arenaria congesta** Nutt., Fig. 57. Very common on the west slope of the mountains, not yet reported in our range but to be expected.

2b. Sepals about 6 mm long; flowering stems rarely over 10 cm tall. **Arenaria hookeri** Nutt. (for W. J. Hooker), Fig. 57. Chaparral belt on mesas and foothills along the north and south edge of our area, and on the plains of eastern Colorado.

CERASTIUM. MOUSE-EAR

1a. Petals conspicuous, at least half again as long as the sepals; capsule only slightly longer than the sepals; native perennial . . . . (2)

1b. Petals about as long as the sepals or slightly exceeding them; capsule about twice as long as sepals; annual or weedy biennial or perennial
. . . . (3)

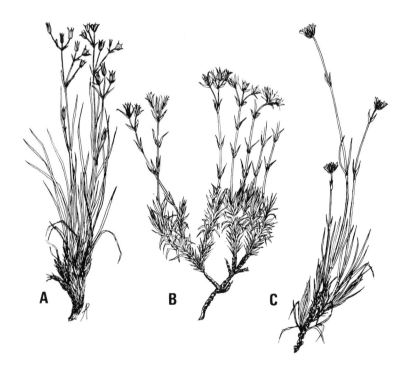

Fig. 57. A, **Arenaria fendleri**; B, **A. hookeri**; C, **A. congesta**

2a. Bracts of the inflorescence not at all scarious; leaves of flowering stems usually without leafy tufts in their axils; calyx glandular with long multicellular hairs; plants low and loosely matted. Alpine. *C. beeringianum* Cham. & Schlecht. ssp. *earlei* (Rydb.) Hultén, ALPINE MOUSE-EAR, Fig. 61. Tundra and alpine rockslides.

2b. Bracts of the inflorescence scarious-margined; flowering stems with tufts of leaves of sterile shoots in the leaf axils; plants with tall erect flowering stems. Plant of mesas to subalpine. *Cerastium arvense* L., FIELD MOUSE-EAR, Fig. 61. Abundant in early summer from the mesas to near timberline.

3a. Annual blooming in early spring; stem ascending or erect, not matted or rooting at the nodes; petals usually equalling or slightly longer than the sepals. *Cerastium nutans* Raf. var. *brachypodum* Engelm. (nodding, short-stalked). Frequent in gulches on the mesas, usually in moist places.

3b. Perennial weed of gardens and disturbed shady sites; stem weak and trailing, often matted and rooting at the nodes; petals about equalling the sepals. *Cerastium vulgatum* L., COMMON MOUSE-EAR. European workers suggest that the correct name for this is *C. fontanum* Baumg.

DIANTHUS. PINK

One species, *Dianthus deltoides* L. (triangular, possibly referring to the shape of the bract), MAIDEN PINK, Fig. 58. A European species locally established along the roadsides near Nederland. Cultivated species: *Dianthus barbatus* L. is the Sweet William of gardens; *D. plumarius* L. is the Garden Pink, which resembles a carnation without double corollas, and *D. caryophyllus* L. is the commercial Carnation. The genus *Dianthus* is extremely diversified in central and southeastern Europe. The flowers of most species have a characteristic clove-like scent.

GYPSOPHILA. BABY'S BREATH

One species, *Gypsophila paniculata* L., Fig. 58. Locally abundant as an escape from cultivation, foothill canyons. Where it occurs it may be extremely conspicuous, forming bushy intricately branched grayish-whitish massed stems with myriads of tiny blossoms. Native in Eastern Europe, and probably escaped here from old-fashioned gardens.

MELANDRIUM. CAMPION

1a. Dwarf alpine plants, usually less than 10 cm tall .... (2)
1b. Taller plants of various altitudes .... (3)

2a. Flowers nodding; petals included or barely exserted; calyx inflated like a Japanese lantern. *Melandrium apetalum* (L.) Fenzl, Fig. 59. Rare, on alpine tundra and scree slopes. Seeds 1.5-2.0 mm, rounded.

2b. Flowers erect; petals included, barely exserted, or conspicuously exserted; calyx cylindric, only slightly inflated. Alpine tundra, rare. *Melandrium kingii* (S. Wats.) Tolmatchev. Various Arctic specialists

Fig. 58. A, **Gypsophila**; B, **Vaccaria**; C, **Dianthus**; D, **Saponaria**

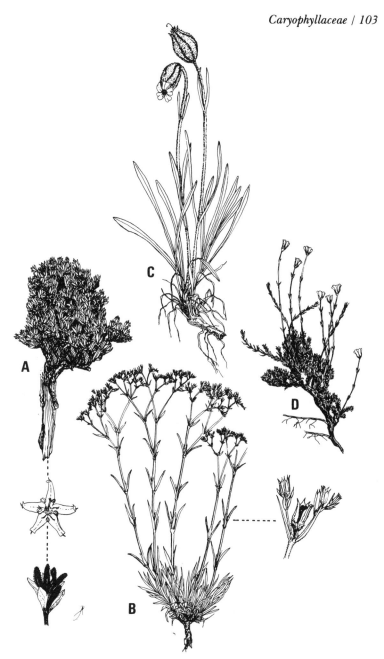

Fig. 59. A, *Paronychia pulvinata*; B, *P. jamesii*; C, *Melandrium apetalum*; D, *Minuartia obtusiloba*

have suggested that this is equivalent to *M. furcatum* or related species, but there has been no serious revision recently and the relationships are still not at all clear. Seeds 0.5-1.0 mm, angular.

3a. Perennial; flowers perfect. ***Melandrium drummondii*** (Hook.) Hultén (for Thomas Drummond, who collected plants in the Canadian Rockies). Dry slopes, foothills to subalpine; very similar in general appearance to *Silene scouleri.*
3b. Annual or biennial; flowers unisexual. ***Melandrium dioicum*** (L.) Coss. & Germ., WHITE CAMPION. A European weed, established locally in fields and along roadsides in the montane zone. There have been extensive discussions as to whether this and *M. album* are distinct species. They cross quite freely and most American material is said to contain genes of both entities.

MINUARTIA

1a. Stems stiff, often somewhat woody below; plants perennial; stems one-flowered, rarely few-flowered; sepals cucullate . . . . (2)
1b. Stems soft, not rigid, not at all woody; annual or short-lived perennials from slender taproots; stems terminated by few-flowered cymes; sepals acute . . . . (3)

2a. Petals only slightly exceeding the sepals, not conspicuous; stems not densely matted or very woody, not forming extensive clumps. ***Minuartia biflora*** (L.) Schinz & Thell. Uncommon, in open gravels or frost-disturbed tundra sites (*Arenaria sajanensis* Willd.).
2b. Petals twice as long as the sepals, conspicuous; stems densely matted, often more or less woody, the old leaves persistent on the lower part; plants forming extensive, tight clumps. ***Minuartia obtusiloba*** (Rydb.) House, Fig. 59. ALPINE SANDWORT. Very abundant on well-developed tundra.

3a. Pedicels and calyx glandular-pubescent. ***Minuartia rubella*** (Wahlenb.) Graebn. On moraines, gravel-bars, and unstable tundra slopes, subalpine and alpine.
3b. Entire plant glabrous . . . . (4)

4a. Petals short, inconspicuous; plants only a few cm diam. ***Minuartia stricta*** (Sw.) Hiern. Rare, frostscars, Mt. Evans.
4b. Petals exceeding the sepals, broad and conspicuous; plants much-branched, forming loose, rounded clumps. ***Minuartia macrantha*** (Rydb.) House. Tundra, from Grays Peak west into the inner ranges.

MOEHRINGIA

One species, ***Moehringia lateriflora*** (L.) Fenzl. Frequent in moist or swampy forests, montane and subalpine. Stems very slender and delicate, very finely pubescent with recurved hairs; leaves about as long as the internodes. Not particularly rare, but rarely occurring in large stands, usually one or two stems in a site. On the western slope, a second species, *M. macrophylla* (Hook.) Torr. occurs, characterized by broader, ovate-oblong leaves with distinct points.

PARONYCHIA. Nailwort

1a. Densely matted alpine plants; leaves elliptic, rounded or obtuse; flowers sessile. **Paronychia pulvinata** Gray, Fig. 59.
1b. Plants freely branching or depressed, not alpine; leaves linear, sharp-pointed .... (2)

2a. Flowers solitary or in pairs; leaves and bracts of equal length; leaves and stipules 4-6 mm long. **Paronychia sessiliflora** Nutt. Infrequent on high plains and open mountain parks.
2b. Flowers numerous, in branched cymes; leaves 6-20 mm long, longer than the bracts and stipules. **Paronychia jamesii** T. & G., Fig. 59. Abundant in pine forests of the foothills and on the higher eastern plains.

SAGINA. Pearlwort

One species, **Sagina saginoides** (L.) Karst., Arctic Pearlwort. Rather rare, or overlooked because of its small size; found among rocks, subalpine and alpine, sometimes on muddy shores of ponds.

SAPONARIA. Soapwort; Bouncing Bet

One species, **Saponaria officinalis** L. (of the shops), Fig. 58. Commonly escaped from cultivation and very well established in dense stands along roadsides, mesas and foothills, flowering in midsummer. The leaves make a fair lather when crushed and rubbed under water. Double-flowered sports are frequent.

SILENE. Catchfly; Campion

1a. Plant low and densely matted, moss-like; flowers scarcely higher than the short basal leaves. **Silene acaulis** L. ssp. **subacaulescens** (F. N. Williams) C. L. Hitchc. & Maguire, Moss-pink, Fig. 60. Flowers pink, very rarely white. Common on tundra. Races of this species are found in the Arctic and in practically all tundra areas in the Northern Hemisphere.
1b. Plants with tall, leafy stems, or at least not matted or moss-like; growing at various altitudes .... (2)

2a. Calyx small, less than 5 mm long; low, dichotomously branched. **Silene menziesii** Hook. (for Archibald Menzies, early collector in coastal Pacific Northwest). Plants sticky-hairy. Common in western Colorado, but only a few specimens reported from our area.
2b. Calyx more than 5 mm long .... (3)

3a. Perennial; petals deeply cleft .... (4)
3b. Annual weed; petals entire or shallowly cleft .... (5)

4a. Plant glabrous and glaucous, tall and branched; leaves ovate; calyx smooth, inflated, with 20 pale and inconspicuous veins. *Silene vulgaris* (Moench) Garcke. A European weed, established in pastures in the foothills.
4b. Plant glandular-pubescent above, little branched; leaves narrow; calyx little expanded, with 10 dark veins. *Silene scouleri* Hook. ssp. *hallii* (Wats.) C. L. Hitchc. & Maguire. Dry slopes, montane and subalpine.

5a. Stems with localized dark bands of sticky fluid on the upper internodes; calyx 0.5-1.0 cm long. *Silene antirrhina* L. (with leaves resembling snapdragon), SLEEPY CATCHFLY. Dry slopes, mesas and foothills.
5b. Plants glandular-pubescent throughout; localized sticky bands lacking; calyx 1.5-2.0 cm long. *Silene noctiflora* L., NIGHT-FLOWERING CATCHFLY. Vacant lots and abandoned fields in suburban areas.

Alert observers will notice that the petals of *Silene acaulis*, *Minuartia obtusiloba* and probably several other caryophylls will vary a great deal in length and showiness from plant to plant in the same population. Careful examination will reveal differences in the sizes and development of the stamens and carpels. Plants with small petals, often hardly longer than the sepals, will tend to have abortive and nonfunctional anthers but

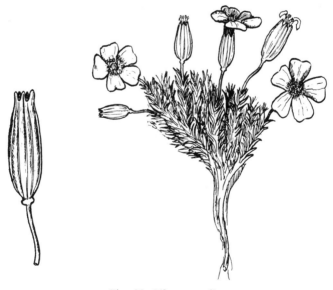

Fig. 60. *Silene acaulis*

well-developed ovaries, while plants with showy petals often have well-developed anthers and poorly developed ovaries. In other words, different plants will show different degrees of "maleness" and "femaleness" and in fact may be quite dioecious. The phenomenon is very common in certain families and is especially well developed in the Caryophyllaceae and Umbelliferae, where the variation in floral structure will occur on the same plant and within the same umbel!

SPERGULARIA. Sand Spurry

1a. Plants perennial; stamens 7 to 10; seeds winged. ***Spergularia media*** (L.) Presl. Muddy streambanks on the plains and piedmont valleys.
1b. Plants annual; stamens 2 to 10; seeds winged or wingless ..... (2)

2a. Stamens usually 10, rarely as few as 6 or 7 .... (3)
2b. Stamens 2 to 5; seeds not winged. ***Spergularia marina*** (L.) Griseb. Alkaline flats on the plains and the piedmont valleys.

3a. Sepals glabrous; seeds usually conspicuously winged. ***Spergularia media*** (L.) Presl. This plant behaves variously as an annual or short-lived perennial. Plains and piedmont valleys.
3b. Sepals glandular-hairy; seeds never winged. ***Spergularia rubra*** (L.) J. & C. Presl. A weed often following lumbering operations in forest clearings, growing prostrate on the ground and bearing small pink flowers.

STELLARIA. Chickweed

1a. Leaves ovate, or at least the lower ones petiolate (abruptly truncated to a distinct petiole); petal number and stamen number variable; stem with two lines of hairs. ***Stellaria media*** (L.) Vill., Fig. 61. Common introduced weed of poorly drained and shady lawns in towns. Probably better regarded as a distinct genus, *Alsine media* L.
1b. Leaves never distinctly petiolate, the blades elliptic or lanceolate to linear .... (2)

2a. Plant glandular-pubescent, at least in the inflorescence; petals 6-8 mm long, about twice as long as the sepals, cleft not more than half-way to the base; leaves lanceolate, 3-10 cm long. ***Stellaria jamesiana*** Torr., Tuber Starwort, Fig. 61. Common in open forests, foothills and montane. Possibly an American counterpart of the European *S. holostea* L.
2b. Plant not glandular-pubescent; petals not over 5 mm long; leaves various .... (3)

3a. Flowers subtended by scarious bracts (in *S. umbellata* the inflorescence may be condensed so as to hide the bracts somewhat) .... (4)
3b. Flowers subtended by green leaves .... (7)

4a. Leaves elliptic-oblong; inflorescence sub-umbellate and condensed or cymose and open, the flowers tending to be reflexed; petals lacking. ***Stellaria umbellata*** Turcz., Fig. 61. Infrequent, in moist, shady

Fig. 61. A, *Stellaria jamesiana*; B, *S. media*; C, *S. umbellata*; D, *Cerastium arvense*; E, *C. beeringianum*

subalpine forests. A dwarf alpine form has been called *S. weberi* Boivin.

4b. Leaves lanceolate or lance-linear; inflorescence cymose, the pedicels ascending or divaricate but rarely actually reflexed .... (5)

5a. Calyx 2-3 mm long, broadly acute or obtuse, the sepals almost nerveless; cymes commonly axillary as well as terminal; leaves very minutely tuberculate on the margins (high power lens); leaves dull. *Stellaria longifolia* Muehl. *ex* Willd. Wet meadows, upper montane and subalpine.

5b. Calyx 4-8 mm long, sharply acute or acuminate; strongly 3-nerved; cymes terminal; leaves with smooth margins, shiny, sometimes slightly ciliate at base .... (6)

6a. Stems very sharply 4-angled, the areas between the angles deeply concave; sepals ciliate. *Stellaria graminea* L. A weed occasionally found along irrigation ditches.

6b. Stems obtusely angled, not strongly shrunken between the angles; sepals not ciliate; leaves smooth and shining as if lacquered, strongly keeled; native species. *Stellaria longipes* Goldie, LONG-STALKED STITCHWORT. Common in wet ground, upper montane and subalpine.

7a. Stem copiously pilose with multicellular hairs; leaves strongly ciliate, elliptic-oblong, acute; petals vestigial (1 mm long) with narrowly oblong divisions. *Stellaria simcoei* (Howell) C. L. Hitchc. Rare, subalpine meadows and willow thickets.

7b. Stem glabrous or very nearly so; leaves smooth or somewhat ciliate at the base, lanceolate to lance-linear; petals various, from well developed to lacking .... (8)

8a. Leaves firm, thick and keeled, shining green or glaucous; stem usually with a single terminal flower, sometimes irregularly cymose; sepals smooth or rarely ciliate; petals about twice as long as the sepals. *Stellaria laeta* Rich. Subalpine and alpine (*S. monantha* Hultén).

8b. Leaves not shining, flat, not keeled; flowers solitary or in cymes; petals equalling or shorter than the sepals or lacking .... (9)

9a. Margins of the leaves smooth and the surfaces glabrous. *Stellaria crassifolia* Ehrh. Rare, subalpine meadows.

9b. Margins of the leaves ciliate, at least on the lower half. *Stellaria calycantha* (Ledeb.) Bong. Infrequent, subalpine meadows and willow thickets.

VACCARIA. Cow Cockle

One species, *Vaccaria pyramidata* Medicus, Fig. 58. Common weed in grain fields, mesas and plains (*V. segetalis* [Neck.] Garcke).

CELASTRACEAE—STAFF-TREE FAMILY

This small family includes Bittersweet, *Celastrus scandens*, a woody vine noted for its seed encased in a brilliant orange aril. The dry capsules dehisce, exposing but not releasing the seed. Sprays of Bittersweet are gathered in autumn for dry arrangements. *Euonymus*, the Spindle-tree, includes several species, either evergreen or deciduous, with similar arillate seeds. These are desirable ornamentals, often having cork-ridged stems. The fine-grained hard wood was used in making spindles. Possibly the name "Staff-tree" derives not from a walking stick, but from the spinning distaff.

One genus and species, ***Pachistima myrsinites*** (Pursh) Raf. (myrtle-like), MOUNTAIN-LOVER, Plate 2, Fig. 62. A low, evergreen shrub with opposite crenate leaves and inconspicuous reddish flowers. Common in forests west of the Continental Divide, but infrequent within our area. This is one of our Tertiary relics, with a close relative, *P. canbyi*, found in the southern Appalachians. The original spelling of the name was *Paxistima*, but scholars believe this was an error. *Pachystima* also evidently is incorrect.

Fig. 62. ***Pachistima myrsinites***

CERATOPHYLLACEAE—HORNWORT FAMILY

One genus and species, ***Ceratophyllum demersum*** L. (submerged), HORNWORT, Fig. 302. Lakes and ponds in the piedmont valleys. The whorled leaves are dichotomously branched with narrowly linear divisions, very densely grouped toward the stem apex. The similar *Ranunculus trichophyllus* has alternate leaves and the green alga *Chara* has distinctly jointed stems and a fetid odor.

CHENOPODIACEAE—GOOSEFOOT FAMILY

Disturbed soils, particularly in urban, roadside or rural sites, assume a late summer and fall aspect characterized by a welter of unattractive hairy, white-mealy or spiny plants with inconspicuous greenish flowers, most of which belong to the Goosefoot family. Most amateurs ignore them because they are nondescript and presumably difficult. But chenopods make up such an important part of the landscape and mean so much in terms of interpreting the condition of the land that everyone should know the common species. Chenopods find their way to the dining table too. *Beta vulgaris* (Red Beets, Swiss Chard and Sugar Beets) and Spinach (*Spinacia oleracea*) belong here. The fruits of Spinach have several spines or prickles, hence the old name Spinage.

1a. True shrubs; twigs ending in stiff spine-like tips; fruits with four chaffy wings. ***Atriplex***, SALTBUSH, page 112.
1b. Herbs, sometimes somewhat woody at the base, but never tall shrubs
....(2)

2a. Leaves linear, up to 4 cm long, withering early and replaced by green spine-tipped bracts which cover the stem; tumbleweeds. ***Salsola***, RUSSIAN-THISTLE, page 118.
2b. Plants not spiny ....(3)

3a. Plants pubescent or woolly ....(4)
3b. Plants glabrous or granular-mealy (farinose) pubescent .... (6)

4a. Plants white-woolly all over, the leaves linear, revolute, the hairs turning golden-brown in age; perennials, woody at base. ***Ceratoides***, WINTERFAT, page 113.
4b. Plants green, pilose or tomentose in the inflorescence only; weedy annuals, flowering in late summer ....(5)

5a. Leaves thin, pilose; sepals naked or developing a blunt knob or wide papery horizontal wing. ***Kochia***, BURNING-BUSH, page 118.
5b. Leaves thick, glabrous; sepals each developing a hooked spine on the back. ***Bassia***, page 113.

6a. Leaves narrowly linear ....(7)
6b. Leaves of various shapes, never narrowly linear ....(8)

7a. Leaves thick and fleshy; plants of alkaline flats. *Suaeda*, Sea Blite, page 118.
7b. Leaves thin; tumbleweed of sandy plains. *Corispermum*, Bugseed, page 117.

8a. Ovary contained within a green, 5-lobed calyx or a single small bract
. . . . (9)
8b. Ovary contained within two specially shaped, usually enlarged, bracts or a peculiarly winged calyx . . . . (10)

9a. Perianth of a single bract-like greenish segment; flowers in sessile axillary clusters; plants fleshy, glabrous, prostrate, with oblong or coarsely lobed leaves. *Monolepis*, Povertyweed, page 118.
9b. Perianth of several calyx-lobes, closely investing the ovary; flowers either in axillary or terminal clusters; plant usually with some farinose pubescence. *Chenopodium*, Pigweed, page 115.

10a. Fruiting calyx with conspicuous, continuous horizontal wing producing a saucer-shaped fruit; plant a much-branched tumbleweed with sinuate, early-deciduous leaves, the fruits soon becoming the only conspicuous structures along the stem. *Cycloloma*, Winged Pigweed, page 117.
10b. Ovary lacking a perianth, enclosed instead by two bracts which may be more or less fused and with characteristic shapes . . . . (11)

11a. Fruit triangular-conical, the bracts fused and folded sideways, the apex two-toothed; leaves broadly ovate, coarsely toothed; plants prostrate, extremely variable, in unfavorable sites often reduced to two cotyledons and a small cluster of fruits. *Suckleya*, page 118.
11b. Fruit variously shaped, the bracts separate or fused, not folded, often ornamented on the back and margins with tubercles or teeth; leaves lanceolate to triangular-hastate. *Atriplex*, page 112.

ATRIPLEX. Saltbush, Orache
1a. Shrubs, or at least the lower parts woody and perennial . . . . . . (2)
1b. Weedy annual herbs with a tap-root . . . . (3)

2a. True shrubs, woody throughout; fruiting bractlets enlarged, the margins forming four divergent wings. *Atriplex canescens* (Pursh) Nutt., Four-winged Saltbush, Fig. 63. Locally frequent in sandy soil on mesas and plains.
2b. Subshrubs, woody only at the base, the herbaceous stems simple, erect; fruiting bractlets variously ornamented with lumps or teeth; not as above. *Atriplex gardneri* (Moq.) D. Dietr. (for Alexander Gordon, the first collector, his name misspelled by Moquin!). In alkaline flats, mostly on the extreme northeastern limits of our area in Weld County (*Atriplex nuttallii* Wats.).

3a. Fruiting bractlets orbicular, not fused, up to 1 cm in diameter ... (4)
3b. Fruiting bractlets triangular or irregularly shaped, partly fused, 5 mm or less in diameter .... (5)

4a. Carpellate flowers dimorphic, some with horizontal seed surrounded by a 4-5-lobed perianth, the rest with vertical seeds surrounded by the large (to 1 cm) orbicular bractlets, both types mixed on the same branch; upper leaves alternate, entire. *Atriplex hortensis* L., GARDEN ORACHE. An uncommon weed conspicuous in late summer, the plants up to 3 meters high with massive clusters of pink fruits.
4b. Carpellate flowers all alike, with orbicular bracts less than 5 mm diameter; upper leaves opposite, hastate, coarsely dentate. *Atriplex heterosperma* Bunge. A Eurasian weed, recently introduced.

5a. Leaves green, often somewhat fleshy, with little or no farinose pubescence; stem with prominent parallel ridges; fruits in dense, essentially leafless interrupted spikes. *Atriplex hastata* L. (spreading), SPEAR ORACHE. Common weed in cultivated ground and drying pond margins on the plains, late summer.
5b. Leaves farinose; stem pale, without prominent parallel ridges; fruits in leafy-bracted clusters .... (6)

6a. Bractlets inversely triangular or goblet-shaped, broadest at the apex, prominently 3-nerved, crowned with a few shallow teeth. *Atriplex truncata* (Torr.) Gray (cut off, referring to the flat-topped bractlets). Alkali flats and drying pond margins on the plains.
6b. Bractlets diamond-shaped or deeply lobed and toothed, pointed at the apex, toothed on the sides and back .... (7)

7a. Leaves not strongly farinose, narrowly ovate, coarsely toothed; bractlets triangular, veiny, not strongly farinose, the teeth not obscuring the general outline. *Atriplex rosea* L. A Eurasian weed of irrigated lands.
7b. Leaves strongly farinose, broadly rounded-ovate with a few large basal teeth or lobes; bractlets strongly farinose, deeply incised by slender teeth on the margins and back. *Atriplex argentea* Nutt. A native weedy species of alkaline soil.

BASSIA

One species, *Bassia hyssopifolia* (Pallas) Kuntze. A Eurasian weed established in alkaline areas in the piedmont valleys. Besides the characteristic hooked sepals, the plant is recognized by its long, slenderly ropelike, stiffly-spreading branches and tiny leaves little longer than the flowers.

CERATOIDES. WINTERFAT

One species, *Ceratoides lanata* (Pursh) J. T. Howell, Fig. 63. Common on dry mesas and plains. At first glance this resembles a very white, woolly sagebrush (*Eurotia* of Ed. 4).

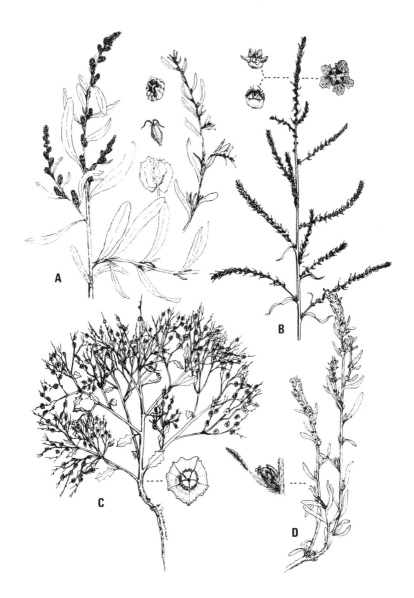

Fig. 63. A, *Atriplex canescens*; B, *Kochia*; C, *Cycloloma*; D, *Ceratoides*

CHENOPODIUM. Goosefoot

1a. Plant pubescent with glandular hairs, aromatic; leaves pinnately lobed; flowering branches curving out and down, forming a narrow pyramid. *Chenopodium botrys* L.(bunch of grapes), Jerusalem-oak, Fig. 64. Gravelly roadsides in the foothills, introduced weed.
1b. Plants glabrous or farinose, at least on the young growth, neither glandular nor aromatic .... (2)

2a. Seeds vertical (standing erect in the flower), except occasionally in the terminal flower or a cluster; inflorescence glabrous; flowers in axillary clusters, the calyx never keeled .... (3)
2b. Seeds usually all horizontal; inflorescence usually farinose; flowers in interrupted terminal spikes; calyx sometimes keeled .... (6)

3a. Leaves densely glaucous-farinose beneath. *Chenopodium glaucum* L., Fig. 64. Shores of drying ponds, late summer.
3b. Leaves green or reddish, glabrous beneath .... (4)

4a. Flowers in sessile axillary clusters .... (5)
4b. Flowers in axillary and terminal spikes. *Chenopodium rubrum* L., Red Goosefoot. Margins of ponds in the piedmont valleys, late summer.

5a. Fruiting clusters becoming bright red at maturity. *Chenopodium capitatum* (L.) Asch., Strawberry Blite, Fig. 65. Roadsides and burned forests, montane and subalpine. Leaves hastate, coarsely toothed.
5b. Fruiting clusters remaining green even in late maturity. *Chenopodium overi* Aellen (for W. H. Over, South Dakota botanist). More slender than the last; leaves often rounded-ovate and sparingly toothed.

6a. Leaves thin, large, truncate at the base, very coarsely few-toothed or lobed (like a webbed foot); flower clusters widely separated on slender branches; seeds up to 2 mm diameter, with coarse pits. *Chenopodium hybridum* L., Maple-leaved Goosefoot. Frequent in open forests and clearings, mesas and foothills.
6b. Leaves thick or small, cuneate at the base; flower clusters in more dense interrupted spikes; seeds smaller than 2 mm .... (7)

7a. Principal leaves linear to narrowly ovate or oblong, usually less than 15 mm broad; sepals without definite apiculate tips .... (8)
7b. Principal leaves deltoid to deltoid-rhombic or ovate, 1-3 times as long as broad; sepals with definite apiculate tips .... (9)

8a. Principal leaves oblong to lanceolate or ovate-lanceolate, from thin to almost fleshy, entire or basally lobed; pericarp free from the seed. *Chenopodium desiccatum* Nels. Disturbed and compacted ground, piedmont valleys.
8b. Principal leaves linear, one-nerved, the margins entire; pericarp firmly attached to the seed. *Chenopodium leptophyllum* Wats. Disturbed

soil, often in forested areas of the foothills. A difficult group of species may be covered by this name.

9a. Leaf-blades deltoid to rhombic-deltoid or variously ovate but otherwise nearly entire .... (10)
9b. Leaf-blades as above but at least the lower ones deeply or shallowly toothed above the basal lobes .... (11)

Fig. 64. A, ***Chenopodium album***; B, ***C. fremontii***; C, ***C. glaucum***; D, ***C. botrys***

10a. Plants widely branched, stiff and very white-mealy; leaves thick. **Chenopodium incanum** (Wats.) Heller. On sun-baked flats on the plains and piedmont valleys.

10b. Plants slender, often weak, green or lightly farinose; leaves thin, broad with often rounded apex and broad basal lobes. **Chenopodium fremontii** Wats., Fig. 64. Usually in openings in forests, campgrounds etc., in the foothills.

11a. Seeds distinctly pitted (high magnification); leaves broadly triangular-ovate, three-nerved. **Chenopodium acerifolium** Andrz. Locally abundant around Boulder. A Eurasian weed.

11b. Seeds with fine concentric lines or ridges, not pitted; leaves various. **Chenopodium album** L., Common Pigweed, Fig. 64. Abundant late summer weed. Under this name are undoubtedly included several unrecognized Eurasian weeds. Further studies are needed in this group.

CORISPERMUM. Bugseed

One species, **Corispermum hyssopifolium** L., Common Bugseed. Sandy soil on the plains.

CYCLOLOMA. Winged Pigweed

One species, **Cycloloma atriplicifolium** (Spreng.) Coulter, Fig. 63. Sandy places on the plains. A common tumbleweed, pale green, becoming bright red in the fall.

Fig. 65. *Chenopodium capitatum*

KOCHIA. Burning-bush

One species, **Kochia iranica** Bornmueller, Fig. 63. Probably the most abundant weed in Colorado, everywhere in late summer along roadsides and waste places. This has been confused with *K. scoparia*, another weedy Eurasian plant, but differs by having large papery wings developing on the calyx; only the later-blooming flowers develop wings.

MONOLEPIS. Poverty Weed

One species, **Monolepis nuttalliana** (R. & S.) Greene. In mud or sand, especially in wet ground, foothills to subalpine.

SALSOLA. Russian-thistle

1a. Bracts broad-based, with stiffly flaring spine-tips; plant extremely prickly, difficult to handle, the branches stiffly spreading. **Salsola iberica** Sennen & Pau, Fig. 66. Abundant tumbleweed, roadsides and fallow fields (*S. kali* of Ed. 4).

1b. Bracts narrow-based, the tips directed forward; plant easily handled, the branches elongate, gracefully curving. **Salsola collina** Pallas, Fig. 66. Similar distribution, not quite so abundant as the preceding.

SUAEDA. Sea-blite

1a. Calyx with a fleshy conical outgrowth on the back of one or more sepals, this shriveling in age, giving the flower a contorted appearance. **Suaeda depressa** (Pursh) Wats. Common on margins of drying ponds and on alkali flats, plains.

1b. Calyx with thin sepals, not developing as above. **Suaeda nigra** (Raf.) Macbr. Similar habitats, but apparently uncommon.

SUCKLEYA

One species, **Suckleya suckleyana** (Torr.) Rydb. Drying pond borders and alkaline soil in the Denver area.

CISTACEAE — ROCK-ROSE FAMILY

A small family notable for the genus *Cistus*, a group of showy ornamental shrubs of the Mediterranean region, and the American genus *Houstonia*, a heath-like low shrub important in stabilizing sand dunes along the Atlantic coast. Our single species of *Helianthemum* represents what we believe was a Pleistocene westward movement of the midwestern prairie-woodland flora to the base of the Rockies, of which only a few local colonies now remain after the climatic changes resulting in the present flora of the high plains.

One genus and species, **Helianthemum bicknellii** Fernald (for Eugene P. Bicknell). A small herbaceous plant with alternate, elliptic leaves clothed with minute stellate hairs. The flowers are yellow, resembling cinquefoil. Very rare, in the Black Forest near Palmer Lake and in foothills north of Boulder.

COMPOSITAE (ASTERACEAE)— SUNFLOWER FAMILY

Except for the cockleburs and ragweeds, which one simply has to accept as composites, this family is easily recognized if one can think of a Dandelion and a Sunflower as being representative of the group. The family illustrates a very interesting evolutionary tendency: when the number of flowers in an inflorescence is enormously increased at the same time as the flower size is decreased, the visibility of the flowers to pollinating insects is probably also decreased. This disadvantage is often compensated for in certain plant families by massing the flowers into tight clusters, and setting up a division of labor among the flowers. This is usually accomplished by enlarging and changing the shape of the marginal flowers of a cluster in such a way as to cause the entire flower cluster to resemble a single flower and thus restore the visibility of the inflorescence. The composites achieve this in a variety of ways, making them a very complex and diverse family.

1a. Flowers all strap-shaped (ligulate) and perfect; juice milky. **Key A,** page 120.
1b. Flowers not all ligulate; ray (ligulate) flowers, when present, marginal, either with stigmas only or with neither stigmas nor stamens (neuter); juice usually watery .... (2)

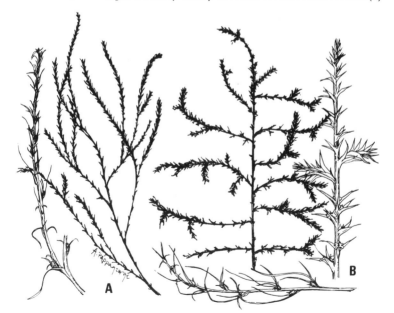

Fig. 66. A, *Salsola collina*; B, *S. iberica* (juvenile shoot below)

2a. Heads with ray-flowers .... (3)
2b. Heads with only disk flowers .... (5)

3a. Rays yellow or orange (sometimes marked with purple or reddish-brown at the base) .... (4)
3b. Rays white, pink, purple, red, or blue. **Key B**, page 122.

4a. Pappus chaffy or of firm awns, or absent; receptacle chaffy, bristly, or naked. **Key C,** page 123.
4b. Pappus partly or wholly of numerous capillary, sometimes plumose, bristles; receptacle naked. **Key D**, page 125.

5a. Pappus partly or wholly of numerous capillary, sometimes plumose, bristles. **Key E**, page 126.
5b. Pappus of scales or awns or very short, chaffy bristles or of a few low teeth, never plumose. **Key F**, page 127.

KEY A

1a. Flowers blue, pink, purple, or white .... (2)
1b. Flowers yellow or orange (sometimes drying pinkish) .... (9)

2a. Flowers sky-blue, sessile on nearly leafless, much-branched stems; pappus a crown of blunt scales. *Cichorium*, CHICORY, page 143.
2b. Flowers some shade of pink, lavender or purple, rarely white; pappus of capillary bristles .... (3)

3a. Pappus bristles plumose .... (4)
3b. Pappus bristles simple .... (5)

4a. Leaves elongate, grasslike; stems tall, relatively unbranched; heads large, with swollen peduncle. *Tragopogon*, SALSIFY, page 171.
4b. Leaves short, inconspicuous; stem richly branched, wiry; heads small, peduncles not swollen. *Stephanomeria*, WIRE-LETTUCE, page 170.

5a. Stems low, branched; leaves narrowly linear or bract-like........ (6)
5b. Stems tall, simple, leafy at least at the base .... (7)

6a. Annual; fruit with a beak; pappus snow-white. *Shinnersoseris*, BEAKED SKELETON-WEED, page 168.
6b. Perennial; fruit beakless; pappus tawny. *Lygodesmia*, SKELETON-WEED, page 161.

7a. Leaves lanceolate, tapered to a point, entire or variously toothed or lobed; fruits flattened. *Lactuca*, LETTUCE, page 157.
7b. Leaves oblanceolate, rounded, very shallowly if at all toothed .... (8)

8a. Leaves glabrous and glaucous; flower heads nodding, in a raceme. *Prenanthes*, page 164.

8b. Leaves hirsute; flower heads few, erect in an open panicle. *Hieracium*, HAWKWEED, page 155.

9a. Leaves primarily basal, the stem leaves near the base of the plant and greatly reduced upwards .... (10)
9b. Leaves not primarily basal, the stem leaves well developed ..... (17)

10a. Pappus of plumose bristles .... (11)
10b. Pappus of simple bristles .... (12)

11a. Fruits truncate at the apex, not beaked; native plant of the mountains. *Microseris*, page 162.
11b. Leaves hirsute; fruits with long beaks; weed of lawns. *Hypochaeris*, page 157.

12a. Pappus composed of 10 to 15 small oblong scales and an inner group of long capillary bristles. *Krigia*, page 157.
12b. Pappus consisting only of capillary bristles .... (13)

13a. Head solitary on a leafless scape .... (14)
13b. Heads (or buds) few to numerous, rarely solitary; stem usually with one or more well-developed leaves .... (16)

14a. Leaves linear, entire, the edges more or less wavy and crinkly-white hairy. *Nothocalais*, page 162.
14b. Leaves broader, or if narrow, often toothed or pinnately lobed; leaf margins neither wavy nor hairy .... (15)

15a. Fruits 10-ribbed or 10-nerved, without minute spines on the surface; outer phyllaries erect. *Agoseris*, FALSE DANDELION, page 130.
15b. Fruits 4- to 5-ribbed, with minute spines at least near the apex; phyllaries reflexed (except in some rare alpine species). *Taraxacum*, DANDELION, page 170.

16a. Pappus white; fruits tapering upwards; phyllaries more or less thickened at base and on the midrib. *Crepis*, HAWKSBEARD, page 145.
16b. Pappus brownish or reddish; fruits not tapering upwards; bracts not thickened. *Hieracium*, HAWKWEED, page 155.

17a. Leaves simple, grasslike, not toothed or divided. *Tragopogon*, SALSIFY, page 171.
17b. Leaves toothed, lobed or pinnatifid .... (18)

18a. Pappus plumose; leaves pinnatifid. *Podospermum*, page 164.
18b. Pappus simple; leaves toothed or lobed .... (19)

19a. Fruits beaked; involucre cylindric or ovoid-cylindric. *Lactuca*, LETTUCE, page 157.
19b. Fruits not beaked; involucre turbinate or hemispheric. *Sonchus*, SOW-THISTLE, page 169.

KEY B

1a. Leaves alternate; plants annual or usually perennial .... (2)
1b. At least the lower leaves opposite; plants annual .... (13)

2a. Rays very short, deep maroon-red; receptacle short-cylindric. ***Ratibida***, Cone-flower, page 164.
2b. Rays not short and maroon-red .... (3)

3a. Receptacle chaffy, at least in the middle; rays white (very rarely pink) .... (4)
3b. Receptacle naked .... (5)

4a. Rays few, commonly 3 to 5, short and broad, less than 5 mm long; perennial. ***Achillea***, Yarrow, page 129.
4b. Rays numerous, mostly 5-10 mm long; annual weed. ***Anthemis***, page 132. See Addenda.

5a. Pappus of the disk-flowers composed partly or wholly of capillary bristles .... (6)
5b. Pappus of stiff bristles, or lacking .... (12)

6a. Plants with cordate, sagittate, long-petiolate leaves, white beneath, the stem leaves reduced to bracts. ***Petasites,*** page 163.
6b. Plants without cordate leaves .... (7)

7a. Rays very numerous, filiform and short, scarcely surpassing the disk-flowers; annual weeds .... (8)
7b. Rays linear or broader, obviously flattened, longer than the disk-flowers; usually not weedy annuals .... (9)

8a. Involucre 5-10 mm high; pappus longer than the flowers, conspicuous in fruiting condition (white powderpuff). ***Brachyactis***, page 142.
8b. Involucre less than 5 mm high; pappus not longer than the flowers. ***Conyza***, Horseweed, page 145.

9a. Phyllaries subequal or more or less imbricate, often green in part but neither definitely leaflike nor with chartaceous base and herbaceous green tip; style branches lanceolate or broader, acute to obtuse, 0.5 mm long or less; plants blooming chiefly in spring and early summer (midsummer at higher elevations). ***Erigeron***, Fleabane, page 146.
9b. Phyllaries either subequal and the outer leaflike, or more commonly imbricate, with chartaceous base and evident green tip, sometimes chartaceous throughout; style branches lanceolate or narrower, acute or acuminate, ordinarily more than 0.5 mm long; plants blooming chiefly in late summer and fall .... (10)

10a. Leaves linear, less than 1 cm long; ray-flowers white; plants much branched, forming rounded low clumps. ***Leucelene***, page 158.
10b. Leaves broader; ray-flowers white or colored; plants not as above .... (11)

11a. Leaves entire; ray-flowers always purplish or white, never yellow. **Aster**, page 138. (Note: *Aster*, with very few exceptions, may be distinguished from *Erigeron* by the broader ray-flowers.)
11b. Leaves toothed or divided; ray-flowers either lavender or yellow. **Machaeranthera**, page 162.

12a. Pappus of the disk-flowers of about 10 or more flattened bristle-like scales; leaves entire. **Townsendia**, page 171.
12b. Pappus lacking; leaves toothed or slightly pinnatifid. **Leucanthemum**, Ox-eye Daisy, page 158. See Addenda.

13a. Ray-flowers large, pink, deeply 3-cleft; pappus of disk-flowers consisting of long papery scales, that of the rays a few short teeth. **Palafoxia**, page 163.
13b. Ray-flowers small, white, shallowly notched; pappus similar, but inconspicuous because of the very small size of the heads. **Galinsoga**, page 152.

KEY C

1a. Phyllaries extremely sticky-gummy, the tips recurved. **Grindelia**, Gumweed, page 152.
1b. Phyllaries not sticky-gummy all over; glands present in some, however .... (2)

2a. Receptacle chaffy or bristly .... (3)
2b. Receptacle naked .... (13)

3a. Phyllaries in two distinct, dissimilar series; fruits strongly flattened at right angles to the radius of the head .... (4)
3b. Phyllaries in one or more series, all more or less similar; fruits either not flattened, or flattened parallel to the radius of the head ..... (6)

4a. Pappus of 2 to 4 firm, retrorsely-barbed awns; leaves entire to pinnatifid or pinnately compound. **Bidens**, Beggars Tick, page 141.
4b. Pappus of two minute teeth, or lacking; leaves pinnately dissected (5)

5a. Lobes of disk-corollas equal, triangular, about twice as long as wide, shorter than the widened upper part of the tube. **Coreopsis**, page 145.
5b. Lobes of disk-corollas unequal, oblong or linear-lanceolate, more than twice as long as wide, equalling or longer than the widened upper part of the tube. **Thelesperma**, page 171.

6a. Receptacle merely bristly; ray-flowers broad, yellow or with red bases, deeply notched. **Gaillardia**, Blanket-flower, page 151.
6b. Receptacle chaffy, with stiff bracts on the receptacle .... (7)

7a. Receptacle conic or columnar (remove the flowers to see this); cauline leaves all alternate .... (8)
7b. Receptacle flat or nearly so; cauline leaves, at least the lower ones, opposite .... (9)

8a. Ray-flowers subtended by receptacular chaffy bracts; fruits flattened, with 2 sharp and 2 blunt angles; leaves pinnatifid; receptacle elongate. ***Ratibida***, CONE-FLOWER, page 164.

8b. Ray-flowers not subtended by receptacular bracts; fruits quadrangular; leaves entire to pinnatifid; receptacle conical. ***Rudbeckia***, BLACK-EYED SUSAN, page 165.

9a. Ray-flowers with well-developed styles, fertile and producing seeds .... (10)

9b. Ray-flowers lacking functional styles, not producing fruits ..... (11)

10a. Leaves mostly opposite, green and scabrous; rays persistent, becoming papery in age. ***Heliopsis***, OX-EYE, page 155.

10b. Leaves mostly alternate, white-pubescent beneath; rays shriveling in age; achenes flattened, with 2 corky wings on the sides. ***Verbesina***, CROWN-BEARD, page 172.

11a. Pappus lacking; ray-flowers up to 1.5 cm long. ***Heliomeris***, page 155.

11b. Pappus present, although sometimes falling when the fruit is ripe; ray-flowers longer .... (12)

12a. Pappus persistent; disk-achenes strongly flattened, thin-edged. ***Helianthella***, LITTLE-SUNFLOWER, page 154.

12b. Pappus deciduous; fruits only slightly compressed, plump. ***Helianthus***, SUNFLOWER, page 154.

13a. Leaves simple and undivided .... (14)

13b. Leaves pinnatifid or ternately divided .... (18)

14a. Plants scapose with linear basal leaves. ***Hymenoxys***, page 156.

14b. Plants with leafy stems .... (15)

15a. Rays well developed and showy, mostly 5-30 mm long .... (16)

15b. Rays short and inconspicuous, mostly 1-5 mm long .... (17)

16a. Leaves not decurrent on the stem; top of peduncle lanate. ***Dugaldia***, ORANGE SNEEZEWEED, page 146.

16b. Leaves decurrent on the stem; top of peduncle not lanate. ***Helenium***, SNEEZEWEED, page 153.

17a. Plant bushy-branched from the base, with tiny heads; phyllaries imbricate in several series. ***Gutierrezia***, SNAKEWEED, page 152.

17b. Plant simple and little-branched with few medium-sized heads; phyllaries in one series, each one folded around an achene. ***Madia***, page 162.

18a. Phyllaries with large reddish glandular dots; annual. ***Dyssodia***, page 146.

18b. Phyllaries lacking large glandular dots; perennial .... (19)

19a. Low matted plants with three-parted opposite gray-pubescent

leaves; rays short and inconspicuous. *Picradeniopsis*, page 164.
19b. Erect plants with a single or few main leafy stems and alternate stem leaves; rays well developed .... (20)

20a. Basal rosette leaves with rounded tips and many divisions. *Bahia*, page 141.
20b. Basal rosette leaves with linear, pointed divisions. *Hymenoxys*, page 156.

KEY D

1a. Shrubs. "*Haplopappus*," page 152.
1b. Herbaceous .... (2)

2a. Leaves mostly opposite. *Arnica*, page 133.
2b. Leaves alternate or basal .... (3)

3a. Phyllaries equal, narrow, in one series (except for one or two outer ones at the base of the head). .... (4)
3b. Phyllaries in 2 or more series, equal or imbricate .... (5)

4a. Heads turbinate, nodding, succulent; leaves succulent, coarsely dentate, often with purplish and clasping petiole bases; roots little-branched, rope-like; plants with a strong lemon scent when crushed or after drying. *Ligularia*, page 159.
4b. Heads not turbinate or nodding, rarely succulent; leaves not as above; roots fibrous-branched; plants lacking lemon scent. *Senecio*, page 165.

5a. Heads usually very small and numerous, in erect or flat-topped panicles; phyllaries rarely distinctly herbaceous at the apex ...... (6)
5b. Heads usually few and relatively large .... (8)

6a. Leaves linear throughout the stem; stems strictly erect, topped by flat clusters of heads, the heads 4-6 mm high including the flowers. *Euthamia*, page 151.
6b. Leaves broader, or only the uppermost linear; stems erect or the base decumbent; inflorescence spike-like or if flat-topped, the sprays more or less one-sided; heads larger .... (7)

7a. Phyllaries longitudinally striate (having parallel ribs in addition to the midvein). *Oligoneuron*, page 162.
7b. Phyllaries not longitudinally striate. *Solidago*, GOLDENROD, page 168.

8a. Leaves serrate or pinnatifid. *Machaeranthera*, page 162.
8b. Leaves entire .... (9)

9a. Pappus in 2 sets, the outer of small scales or bristles, the inner of longer, scabrous bristles. *Heterotheca*, GOLDEN ASTER, page 155.
9b. Pappus of subequal bristles, not double. "*Haplopappus*," page 152.

KEY E

1a. Leaves either more or less spiny or thistle-like, or heads with densely bristly receptacle, or both .... (2)
1b. Leaves not at all thistle-like; receptacle naked (or with a few chaffy bracts near the margin in *Evax*) .... (5)

2a. Plants thistle-like, with spiny-margined leaves and usually spiny involucre .... (3)
2b. Plants scarcely thistle-like, the leaves not spiny-margined. *Centaurea*, page 142.

3a. Pappus bristles plumose; receptacle densely bristly. *Cirsium*, THISTLE, page 143.
3b. Pappus bristles merely barbellate .... (4)

4a. Receptacle densely bristly, neither honeycombed nor obviously fleshy. *Carduus*, page 142.
4b. Receptacle fleshy, conspicuously honeycombed, not bristly or only sparsely and very shortly so. *Onopordum*, page 163.

5a. Shrubs .... (6)
5b. Herbs .... (7)

6a. Phyllaries aligned in more or less vertical ranks; leaves linear to oblong. *Chrysothamnus*, RABBITBRUSH, page 143.
6b. Phyllaries not aligned in vertical ranks. *Macronema*, page 153.

7a. Leaves opposite or whorled .... (8)
7b. Leaves alternate or basal .... (10)

8a. Flowers yellow. *Arnica*, page 133.
8b. Flowers white or purplish .... (9)

9a. Leaves opposite; flowers white or cream-colored; involucres 2-4 mm long, the phyllaries almost nerveless. *Ageratina*, page 129.
9b. Leaves whorled; flowers lavender; involucres about 1 cm long, the phyllaries strongly several-nerved. *Eupatorium*, page 151.

10a. Flowers all alike, perfect and fertile .... (11)
10b. Outer flowers of the head carpellate or, in some heads, all carpellate, or plants dioecious, with staminate and carpellate heads on different plants .... (16)

11a. Flowers yellow .... (12)
11b. Flowers lavender, purple, white, or cream-colored .... (14)

12a. Phyllaries in one series, elongate, equal, with a few outer ones (not in a whorl) near the base of the head .... (13)
12b. Phyllaries more or less imbricate in two or more series (rayless forms of *Aster* or *Erigeron*, see Key B: 8a *et seq.*).

13a. Heads turbinate, nodding, succulent; leaves succulent, coarsely dentate, often with purplish and clasping petiole bases; roots little-branched, rope-like; plants with a strong lemon scent after drying. *Ligularia*, page 159.

13b. Heads not turbinate or nodding, rarely succulent; leaves not as above; roots fibrous-branched; plants lacking lemon scent. *Senecio*, page 165.

14a. Flowers lavender or purple; heads in spikes. *Liatris*, BLAZING STAR, page 158.

14b. Flowers white or cream-colored to pale pinkish; heads in loose panicles .... (15)

15a. Pappus plumose. *Kuhnia*, page 157.

15b. Pappus smooth or only barbellate. *Brickellia*, page 142.

16a. Basal leaves over 10 cm long, triangular-cordate, white beneath. *Petasites*, page 163.

16b. Basal leaves not as above .... (17)

17a. Foliage and stems more or less white-woolly; phyllaries with dry, scarious tips .... (18)

17b. Foliage and stems not white-woolly; phyllaries not scarious (rayless forms of *Erigeron* and *Aster*, see Key B: 8a *et seq.*).

18a. Plants with tap-root, annual or perennial; heads all with outer carpellate and inner perfect flowers .... (19)

18b. Plants fibrous-rooted, perennial, often with rhizomes or stolons, without tap-root; dioecious or nearly so, the heads on some of the plants wholly staminate or wholly carpellate .... (20)

19a. Receptacle naked; phyllaries with more or less conspicuous scarious or hyaline tips; annual or perennial. *Gnaphalium*, page 152.

19b. Receptacle with a few carpellate flowers borne between series of phyllaries; phyllaries with strongly green midrib nearly to the tip; annual. *Evax*, page 151.

20a. Basal leaves forming a conspicuous, persistent tuft; stem seldom very leafy, often with stolons or rhizomes; strictly dioecious, the staminate and carpellate plants often very different in appearance. *Antennaria*, PUSSYTOES, page 131.

20b. Basal leaves soon withering, not larger than the numerous stem leaves; plants with rhizomes but never stolons; carpellate plants commonly with a few centrally-located staminate flowers in each head. *Anaphalis*, PEARLY EVERLASTING, page 131.

KEY F

1a. Phyllaries extremely sticky-gummy, the tips recurved. *Grindelia*, GUMWEED, page 152.

1b. Phyllaries not sticky-gummy nor with recurved tips .... (2)

2a. Heads of two kinds, staminate and carpellate; involucre of the carpellate heads burlike or nutlike, provided with hooked prickles, spines
or tubercles; staminate involucres unarmed; corollas small and inconspicuous .... (3)
2b. Heads all alike .... (4)

3a. Carpellate involucre with hooked prickles. *Xanthium*, Cocklebur,
page 172.
3b. Carpellate involucre with tubercles or straight spines. *Ambrosia*,
page 130.

4a. Phyllaries terminating in slender hooked bristles. *Arctium*, Burdock,
page 133.
4b. Phyllaries not burlike .... (5)

5a. Receptacle chaffy or bristly throughout .... (6)
5b. Receptacle not chaffy or bristly, sometimes with hairs .... (9)

6a. Heads very small, the involucre up to 4 mm high, the disk to about
5 mm wide. *Iva*, Marsh-elder, page 157.
6b. Heads larger; involucre 6-40 mm high, the disk seldom less than
1 cm wide .... (7)

7a. Receptacle chaffy; phyllaries in two series, the inner and outer well
differentiated .... (8)
7b. Receptacle bristly; phyllaries not divided into two distinct series;
involucre sometimes spiny. *Centaurea*, Knapweed, page 142.

8a. Inner phyllaries united to form a cup, the outer row shorter.
Thelesperma, page 171.
8b. Inner phyllaries not united, the outer often longer than the inner.
Bidens, Beggars Tick, page 141.

9a. Leaves opposite .... (10)
9b. Leaves alternate .... (11)

10a. Leaves simple, triangular with long slender tips; tall bushy-branched
shrub. *Pericome*, page 163.
10b. Leaves pinnatifid or ternate; low herb with glandular dots on
leaves and phyllaries. *Dyssodia*, page 146.

11a. Pappus of scales .... (12)
11b. Pappus absent or a minute crown of teeth .... (13)

12a. Phyllaries with broad papery tips. *Hymenopappus*, page 156.
12b. Phyllaries with narrow, green tips. *Chaenactis*, page 142.

13a. Phyllaries in one equal series, each enclosing an achene; linear-
leaved annuals with glandular heads. *Madia*, Tarweed, page 162.
13b. Phyllaries in several series, not individually enclosing the achenes;
annuals, perennials, or shrubs .... (14)

14a. Heads greenish-yellow, in spikes, panicles or racemes. **Artemisia**, Sagebrush, Sagewort, page 135.
14b. Heads yellow, in flat-topped clusters or solitary ....(15)

15a. Low herb less than a half-meter high, with odor of pineapples. **Chamomilla**, Pineapple-weed, page 143.
15b. Tall herb over a meter high, with a distinctive aroma of its own. **Tanacetum**, Tansy, page 170.

ACHILLEA. Yarrow

One native species, **Achillea lanulosa** Nutt. (woolly), Fig. 67. Common weedy perennial with very finely dissected leaves, often mistaken for a fern when in the rosette stage. Flowers white, rarely pink, in a rounded cluster of small heads. Plains to alpine. The cultivated, and escaped weedy relative is *A. millefolium* L., recognized by its relatively smooth stem and foliage, and its more flat-topped inflorescence.

AGERATINA

One species, **Ageratina herbacea** (Gray) King & H. Robinson, in forests of the foothills from Colorado Springs southward into New Mexico (*Eupatorium herbaceum* of Ed. 4).

Fig. 67. *Achillea lanulosa*

AGOSERIS. False dandelion

1a. Beak of the fruit comparatively stout, nerved throughout, much shorter than the body; flowers yellow, often drying pinkish. *Agoseris glauca* (Pursh) Raf., Pale Agoseris, Fig. 68. Common plants, resembling dandelions, but differing in the technical characters of the fruit and involucre. This and the next species are very variable in leaf outline and plant size. Montane and subalpine.

1b. Beak of the fruit slender, not nerved throughout, elongate; flowers burnt-orange, often drying purplish. *Agoseris aurantiaca* (Hook.) Greene, Orange Agoseris. Meadows and forest openings, montane, subalpine.

AMBROSIA. Rag-weed; Sand-bur

1a. Leaves entire to palmately 3- to 5-lobed; involucre of staminate heads 3- to 4-ribbed. *Ambrosia trifida* L., Giant Ragweed, Fig. 69. Abundant in cultivated ground, along roadsides and in vacant lots. An important hay-fever plant.

Fig. 68. *Agoseris glauca*   Fig. 69. *Ambrosia trifida*

1b. Leaves once to thrice pinnatifid; involucre of staminate heads not
   ribbed .... (2)

2a. Fruiting involucre naked or with a few very short knobs or spines (3)
2b. Fruiting involucre burlike, with long, sharp spines .... (4)

3a. Annual; leaves thin; fruiting involucre with short spines near the
   summit. ***Ambrosia artemisiifolia*** L., ROMAN WORMWOOD. Common
   weed in neglected ground, plains and mesas. Introduced.
3b. Perennial from deep-seated creeping rhizomes; leaves thick; fruiting
   involucre naked or with a few short knobs. ***Ambrosia psilostachya*** DC.
   (naked-spiked), WESTERN RAGWEED. The native counterpart of the last,
   occurring in the same areas. Easily mistaken for the last species
   because the stems break when pulled from the ground, leaving the
   rhizome intact.

4a. Leaves ovate or deltoid in general outline, once- to thrice- pinnatifid,
   green or only slightly paler beneath; fruit 1-beaked, armed with 6 to 30
   strongly flattened, straight, spreading spines 2-5 mm long; annual.
   Ambrosia acanthicarpa Hook. (spiny-fruited), SAND-BUR. Common
   weed on the plains (*Franseria* of Ed. 4).
4b. Leaves oblong in outline, interruptedly pinnatifid, with a strongly
   toothed or lobed rachis, green above, densely white-pubescent beneath;
   fruit 2- or 3-beaked, bearing about 4 to 9 thick-subulate spines 1-2 mm
   long and flattened only at the base; perennial from rhizomes.
   Ambrosia tomentosa Nutt. In similar habitats, sometimes in gardens,
   where it is difficult to eradicate because of the deep-seated rhizomes
   (*Franseria discolor* of Ed. 4).

ANAPHALIS. PEARLY EVERLASTING

   One species, ***Anaphalis margaritacea*** (L.) B. & H. (pearly). Common
in meadows and forest openings, foothills to subalpine.

ANTENNARIA. PUSSYTOES

1a. Plants not producing prostrate leafy stolons; leaves linear-lanceolate
   or lanceolate, over 5 cm long. ***Antennaria pulcherrima*** (Hook.) Greene
   ssp. ***anaphaloides*** (Rydb.) W. A. Weber. As implied by the name, this
   closely resembles the Pearly Everlasting, *Anaphalis*, but has the leaves
   uniformly pubescent on both sides, while *Anaphalis* has strongly
   bicolored leaves. Common in upper montane and subalpine.
1b. Plants producing leafy stolons; leaves usually shorter .... (2)

2a. Phyllaries green or brown at the tips. ***Antennaria alpina*** (L.) Gaertn.,
   ALPINE PUSSYTOES. Dwarf plants, alpine and subalpine.
2b. Phyllaries with white or pink tips .... (3)

3a. Leaves of stem, rosettes, and stolons linear-oblanceolate, not abruptly
   pointed; phyllaries with dark spots at their bases; heads 5-8 mm high.
   Antennaria corymbosa E. Nels. (having a flat-topped inflorescence).
   Infrequent, wet meadows and lake shores, subalpine.

3b. Leaves of at least the basal rosette obovate or spatulate, rounded at the tip, abruptly pointed, or otherwise not as above .... (4)

4a. Tomentum soon rubbing off the upper surface of the basal leaves; leaves of stolons much narrower than those of the rosette. **Antennaria neglecta** Greene (overlooked). Frequent on the mesas and lower foothills.

4b. Tomentum permanent on both leaf surfaces; leaves of stolons usually similar to rosette leaves .... (5)

5a. Involucres 4-6 mm high (heads comparatively small). **Antennaria rosea** Greene, Fig. 70. The most obvious mark of this species is the pink color of the phyllaries, but these may be either white or pink in different individuals. Probably the most common Pussytoes, found from the mesas to timberline.

5b. Involucres 7-9 mm high (heads relatively large). **Antennaria parvifolia** Nutt. (small-leaved). Mesas to subalpine.

ANTHEMIS. CHAMOMILE

One species, **Anthemis cotula** L. (resembling the genus *Cotula*), DOG FENNEL. Occasional as a weed in cultivated ground, farmyards, etc.

Fig. 70. *Antennaria rosea*

ARCTIUM. Burdock

One species, **Arctium minus** (Hill) Bernh. (small). Common tall, rank weed in cultivated or neglected ground. The fruits stick to clothing.

ARNICA

1a. Pappus pure white .... (4)
1b. Pappus tawny, or reddish-brown, never white .... (2)

2a. Phyllaries obtuse or sometimes acutish, the tips pilose on the inner surface; rhizomes elongate, fleshy, naked, brown, not rooting the first year. **Arnica chamissonis** Less. ssp. **foliosa** (Nutt.) Maguire (for A. von Chamisso), Leafy Arnica. Wet meadows and lake shores, upper montane, subalpine.
2b. Phyllaries acute, the tips not pilose; rhizomes shorter, branched, rooting the first year .... (3)

3a. Heads without rays, the immature heads nodding. **Arnica parryi** Gray (for C. C. Parry). Spruce-fir forests and aspen groves, subalpine.
3b. Heads with rays, the immature heads erect. **Arnica mollis** Hook. (soft). Meadows and forest openings, subalpine.

Fig. 71. **Podospermum laciniatum**

4a. Leaves ovate, at least the basal ones with petioles equalling the blades; rhizomes naked or clothed with overlapping scales and leaf-bases only near the apex, characteristically 3-branched near the apex ....(5)

4b. Leaves lanceolate, sessile or with petioles shorter than the blades; rhizomes clothed with overlapping scales and leaf-bases, characteristically unbranched near the apex ....(6)

5a. Stem leaves about 3 pairs, sessile, or if short-petioled, the petioles winged; plant sparingly hairy, often quite green and glabrous; basal leaves not cordate, but ovate-truncate. ***Arnica latifolia*** Bong. Subalpine forests. Intermediates connect this with the next, probably through hybridization, and some individuals are impossible to assign to one species or the other. The extreme keyed here, however, is unmistakable.

5b. Leaves ovate, tending to be cordate; basal and stem leaves distinctly petiolate; plant hairy, the involucre usually rather densely so. ***Arnica cordifolia*** Hook., Fig. 72. Dry forests, montane, subalpine.

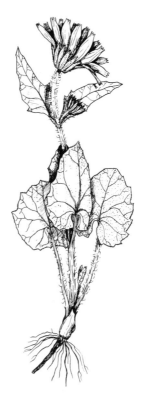

Fig. 72. ***Arnica cordifolia***

6a. Old leaf-bases at base of stem with tufts of tawny hairs in their axils; lower stem-leaves petioled; plants of the mesas. ***Arnica fulgens*** Pursh (shining), Orange arnica. Abundant in late spring in grassy meadow slopes on the mesas.

6b. Old leaf-bases at base of stem lacking tufts of tawny hairs; lower stem leaves sessile; subalpine or alpine species. ***Arnica rydbergii*** Greene. Infrequent on rocky meadow slopes near timberline.

ARTEMISIA. Sagebrush

1a. Plant an herb; stem often thickened and perennial at base but never decidedly woody .... (4)

1b. Plant a shrub, sometimes low but always decidedly woody at the base .... (2)

2a. Leaves deeply lobed or pinnatifid, the lobes repeatedly dissected. ***Artemisia frigida*** Willd. (of cold places), Pasture Sagebrush, Fig. 73. Very common and widespread on gravelly hillsides, mesas to subalpine. Vegetative shoots are seldom more than a few inches tall, white-pubescent.

2b. Leaves entire or merely 3-cleft at the apex .... (3)

Fig. 73. *Artemisia frigida*

3a. Leaves simple or deeply cleft into 3 linear lobes. **Artemisia filifolia**
Torr. (thread-leaved), SILVERY WORMWOOD. Tall shrub with elongate,
linear leaves. The common sagebrush of sandy places on the plains.
West of our range, in the mountain parks, the common entire-leaved
sagebrush is *Artemisia cana* Pursh, Fig. 74. This has lanceolate or
elliptic-lanceolate leaves, and is a low shrub.

3b. Leaves shallowly 3-cleft or 3-toothed at the apex. **Artemisia tridentata**
Nutt. ssp. **vaseyana** (Rydb.) Beetle, MOUNTAIN SAGEBRUSH, Fig. 75.
Upper montane and subalpine on dry hillsides and floors of mountain
parks, infrequent in our range but abundant in Middle Park. Replaced
at lower altitudes by ssp. **tridentata**, the Big Sagebrush, which
dominates river benches on the Western Slope but occurs rarely in
our area.

4a. Plants annual or biennial; basal leaves withered and not conspicuous
at flowering time .... (5)

4b. Plants perennial; if appearing biennial, with basal leaves and a
taproot, then the basal leaves functional at flowering time ...... (6)

5a. Plants annual, up to 2 or 3 meters tall; weed of waste ground in towns.
Artemisia annua L. Found only once, in Boulder.

Fig. 74. *Artemisia cana*

5b. Plants biennial, less than a meter tall; leaves pinnately compound, with short but slender sharp teeth; disturbed soils in the forests, particularly in logging areas. ***Artemisia biennis*** Willd., BIENNIAL WORMWOOD.

6a. Segments of leaves mostly 2 mm or more wide, linear or lanceolate to ovate, or leaves entire and over 2 mm wide .... (7)
6b. Segments of leaves mostly 1 mm or less wide, linear or filiform, rarely elliptic or ovate in dwarf plants, or leaves entire and less than 2 mm wide .... (9)

7a. Leaves with a dense tomentum or woolly pubescence, at least beneath. ***Artemisia ludoviciana*** Nutt. (of "old" Louisiana), PRAIRIE SAGE. Leaves extremely variable from plant to plant, ranging from lanceolate and entire to variously lobed and deeply cleft. Very common, from plains to subalpine.
7b. Leaves with silky or spreading pubescence, or glabrous .... (8)

8a. Leaves mostly entire or a few cleft into 2 or 3 short ascending lobes, hairy only when young, soon green and glabrous; heads less than 5 mm wide, numerous in a diffuse panicle. ***Artemisia dracunculus*** L. ssp. ***glauca*** (Pallas) Hall & Clements, WILD TARRAGON. Abundant on plains and mesas.

Fig. 75. ***Artemisia tridentata***

8b. Leaves dissected, usually silky-hairy; heads 5 mm or more wide, few, racemosely arranged and nodding. **Artemisia arctica** Less. ssp. **saxicola** (Rydb.) Hultén, ARCTIC SAGE. Usually above timberline. Phyllaries usually purple-margined.

9a. Receptacle not evidently hairy between the flowers ....(10)
9b. Receptacle densely long-hairy between the flowers ....(12)

10a. Leaves mostly entire, a few cleft into 2 or 3 short, ascending lobes, green and glabrous or nearly so. **Artemisia dracunculus** L. (see 8a).
10b. Leaves pinnatifid into 5 to 10 or more spreading divisions, or, if nearly entire, the leaves tomentose ....(11)

11a. Leaves chiefly basal, the stem leaves reduced in size; fruits present only in marginal flowers, those of the central flowers lacking .....(14)
11b. Leaves not chiefly basal, the stem leaves not greatly reduced; fruits present in all flowers of the head. **Artemisia ludoviciana** Nutt. (see 7a).

12a. Stems very leafy; heads usually in panicles; plants of middle and lower altitudes. **Artemisia frigida** Willd. (see 2a).
12b. Stems sparsely leafy; heads in racemes or solitary; dwarf alpine species ....(13)

13a. Heads 5 to 25; leaves mostly twice pinnatifid (i.e., pinnatifid with the first divisions again divided). **Artemisia scopulorum** Gray (of rocks). Fairly common on tundra and in high subalpine meadows.
13b. Heads 1 to 4; leaves only once pinnatifid or cleft. **Artemisia pattersonii** Gray (for Harry N. Patterson), ALPINE SAGE. Apparently rare or only locally abundant, on tundra.

14a. Inflorescence unbranched, spikelike, with the bracts standing out and conspicuously longer than the clusters of heads; involucres quite pubescent, the phyllaries with brown margins. **Artemisia borealis** Pallas ssp. **purshii** (Besser in Hook.) Hultén, BOREAL SAGE. Tundra and upper subalpine slopes. Flowering shoots one or a few together.
14b. Inflorescence distinctly branched, the flower spikes generally not exceeded by the bracts; involucres green, sparsely pubescent. **Artemisia campestris** L. ssp. **caudata** (Michx.) Hall & Clements. Abundant in gravelly fields, open dry meadows and pine woods, plains to subalpine. Stems with many basal leaves and several flowering shoots (*A. canadensis* of Ed. 4).

ASTER
1a. Stems low, usually 10 cm high or less; leaves very small, less than 1 cm long, narrowly linear or the upper scale-like (see **Leucelene**).
1b. Stems taller and leaves much larger, or otherwise not as above ... (2)

2a. Phyllaries glandular-puberulent ....(3)
2b. Phyllaries not glandular although sometimes pubescent ......(5)

3a. Leaves linear or linear-oblanceolate; stems slender, low ......(4)

3b. Leaves broadly lanceolate; plants tall and stout; heads in a crowded flat-topped inflorescence; rays brilliant red-purple. ***Aster novae-angliae*** L., NEW ENGLAND ASTER. Meadows in the piedmont valleys, late summer, possibly originally introduced as an ornamental but thoroughly naturalized.

4a. Stems erect, from creeping rhizomes; heads few, the flowering branches without strongly modified leaves; montane and subalpine. ***Aster campestris*** Nutt.
4b. Stems spreading from a cluster of short caudices; heads numerous, on short branches from the axils of the upper leaves, the branches with many very short leaves. ***Aster fendleri*** Gray. Rare or infrequent, mesas at the base of the mountains, in late summer.

5a. Involucre and stem immediately below it glabrous or very nearly so
. . . . (6)
5b. Involucre and/or peduncle pubescent . . . . (11)

6a. Basal leaves larger than the cauline ones; head solitary at the stem apex . . . . (7)
6b. Basal leaves, if present, not larger than the cauline ones; heads rarely solitary . . . . (8)

7a. Leaves glabrous above, minutely pubescent on the margins and veins beneath; ray-flowers deep lavender. [***Erigeron peregrinus*** (Pursh) Greene ssp. ***callianthemus*** (Greene) Cronquist. Because of its unusually broad ray-flowers, this species is usually mistaken for an *Aster* and probably forms a connecting link between the two genera.]
7b. Leaves short-pubescent on both sides; ray-flowers pink to pale lavender or white. ***Aster alpinus*** L. ssp. ***vierhapperi*** Onno. Very rare, possibly extinct in our area, discovered only once on Berthoud Pass in 1903 by Frank Tweedy. After flowering, the ray-flowers characteristically curl down around the involucre, a good field recognition character. This *Aster* resembles *Erigeron* just as the last species resembles *Aster*.

8a. Leaves predominantly narrowly linear-oblanceolate (less than 1 cm wide); ray-flowers white and heads less than 1 cm high. ***Aster porteri*** Gray (for T. C. Porter). The most common white-flowered aster of the mountains, from the foothills to subalpine, blossoming in late summer.
8b. Leaves broader, more than 1 cm wide . . . . (9)

9a. Heads 5 mm or less high; ray-flowers few; leaves oblong, glaucous; phyllaries obtuse. ***Aster glaucodes*** Blake, GLAUCOUS ASTER. Talus slopes, montane and subalpine.
9b. Heads 1 cm or more high; ray-flowers numerous; leaves lanceolate, broadest near the base; if leaves glaucous, then the phyllaries acute (10)

10a. Ray-flowers white; leaves green, sparsely pubescent, not clasping the stem. ***Aster engelmannii*** Gray (for George Engelmann). Rare in this region, in upper montane and subalpine forests. More common to the northwest.

10b. Ray-flowers blue; leaves glaucous, glabrous, clasping the stem. **Aster laevis** L. (smooth). The common blue aster of late summer, foothills and montane.

11a. Involucre 3-4 mm high; leaves linear or oblong, short; foliage and stem generally stiff-hairy; heads very numerous . . . . (12)
11b. Involucre 5-15 mm high; leaves broader, elongate; foliage usually glabrate except above; heads few . . . . (13)

12a. Stem hairs spreading. **Aster falcatus** Lindl. (sickle-shaped). Abundant weedy aster along roadsides and fencerows in late summer, piedmont valleys and plains.
12b. Stem hairs appressed or ascending. **Aster ericoides** L. (like heather). Not as common as the preceding, in similar habitats.

13a. Pubescence of the stem and branchlets occurring in lines decurrent from the leaf bases, commonly neither uniformly distributed under the heads nor confined to the inflorescence; swampy places, piedmont valleys and plains. **Aster hesperius** Gray (western). A tall, pale blue or white-flowered aster with willow-like leaves, fairly common in swampy places, at low altitudes (*A. coerulescens* of manuals).
13b. Pubescence of the stem uniform, or, if in lines, then either uniform under the heads or very scanty and confined to the inflorescence; foothills and mountains . . . . (14)

14a. Involucres strongly graduated (the outer series of bracts progressively shorter), at least the outer phyllaries obtuse, markedly shorter than the inner, and not foliaceous (leaf-like) . . . . (15)
14b. Involucres not strongly graduated, or, if so, the phyllaries markedly acute; phyllaries acute, or if obtuse, enlarged and foliaceous. (17)

15a. Rays white; plants scabrous-puberulent. **Aster ptarmicoides** (Nees) T. & G. Rare, ponderosa pine forests near Monument.
15b. Rays some shade of pink to lavender; plants not scabrous . . . . (16)

16a. Phyllaries with oblanceolate green tips, or, if nearly wholly green then narrowed at the base. **Aster chilensis** Nees ssp. **adscendens** (Lindl.) Cronquist (Chilean, a misnomer), PACIFIC ASTER. This and the next three species are common in the mountains and are very difficult to identify satisfactorily.
16b. Phyllaries nearly wholly green (at least the outer), not narrowed at the base. **Aster occidentalis** (Nutt.) T. & G., WESTERN ASTER.

17a. Middle stem leaves 1 cm wide or more, mostly less than 7 times as long as wide. **Aster foliaceus** Lindley, LEAFY-BRACTED ASTER.
17b. Middle stem leaves mostly less than 1 cm wide and more than 7 times as long as wide . . . . (18)

18a. Plant caespitose, decumbent, less than 2 dm high; inner and sometimes outer phyllaries purple-tipped and -margined; alpine and subalpine. **Aster foliaceus** var. **apricus** Gray. A dwarfed subalpine form usually having purple-margined phyllaries.

18b. Stems erect, commonly arising singly or in two's or three's from rhizomes, mostly over 2 dm high; phyllaries usually not purple-margined, although often purple-tipped; mostly not alpine. ***Aster occidentalis*** (Nutt.) T. & G.

BAHIA

One species, ***Bahia dissecta*** (Gray) Britt. Common on gravelly soil of canyonsides from the foothills through the montane.

BIDENS. Beggars Tick

1a. Leaves simple, lanceolate or oblanceolate; ray-flowers short but present. ***Bidens cernua*** L., Nodding Bur-marigold. Common in swamps and along irrigation ditches, piedmont valleys and plains.
1b. Leaves divided into three leaflets or deeply dissected; ray-flowers lacking .... (2)

2a. Leaves deeply dissected, the divisions 0.5 cm or less broad. ***Bidens tenuisecta*** Gray (with slender segments), Spanish Needles. Streamsides and floodplains, chiefly south of Denver.
2b. Leaves deeply 3-lobed or usually divided into 3 broad leaflets (3)

3a. Outer phyllaries 5 to 8 in number, sparsely ciliate; inner phyllaries equalling the disk in length. ***Bidens frondosa*** L. (leafy), Fig. 77. Common in swamps and along irrigation ditches, piedmont valleys and plains. The distinctions between this and the next species are seldom satisfactory.

Fig. 76. ***Machaeranthera pattersonii***   Fig. 77. ***Bidens frondosa***

3b. Outer phyllaries 10 to 20, strongly hispid-ciliate; inner phyllaries shorter than the disk. **Bidens vulgata** Greene (common). Habitats similar to the preceding.

BRACHYACTIS

One species, **Brachyactis angusta** (Lindl.) Britt. Margins of ponds on the plains and piedmont valleys, flowering in late summer. The fruiting heads with their copious white pappus resemble powderpuffs. The marginal flowers have no strap-shaped portion and the style is long-exserted from the corolla tube (*Aster brachyactis* of Ed. 4).

BRICKELLIA

1a. Heads large (1 cm or more long), in long-pedunculate nodding clusters from the axils of the upper leaves. **Brickellia grandiflora** (Hook.) Nutt. Common on rocky slopes in the foothill canyons.

1b. Heads small (0.5 cm) in very short-pedunculate clusters. **Brickellia californica** (T. & G.) Gray. Dry, rocky slopes, mesas and lower foothills. Flowering in late summer.

CARDUUS

One species, **Carduus nutans** L. ssp. **macrolepis** (Peterm.) Kazmi. Recently established weed, abundant locally in the piedmont valleys and along roadsides in the mountains (*C. leiophyllus* of Ed. 4). A handsome tall pink thistle with very broad, glabrous, sharp-pointed spreading phyllaries.

CENTAUREA. KNAPWEED; CORNFLOWER

1a. Phyllaries spine-tipped, fringed; flowers mostly white; pappus none; annual or biennial, bushy-branched. **Centaurea diffusa** Lam. One of the most abundant weeds along the major highway from Denver to Colorado Springs, and established in disturbed areas around Boulder, spreading up into the foothills to some extent.

1b. Phyllaries not spine-tipped but may be weakly fringed; flowers blue, lavender or pink, only sporadically white; pappus present .... (2)

2a. Annual; marginal flowers of head enlarged, almost tubular, very showy, blue, lavender or white; phyllaries fringed. **Centaurea cyanus** L., CORNFLOWER. An old-fashioned garden flower locally escaped and established in fields and roadsides.

2b. Perennial; marginal flowers of head not greatly enlarged or showy, pink-lavender; phyllaries not fringed. **Centaurea repens** L., RUSSIAN KNAPWEED. A serious pest of fields and roadsides in the foothills, reproducing by rhizomes.

CHAENACTIS

1a. Plants low or dwarf, growing on alpine rockslides; leaves mostly basal; pappus scales 4 to 6. ***Chaenactis alpina*** (Gray) Jones. Frequent on the slopes of the higher peaks.

1b. Plants tall (2 dm or more), growing in dry, open forests of the foot-hills; plants leafy-stemmed; pappus scales 8 to 14. ***Chaenactis douglasii*** H. & A. (for David Douglas).

CHAMOMILLA. Chamomile

One species, ***Chamomilla suaveolens*** (Pursh) Rydb. (sweet-smelling), Pineapple Weed. Common weed in disturbed soil (picnic areas, parking lots) particularly in the mountains throughout our range. The crushed foliage has a strong pineapple odor (*Matricaria matricarioides* of Ed. 4).

CHRYSOTHAMNUS. Rabbitbrush

1a. Twigs glabrous or puberulent, not closely tomentose. ***Chrysothamnus viscidiflorus*** (Hook.) Nutt. Montane and subalpine. Very abundant in the western part of the state at lower elevations, but apparently uncommon east of the Continental Divide.

1b. Twigs covered with a felt-like tomentum, this sometimes so close as to escape casual observation .... (2)

2a. Heads in leafy spike-like or racemose clusters, these sometimes branching to form panicles; outer phyllaries commonly prolonged into a slender herbaceous tip or appendage. ***Chrysothamnus parryi*** (Gray) Greene (for C. C. Parry). Upper montane, subalpine, in open forests.

2b. Heads cymose at the ends of the branches, the inflorescence some-times compound and elongated; phyllaries obtuse to acute, the outer ones regularly shortened and without an herbaceous tip. ***Chrysotham-nus nauseosus*** (Pallas) Britt. (nauseating), Fig. 78. The most abundant species of *Chrysothamnus* in the area. Plants are very variable as to amount of pubescence and height of stem.

CICHORIUM. Chicory

One species, ***Cichorium intybus*** L. (ancient name for chicory). Introduced and locally established as a roadside weed on the plains and piedmont valleys.

CIRSIUM. Thistle

1a. Perennial plants, reproducing by underground rhizomes (plants growing in patches); heads usually less than 3 cm high .... (2)

1b. Biennials with taproots (plants growing singly or a few together); heads usually 3 or more cm high .... (3)

2a. Plants green, glabrous; heads 1-1.5 cm high. ***Cirsium arvense*** (L.) Scop. (of fields), Canada Thistle. Introduced weed, very difficult to eradicate. Found in fields and roadsides, plains and piedmont valleys.

2b. Plants woolly-pubescent; heads larger. ***Cirsium flodmanii*** (Rydb.) Arthur (for J. H. Flodman). Infrequent, roadside depressions on the plains and piedmont valleys.

3a. Heads usually in dense terminal clusters or sessile along the stem; if not, the phyllaries ragged-fringed at the apex .... (4)
3b. Heads usually on elongate peduncles, the phyllaries never fringed .... (8)

4a. Phyllaries with short, weak spines, these fringed at the upper end, the fringe arising from a dilated apex and pointing upward with the spine. *Cirsium centaureae* (Rydb.) K. Schum. Montane and subalpine forest openings.
4b. Phyllaries with stout spines, if fringed, the fringes seemingly made up of fused hairs which point sideways .... (5)

5a. Phyllaries glabrous or with a bit of matted cobweb along the upper margins, the back covered with minute granular yellowish glands; spines short and broad, flattened; heads with white flowers; plants either reduced to a massive rosette of basal leaves and a cluster of sessile heads, or tall with the heads sessile in the leaf-axils. *Cirsium coloradense* (Rydb.) Cockerell. Mountain meadows and streamsides.
5b. Phyllaries with long multicellular hairs often giving the head a cobwebby appearance; spines long and not strongly flattened .... (6)

6a. Flowers pale lavender; upper leaves long-decurrent; phyllaries with a stout terminal spine but hardly ciliate or spinose on the sides; leaves regularly and deeply pinnatifid. *Cirsium tweedyi* (Rydb.) Petrak. Upper subalpine meadows.
6b. Flowers yellow or greenish-yellow; leaves not decurrent; phyllaries ciliate or with lateral spines .... (7)

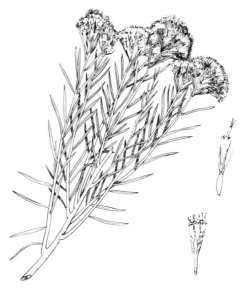

Fig. 78. *Chrysothamnus nauseosus*

7a. Heads in a very dense nodding cluster, exceedingly spinose and with much cobwebby-pubescence; phyllaries with lateral spines; flowers yellow; alpine. **Cirsium scopulorum** (Greene) Cockerell, Plate 29. A handsome heavy-headed alpine thistle on higher mountain slopes.

7b. Heads erect, not always in dense clusters, with loose and relatively inconspicuous hairs; phyllaries with lateral fringes formed by united marginal hairs; flowers greenish-yellow; montane and subalpine. **Cirsium parryi** (Gray) Petrak. Common in the foothill canyons.

8a. Phyllaries cobwebby-pubescent; leaves with decurrent bases, forming narrow wings extending down the stem for several centimeters. **Cirsium vulgare** (Savi) Tenore (common), BULL THISTLE. Introduced weed in pastures on the plains and piedmont valleys (*C. lanceolatum* of manuals).

8b. Phyllaries not cobwebby-pubescent; leaves not or little decurrent (9)

9a. Flowers lavender-purple (occasional white-flowered individuals appear in normal colonies); bases of stem leaves clasping, rarely somewhat decurrent . . . . (10)

9b. Flowers white; bases of stem leaves decurrent. **Cirsium canescens** Nutt. (hoary). Abundant from the plains through the montane.

10a. Leaves shallowly pinnatifid, upper and lower surfaces similar in color, leaf bases not at all decurrent. **Cirsium undulatum** (Nutt.) Spreng., WAVY-LEAVED THISTLE. Abundant on the mesas and plains. Early-flowering plants usually have larger heads.

10b. Leaves deeply pinnatifid, upper leaf surface not as canescent as the lower, slightly decurrent (up to 1 cm below leaf base attachment). **Cirsium ochrocentrum** Gray. Evidently not as common as the last, in the same areas.

CONYZA. HORSEWEED

One common species, **Conyza canadensis** (L.) Cronquist. Disturbed ground, overgrazed areas, trailsides, etc. Leaves linear, flower heads small, in a diffuse panicle. A second species, **C. schiedeana** (Less.) Cronquist, with fewer, larger heads, broader crenate leaves, has been found as a weed near Pikes Peak.

COREOPSIS

One species, **Coreopsis tinctoria** Nutt. Swales in the piedmont valleys, infrequent. It is very similar to *Thelesperma filifolium*, but the phyllaries are usually deeply infused with red.

CREPIS. HAWKSBEARD

1a. Involucres turbinate-campanulate; stem leaves generally all reduced, narrow, inconspicuous or rarely the lowest one similar to the basal leaves; plants of moist situations. **Crepis runcinata** T. & G. (sharply incised). A very common and variable species of wet meadows, montane and subalpine. Easily distinguished from the other *Crepis* species by the broad involucre.

1b. Involucre narrowly or broadly cylindrical; 1 to 3 stem leaves well developed; plants of dry situations ....(2)

2a. Largest heads of the inflorescence with 5 to 7 inner phyllaries; heads 5- to 10-flowered. *Crepis acuminata* Nutt. Dry slopes, montane.
2b. Largest heads of the inflorescence with 8 to 13 inner phyllaries; heads 9- to 40-flowered ....(3)

3a. Fruits yellowish or brownish; lobes of leaves broadly lanceolate or deltoid, or, if narrower, usually toothed or lobed. *Crepis occidentalis* Nutt., WESTERN HAWKSBEARD. Grasslands on the mesas. Leaves usually gray-pubescent.
3b. Fruits deep- or pale-green; lobes of leaves linear or narrowly lanceolate. 0.5-2.5 mm broad, curved, mostly entire. *Crepis atribarba* Heller (black-bearded). Infrequent, canyonsides and in chaparral on the hogbacks. Leaves usually not strongly gray-pubescent.

DUGALDIA. ORANGE SNEEZEWEED

One species, *Dugaldia hoopesii* (Gray) Rydb. (for Thomas Hoopes), Fig. 85. Mountain meadows and aspen groves, montane and subalpine. Very common west of the Divide, but in the Front Range only in the Pikes Peak region. A poisonous plant of major importance to sheep raisers on summer ranges. Nearly 8,000 head are said to die each year in Colorado alone from sneezeweed poisoning. The poisonous principle is a glycoside, dugaldin.

DYSSODIA. FETID MARIGOLD

One species, *Dyssodia papposa* (Vent.) Hitchc. (for its conspicuous pappus). Common roadside weed, easily distinguished by the gland-dotted phyllaries. Ray-flowers short and inconspicuous. Another species, common in the Arkansas River drainage, is *D. aurea* (Gray) Nels., with conspicuous yellow ray-flowers.

ERIGERON. FLEABANE; DAISY

1a. Leaves simple ....(3)
1b. Leaves cleft or lobed ....(2)

2a. Leaves once or twice 3-parted at the apex. *Erigeron compositus* Pursh (compound), Fig. 79. Openings in pine forests in the foothills, to gravelly moraines in the subalpine zone. The majority of the plants have conspicuous white ray-flowers, but rayless forms are fairly common.
2b. Leaves pinnatifid. *Erigeron pinnatisectus* (Gray) Nels. (pinnately-dissected). Meadows and rocky hillsides, subalpine. This and the preceding are low species growing in dense clumps, the leaves chiefly basal. They are easily distinguished by the cutting of the leaves. *E. pinnatisectus* has colored ray-flowers.

3a. Carpellate (ray-flowers) corollas very numerous, with very narrow, short, erect ligules, these sometimes not exceeding the disk, or the inner carpellate corollas tubular and without an expanded ligule (two rare species in the subalpine) .... (4)

3b. Carpellate flowers few to numerous (rarely absent), the ligules, when present, well developed and spreading, not short, narrow, and erect .... (5)

4a. Inner phyllaries usually long-attenuate; inflorescence more or less flat-topped; pappus reddish-brown. ***Erigeron acris*** L. var. ***debilis*** Gray. Rather rare, subalpine meadows.

4b. Inner phyllaries merely acute or acuminate; inflorescence racemose, not flat-topped; pappus usually white. ***Erigeron lonchophyllus*** Hook. (with spear-shaped leaves). Wet meadows and rocky walls of cirques near timberline, subalpine.

5a. Annuals, biennials, or short-lived perennials, without deep-seated rhizome or well developed woody caudex .... (6)

5b. True perennials, often with deep-seated rhizome or well developed woody caudex .... (8)

6a. Plant mostly 3-7 dm high; stems solitary or very few, mostly un-branched; ray-flowers always white. ***Erigeron strigosus*** Muehl. (with straight appressed hairs), DAISY FLEABANE. A tall weedy species found along roadsides and ditches on the plains and sometimes along trails in the mountains. Probably better treated as *Stenactis annua* ssp. *strigosa* (Willd.) Soo.

Fig. 79. ***Erigeron compositus***

6b. Plant usually under 3 dm high; stems branched from near the base, or numerous; ray-flowers blue, pink, or white .... (7)

7a. Stem hairs all spreading; ray-flowers blue or white; plant usually without trailing leafy stolons. **Erigeron divergens** T. & G. SPREADING FLEABANE. Plains and mesas.
7b. Stem hairs appressed or closely ascending; ray-flowers usually white; plant with trailing leafy stolons. **Erigeron flagellaris** Gray (whip-like), TRAILING FLEABANE. Common on grassy slopes, plains to subalpine.

8a. Fruit 4- to 14-nerved; involucre clearly and usually regularly imbricate. **Erigeron canus** Gray (gray-haired). Rather rare in this area and apparently confined to shales on the mesas.
8b. Fruit mostly 2-nerved; if with 4 or more nerves, then the phyllaries about equal .... (9)

9a. Stem leaves simple, usually lanceolate or broader; plants tall and erect, somewhat *Aster*-like .... (10)
9b. Stem leaves usually much reduced, mostly linear or oblanceolate; plants relatively low, often spreading, scarcely *Aster*-like in appearance .... (17)

10a. Involucre woolly-villous with multicellular hairs; leaves entire. **Erigeron elatior** (Gray) Greene (taller), TALL FLEABANE. Forests, montane to subalpine.
10b. Involucre not woolly with multicellular hairs, but often hirsute (*E. coulteri* may be so pubescent as to appear woolly to one unacquainted with *E. elatior*, but the leaves of *E. coulteri* are remotely sharply serrate) .... (11)

11a. Hairs of the involucre with black cross-walls near their bases; ray-flowers white; leaves hairy; pappus simple or nearly so. **Erigeron coulteri** Porter (for J. M. Coulter). Subalpine forests, uncommon east of the Continental Divide.
11b. Hairs of the involucre without black cross-walls; ray-flowers usually colored; leaves and pappus various .... (12)

12a. Ray-flowers mostly 2-3 mm wide; pappus single, rarely double (a double pappus has bristles of two different lengths; usually the outer bristles are very short). **Erigeron peregrinus** (Pursh) Greene (wandering), SUBALPINE DAISY, Fig. 80. A most handsome species of subalpine and alpine meadows.
12b. Ray-flowers about 1 mm wide (1-2 mm in *E. eximius*); pappus double, or rarely single .... (13)

13a. Stem leaves glabrous or glandular, not even ciliate on the margins, comparatively few in number, and little if at all longer than the internodes. **Erigeron eximius** Greene. Moist subalpine forest glades (*E. superbus* Greene).
13b. Stem leaves either obviously pubescent or at least cilate on the

margins, sometimes also glandular, often relatively numerous and longer than their internodes .... (14)

14a. Plant rather equably leafy, the upper leaves gradually instead of abruptly reduced in size, the middle leaves commonly as large as or larger than the lowermost ones .... (15)

14b. Plant rather inequably leafy, the uppermost leaves abruptly reduced in size, the middle ones commonly smaller than the lowermost ones .... (16)

15a. Upper and middle stem leaves glabrous or nearly so except for the ciliate margins; stem glabrous below the inflorescence or bearing a few scattered hairs. ***Erigeron speciosus*** (Lindl.) DC. var. ***macranthus*** (Nutt.) Cronquist, SHOWY DAISY, Fig. 81. Foothills to subalpine.

15b. Upper and middle stem leaves obviously hairy, or the stem conspicuously pubescent with long spreading hairs. ***Erigeron subtrinervis*** Rydb. (somewhat 3-nerved). Closely related to the preceding and possibly an ecologic race of it. Found on drier habitats in the same zones.

16a. Stem and involucre glandular and viscid, sometimes also hairy; stem curved at the base. ***Erigeron formosissimus*** Greene (very beautiful). Meadows and forest openings, montane and subalpine.

16b. Stem and involucre more or less hairy, scarcely glandular or viscid; stem usually erect from the base. ***Erigeron glabellus*** Nutt., SMOOTH DAISY. Mountain meadows, aspen groves, montane, subalpine.

Fig. 80. ***Erigeron peregrinus***   Fig. 81. ***Erigeron speciosus***

17a. Involucre woolly-villous with multicellular hairs .... (18)
17b. Involucre variously pubescent or glandular to sometimes glabrous
but not woolly-villous .... (20)

18a. Hairs of the involucre with black or very dark purple cross-walls;
ray-flowers white. ***Erigeron melanocephalus*** Nels., Black-headed Daisy,
Fig. 82. One of the most common dwarf daisies on subalpine slopes and
meadows. Usually tends to be replaced on tundra by *E. simplex*; where
they occur together, the soil is more moist under plants of *E.
melanocephalus.*
18b. Hairs of the involucre with clear cross-walls, or the lowermost
cross-walls sometimes bright reddish-purple; ray-flowers lavender. (19)

19a. Pappus bristles mostly about a dozen, sometimes as many as 15;
outer pappus conspicuous, setose-squamellate; involucre and upper
stem with moderately long hairs, never appearing shaggy or obscuring
the phyllaries. ***Erigeron simplex*** Greene, One-headed Daisy. Common
dwarf species, subalpine and alpine. Most common above timberline.
19b. Pappus bristles mostly 15 to 20; outer pappus obscure; involucre
and upper stem with very long shaggy (3-4 mm) hairs, tending to
obscure the phyllaries. ***Erigeron grandiflorus*** Hook. Uncommon or
rare, our specimens from Grays Peak to Rollins Pass, on tundra.

Fig. 82. ***Erigeron melanocephalus***

Fig. 83. ***Gaillardia aristata***

20a. Caudex with several or many slender, almost rhizomatous branches bearing numerous fibrous roots, without a well-defined taproot or long central axis; base of stem and bases of basal leaves purplish. ***Erigeron ursinus*** D. C. Eaton (from the Bear River). Resembles *E. simplex* and is found in similar habitats, but is distinguished by the slender, elongate, rooting caudex.

20b. Caudex simple or with relatively stout branches, with few or no long fibrous roots; plants with an evident taproot or stout central axis; base of stem, etc., not strongly purplish .... (21)

21a. Basal leaves narrow, linear or narrowly oblanceolate, the blade, if distinguishable, tapering very gradually to the petiole; caudex short .... (22)

21b. Basal leaves relatively broad, broadly oblanceolate or usually broader, the blade well-defined, usually abruptly narrowed to the petiole; caudex slender, elongate. ***Erigeron leiomerus*** Gray (with smooth parts). Rare species of alpine and subalpine rock slides.

22a. Stem and usually leaves glandular; basal leaves linear-oblanceolate, tapering gradually to the base; branches of the caudex very stout. ***Erigeron vetensis*** Rydb., La Veta Daisy. A common dwarf daisy on gravelly slopes or dry meadows of montane and subalpine zones. Known also from a few localities on the mesas.

22b. Stem and leaves not glandular, or, if so, then either with broader leaves or with not very stout caudex, or both. ***Erigeron pumilus*** Nutt., Low Daisy. A common dwarf daisy with white or blue-violet ray-flowers, found on the mesas and plains.

EUPATORIUM. Boneset; Thorough-wort

One species, ***Eupatorium maculatum*** L. (spotted), Joe-pye Weed. Marshy meadows in the piedmont valleys, rare or infrequent. A tall, coarse plant up to 2 meters high or more.

EUTHAMIA

One species, ***Euthamia occidentalis*** Nutt., Western Goldenrod. Infrequent along irrigation ditches in the Denver area (*Solidago occidentalis* of Ed. 4).

EVAX. Fluffweed

One species, ***Evax prolifera*** DC. A common small and inconspicuous weed on badly overgrazed range on the mesas and plains (*Filago prolifera* of Ed. 4).

GAILLARDIA. Blanket-flower

One species, ***Gaillardia aristata*** Pursh (awned), Fig. 83. Dry slopes, mesas and foothills. A handsome plant with yellow ray-flowers and red or orange disk-flowers. Species related to this are cultivated in gardens.

GALINSOGA

One species, **Galinsoga parviflora** Cav. (small-flowered). Uncommon weed of shaded gardens, floodplains, etc. Leaves opposite, ovate; heads small, with white ray-flowers and yellow disk.

GNAPHALIUM. CUDWEED

1a. Heads very small, clustered and imbedded in wool, the clusters leafy-bracted; low annuals, seldom more than 20 cm high. **Gnaphalium exilifolium** Nels. (slender-leaved), LOW CUDWEED. Swampy places, streambanks and pond shores, plains to montane (*G. grayi* Nels. & Macbr.).

1b. Heads medium-sized (5 mm or more wide), not leafy-bracted; plant usually 30 cm or more high (resembling Pearly Everlasting) .... (2)

2a. Plants glandular-pubescent. **Gnaphalium viscosum** H. B. K. Infrequent in forest clearings, foothills.

2b. Plants tomentose but not glandular .... (3)

3a. Phyllaries white or slightly tinged with straw-color. **Gnaphalium wrightii** Gray (for Charles Wright). Gravelly streambanks and seepage areas near cliffs, piedmont valleys and lower foothills.

3b. Phyllaries distinctly yellowish. **Gnaphalium chilense** Spreng. Habitats similar to the preceding.

GRINDELIA. GUMWEED

1a. Cauline leaves mostly oblanceolate and narrowed to a petiole-like base, usually sharply serrate; pappus bristles distinctly barbellate. **Grindelia subalpina** Greene, MOUNTAIN GUMWEED, Fig. 84. Common from the mesas to subalpine, on dry mountain slopes.

1b. Cauline leaves mostly oblong and sessile by a broad, somewhat clasping base, the blades bluntly serrate or serrulate; pappus bristles smooth. **Grindelia squarrosa** (Pursh) Dunal. Extremely abundant weed of late summer on the plains and mesas. The common form has ray-flowers, but rayless individuals are not uncommon.

GUTIERREZIA. SNAKEWEED

One species, **Gutierrezia sarothrae** (Pursh) Britt. & Rusby (for a fancied resemblance to *Hypericum sarothra*). Very common weed of late summer, particularly on over-grazed range on the plains and mesas. Resembles a dwarf, bushy Rabbitbrush with linear leaves and very small heads.

"HAPLOPAPPUS"

Note: After removing the yellow species belonging to *Machaeranthera*, *Haplopappus* in Colorado remains a hopelessly unnatural group, of which probably none is related to the original species described from Chile. While keeping this group under the present heading, I will give them the name I think they should take.

1a. Plants diminutive, alpine; head solitary .... (2)
1b. Plants taller, never alpine; heads several .... (3)

2a. Leaves few, mostly basal, spatulate, not glandular; an alpine cushion plant. ***Tonestus pygmaeus*** (T. & G.) Nels. Common on stony alpine tundra.
2b. Plants taller, leafy-stemmed, not a condensed mat-plant; foliage glandular. ***Tonestus lyallii*** (Gray) Nels. Uncommon, Loveland Pass and scattered localities on higher peaks.

3a. Plants strictly herbaceous; leaves ovate-lanceolate or oblong; ray-flowers present. ***Oreochrysum parryi*** (Gray) Rydb. A forest clearing plant of the subalpine with foliage resembling the leafy-stemmed asters, but with yellow rays.
3b. Plants shrubby or from a woody base; leaves linear or oblanceolate; ray-flowers absent .... (4)

4a. Shrubs with white-felty twigs; leaves oblanceolate; canyons and intermountain parks of foothills and montane. ***Macronema discoideum*** Nutt. A *Chrysothamnus*-like shrub fairly common in the Clear Creek drainage around Georgetown and Mount Evans.
4b. Woody-based herb or subshrub 1-2 dm high, with smooth twigs; leaves narrowly linear, very numerous; plains east of Denver. ***Oonopsis engelmannii*** (Gray) Greene.

HELENIUM. Sneezeweed

One species, ***Helenium autumnale*** L., Sneezeweed. Infrequent, floodplains in the lower foothills, piedmont valleys, and plains.

Fig. 84. *Grindelia subalpina*

HELIANTHELLA. Little Sunflower

1a. Plants tall, up to a meter or more high; leaves leathery, glossy; heads large, the disk 3 cm or more wide, the ray-flowers bright yellow. ***Helianthella quinquenervis*** (Hook.) Gray (5-nerved), Fig. 86. Mountain meadows, aspen groves, montane and subalpine. Leaves with 5 prominent nerves.
1b. Plants low, usually less than 4 dm high; leaves thin, rough-pubescent; heads small, the disk 2 cm or less wide, the ray-flowers very pale yellow. ***Helianthella parryi*** Gray (for C. C. Parry). Ponderosa pine forests in the Rampart Range, vicinity of Pikes Peak, and southward.

HELIANTHUS. Sunflower

1a. Disk-flowers purple .... (2)
1b. Disk-flowers yellow .... (4)

2a. Leaves mostly alternate, broadly ovate; plants annual .... (3)
2b. Leaves mostly opposite, narrowly rhomboidal; plants perennial, from horizontal rhizomes. ***Helianthus rigidus*** (Cass.) Desf. var. ***subrhomboideus*** (Rydb.) Heiser. Common on the mesas in late summer.

Fig. 85. ***Dugaldia hoopesii***

Fig. 86. ***Helianthella quinquenervis***

3a. Phyllaries hispid-ciliate, ovate or obovate, with acuminate tips. **Helianthus annuus** L., COMMON SUNFLOWER. Very abundant and variable weed. The showy flowers dominate the landscape of eastern Colorado in late summer.

3b. Phyllaries not ciliate, appressed short-hairy, lanceolate. **Helianthus petiolaris** Nutt., PRAIRIE SUNFLOWER. Similar to the preceding and commonly hybridizing with it.

4a. Plants low, very rough-hirsute; leaves mostly opposite, ovate. **Helianthus pumilus** Nutt. (low). The most abundant perennial sunflower on the mesas and lower foothills, on dry slopes.

4b. Plants tall, up to 3 meters high, not harshly pubescent; leaves mostly alternate, lanceolate. **Helianthus nuttallii** T. & G. (for Thomas Nuttall). Common in sloughs and along irrigation ditches, piedmont valleys and plains.

HELIOMERIS

One species, **Heliomeris multiflora** Nutt. A very common small-headed sunflower of roadsides in the foothills and montane. Leaves opposite, usually narrowly elliptic. Heads numerous, cymosely arranged. Flowering in late summer (*Gymnolomia multiflora* of Ed. 4).

HELIOPSIS. Ox-EYE

One species, **Heliopsis helianthoides** (L.) Sweet (like *Helianthus*). Frequent in open woods, foothills from Colorado Springs southward.

HETEROTHECA. GOLDEN ASTER

1a. Heads less than 9 mm high and wide, foliage green, very densely glandular; heads strongly peduncled. **Heterotheca horrida** (Rydb.) Harms. Foothills canyons.

1b. Heads larger, or if smaller, then the glands if present inconspicuous
....(2)

2a. Heads conspicuously subtended by large leaflike bracts; plants usually with appressed pubescence. **Heterotheca fulcrata** (Pursh) Shinners. Upper montane and subalpine.

2b. Heads not with conspicuous foliar bracts; plants usually with spreading pubescence. **Heterotheca villosa** (Pursh) Shinners. Widespread except at high altitudes. Hybrids seem to be common.

HIERACIUM. HAWKWEED

1a. Leaves glabrous (with very minute stalked glands) and glaucous; inflorescence a loose raceme; involucre glandular-pubescent with black hairs. **Hieracium gracile** Hook., SLENDER HAWKWEED. Subalpine spruce-fir forests.

1b. Leaves pubescent; inflorescence a cyme or panicle of heads; involucre not glandular-pubescent ....(2)

2a. Corollas white; heads numerous (over 20); involucre 8-10 mm high, campanulate; fruits 3 mm long excluding pappus; phyllaries with a prominent dark median line. *Hieracium albiflorum* Hook. (white-flowered). Common in wooded canyons in the foothills and montane.

2b. Corollas yellow; heads few (less than 10); involucre 12-15 mm high, cylindric; fruits 6 mm long; phyllaries green, without a dark median line. *Hieracium fendleri* Sch.-Bip. (for August Fendler). Rare or infrequent, montane and subalpine.

HYMENOPAPPUS

One species, *Hymenopappus filifolius* Nutt. (thread-leaved). Common on mesas and plains.

HYMENOXYS

1a. Leaves simple, basal, entire; heads small, the disk 1.5-2.0 cm wide. *Hymenoxys acaulis* (Pursh) Parker (stemless). The typical form of the mesas has an elongate scape. The alpine variety *caespitosa* (Nels.) Parker has the scape not much longer than the basal leaves, and is very dwarfed. The species is apparently absent in the montane and subalpine.

1b. Leaves pinnatifid; stems leafy to the inflorescence .... (2)

2a. Inflorescence loosely woolly-pubescent; heads large, the disk 3 cm wide or more, solitary, nodding; plants of alpine tundra. *Hymenoxys grandiflora* (Pursh) Parker (large-flowered), RYDBERGIA; OLD-MAN-OF-THE-MOUNTAIN, Fig. 87.

Fig. 87. *Hymenoxys grandiflora*

2b. Inflorescence not loosely woolly-pubescent; heads much smaller, several, erect; plants of mountain parks and plains. *Hymenoxys richardsonii* (Hook.) Cockerell (for Sir John Richardson).

HYPOCHAERIS. CATS-EAR

One species, *Hypochaeris radicata* L. (rooted), SPOTTED CATS-EAR. An uncommon weed in lawns, apparently only recently introduced into Colorado. Leaves resemble those of dandelion but are rough-pubescent, and there are several heads on a tall scape.

IVA. MARSH-ELDER

1a. Leaves oblong or spatulate, entire; heads solitary or few, axillary, short-peduncled. *Iva axillaris* Pursh, SMALL-FLOWERED MARSH-ELDER. Abundant on drying shores of temporary reservoirs on the plains.
1b. Leaves broadly ovate, serrate; heads in axillary and terminal spikes. *Iva xanthifolia* Nutt. (with leaves like *Xanthium*), TALL MARSH-ELDER. Very common weed of late summer, in cultivated ground on the plains. Resembles Giant Ragweed as to the flowers, and Common Sunflower as to the leaves.

KRIGIA

One species, *Krigia biflora* (Walt.) Blake. Very rare, in meadows of the Black Forest northeast of Colorado Springs.

KUHNIA. FALSE BONESET

1a. Stem leaves all narrowly linear and entire, not over 3 mm wide, the inflorescence broad and open, the branches slender. *Kuhnia rosmarinifolia* Vent. var. *chlorolepis* (Woot. & Standl.) Blake (green-scaled). Common in late summer on the plains and mesas.
1b. Leaves of at least the main stem broader, lanceolate to rhombic, with prominent teeth, the inflorescence usually dense and the branches stout. *Kuhnia eupatorioides* L. (like *Eupatorium*), FALSE BONESET. Habitats similar to the preceding.

LACTUCA. LETTUCE

1a. Leaves spiny-margined and often with spines along the midrib and veins. *Lactuca serriola* L. (an Arabic name), PRICKLY LETTUCE, Fig. 88. Common weed in fields and gardens (*L. scariola* of manuals). Flowers yellow. Hybridizes in nature with the cultivated lettuce.
1b. Leaves not spiny-margined .... (2)

2a. Flowers blue or purplish .... (3)
2b. Flowers yellow. *Lactuca canadensis* L., CANADIAN WILD LETTUCE. Infrequent, in canyons of the lower foothills.

3a. Perennial; pappus white; leaves rather narrow, lance-linear, many of them almost entire. *Lactuca tatarica* (L.) C. A. Mey. ssp. *pulchella*

(Pursh) Stebbins (of Tartary, in Asia), Large-flowered Blue Lettuce. Abundant in roadside ditches on the plains (*L. pulchella* [Pursh] DC.).

3b. Annual or biennial; pappus brown; leaves broad, deeply and coarsely pinnatifid. *Lactuca biennis* (Moench) Fern., Tall Blue Lettuce. In clearings in the foothill canyons, not common.

LEUCANTHEMUM. Ox-eye Daisy

One species, *Leucanthemum vulgare* Lam., Fig. 91. Escaped from gardens and well established, particularly around mines and ghost towns in the mountains. The common daisy of the eastern U.S.

LEUCELENE

One species, *Leucelene ericoides* (Torr.) Greene. Common on arid gravelly or clayey semi-desert sites on the plains and mesas (*Aster arenosus* of Ed. 4).

LIATRIS. Blazing Star

1a. Heads numerous, small, longer than broad (cylindric); individual flowers few; leaves linear. *Liatris punctata* Hook. (with translucent dots), Blazing Star, Fig. 92. Abundant in late summer, on mesas and plains. Flowers pink.

1b. Heads few, as broad as or broader than long (hemispheric); individual flowers numerous; leaves spatulate or oblanceolate. *Liatris*

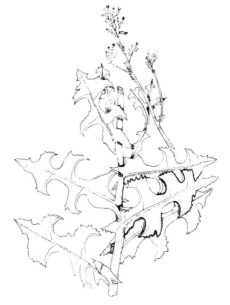

Fig. 88. *Lactuca serriola*

ligulistylis (Nels.) K. Sch. (with strap-like styles), ROCKY MOUNTAIN BLAZING STAR. Rare or infrequent, wet bottomlands in the lower foothills and valleys.

LIGULARIA.

1a. Dwarf alpines, or, if taller and subalpine, the heads with ray-flowers
....(2)
1b. Tall plants of montane forests; ray-flowers absent; leaves several on the stem ....(5)

2a. Plants glabrous ....(3)
2b. Plants cobwebby-pubescent. ***Ligularia taraxacoides*** (Gray) W. A. Weber (like dandelion), Fig. 90. Rare, on high rocky alpine slopes. Leaves commonly pinnatifid.

3a. Leaves chiefly basal, present at flowering time, all leaves rounded or cordate, with distinct petioles; alpine ....(4)
3b. Basal leaves withering by flowering time, the cauline leaves elongate, usually sessile and clasping the stem (rarely tapered to a narrow base). ***Ligularia amplectens*** (Gray) W. A. Weber (clasping), Fig. 90. Subalpine meadows and forest openings.

4a. Leaves broadly rounded at apex, abruptly narrowed to the petiole, the teeth remote or almost lacking; ray-flowers short and not twice as

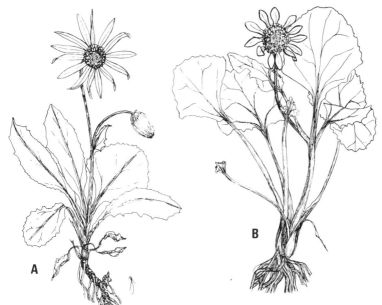

Fig. 89. A, *Ligularia holmii*; B, *L. soldanella*

Fig. 90. A, *Ligularia amplectens*; B, *L. taraxacoides*; C, *L. pudica*; D, *L. bigelovii*

long as the involucre; plant thick and fleshy, strongly reddish-tinged. *Ligularia soldanella* (Gray) W. A. Weber (for a resemblance to the Alpine genus *Soldanella*), Fig. 89. Rare, on boulderfields and screes of the higher peaks.

4b. Leaves more tapered to base and apex, usually strongly dentate; ray-flowers twice as long as the involucre, showy; plant not strongly fleshy, green or reddish-tinged on the petioles. *Ligularia holmii* (Greene) W. A. Weber (for Theodor Holm), Fig. 89. Frequent on alpine tundra.

5a. Heads large, turbinate, thick and fleshy, on stout peduncles, mostly racemosely arranged. *Ligularia bigelovii* (Gray) W. A. Weber (for Jacob Bigelow), Fig. 90. Aspen groves, montane and subalpine.

5b. Heads small, cylindric, not fleshy, on slender peduncles, mostly arranged in panicles. *Ligularia pudica* (Greene) W. A. Weber (modest), Fig. 90. Canyons in the foothills and montane. Not common.

LYGODESMIA. SKELETON-WEED

One species, *Lygodesmia juncea* (Pursh) D. Don (rush-like). Common on the plains and piedmont valleys. Stem much-branched, appearing leafless or nearly so, hence the common name.

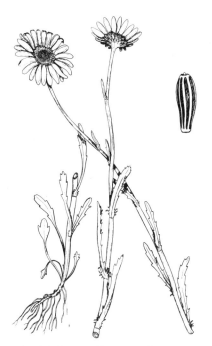

Fig. 91. *Leucanthemum vulgare* Fig. 92. *Liatris punctata*

MACHAERANTHERA

1a. Leaves pinnatifid .... (2)
1b. Leaves merely toothed .... (3)

2a. Ray-flowers lavender or purple; plant annual. **Machaeranthera tanacetifolia** (H. B. K.) Nees (tansy-leaved). Sandy soil on the plains *(Aster tanacetifolius* of Ed. 4).
2b. Ray-flowers yellow; perennial with a woody crown. **Machaeranthera pinnatifida** (Hook.) Shinners. A common weedy plant in dry over-grazed range *(Haplopappus spinulosus* of Ed. 4).

3a. Ray-flowers yellow; plant annual. **Machaeranthera phyllocephala** (DC.) Shinners. A common weed in overgrazed pastures, piedmont valleys and plains *(Haplopappus phyllocephalus* of Ed. 4).
3b. Ray-flowers purple or lavender; biennial or perennial .... (4)

4a. Foliage green, sparingly pubescent to glabrous, leaves usually broadly oblong; phyllaries glandular all over. **Machaeranthera pattersonii** (Gray) Greene (for Harry N. Patterson), Fig. 76. Abundant on roadsides, foothills to subalpine. Leaves extremely variable in size and shape *(Aster bigelovii* of Ed. 4).
4b. Foliage canescent (finely pubescent); phyllaries glandular mostly on the margins. **Machaeranthera canescens** (Pursh) Gray. Occasional, piedmont valleys and plains. This is a complex species and needs more study. Species of this type are abundant on the plains and on the western slope *(Aster canescens* of Ed. 4).

MADIA. Tarweed

One species, **Madia glomerata** Hook. (clustered). Infrequent weed, invading badly overgrazed range, chiefly in the mountains. Plants sticky-hairy.

MICROSERIS

One species, **Microseris nutans** (Hook.) Sch.-Bip. (nodding). Dry wooded slopes and meadows, subalpine. Resembles *Agoseris*, but has several heads per flower stalk, nodding at least in bud *(Ptilocalais* of Ed. 4).

NOTHOCALAIS. False Dandelion

One species, **Nothocalais cuspidata** (Pursh) Greene (pointed). A very common spring flower of the mesas and plains, superficially resembling a dandelion but easily distinguished by the entire, linear leaves with undulate margins bordered by short white hairs *(Microseris* of Ed. 4). The nomenclature of this and the last genus has been and probably will continue to be confusing, since generic lines are difficult to draw.

OLIGONEURON. Stiff Goldenrod

One species, **Oligoneuron rigidum** (L.) Small. Common species blooming in late summer and fall on the mesas and plains. This is usually included in the goldenrods *(Solidago)* but is anomalous there not only because of the several-veined phyllaries but by the stiff hirsute broad rounded leaves unlike those of the other species.

ONOPORDUM. Scotch Thistle

One species, ***Onopordum acanthium*** L. Established locally north of Fort Collins and south of our area near Walsenburg. Leaves tomentose, strongly decurrent. A second species, *O. tauricum* L., with glabrous foliage, is established near Pueblo and might be expected in the Denver area.

PALAFOXIA

One species, ***Palafoxia sphacelata*** (Nutt.) Gray (poisoning). A common and attractive species of the plains chiefly east of our area but occasionally found on the hogbacks west of Denver. Flowering in midsummer.

PERICOME

One species, ***Pericome caudata*** Gray (tailed), Fig. 93. On rockslides in the lowermost foothills. Plants bushy-branched, with small yellow flower-heads. The triangular leaves with long and narrow pointed apex are diagnostic.

PETASITES. Sweet Coltsfoot

One species, ***Petasites sagittata*** (Pursh) Gray (arrow-shaped). Very rare, in subalpine bogs. Leaves triangular-heart-shaped, green above, white-woolly beneath.

Fig. 93. *Pericome caudata*

PICRADENIOPSIS

One species, ***Picradeniopsis oppositifolia*** (Nutt.) Rydb. Leaves opposite, simple or few-lobed; stem leafy to the inflorescence, branched from the base, forming a low, bushy plant. Chiefly on the plains, but moving into the piedmont valleys along major roads.

PODOSPERMUM. FALSE SALSIFY

One species, ***Podospermum laciniatum*** L., a southeastern European weed that has suddenly become established and extremely abundant in the Boulder area. It resembles a small-headed *Tragopogon* but has pinnatifid leaves and truncate fruits, swollen at the base (*Scorzonera* of Ed. 4), Fig. 71.

PRENANTHES

One species, ***Prenanthes racemosa*** Michx., GLAUCOUS WHITE-LETTUCE. Rare or infrequent, subalpine bogs.

RATIBIDA. CONE-FLOWER

1a. Receptacle and disk elongate-oblong; rays elongate, yellow or sometimes with purple at the base. ***Ratibida columnifera*** (Nutt.) Woot. & Standl., PRAIRIE CONE-FLOWER, Fig. 94. Common on the mesas and lower foothills.

Fig. 94. ***Ratibida columnifera***   Fig. 95. ***Rudbeckia hirta***

1b. Receptacle short, the disk thimble-shaped; rays very short, deep maroon. **Ratibida tagetes** (James) Barnhart (after *Tagetes*, the Marigold). Plains, Denver southward. Variation in color of rays of *R. columnifera* is evidently due to past hybridization with *R. tagetes*.

RUDBECKIA

1a. Plant low; leaves hairy, simple, entire, or shallowly toothed; disk purple, low conical. **Rudbeckia hirta** L. (rough), BLACK-EYED SUSAN, Fig. 95. Dry meadows and mountain-sides, mesas to montane.

1b. Plant tall; leaves glabrous, deeply palmately lobed, cleft, or divided; disk greenish-brown, egg-shaped. **Rudbeckia laciniata** L. var. **ampla** (Nels.) Cronquist, TALL CONE-FLOWER. Common on streambanks in the foothills. A double-flowered form in cultivation is called Golden-glow.

SENECIO. BUTTERWEED; GOLDEN RAGWORT

1a. Leaves all linear, either entire or pinnately divided into long, linear lobes; plants very leafy throughout, usually woody at the base, flowering in late summer and fall. **Senecio spartioides** T. & G. (broom-like). Common on the mesas and plains.

1b. Leaves neither all narrowly linear nor with linear lobes . . . . (2)

2a. Basal leaves largest; stem leaves progressively or abruptly reduced upwards . . . . (8)

2b. Middle stem leaves largest, or all leaves approximately equal . . . . (3)

3a. Leaves pinnatifid. **Senecio eremophilus** Rich. var. **kingii** (Rydb.) Greenman (loving solitude). Abundant weedy species along roadsides and on gravelly slopes, montane and subalpine.

3b. Leaves merely serrate or dentate . . . . (4)

4a. Ray-flowers lacking. **Senecio rapifolius** Nutt. (with leaves like *Brassica rapa*). Infrequent in the foothill canyons.

4b. Ray-flowers present . . . . (5)

5a. Leaves finely serrate, lance-linear in outline. **Senecio serra** Hook. var. **admirabilis** (Greene) Nels. Subalpine streamsides and meadows.

5b. Leaves dentate or denticulate; leaves broader . . . . (6)

6a. Leaves narrowly triangular in outline; tall, unbranched plants of wet places. **Senecio triangularis** Hook., Fig. 96. Subalpine swamps and forest streamsides, abundant. The young succulent shoots are tempting but very poisonous.

6b. Leaves obovate to elliptic, not triangular . . . . (7)

7a. Plant erect, unbranched; leaves denticulate, elongate. **Senecio crassulus** Gray (thick). Subalpine meadows and lake shores.

7b. Plant spreading, branched from the base; leaves very coarsely dentate, short and broad. **Senecio fremontii** T. & G. var. **blitoides** (Greene) Cronquist (for John C. Frémont; resembling *Blitum*, a cheno-podium). Subalpine and alpine rockslides.

8a. Ray-flowers lacking; leaves coarsely dentate, the upper clasping the stem, the lower narrowed to a long petiole. **Senecio rapifolius** Nutt. Infrequent in the foothill canyons.

8b. Ray-flowers present; leaves various ....(9)

9a. Leaves glabrous and strongly glaucous, thickish, spatulate and narrowed to a winged petiole which broadens at the base. **Senecio wootonii** Greene (for E. O. Wooton, New Mexican botanist). Frequent on gravelly soils in open subalpine forests.

9b. Leaves either pubescent or not strongly glaucous or otherwise not as above ....(10)

10a. Rhizome well-developed, horizontal or ascending, woody; stem leaves (except in *S. atratus*) usually much reduced; some leaves commonly pinnatifid ....(11)

10b. Rhizome very short, erect (really only a caudex), of short duration, with numerous fleshy-fibrous roots; stem-leaves usually more gradually reduced; leaves either dentate or entire, never pinnatifid ....(20)

11a. Stem scapose (the stem leaves reduced to linear or bract-like vestiges), less than 2 dm high. **Senecio werneriaefolius** Gray (with leaves like genus *Werneria*, of the Andes). Rocky subalpine and alpine ridges.

11b. Stem with at least a few well-developed leaves ....(12)

Fig. 96. **Senecio triangularis**   Fig. 97. **Senecio atratus**

12a. Stem stout; leaves denticulate, oblanceolate; phyllaries black-tipped. *Senecio atratus* Greene (clothed in black), Fig. 97. Gravelly slopes and rockslides, subalpine, forming large handsome clumps on roadside cutbanks.
12b. Stems slender; leaves not denticulate; stem leaves in the larger forms usually pinnatifid ....(13)

13a. Basal leaves entire, more or less permanently white-pubescent. *Senecio canus* Hook. (grayish). Gravelly moraines and alpine ridges.
13b. Basal leaves, at least some of them, toothed or pinnatifid, glabrous or becoming so in age ....(14)

14a. Lower leaves strongly pinnatifid; leaves and stems more or less floccose (cobwebby pubescent) when young, becoming glabrous in age ....(15)
14b. Lower leaves rarely pinnatifid; leaves and stems glabrous or only slightly floccose when young ....(16)

15a. Terminal lobe or lower leaves much larger than the lateral lobes (some basal leaves scarcely lobed); plant not rhizomatous. *Senecio plattensis* Nutt. (of the Platte River). Common on the plains and mesas, flowering in very early spring.
15b. Leaves commonly regularly pinnatifid, rarely almost entire, the terminal lobe never conspicuously larger; plant usually rhizomatous, forming rosettes at the ends of the rhizomes. *Senecio fendleri* Gray (for August Fendler). Common and variable, in gravelly soils of dry forests along the mesas through the subalpine.

16a. Basal leaves oval or cordate, on long slender petioles, regularly crenate ....(17)
16b. Basal leaves narrower, on winged petioles, irregularly toothed or lobed or entire ....(18)

17a. Basal leaves thick and leathery, oval and cuneate at base; plants of dry coniferous forests. *Senecio streptanthifolius* Greene (with leaves like *Streptanthus*, a crucifer).
17b. Basal leaves relatively thin, cordate-ovate; plants of wet streamsides in the foothills. *Senecio pseudaureus* Rydb. (mimicking *S. aureus* of eastern North America).

18a. Basal leaves narrowly oblanceolate, commonly 3-toothed at the apex, the upper stem leaves without greatly enlarged bases; plants forming many-stemmed clumps. *Senecio tridenticulatus* Rydb. Common on dry sites on the plains.
18b. Basal leaves broader, entire or crenulate, with broad winged petioles; upper leaves with enlarged, clasping bases; stems solitary or a few together ....(19)

19a. Ray-flowers yellow; plants of gravelly forest margins; subalpine. *Senecio dimorphophyllus* Greene (with two shapes of leaves).
19b. Ray-flowers deep orange; plants of moist meadows, subalpine and montane. *Senecio crocatus* Rydb. (saffron-colored).

20a. Tall bog plants, 5-15 dm high; basal leaves long-petioled. ***Senecio hydrophilus*** Nutt. (water-loving). Although this plant is extremely abundant along the meandering streams of North and Middle Park, it probably does not occur east of the Continental Divide. A single specimen allegedly from Boulder County was probably not collected there.

20b. Meadow or woodland plants, 2-5 dm high; basal leaves relatively short-petioled .... (21)

21a. Foliage and stem glabrous from the beginning; upper leaves not greatly reduced. ***Senecio crassulus*** Gray. Subalpine meadows and lake shores.

21b. Foliage and stem leaves somewhat cobwebby-pubescent, at least when young; stem leaves usually much smaller than the basal. ***Senecio integerrimus*** Nutt. (very entire). Mesas and foothills to lower subalpine.

SHINNERSOSERIS. BEAKED SKELETON-WEED

One species, ***Shinnersoseris rostrata*** (Gray) Tomb. In sandy soil on the plains. The generic name commemorates Lloyd M. Shinners, botanist of Southern Methodist University (*Lygodesmia* in part, of Ed. 4).

SOLIDAGO. GOLDENROD

1a. Heads in a terminal simple or branched thyrsus (oblong spike-like panicle), the branches not at all one-sided or scarcely so .... (2)

1b. Heads in a terminal, usually large, spreading panicle, its branches arching or recurved, and distinctly one-sided (with the heads arranged along the upper side) .... (5)

2a. Foliage glabrous or nearly so .... (3)

2b. Foliage densely short-pubescent. ***Solidago nana*** Nutt., LOW GOLDEN-ROD. Frequent on mesas and in canyons of the lower foothills. Very similar to *Solidago mollis*, which may be distinguished by its distinctly 3-nerved leaves which are usually serrate and its one-sided branches of the inflorescence. *S. mollis* is definitely a species of the plains.

3a. Leaves pale, somewhat glaucous; stems tall (4-8 dm); phyllaries obtuse. ***Solidago speciosa*** Nutt. var. ***pallida*** Porter, SHOWY GOLDENROD. Common on gravelly slopes in the lower foothills.

3b. Leaves deep green, not glaucous; stems low (1-4 dm); phyllaries acute .... (4)

4a. Lowermost leaves with ciliate-margined petioles; ray-flowers mostly about 13 (or more numerous on the terminal head); phyllaries not very imbricate. ***Solidago multiradiata*** Ait. (many-rayed). Subalpine.

4b. None of the leaves with ciliate-margined petioles; ray-flowers mostly about 8; phyllaries evidently imbricate. ***Solidago spathulata*** DC. (spatulate). Montane and subalpine. Alpine plants belong to var. *nana* (Gray) Cronquist, those of lower altitudes to var. *neomexicana* (Gray) Cronquist.

5a. Leaves, at least the lower ones, oblanceolate, spatulate, or obovate, the upper leaves usually smaller, never regularly sharply serrate .. (6)
5b. Stem rather equably leafy, the basal leaves not larger than the middle stem leaves; leaves all lanceolate, often or usually sharply serrate ... (8)

6a. Plant glabrous or nearly so, the leaves somewhat leathery in texture. **Solidago missouriensis** Nutt., SMOOTH GOLDENROD. The common low-growing smooth goldenrod of the plains, foothills and montane.
6b. Plant short-pubescent, the leaves thin, or at least not leathery in texture .... (7)

7a. Stem low, usually less than 3 dm high; leaves short and broadly oblanceolate; plants of the plains. **Solidago mollis** Bartl. (soft).
7b. Stem tall and slender, often over 4 dm high; leaves narrowly oblanceolate, the upper leaves usually very small; plants of the foothills and mesas. **Solidago sparsiflora** Gray (few-flowered).

8a. Stem glabrous up to the inflorescence. **Solidago gigantea** Ait., LATE GOLDENROD. A very tall goldenrod found in wet places in the piedmont valleys and plains.
8b. Stem more or less pubescent .... (9)

9a. Involucres 2-3 mm high. **Solidago canadensis** L., CANADA GOLDENROD. Wet meadows and streamsides, piedmont valleys and lower foothill canyons.
9b. Involucres 3.5-5.0 mm high. **Solidago altissima** L., TALL GOLDENROD. Habitats similar to the preceding.

SONCHUS. SOW-THISTLE
1a. Annual; involucre glabrous .... (2)
1b. Perennial from deep-seated rhizomes; involucre glandular-pubescent or with glandular dots .... (3)

2a. Fruit strongly 3- to 5-ribbed on each face, thin-margined, not transversely wrinkled; auricles of the leaf-base rounded. **Sonchus asper** (L.) Hill (harsh), SPINY SOW-THISTLE. Introduced weed in gardens and disturbed sites.
2b. Fruits striate and also strongly wrinkled transversely, not thin-margined; auricles of the leaf-base acute. **Sonchus oleraceus** L. (vege-table-like), ANNUAL SOW-THISTLE. Introduced weed, similar sites.

3a. Involucre glandular-pubescent with spreading yellowish hairs. **Sonchus arvensis** L. (of fields), PERENNIAL SOW-THISTLE. Tall weed over 1 meter tall, in cultivated ground.
3b. Involucre glabrous and usually with large glandular spots. **Sonchus uliginosus** Bieb., SWAMP SOW-THISTLE. Similar to the last, in wet meadows and along irrigation ditches. The species of *Sonchus* resemble Prickly Lettuce (*Lactuca serriola*), but the involucres are broad at the base instead of narrowly cylindric.

STEPHANOMERIA. Wire-lettuce

One species, ***Stephanomeria pauciflora*** (Torr.) Nels. (few-flowered). Common in dry, sandy places, roadsides, pastures, etc., on the plains. A wiry, much-branched weedy plant resembling Skeleton-weed (*Lygodesmia*) but differing in having a plumose pappus.

TANACETUM. Tansy

One species, ***Tanacetum vulgare*** L. Introduced weed, locally established around farms in the piedmont valleys.

TARAXACUM. Dandelion

1a. Outer phyllaries recurved-spreading; weeds of disturbed areas (2)
1b. Outer phyllaries appressed, erect; plants of alpine regions .... (3)

2a. Fruits bright reddish-brown, the murications (spines or knobs on the upper part) very sharp and comparatively long. ***Taraxacum erythrospermum*** Andrz., Red-seeded Dandelion.
2b. Fruits greenish, the murications less acute and quite short. ***Taraxacum officinale*** Wiggers, Common Dandelion, Fig. 98. Abundant and ever-present weed in lawns and overgrazed meadows and pastures.

3a. Mature fruits mostly muricate nearly to the base, the spines crowded

Fig. 98. ***Taraxacum officinale***   Fig. 99. ***Townsendia grandiflora***

at least in the upper half; phyllaries blackish-green; leaves almost entire. *Taraxacum phymatocarpum* J. Vahl. Very rare, tundra.

3b. Mature fruits sparingly tuberculate only in the upper half, sometimes almost smooth . . . . (4)

4a. Outer phyllaries with horn-shaped swellings at the tips; plants large (over 5 cm tall); phyllaries green; heads large; leaves broad, entire or shallowly sinuate-dentate. *Taraxacum ceratophorum* DC. The common species of grassy tundra slopes in the alpine.

4b. Outer phyllaries lacking horns; plants minute (1-5 cm tall); phyllaries dark blackish-green; heads very small (about 1 cm); leaves regularly sinuate-lobed. *Taraxacum lyratum* (Ledeb.) DC. Very rare, in gravelly places among boulders, on the highest peaks, never in grassy tundra.

THELESPERMA

1a. Ray-flowers present. *Thelesperma filifolium* Gray. Plains and mesas, mostly from Denver southward. The genus is easily recognized by the peculiar involucre, which has the inner phyllaries fused to form a cup. These plants superficially resemble some of the cultivated species of *Coreopsis.*

1b. Ray-flowers lacking. *Thelesperma megapotamicum* (Spreng.) Kuntze (of the Rio Grande). Generally distributed on plains and mesas, but nowhere very abundant (*T. gracile* [Torr.] Gray).

TOWNSENDIA. EASTER DAISY

1a. Stems several centimeters tall; phyllaries acuminate; plant flowering in summer. *Townsendia grandiflora* Nutt., Fig. 99. Dry slopes of mesas and foothills, common.

1b. Stem lacking (the flowers produced in a cluster of linear basal leaves on the surface of the ground); flowering in very early spring . . . . . . (2)

2a. Phyllaries linear, acuminate, with a tuft of tangled cilia at the apex; involucre about 1.5 cm wide, disk corollas 5 mm long, disc pappus hardly longer than the corolla. *Townsendia hookeri* Beaman, Fig. 100. Abundant on the mesas in early spring, coming into flower with the first warm days.

2b. Phyllaries narrowly lanceolate, acute, without a tuft of tangled cilia; involucre about 2.2 cm wide, disk corollas 9-10 mm long; disk pappus conspicuously longer than the corolla. *Townsendia exscapa* (Rich.) Porter (stemless). Not as common as the last, in similar habitats. The species intergrade in our area.

TRAGOPOGON. SALSIFY; OYSTER-PLANT

1a. Flowers pale to deep violet-purple. *Tragopogon porrifolius* L. Common dandelion-like weed with grass-like leaves on a tall stem. Mesas and plains.

1b. Flowers yellow . . . . (2)

2a. Flowers pale lemon yellow, all shorter than the phyllaries; phyllaries about 13 (sometimes as many as 17 on the first head of vigorous plants or as few as 8 on the latest heads), long and narrow, not margined with purple, longer than the outer flowers; peduncles strongly inflated in fruit; heads averaging well over 100 flowers. ***Tragopogon dubius*** Scop. (uncertain), Fig. 101. Common weed, to be expected anywhere.

2b. Flowers chrome yellow, the outer ones about equalling the phyllary length; phyllaries about 8 or 9 on the first head, rarely as many as 13, broad and short, margined with purple, about equalling the outer flowers in length. ***Tragopogon pratensis*** L. (of meadows). In more moist sites, often in mountain pastures.

VERBESINA. CROWNBEARD; COW-PEN DAISY

One species, ***Verbesina encelioides*** (Cav.) Benth. & Hook. (like *Encelia*). A sunflower-like plant native to much of the western U.S., but in our area behaving as a weed in cultivated fields on the plains.

XANTHIUM. COCKLEBUR

One species, ***Xanthium strumarium*** L. (reference to medical use of the roots). Abundant in late summer in waste ground, shores of temporary reservoirs, etc., on the plains.

CONVOLVULACEAE—MORNING-GLORY FAMILY

Morning-glories are favorite ornamental climbers for porches and patios, but several members of the family are used in other important ways. *Dichondra repens* is used as a ground cover in place of grass for lawns in southern California. *Ipomoea batatas* is the true Sweet-potato (as opposed to the Yam, *Dioscorea*, which is a monocot in the Dioscoreaceae). It is a staple crop in Melanesia, and its introduction, probably from America, is thought to have been effected through Polynesian migrations. *Ipomoea tuberosa* is the curious "Wooden-rose" of dry bouquets.

1a. Plants yellow or orange, without green color; stems stringy, the leaves reduced to inconspicuous scales; parasitic on stems of various kinds of plants (dodders) ....(2)

1b. Plants green; leaves well-developed ....(4)

2a. Stigmas elongated; styles equal; inflorescence glomerate (the flowers in tight balls). ***Cuscuta approximata*** Bab. (close together). Rare, vicinity of Boulder.

2b. Inflorescence loose, the flowers not in tight clusters ....(3)

3a. Flowers 2-3 mm long; stems very slender and thread-like. ***Grammica indecora*** (Choisy) W. A. Weber (not ornamental), Fig. 102. Climbing over herbs and shrubs in the piedmont valleys and plains (*Cuscuta* of Ed. 4).

3b. Flowers 4 mm or more long; stems relatively stout. ***Grammica umbrosa*** (Hook.) W. A. Weber (shady). One old record from Dome Rock in Platte Canyon (*Cuscuta curta* of Ed. 4).

4a. Stems twining or climbing; leaves sagittate ....(5)
4b. Stems erect; leaves oblong, elliptic, or linear ....(6)

5a. Bracts larger than the calyx and enclosing it; flowers 3-6 cm long. **Calystegia sepium** (L.) R. Br. ssp. **americanum** (Sims) Brummitt, HEDGE BINDWEED. Fencerows and roadsides, mesas and plains. Flowers usually white in our region *(Convolvulus interior* House).
5b. Bracts much smaller than the calyx and not enclosing it; flowers 1.5-2.5 cm long. **Convolvulus arvensis** L. (of fields), SMALL BINDWEED; MORNING-GLORY; CREEPING JENNY, Fig. 102. A bad weed in cultivated ground, with very deep brittle rhizomes, very abundant on the plains and piedmont valleys.

6a. Plant low, the leaves densely appressed-pubescent, oblong or elliptic; flowers pale violet, less than 1 cm across. **Evolvulus nuttallianus** R. & S. (for Thomas Nuttall), EVOLVULUS, Fig. 102. Frequent on the mesas and plains. Except for the small morning-glory flowers, there is little to indicate that this plant belongs in the family.
6b. Plant tall, bushy-branched, with linear-glabrous leaves; flower large, red or purplish. **Ipomoea leptophylla** Torr. (narrow-leaved), BUSH MORNING-GLORY, Fig. 102. Common on sandy places on the plains. The enormous root suggests the name, Old-man-of-the-earth.

Fig. 100. *Townsendia hookeri*   Fig. 101. *Tragopogon dubius*

Fig. 102. A, *Evolvulus*; B, *Ipomoea leptophylla*; C, **Grammica**; D, **Convolvulus arvensis**

CORNACEAE—DOGWOOD FAMILY

The name "dogwood" is given to a great number of unrelated trees, and the origin of the name is unknown. An old Century Dictionary mentions that the wood is so free from scratchy silica that jewelers used small splinters of it to clean out the pivot-holes in watches, and opticians for removing dust from small deep-seated lenses. Flowering dogwoods are found in the ancient relictual Tertiary forests of eastern and far western North America and Japan.

1a. Shrub with red branches; inflorescence not subtended by petal-like bracts; leaves opposite. ***Cornus stolonifera*** Michx. (bearing runners), RED-OSIER DOGWOOD. Common along streams, from foothills to subalpine. If the Flowering Dogwood is considered a genus separate from ours, our plant should be called *Swida sericea* (L.) Holub.

1b. Stems herbaceous (only 10-20 cm tall) from a woody rhizome; inflorescence subtended by 4 to 5 white, petal-like bracts (a miniature "flowering dogwood"); leaves in a whorl at the top of the stem. ***Cornus canadensis*** L., BUNCHBERRY; DWARF CORNEL, Fig. 103. Rather rare, in deep shade of subalpine forests. Eurasian authors tend to place this species in a separate genus, as *Chamaepericlymenum canadense* (L.) Asch. & Graebn.

Fig. 103. ***Cornus canadensis***   Fig. 104. ***Sedum lanceolatum***

CRASSULACEAE—STONECROP FAMILY

Most sedums are succulents, but not all succulents are *sedums*. Desert and alpine areas over the world have evoked the succulent habit in several unrelated families. The Mesembryanthemaceae of South Africa are famous for their leaf rosettes that often resemble piles of pebbles, North African euphorbias resemble our Saguaro cacti, and many chenopods of saline ground are succulents.

1a. Flowers yellow; leaves fleshy, almost round in cross-section; leaves crowded on short basal shoots. ***Sedum lanceolatum*** TORR., STONECROP, Fig. 104. Abundant on dry, rocky hillsides, from foothills to alpine.
1b. Flowers purple, pink or white; leaves thin, evenly distributed on the main flowering stem . . . . (2)

2a. Petals pink or white; flowers clustered in the axils of the upper stem leaves; midrib prominent on underside of leaf. ***Clementsia rhodantha*** (Gray) Rose (for Frederic E. Clements, Colorado ecologist), ROSE CROWN, Fig. 105. Common along subalpine rivulets and in peat bogs (*Sedum rhodanthum* of Ed. 4). This species is endemic in the southern Rockies, but has a close relative almost identical to it in the mountains of central Asia, known there as *Rhodiola semenovii*.
2b. Petals deep red-purple; flowers in a flat-topped terminal cluster; midrib imbedded and not easily visible. ***Rhodiola integrifolia*** Raf., KINGS CROWN, Fig. 106. Moist slopes and tundra, usually at higher altitudes than the preceding but often growing with it. The arctic relative, *Rhodiola rosea*, with yellow flowers, is now considered distinct by most botanists (*Sedum rosea* of Ed. 4).

CRUCIFERAE (BRASSICACEAE)—MUSTARD FAMILY

Crucifers are distinctive because of their cross-shaped flowers but they can be confused with the Onagraceae, which also have four petals in that arrangement, but an inferior ovary. Crucifers typically have the flowers in racemes, and usually there are no subtending bracts. Many crucifers are used in gardens (Sweet Alyssum, Rocket, Silver-dollar plant) and many are standard table vegetables: *Brassica oleracea* in its many varieties gives us Kale, Brussels Sprouts, Cabbage, Broccoli, Cauliflower and Kohlrabi. Other brassicas include Rutabaga, Turnip, Rape, White and Black Mustard, and many Chinese vegetables. Water-cress is *Nasturtium officinale*, no relative of the garden Nasturtium flower. The foliage or seeds of most crucifers have distinctive tart flavors.

1a. Silique (the name given to the fruits of mustards) with a long stalk (stipe) between the point of attachment of the petals and the seed-bearing portion of the ovary; tall, showy yellow-flowered plants of the plains and mesas, particularly on shale outcrops. ***Stanleya***, PRINCES PLUME, page 190.
1b. Silique sessile on the pedicel or nearly so . . . . (2)

2a. Silique short (called a silicle), hardly more than twice as long as broad ....(3)
2b. Silique at least 3 times as long as broad ....(13)

3a. Silicle not flattened, but spherical and sometimes strongly inflated and papery in texture ....(4)
3b. Silicle flattened ....(8)

4a. Silicle inflated and papery-textured ....(5)
4b. Silicle neither strongly inflated nor papery, never appearing double
....(6)

5a. Fruit of twin papery sacks, the ovary constricted down the middle; flowers yellow; plants low with rosettes of basal leaves. ***Physaria,*** DOUBLE BLADDER-POD, page 188.
5b. Fruit spherical, the ovary not constricted; flowers white; plants tall with leafy stems from underground rhizomes. ***Cardaria,*** WHITEWEED, page 182.

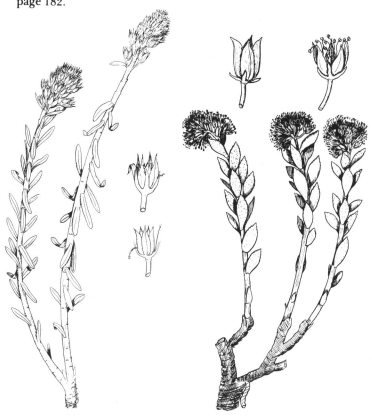

Fig. 105. *Clementsia rhodantha*   Fig. 106. ***Rhodiola integrifolia***

6a. Plants of marshy places and moist ditches; leaves often deeply pinnatifid. *Rorippa*, CRESS, page 188.
6b. Plants of dry sites; leaves never pinnatifid .... (7)

7a. Annual; stem simple, silicle pear-shaped; introduced weed. *Camelina*, FALSE FLAX, page 181.
7b. Perennial, branched from the base; silicle spherical or elliptical; native. *Lesquerella*, BLADDER-POD, page 186.

8a. Silicle flattened parallel to the papery internal partition (replum), i.e., the shape of the replum is also the shape of the silicle in face view .... (9)
8b. Silicle flattened perpendicular to the replum, i.e., the replum bisects the silicle in face view .... (11)

9a. Silicle round in face view. *Alyssum*, page 180.
9b. Silicle oblong, ovate, or elliptical, never round .... (10)

10a. Silicle oval, not more than twice as long as wide; styles 2-3 mm long; petals white, deeply bilobed; tall leafy roadside weed over 3 dm high. *Berteroa*, page 181.
10b. Silicle longer and narrower, or styles shorter; petals white or yellow, not deeply bilobed; low, often scapose herbs, seldom more than 1 dm high. *Draba*, WHITLOW-WORT, page 183.

11a. Silicle triangular-obovate or obcordate .... (12)
11b. Silicle elliptic or oval, rarely triangular (in which event the triangle is broadest at the base). *Lepidium*, PEPPER-GRASS, page 185.

12a. Basal leaves pinnatifid; silicle triangular-obovate. *Capsella*, SHEPHERDS PURSE, page 182.
12b. Basal leaves entire or merely toothed; silicle obcordate. *Thlaspi*, PENNY-CRESS, page 190.

13a. Silique terete or four-angled .... (17)
13b. Silique flattened parallel to the replum .... (14)

14a. Valves (carpel walls) veinless .... (15)
14b. Valves veined .... (16)

15a. Leaves either pinnately compound or triangular-cordate; silique always elongate. *Cardamine*, BITTER-CRESS, page 182.
15b. Leaves always simple, usually lanceolate; silique never more than 5-6 times as long as wide. *Draba*, WHITLOW-WORT, page 183.

16a. Silique short, usually less than 5-6 times as long as wide, ovate to linear-oblong. *Draba*, WHITLOW-WORT, page 183.
16b. Silique elongate (over 10 times as long as wide), linear. *Arabis*, ROCK-CRESS, page 180.

17a. Leaves entire, glabrous or glaucous; basal leaves also entire, neither

pinnatifid nor lobed ....(18)
17b. Leaves (at least some) dentate, pinnatifid, or lobed, or plants
without the above combination of characteristics ....(19)

18a. Leaves linear; raceme elongate, narrow, with small purplish flowers
(petals 3-4 mm) widely spaced; pod terete; rare native perennial on
cliffs, slope of Pikes Peak. *Pennellia*, page 186.
18b. Leaves broad, obtuse, glaucous, clasping the stem; flowers white,
the petals 8 mm long; pod 4-angled; annual weed of fields and roadsides. *Conringia*, HARES EAR, page 183.

19a. Silique with a stout beak extending much beyond the ovule-
bearing portion, indehiscent ....(20)
19b. Silique without a beak, or with a beak not more than 3 mm long,
dehiscent ....(23)

20a. Flowers white or yellow; silique without transverse partitions
between the seeds; lower leaves often pinnatifid ....(21)
20b. Flowers pink or purplish; silique with transverse partitions and
usually constricted between the seeds; basal leaves merely dentate (22)

21a. Valves of the silique one-nerved. *Brassica*, page 181.
21b. Valves of the silique with 3 to 7 veins. *Sinapis*, page 189.

22a. Plant very sparsely glandular pubescent with simple hairs; low,
early spring-blooming weed of open fields in the piedmont valleys and
plains. *Chorispora*, BLUE MUSTARD, page 183.
22b. Plant pubescent with forked or stellate hairs; summer-blooming
tall escaped garden plant. *Hesperis,* DAMES-VIOLETS, page 185.

23a. Pubescence of forked or stellate hairs ....(24)
23b. Pubescence of simple hairs, or none (look closely here; there are
some mustards with forked hairs in which the forks are in a straight
line with each other, the hair being attached by the middle; these often
look like simple hairs, but will be pointed at each end) ....(25)

24a. Leaves pinnately or bipinnately divided or very deeply pinnatifid;
pubescence often partly glandular ....(28)
24b. Leaves entire to moderately pinnatifid; glandular hairs absent.
Erysimum, WALLFLOWER, page 185.

25a. Silique somewhat four-angled, elongate. *Barbarea*, WINTER-CRESS,
page 181.
25b. Silique terete, elongate or club-shaped ....(26)

26a. Silique 3 cm or more long, about 1 mm wide; roadside weed of dry
land. *Sisymbrium*, page 190.
26b. Silique not more than 2 cm long, often more than 1 mm wide;
aquatic or marsh plants ....(27)

27a. Flowers white; leaves succulent, with rounded leaflets. **Nasturtium**, Water-cress, page 186.
27b. Flowers yellow, leaves not especially succulent, with acute lobes or leaflets. **Rorippa**, Cress, page 188.

28a. Weedy annuals with yellow flowers. **Descurainia**, Tansy Mustard, page 183.
28b. Native perennials with white or pinkish flowers; alpine. **Smelowskia**, page 190.

ALYSSUM

1a. Silicle completely glabrous. **Alyssum desertorum** Stapf. An abundant weed in dry disturbed areas on the western slope, and recently discovered in the Denver area.
1b. Silicle with stellate hairs .... (2)

2a. Styles 0.5 mm long; foliage and siliques with very fine pubescence; sepals persistent; filaments uniform, with two basal filiform appendages. **Alyssum alyssoides** (L.) L. Introduced weed in city lots, and on overgrazed forest openings in the foothills.
2b. Styles 1.5-2.0 mm long; foliage and siliques coarsely stellate-pubescent; sepals falling from the ripe fruit; filaments narrowly winged. **Alyssum minus** (L.) Rothmaler. Similar sites. All of our species are introductions. *A. minus* appeared only a few years ago and is now one of the most abundant spring-flowering plants, forming solid stands on major highway rights-of-way.

ARABIS. Rock-cress

Caution: collection of *Arabis* should always include mature fruits and basal leaves. Positive identification without these is often impossible.

1a. Basal leaves ovate to broadly oblanceolate, obtuse at apex; blades nearly as broad as long, glabrous or hirsute with simple or forked hairs; siliques erect .... (2)
1b. Basal leaves linear to linear-oblanceolate (if broader, then minutely pubescent, or siliques reflexed, or both) .... (3)

2a. Seeds in 2 rows on each side of the replum (biseriate). **Arabis glabra** (L.) Bernh., Tower Mustard. Introduced weed, present in disturbed ground at medium altitudes.
2b. Seeds in one row on each side of the replum (uniseriate). **Arabis hirsuta** (L.) Scop., Hairy Rock-cress. Grassy slopes, foothills and mesas, to subalpine.

3a. Mature fruiting pedicels erect or ascending, never diverging at right angles or descending; siliques erect, ascending, straight or rarely curved .... (4)
3b. Mature fruiting pedicels diverging at right angles or sharply reflexed; siliques curved or straight, diverging at right angles or sharply

reflexed . . . . (5)

4a. Siliques erect, blunt; seeds biseriate, winged along one side only; hairs of basal leaves attached at their middles. *Arabis drummondii* Gray (for Thomas Drummond). Common in forests and meadows, montane, subalpine.

4b. Siliques spreading, acute; seeds uniseriate, winged all around; hairs variously branched or simple, not attached in the middle. *Arabis divaricarpa* Nels. (spreading-fruited). Dry slopes, montane, subalpine.

5a. Basal leaves definitely ciliate with large, simple or forked hairs, rarely glabrous; blades sparsely hirsute with simple or forked hairs, or glabrous; pedicels glabrous, gently curving downward. *Arabis fendleri* (Wats.) Greene (for August Fendler). Dry slopes, foothills and mesas, to subalpine.

5b. Basal leaves densely pubescent with fine to coarse branched hairs; blades always pubescent, never merely sparsely hirsute with simple or forked hairs; pedicels pubescent to glabrous, spreading at right angles to usually sharply reflexed. *Arabis holboellii* Hornem. (for F. L. Holboell, Danish botanist). Talus slopes, gravelly streambanks, etc., montane, subalpine.

BARBAREA. Winter-cress

1a. Style 2-3 mm long, distinctly slender and beak-like. *Barbarea vulgaris* R. Br. Eurasian weed; one record, Left Hand Canyon near Boulder.

1b. Style stubby, 0.5-1.5 mm long, not slender or beak-like. *Barbarea orthoceras* Ledeb. Abundant weed in moist fields and ditches.

BERTEROA

One species, *Berteroa incana* (L.) DC. Sparingly established in the foothills along roadsides; a Eurasian weed.

BRASSICA. Mustard

1a. Upper leaves clasping the stem. *Brassica rapa* L. ssp. *campestris* (L.) Janchen, Bird Rape; Field Mustard. Frequent as a weed in fields on the plains and piedmont valleys (*B. campestris* L.).

1b. Upper leaves petiolate, not clasping . . . . (2)

2a. Pods slender, 10-20 mm long, appressed to the stem; pedicels 2 mm long; lower leaves often hispid, their segments serrate. *Brassica nigra* (L.) Koch, Black Mustard. Introduced weed in fields.

2b. Pods 25-50 mm long but not appressed; pedicels 3-5 mm long; plant glabrous and glaucous throughout. *Brassica juncea* (L.) Coss. (rush-like), India Mustard. Introduced weed.

CAMELINA. False Flax

One species, *Camelina microcarpa* Andrz. (small fruited). A very common introduced weed.

CAPSELLA. Shepherds Purse

One species, *Capsella bursa-pastoris* (L.) Medic, Fig. 107. Introduced weed.

CARDAMINE. Bitter-cress

1a. Leaves simple, broad, somewhat cordate. *Cardamine cordifolia* Gray (heart-leaved), Bitter-cress, Fig. 108. Streamsides and wet forest floors, montane, subalpine.
1b. At least some of the leaves compound ....(2)

2a. Petals 3-7 mm long; perennial with rhizomes. *Cardamine breweri* Wats. (for William H. Brewer). Rare, Fort Collins northward in the foothill valleys.
2b. Petals 2-4 mm long; annual or biennial with tap root. *Cardamine pensylvanica* Muehl. *ex* Willd. Moist places, subalpine.

CARDARIA. Whiteweed

1a. Silicles glabrous. *Cardaria draba* (L.) Desv. (for the genus *Draba*). Introduced weed, forming dense stands along roadsides, the white

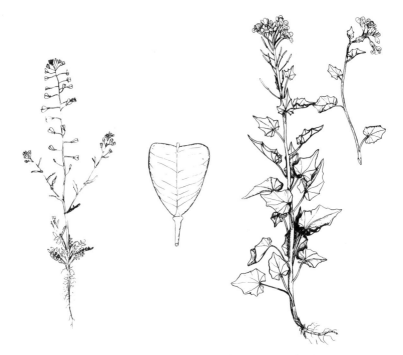

Fig. 107. *Capsella bursa-pastoris*   Fig. 108. *Cardamine cordifolia*

masses of flowers being visible at some distance. Plains.
1b. Silicles pubescent. ***Cardaria pubescens*** (Mey.) Rollins. Similar habitats, plains and mesas.

CHORISPORA. BLUE MUSTARD
One species, ***Chorispora tenella*** (Pallas) DC. (very slender). Abundant weed in fallow grain fields on the plains.

CONRINGIA. HARES EAR
One species, ***Conringia orientalis*** (L.) Dumort. (eastern). Introduced weed of grainfields, plains.

DESCURAINIA. TANSY MUSTARD
1a. Siliques slender, less than 1 mm broad ....(2)
1b. Siliques thick, club-shaped, over 1 mm broad. ***Descurainia pinnata*** (Walt.) Britt., TANSY MUSTARD. Weed in disturbed ground, plains to montane.

2a. Leaves 2 to 3 times pinnately compound; siliques 20- to 40-seeded. ***Descurainia sophia*** (L.) Webb (*Sophia*, an old generic name), FLIXWEED. Habitats similar to the above.
2b. Leaves simply pinnate, the leaflets often deeply incised; siliques 4- to 30-seeded. ***Descurainia richardsonii*** (Sw.) O. E. Schulz (for John Richardson), WESTERN TANSY MUSTARD. Common weed in disturbed ground, plains to montane.

DRABA. WHITLOW-WORT
1a. Annual or winter annual ....(2)
1b. Biennial or perennial ....(5)

2a. Flowering stems devoid of leaves, all the leaves in a basal rosette (often 30 or more). ***Draba crassifolia*** R.Grah.Common on moist subalpine and alpine slopes. Flowers pale yellowish (thick-leaved).
2b. Flowering stems bearing one or more leaves ....(3)

3a. Pedicels usually at least 1½ times as long as the fruits. ***Draba nemorosa*** L. (of woods). Open slopes, mesas and foothills, blooming in early spring. Flowers yellow.
3b. Pedicels usually only a little longer than the fruits, or just as long
....(4)

4a. Siliques evenly spaced, in a long raceme; plants possibly biennial (at least winter annual), montane. ***Draba albertina*** Greene (of Alberta). Flowers yellow.
4b. Siliques crowded in an umbel-like raceme; spring-flowering annuals of lower elevations. ***Draba reptans*** (Lam.) Fern. (creeping), CAROLINA WHITLOW-GRASS. Plains and foothills. Flowers white.

5a. Flowering stems naked except for one or two leaves occasionally at the base .... (6)

5b. Flowering stems leafy .... (11)

6a. Styles at least 0.5 mm long or, if shorter, the plants with thick main roots 2-3 mm in diameter; flowers yellow or white .... (8)

6b. Styles less than 0.5 mm long, often hardly visible; plants slender, the roots small and not fleshy .... (7)

7a. Flowers very pale yellow; plants with a single basal rosette of leaves from a very slender taproot. ***Draba albertina*** Greene. Common on moist subalpine and alpine slopes (*D. crassifolia* of Ed. 4).

7b. Flowers white; plants with several to many rosettes from slender caudices, with a stouter root system. ***Draba fladnizensis*** Wulf. (of Fladnitz, Austria), WHITE ARCTIC DRABA. Infrèquent but widely distributed on high tundra.

8a. Larger basal leaves 3-10 mm broad, often as much as 7-8 cm long, thick and leathery; petals yellow. ***Draba crassa*** Rydb. (thick). Rocky alpine slopes, ridges, and summits; rather rare.

8b. Larger basal leaves seldom as much as 3 mm broad, not over 4 cm long; petals yellow or white .... (9)

9a. Petals white. ***Draba nivalis*** Lilj., SNOW DRABA. Rare, on high tundra.

9b. Petals yellow .... (10)

10a. Petals very broad, abruptly narrowed to a distinct claw; sepals and petals falling early from the young capsule; stems conspicuously pubescent. ***Draba grayana*** (Rydb.) C. L. Hitchc. (of Grays Peak). Rare, on alpine summits of the higher peaks.

10b. Petals more oblong, without a claw; sepals and petals remaining appressed to the fruits until well developed; stems glabrous or nearly so. ***Draba exunguiculata*** (Schulz) C. L. Hitchc. (without claws). Frequent on gravelly slopes at high altitudes, alpine.

11a. Flowers white; fruits flat or but slightly contorted; pubescence consisting entirely of much-branched hairs. ***Draba cana*** Rydb. Frequent, subalpine and alpine, near and above timberline (*D. lanceolata* of Ed. 4).

11b. Flowers yellow; fruits contorted or twisted; pubescence of simple or forked hairs .... (12)

12a. Styles 1.5 mm long or less; fruits contorted but not regularly twisted; pubescence of basal leaves fine. ***Draba aurea*** Vahl, GOLDEN DRABA. The most abundant yellow draba, upper montane to alpine. Blooms in midsummer.

12b. At least some of the styles over 1.5 mm long; fruits regularly twisted; pubescence of basal leaves coarse, hirsute. ***Draba streptocarpa*** Gray (twisted-fruit). Less common than the preceding, subalpine and lower alpine.

ERYSIMUM. WALLFLOWER

1a. Petals 12-20 mm long, yellow, orange or lavender; biennial or perennial .... (2)
1b. Petals usually less than 10 mm long; annual or biennial ...... (3)

2a. Biennial; stem usually tall, solitary or a few together; common throughout the foothills and onto the plains. **Erysimum asperum** (Nutt.) DC. (harsh), WESTERN WALLFLOWER. Two extremes of variation may be recognized: (1) siliques stiffly erect or ascending, flowers orange with the petals often brown outside, plants of the foothills; (2) siliques wide-spreading, the flowers clear yellow, plants of the plains. These types seem to hybridize along the lower foothills. Their nomenclature as well as their breeding behavior has not been resolved.
2b. Perennial; stems low, caespitose; alpine tundra. **Erysimum nivale** (Greene) Rydb. (of the snows), ALPINE WALLFLOWER. Typically, the flowers are clear yellow, but a lavender form, which has been called *Erysimum amoenum* (Greene) Rydb., is common on some of the higher peaks such as Mount Evans.

3a. Petals 4-5 mm long; stem tall, little-branched; silique 2-3 cm long; leaves almost entire; biennial. **Erysimum cheiranthoides** L. ssp. **altum** Ahti, WORMSEED MUSTARD. Introduced weed, plains and foothills.
3b. Petals 6-10 mm long; stem low, widely branched (when well developed); silique 4-8 cm long; leaves sinuate-dentate; annual. **Erysimum repandum** L. (repand=sinuate), SPREADING WORMSEED. Introduced weed, common in fallow fields on the plains.

HESPERIS. DAMES-VIOLETS

One species, **Hesperis matronalis** L. ssp. **cladotricha** (Borbas) Hayek. A common plant of informal gardens, this has escaped and is established along roadsides in the lower foothills.

LEPIDIUM. PEPPER-GRASS

1a. Leaves of two strikingly different types, the lower pinnately dissected, the upper simple, clasping the stem. **Lepidium perfoliatum** L., CLASPING PEPPER-GRASS, Fig. 109. Abundant roadside weed in arid plains areas. The clasping "leaves" are really enlarged leaf-bases. The normal lower leaves show complete transitions to the upper perfoliate ones.
1b. Leaves not of two different types .... (2)

2a. Leaves entire, with clasping bases; fruit with winged margin and apex, the surfaces minutely whitish-pustulate. **Lepidium campestre** (L.) R. Br. (of fields), FIELD-CRESS. Introduced weed in waste ground.
2b. Leaves not entire nor with clasping bases .... (3)

3a. Perennial from rhizomes; silicle not notched at the apex; fruit somewhat pilose; stem glabrous or nearly so. **Lepidium latifolium** L., PERENNIAL PEPPER-GRASS. Introduced weed established near Boulder adjacent to the railroad and spreading rampantly along borrow ditches, a tall coarse plant difficult to eradicate.

3b. Annual or biennial, with a tap root; silicle notched at the apex; fruits usually glabrous; stem usually somewhat hairy . . . . (4)

4a. Style longer than the notch of the silique; plants biennial or perennial; flowers showy, white. *Lepidium montanum* Nutt. ssp. *alyssoides* (Gray) C. L. Hitchc. Common on plains and valley floors south of the Arkansas Divide; very abundant in the San Luis Valley.

4b. Style shorter than the notch of the silique; plants annual or biennial . . . . (5)

5a. Petals usually conspicuous, 1-3 mm long; silicles completely glabrous, almost orbicular. *Lepidium virginicum* L., PEPPER-GRASS. A roadside weed, not as abundant as the next. The silicles of all *Lepidium* species are mildly peppery if chewed.

5b. Petals inconspicuous or lacking, not longer than the sepals; silicles puberulent at least on the margins, more elliptic than orbicular . . . (6)

6a. Inflorescence a single raceme or only a few; silicles 3-3.5 x 2.5-3 mm, round-obcordate to short oblong-obovate, rounded or abruptly curved into obtuse apical teeth. *Lepidium densiflorum* Schrad. A very common weed in towns and along roadsides, usually at low altitudes.

6b. Inflorescence congested into numerous axillary racemes as well as terminal ones; silicles 2.5-3 x 1.5-2 mm, nearly elliptic, narrowed into acute apical teeth. *Lepidium ramosissimum* Nels. Abundant in the mountain valleys in middle and late summer, a coarse yellowish-green plant.

LESQUERELLA. BLADDER-POD

1a. All the leaves narrow (linear or oblanceolate); siliques globose or nearly so. *Lesquerella ludoviciana* (Nutt.) Wats. (of "old" Louisiana), SILVERY BLADDER-POD, Fig. 109. Sandy soil, plains. Usually silvery-pubescent.

1b. Some leaves broad (orbicular to obovate); siliques ovate to oblong. *Lesquerella montana* (Gray) Wats., MOUNTAIN BLADDER-POD, Fig. 109. Common on dry slopes, foothills and montane.

NASTURTIUM. WATER-CRESS

One species, *Nasturtium officinale* R. Br. Abundant in slow water-courses and irrigation ditches. Excellent for salads, but unless the water in which it grows is free from pollutants it may be wisest to buy greenhouse-grown plants.

PENNELLIA

One species, *Pennellia micrantha* (Gray) Nieuwl., found only once, on the lower slopes of Pikes Peak. Most common southwest of our area, in New Mexico.

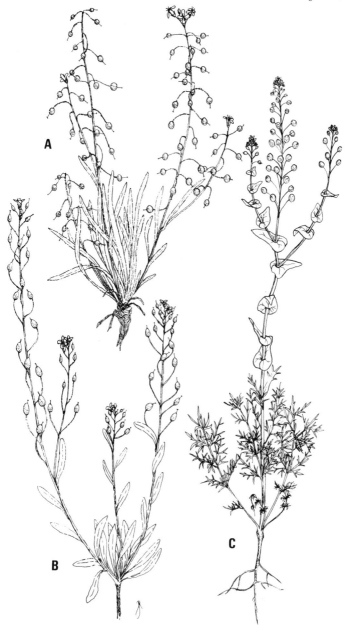

Fig. 109. A, *Lesquerella ludoviciana*; B, *L. montana*; C, *Lepidium perfoliatum*

PHYSARIA. Double Bladder-pod

1a. Constriction separating the locules equally deep above and below; locules globose; leaves broadly obovate, obtuse at the apex, rarely toothed or lobed. ***Physaria bellii*** Mulligan, Fig. 110. Restricted to shales, mesas near Boulder.

1b. Constriction separating the locules much deeper above than below; locules angular; leaves fiddle-shaped. ***Physaria vitulifera*** Rydb., (of calves, probably alluding to the resemblance of the siliques to "Rocky Mountain Oysters"), Fig. 111. Common on gravelly slopes of the foothill canyons.

RORIPPA. Cress

1a. Perennial with creeping rhizomes; petals well exceeding the sepals; leaves regularly pinnatifid .... (2)

1b. Annual or biennial with a tap root; petals scarcely exceeding the sepals; leaves lyrate-pinnatifid or only toothed .... (3)

2a. Beak of silique 1.3-2.5 mm long. ***Rorippa sinuata*** (Nutt.) Hitchc. Abundant along dry roadsides as well as low wet ground on the plains.

2b. Beak of silique 0.5-1.0 mm long. ***Rorippa sylvestris*** (L.) Bess. Wet margins of ditches, piedmont valleys, and in poorly drained lawns.

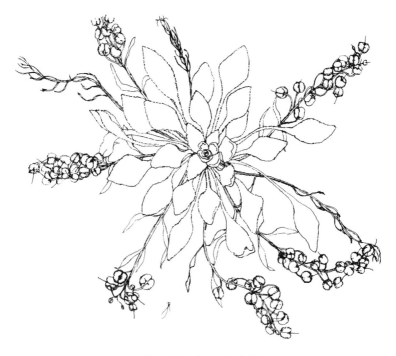

Fig. 110. ***Physaria bellii***

3a. Siliques spherical, the replum also circular. ***Rorippa sphaerocarpa*** (Gray) Britt. Infrequent in the piedmont valleys.
3b. Siliques oblong ....(4)

4a. Stem leaves unlobed, the margin entire or crenate or serrate; low, spreading plant. ***Rorippa curvipes*** Greene var. ***alpina*** (Wats.) Stuckey. Common on muddy shores of drying ponds and streams, montane to subalpine.
4b. Stem leaves pinnatifid; mostly tall and erect plants ....(5)

5a. Upper leaf surface and stems with scattered "vesicular trichomes" (these appear as small round blisters on the leaf-surface); seeds less than 0.5 mm long. ***Rorippa teres*** (Michx.) Stuckey. Common in muddy places, plains to montane.
5b. Upper leaf surface and stems lacking vesicular trichomes, but usually with other hairs; seeds more than 0.5 mm long. ***Rorippa palustris*** (L.) Bess. ssp. ***hispida*** (Desv.) Jonsell. Similar habitats.

SINAPIS. Charlock
One species, ***Sinapis arvensis*** L. A. common introduced weed in fields (*Brassica kaber* of Ed. 4).

Fig. 111. *Physaria vitulifera*

SISYMBRIUM

1a. Siliques closely appressed to the stem; petals 3-4 mm long. *Sisymbrium officinale* (L.) Scop. A garden and roadside weed in the Denver area.
1b. Siliques spreading to erect, if tending to be erect, then the pedicels spreading; petals 5-8 mm long .... (2)

2a. Flowers pale yellow; pedicels stout, 4-10 mm long, nearly as thick as the fruit; silique widely spreading, rigid, 5-10 cm long. *Sisymbrium altissimum* L. (very tall), JIM HILL MUSTARD. Very abundant tall tumbleweed. The leaves are pinnatifid and wither early. Plains and mesas, believed to have spread into the West by way of the railroads (Jim Hill was an early railroad magnate).
2b. Flowers bright yellow; pedicels slender, 7-20 mm long, not as thick as the fruit; siliques ascending to erect, 2-3.5 cm long. *Sisymbrium loeselii* L. (for J. A. Loiseleur-des-Longchamps). Infrequent weed of gardens in the cities along the Front Range.

SMELOWSKIA

One species, *Smelowskia calycina* (Desv.) C. A. Mey. (cup-like), SIBERIAN SMELOWSKIA. On scree slopes, alpine tundra. Rare in our region (Grays Peak area).

STANLEYA. PRINCES PLUME

One species, *Stanleya pinnata* (Pursh) Britt., Plate 17, Fig. 112. Locally abundant on shales, mesas and plains. Flowers yellow, in elongate, showy spikes. The presence of *Stanleya* is a good indication that the poisonous element, selenium, is present in the soil.

THLASPI. PENNY-CRESS

1a. Silicle large, orbicular; introduced annual weed. *Thlaspi arvense* L. (of cultivated land), FANWEED; PENNY-CRESS. Abundant in cultivated ground.
1b. Silicle obovate or oblong-cuneate, less than 1 cm long; plants perennial, native in the mountains. *Thlaspi montanum* L., WILD CANDYTUFT, Fig. 113. Abundant from the foothills to alpine, blooming from early spring to midsummer.

CUCURBITACEAE—GOURD FAMILY

Cultivated cucurbits are a legacy to us from aboriginal man, who used them not only for food but for all sorts of kitchen utensils, musical rattles, floats for fish-nets, and drinking cups. To learn their importance in our culture, one only has to list a few: Squash, Gourd, Pumpkin, Watermelon, Canteloupe, Cucumber. Besides these, there are dozens of cucurbits used throughout the tropical regions that are quite unknown to northerners. The inner spongy pulp of the genus *Luffa* is the original "chore-boy," called Dishcloth Gourd. Flowers of cucurbits are usually either staminate or carpellate, rarely perfect. Food crops depend on pollination by honeybees and solitary bees.

1a. Vine trailing over the ground and over low plants; leaves rough-pubescent, ovate or triangular, denticulate; flower yellow, about 10 cm long, solitary; fruit a woody dry striped baseball-shaped gourd. ***Cucurbita foetidissima*** H. B. K. (stinking), WILD GOURD, CALABAZILLA, Fig. 114. Common in sandy soil on the plains, particularly in southern Colorado. The plants form a huge spreading cover on roadside embankments.

1b. Vine climbing over fences and on tall shrubs; leaves palmately 5-lobed, glabrous; flowers small, white, in racemes or panicles; fruit prickly, papery-balloon-like with a spongy center. ***Echinocystis lobata*** (Michx.) T. & G., WILD BALSAM-APPLE; MOCK CUCUMBER, Fig. 114. Common along irrigation ditches on the piedmont valleys and plains.

DIPSACACEAE—TEASEL FAMILY

The teasel head is a perfect device for raising the nap on woolen fabrics. The process, called "fulling," has been used since ancient Roman times, and the English surname, Fuller, comes from this operation. Although teasels are still grown for this purpose, modern technology has found metal substitutes. To be a satisfactory teasel, the bristles on the head need to be hooked and stiff enough to stand up to tension without

Fig. 112. ***Stanleya pinnata***   Fig. 113. ***Thlaspi montanum***

shattering and getting caught in the wool. *Dipsacus sativus* is the commercial teasel. Our weedy species has straight bristles and is of little use. The family name comes from the Greek *dipsa* = thirst, alluding to the water-catching cup formed by the fused bases of the opposite leaves in some species. "Dipsomaniac" comes from the same stem. When one

Fig. 114. A, *Echinocystis*; B, *Cucurbita foetidissima*

speaks of "teasing" something apart, or of "teasing" some one in the sense of annoying, the word comes from the same source as "teasel." The wild teasels are commonly silvered or gilded and make striking additions to winter bouquets.

One genus and species, ***Dipsacus sylvestris*** Huds., WILD TEASEL, Fig. 115. An introduced weed, established along streams and irrigation ditches in the piedmont valleys. The hooked spines on the stems and leaves make this a formidable plant to collect or to struggle past in the field. Flowering begins midway in the head, proceeding upwards and downwards so that two rings of blossoms gradually move farther and farther apart.

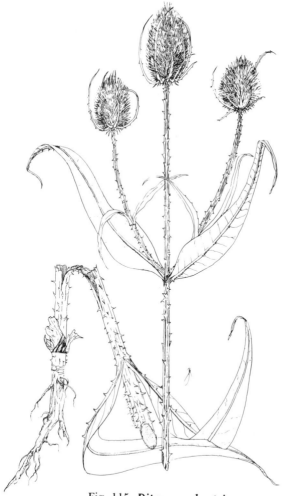

Fig. 115. *Dipsacus sylvestris*

ELAEAGNACEAE—OLEASTER FAMILY

This family is unique because of the peculiar peltate scales that cover the leaves and fruits, giving the foliage a satiny sheen or a rusty tint. All are trees or shrubs and many are ornamental cultivars of which the best known is the Russian-olive, one of the hardiest introduced trees on the Great Plains. Deserted homesteads are often recognizable by the persisting windrows of Russian-olive trees.

1a. Leaves and branches opposite .... (2)
1b. Leaves and branches alternate .... (3)

2a. Leaves silvery on both sides, oblong-elliptic; berries silvered. ***Shepherdia argentea*** (Pursh) Nutt., SILVERBERRY. Abundant in river-bottoms and along irrigation ditches on the western slope, but there are a few old records from the plains along the Platte drainage.

2b. Leaves green, broadly elliptic with rusty scales; berries red. ***Shepherdia canadensis*** (L.) Nutt., BUFFALO-BERRY, Plate 3, Fig. 117. Open lodgepole pine forests and rocky slopes and summits, montane and subalpine. Flowers unisexual, appearing in early spring before the leaves.

3a. Leaves silvery-scaly on both surfaces .... (4)
3b. Leaves stellate-pubescent above or becoming glabrous, greener above than below .... (5)

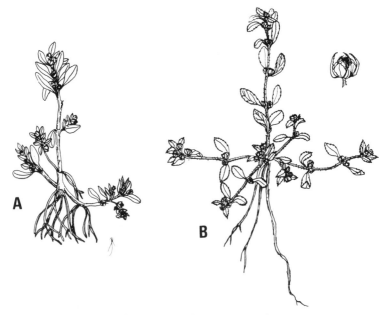

Fig. 116. A, *Elatine*; B, *Bergia*

4a. Leaves narrow; twigs of the year silvery-scaly as the leaves; cultivated tree becoming naturalized. **Elaeagnus angustifolia** L., Russian-olive.
4b. Leaves broad; twigs of the year with many rusty scales; shrub. **Elaeagnus commutata** Bernh., Silverberry. Native north of our range but cultivated as a highway ornamental some years ago and persisting. Probably not native in Colorado.

5a. Leaves softly stellate-pubescent above, the underside often with more hairs than scales; leaves not undulate-margined; berry silvered. **Elaeagnus orientalis** L. The leaves are usually broader and more rounded at the base than the Russian-olive, and are distinctly bicolored.
5b. Leaves becoming glabrous above, with impressed nerves; leaves undulate-margined; berry pinkish under the silver sheen. **Elaeagnus parvifolia** Royle. A very spiny species in cultivation and escaping just as Russian-olive. The twigs soon become naked and reddish-brown.

ELATINACEAE—WATERWORT FAMILY

A small family of semiaquatic plants, containing only the two genera listed below. They are infrequent and inconspicuous and of no economic importance whatever. *Elatine* is so rarely collected that we do not know if we have one or more species, or what their correct names are. Anyone collecting *Elatine* should try to deposit specimens with the Museum.

1a. Sepals and petals 5; sepals conspicuously scarious-margined and midrib clearly visible; foliage glandular-pubescent. **Bergia texana** (Hook.) Seub., Fig. 116. Drying pond margins on the plains and piedmont valleys.
1b. Sepals 2, petals 3; sepals not scarious-margined, without evident midrib; foliage glabrous. **Elatine rubella** Rydb. (reddish), Fig. 116. Mud flats, plains and piedmont valleys (*E. americana* of Harrington Manual).

ERICACEAE—HEATH FAMILY

Heaths or heathers are characteristic plants of almost every mountain region of the world, but they are mostly absent from our tundra because of our arid continental climate and the lack of acidity in the tundra soils. Even the blueberries (incorrectly called huckleberries) rarely set abundant fruit, possibly because of unseasonal frosts at flowering time. The flowers of ericads are beautiful creations, like porcelain easter-eggs into which one looks to see exotic scenes, and exotic they are, for the stamens have anthers that open by terminal pores and are often adorned with peculiar horns.

1a. Green leaves absent; plant saprophytic, reddish-brown or pink .. (2)
1b. Green leaves present ....(3)

2a. Stems stiffly erect, 3-8 dm high, with an elongate raceme of many pink or purplish brown flowers; petals united. ***Pterospora andromedea*** Nutt. (like the genus *Andromeda*), PINEDROPS, Fig. 118. Common in pine forests, foothills.

2b. Stems quite fleshy, often nodding at the top, 1-2 dm high, few-flowered; petals separate. ***Monotropa hypopitys*** L. var. ***latisquama*** (Rydb.) Kearney & Peebles (under pines; broad-scaled), PINESAP. Rare in forests from foothills to subalpine; an endangered species.

3a. Stems distinctly woody .... (4)
3b. Stems herbaceous, although the leaves sometimes evergreen .... (9)

4a. Trailing plants .... (5)
4b. Erect shrubs .... (6)

5a. Leaves thick, oblanceolate, the lateral veins inconspicuous; bark of older twigs peeling. ***Arctostaphylos uva-ursi*** (L.) Spreng. ssp. ***adeno-tricha*** (Fern. & Macbr.) Calder & Taylor (bears-grape; gland-hairs), KINNIKINNIK; BEARBERRY, Fig. 119. Abundant evergreen ground cover in open coniferous woods from foothills to subalpine; flowers white or pink, urn-shaped. The glandular-hairy race is most common but ssp. *coactilis* (Fern. & Macbr.) Löve & Kapoor, without glandular twigs, occurs less frequently.

5b. Leaves thin, almost round, the lateral veins prominent; bark of older twigs not peeling; twigs extremely fine and slender. ***Gaultheria humifusa*** (Graham) Rydb. (dwarf, spread out), CREEPING WINTERGREEN, Fig. 120. In cold mossy subalpine forests. Flowers inconspicuous, greenish-white. Berries red in both species.

Fig. 117. ***Shepherdia canadensis***   Fig. 118. ***Pterospora andromedea***

6a. Leaves evergreen, entire, pale beneath, with revolute margins; flowers showy, deep pink, parasol-shaped. *Kalmia polifolia* Wang. ssp. *microphylla* (Hook.) Calder & Taylor (with leaves like genus *Polium*), PALE or SWAMP LAUREL, Fig. 121. Infrequent but locally abundant on pond and stream borders, subalpine. Per Kalm was Linnaeus' plant collector in America.

6b. Leaves deciduous, usually at least finely serrate; flowers urn-shaped, pink or white, relatively inconspicuous .... (7)

7a. Leaves broadest above the middle, crenulate-serrate above the middle; branchlets not angled. *Vaccinium cespitosum* Michx. (in clumps), DWARF BILBERRY. Mossy forest floors and shores of ponds, subalpine. *Cespitosum* was the original spelling and must be retained.

7b. Leaves broadest at or below the middle, sharply serrate or serrulate from base to apex; branchlets angled .... (8)

8a. Leaves more than 10 mm long; berry blue-black when ripe; branches spreading, not crowded. *Vaccinium myrtillus* L. ssp. *oreophilum* (Rydb.) Löve, Löve & Kapoor, MYRTLE BLUEBERRY, Fig. 122. Very common in upper montane and subalpine forests under spruces.

8b. Leaves less than 10 mm long; berry red when mature; branches erect, crowded as straw in a broom. *Vaccinium scoparium* Leiberg,

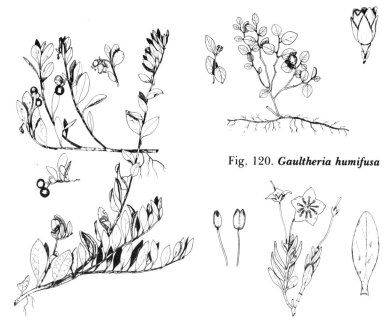

Fig. 120. *Gaultheria humifusa*

Fig. 119. *Arctostaphylos uva-ursi*   Fig. 121. *Kalmia polifolia*

BROOM HUCKLEBERRY. Usually found at higher altitudes than the preceding, frequently above timberline.

9a. Stems bearing several whorls of sharply serrate, oblanceolate, leathery leaves; inflorescence almost umbellate. *Chimaphila umbellata* (L.) Bart. ssp. *occidentalis* (Rydb.) Hultén, PIPSISSEWA; PRINCES PINE, Plate 11, Fig. 123. Frequent in cool ravines in deep shade, foothills to subalpine.
9b. Stems leafy only at or near the base; leaves ovate or round; inflorescence a raceme, or flower solitary .... (10)

10a. Flower large, solitary, extremely fragrant. *Moneses uniflora* (L.) Gray, ONE-FLOWERED WINTERGREEN, Fig. 124. Cold mossy forests, usually near streams.
10b. Flowers several on a stem .... (11)

11a. Leaves basal; inflorescence not distinctly one-sided .... (12)
11b. Leaves scattered along lower third of stem; inflorescence distinctly one-sided. *Ramischia secunda* (L.) Garcke, ONE-SIDED WINTERGREEN, Fig. 125. Mossy forest floors, cool ravines in the foothills, montane and subalpine.

12a. Style straight. *Pyrola minor* L., LESSER WINTERGREEN. Subalpine spruce-fir forests.
12b. Style curved downward and outward .... (13)

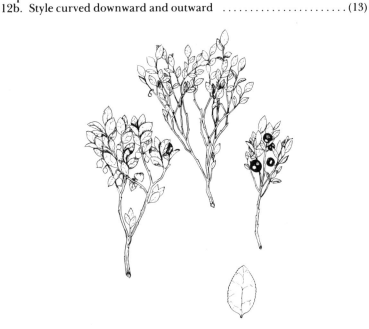

Fig. 122. *Vaccinium myrtillus*

13a. Leaves mottled or blotched with white, the blades ovate, acute at the tip. ***Pyrola picta*** Smith (painted), WHITE-VEINED PYROLA. Rare, foothills near Boulder and Colorado Springs.
13b. Leaves not mottled or blotched, the blades almost round ......(14)

14a. Flowers greenish; petals 4-5 mm long; scape usually less than 20 cm long; leaves 2-3 cm in diam. ***Pyrola chlorantha*** Swartz, Green-flowered Pyrola. Upper montane and subalpine forests (*P. virens* of Ed. 4).
14b. Flowers pink; petals 7-8 mm long; scape tall, up to 40 cm long; leaves commonly over 3 cm in diam. ***Pyrola asarifolia*** Michx. var. ***purpurea*** (Bunge) Fern. (with leaves like *Asarum*), SWAMP WINTER-GREEN. Boggy streambanks, subalpine forests.

EUPHORBIACEAE—SPURGE FAMILY

In this family a curious evolutionary trend is demonstrated in fantastic variety. Whole flower clusters are reduced to one essential part (one stamen or one gynoecium). Bracts take the place of the sepals, and colored glands the place of petals. Yet each flower cluster assumes the aspect of a single flower. Look closely at the stamen or the gynoecium and you will see that it has its own stalk, marked by a joint, so each is a separate flower and not a floral part! Next Christmas, examine the Poinsettia and learn that the beautiful red "petals" are not petals at all but colored leaves surrounding a number of these strange flower clusters or "cyathia."

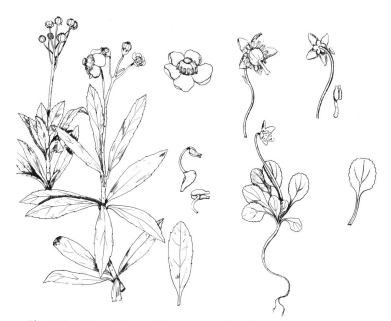

Fig. 123. ***Chimaphila umbellata***   Fig. 124. ***Moneses uniflora***

1a. Foliage covered by stellate hairs; leaves and stems silvery. ***Croton texensis*** (Klotsch) Muell.-Arg., CROTON, Fig. 127. Very common on the plains.
1b. Foliage glabrous or with simple hairs .... (2)

2a. Foliage bristly with stinging hairs (Sorry!); leaves sharply serrate; a true calyx present. ***Tragia urticifolia*** Michx. (nettle-leaved), Fig. 127. Grassy hillsides, mesas and lower foothills.
2b. Foliage without stinging hairs; leaves entire, dentate, or obscurely serrate; flowers surrounded by an involucre; true calyx absent ... (3)

3a. Stem leaves without united or connected stipules, spirally or radially arranged, alternate, opposite or whorled; main stem well developed, longer than the branches .... (4)
3b. Stem leaves opposite, with united or connected stipules, 2-ranked; main stem much shorter than the branches, or absent, the plant apparently many-stemmed (branched from the base) .... (11)

4a. Uppermost leaves and bracts with white margins. ***Agaloma marginata*** (Pursh) Löve & Löve, SNOW-ON-THE-MOUNTAIN, Fig. 126. Common on mesas and plains in midsummer, native here but a favorite under cultivation elsewhere.
4b. Uppermost leaves and bracts not white-margined .... (5)

Fig. 125. ***Ramischia secunda***   Fig. 126. ***Agaloma marginata***

5a. Perennials with woody bases or underground rhizomes .... (6)
5b. Annuals with taproots .... (9)

6a. Leaves linear, not thick and leathery .... (7)
6b. Leaves oblong or oblanceolate, thick and fleshy or leathery ..... (8)

Fig. 127. A, *Chamaesyce glyptosperma*; B, *Euphorbia robusta*; C, *Tragia*; D, *Croton*

7a. Leaves narrowly linear, less than 3 mm wide; plants low, less than a half-meter tall. **Euphorbia cyparissias** L., Cypress Spurge. Locally established as an escape from cultivation in dry open waste ground.

7b. Leaves broadly linear, over 5 mm wide; plants often more than a meter tall. **Euphorbia esula** L. (from old Celtic word esu = sharp, from the acrid juice). A pernicious weed in pastures and moist roadsides from the plains through the montane.

8a. Leaves broadest below the middle, less than 1 cm wide; native species. **Euphorbia robusta** (Engelm.) Small, Rocky Mountain Spurge, Fig. 127. Rocky mesas and hillsides, plains to montane.

8b. Leaves broadest above the middle, over 1 cm wide; garden species locally naturalized. **Euphorbia myrsinites** L. Locally established south of Boulder near Marshall and extremely abundant there.

9a. Leaves entire. **Euphorbia peplus** L. An introduced weed locally naturalized and abundant near Golden.

9b. Leaves toothed, sometimes obscurely so .... (10)

10a. Leaves coarsely dentate; petioles up to half the length of the blades; leaves opposite, often with a central dark spot. **Poinsettia dentata** (Michx.) Klotsch & Garcke. Weed of roadsides and railroad embankments, plains and piedmont valleys (*Euphorbia dentata* of Ed. 4).

10b. Leaves finely serrate, sessile or with short petioles; leaves alternate or scattered. **Euphorbia spathulata** Lam. Infrequent on the plains and lower foothills (*E. dictyosperma* of Ed. 4).

11a. Annual with a taproot .... (12)

11b. Perennial with deep-seated woody root systems, with a cluster of slender woody stems below ground level. **Chamaesyce fendleri** (T. & G.) Small (for August Fendler). Common in sandy places on the mesas and plains.

12a. Seeds with distinct transverse ridges and furrows. **Chamaesyce glyptosperma** (Engelm.) Small (with engraved seed), Fig. 127. Sandy soil, plains and mesas, cracks in sidewalks.

12b. Seeds smooth or roughened but never with regular transverse furrows and ridges .... (13)

13a. Leaves always entire, 4-5 times as long as wide, oblong; seeds smooth and plump. **Chamaesyce missurica** (Raf.) Shinners. Gravelly slopes, gulches and canyons on the plains and mesas.

13b. Leaves usually serrulate, rarely over 3 times as long as wide, oval. **Chamaesyce serpyllifolia** (Pers.) Small, Thyme-leaved Spurge. A common city weed, often rooted in cracks in sidewalks.

Fagaceae—Oak Family

Our only species of oak is extremely variable in its leaf shape.

Probably some of this variability is the result of ancient hybridization between Gambel Oak and others no longer surviving in our region. The Bur Oak, for example, occurs in the Black Hills of South Dakota and in a small colony in New Mexico and probably once was common in our region. Other southern species still reach north to the Canon City area. The absence of oaks north of the Denver area must indicate a major climatic boundary, possibly having to do with the winter storm tracks.

One genus and species, ***Quercus gambelii*** Nutt. (for Wm. Gambel), Scrub Oak, Fig. 128. A shrub or small tree characteristic of the chaparral belt from Evergreen and Littleton southward, extending into the foothills west of Salida. Acorns planted by Ernest Greenman in the canyons near Boulder have survived for over 30 years.

Fumariaceae—Fumitory Family

Close relatives of our only species of this strange family are the Dutchmans Breeches and Squirrel Corn, well-known spring flowers of the eastern and far-western states, and the ornamental species of rose-colored *Dicentra*, the best-known of which is the Bleeding-heart. All species are noted for their unusual spurred flowers.

One genus and species, ***Corydalis aurea*** Willd., Golden Smoke, Fig. 129. Abundant on mesas, plains, and lower foothills in early spring,

Fig. 128. *Quercus gambelii*

blossoming later along roadsides in the montane. Flowers very irregular, the sepals 2, minute, one of the 2 outer petals spurred, enclosing the nectary, the two inner petals united at the top, covering the six stamens which are united in threes.

GENTIANACEAE—GENTIAN FAMILY

Gentians are characteristic and often among the choicest of alpine wildflowers in the high mountains of the world. In the Rockies we lack the deep blue low gentians of the Swiss Alps, but have some specialties of our own. And we share some of ours with the mountains of Eurasia: *Ciminalis prostrata*, *Swertia perennis*, *Comastoma tenellum* and *Gentianodes algida*. I have seen species of *Ciminalis* even in the highest mountains of New Guinea.

1a. Corolla lobed to near the base, rotate, never distinctly tubular (2)
1b. Corolla distinctly tubular .... (5)

2a. Flowers large, each corolla-lobe 3 cm or more long, blue or purple.
  Eustoma, TULIP GENTIAN, page 206.
2b. Flowers with corolla-lobes less than 2 cm long, blue, white or greenish
.... (3)

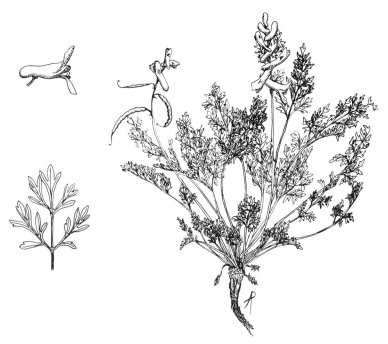

Fig. 129. *Corydalis aurea*

3a. Plant stout, up to 2 meters high; leaves fleshy, in whorls, flowers greenish-white. *Frasera*, MONUMENT PLANT, page 206.
3b. Plant slender; leaves opposite or basal; flowers blue or white .... (4)

4a. Annual; flowers white, rarely light blue; several pairs of opposite stem leaves present. *Lomatogonium*, MARSH FELWORT, page 207.
4b. Perennial; flowers deep blue; leaves chiefly basal, elliptic or oblanceolate. *Swertia*, STAR GENTIAN, page 209.

5a. Distinctly perennial, without a taproot; corolla never with fringed lobes, usually over 2.5 cm long .... (6)
5b. Annual or biennial or, if a short-lived perennial, having a taproot; corolla usually small, but if larger than 2.5 cm, then with fringed lobes .... (7)

6a. Flowers white with dull purplish pleats. *Gentianodes*, ARCTIC GENTIAN, page 207.
6b. Flowers blue or purple. *Pneumonanthe*, BLUE GENTIAN, page 209.

7a. Corolla deep blue, over 2.5 cm long, the lobes marginally fringed. *Gentianopsis*, FRINGED GENTIAN, page 207.
7b. Corolla white, pale or deep blue, less than 2 cm long, the principal lobes not fringed on the margin .... (8)

8a. Sinuses of the corolla plicate, with a smaller tooth-like lobe between the principal ones; leaf pairs connate into a tubular base; leaves less than 1 cm long, rounded-oblanceolate or obovate, white-edged. *Ciminalis*, SIBERIAN GENTIAN, page 205.
8b. Sinuses of the corolla not plicate, without subsidiary lobes; leaves larger, not connate-based, never white-edged .... (9)

9a. Corolla-lobes with two fringed scales within; flowers on long naked peduncles. *Comastoma*, LAPPLAND GENTIAN, page 206.
9b. Corolla-lobes with a single row of hairs forming a fringe inside (occasionally lacking in very late-blooming plants); flowers subtended by bracts, usually in clusters on the stem. *Gentianella*, LITTLE GENTIAN, page 206.

CIMINALIS. SIBERIAN GENTIAN

1a. Corolla deep blue, 12-15 mm long; capsule 8-10 mm long, ca. 1.5 mm broad, usually included, the valves not markedly divergent; tundra plant; corolla very sensitive to changes in light, closing quickly when shaded by a cloud or a hand. *Ciminalis prostrata* (Haenke) Löve & Löve (*Ericoila* of Ed. 4), Fig. 130.
1b. Corolla greenish-purple, 7-8 mm long; capsule ca. 5 mm long, almost as wide, long-exserted and with two spreading valves; plants of sedge meadows and swamps in the subalpine; evidently not so sensitive to light changes. *Ciminalis fremontii* (Torr. in Frémont) W. A. Weber. Earlier I believed that these species were variants of each other but now I am convinced I was wrong (*Gentiana fremontii* Torr. in Frém.).

COMASTOMA. Lappland Gentian

One species, **Comastoma tenellum** (Rottb.) Toyokuni (delicate). Rare, alpine tundra (*Gentiana tenella* Rottb.), Fig. 132. Easily recognized by the chiefly basal leaves and long-peduncled flowers. Circumpolar.

EUSTOMA. Tulip Gentian

One species, **Eustoma grandiflorum** (Raf.) Shinners, Plate 9. Formerly common in wet places on the plains, this became scarce with the disappearance of virgin prairie and is now an endangered species (*E. russellianum* of Ed. 4).

FRASERA. Monument Plant; Green Gentian

One species, **Frasera speciosa** Dougl. (splendid), Plate 13, Fig. 131. Common in pine forests and meadows, foothills and montane, a very conspicuous plant with its whorls of glaucous leaves and pale greenish flower clusters. Each petal has a mid-line of stiff glandular hairs and a fringed basal flap covering the nectary.

GENTIANELLA. Little Gentian

One species, **Gentianella amarella** (L.) Boern., Fig. 132. A very variable and widespread species from foothills to subalpine. The usual form has pale blue flowers, but white forms occur, and the sepals are extremely variable in size. In very late-blooming plants the corolla may lack the internal fringe.

Fig. 130. **Ciminalis prostrata**

GENTIANODES. Arctic Gentian

One species, **Gentianodes algida** (Pallas) Iöve & Iöve. A very late summer bloomer in the subalpine and alpine along rills, streambanks and on tundra meadows (*Gentiana algida* of Ed. 4).

GENTIANOPSIS. Fringed Gentian

1a. Annual; flowers on long naked peduncles, not closely bracteate. **Gentianopsis thermalis** (O. Kuntze) Iltis, Rocky Mountain Fringed Gentian, Plate 12, Fig. 134. Locally abundant in wet meadows and snow-melt basins, subalpine (*Gentiana thermalis* Kuntze). The north end of South Park is a prime area for great displays of this species.

1b. Short-lived perennial; flowers short-peduncled in the axils of two bract-like leaves. **Gentianopsis barbellata** (Engelm.) Iltis, Perennial Fringed Gentian. Rare or infrequent, grassy mountainsides, subalpine. Petals narrow, fringed on the sides near the base (*Gentiana barbellata* Engelm.).

LOMATOGONIUM. Marsh Felwort

One species, **Lomatogonium rotatum** (L.) Fries ssp. **tenuifolium** (Griseb.) Porsild, Fig. 132. Infrequent or rare, marshy shores or ponds, subalpine (*Pleurogyne rotata* Griseb.). Our plants have numerous ascending branches and usually white flowers, while the typical Arctic plants have few branches and purplish flowers. Circumpolar.

Fig. 131. *Frasera speciosa*

Fig. 132. A, *Gentianella*; B, *Comastoma*; C, *Swertia*; D, *Lomatogonium*

PNEUMONANTHE. Blue Gentian

1a. Corolla open or at least with evident lobes that are spreading or ascending .... (2)

1b. Corolla closed, the lobes obsolete or nearly so. ***Pneumonanthe andrewsii*** (Griseb.) W. A. Weber (for Henry C. Andrews). An eastern and midwestern species found only once in the early days near Denver, now probably extinct here (*Gentiana andrewsii* of Ed. 4).

2a. Corolla cylindric, the floral leaves narrow, not scarious. ***Pneumonanthe affinis*** (Griseb.) Greene. A common summer-blooming gentian on the mesas and foothills and in the intermountain parks (*Gentiana affinis* of Ed. 4).

2b. Corolla barrel-shaped, the floral leaves broad, scarious. ***Pneumonanthe calycosa*** (Griseb.) Greene (cup-like), Fig. 133. The common large gentian of montane and subalpine forests and meadows (*Gentiana calycosa* of Ed. 4).

SWERTIA. Star Gentian

One species, ***Swertia perennis*** L., Fig. 132. Marshy shores of ponds and streams, subalpine. Rare individuals may have white flowers. Circumpolar.

GERANIACEAE—GERANIUM FAMILY

The geraniums have developed a remarkable method of planting their seeds. The gynoecium splits into 5 one-seeded units (mericarps), each attached to a split length of style, which coils like a spring. Falling to

Fig. 133. ***Pneumonanthe calycosa***   Fig. 134. ***Gentianopsis thermalis***

the ground, the spring coils and uncoils with changes in atmospheric humidity. If it lies against a grass stem or other fixed object, it drills the seed into the earth. Similar devices have evolved, using different materials, in the grasses (*Stipa*) and in the roses (*Cercocarpus*). The potted "geraniums" belong to an African genus, *Pelargonium*.

1a. Leaves pinnately compound and dissected. ***Erodium cicutarium*** (L.) L'Her. (with leaves like *Cicuta*), FILAREE, Fig. 135. Flowers tiny, the petals pink, falling early. One of the earliest flowering weeds of early spring in ruderal sites. A winter annual, its leafy rosette is already well-developed by October.

1b. Leaves palmately lobed ....(2)

2a. Flowers 1 cm or less wide; filaments not long-pilose; annual or biennial. ***Geranium bicknellii*** Britt. (for Eugene P. Bicknell). Infrequent weed around dwellings. Flowers pink.

2b. Flowers 2 cm or more wide; petals and filaments more or less long-pilose ....(3)

3a. Plants with a single or few stems; petals white with purple veins;

Fig. 135. ***Erodium cicutarium***   Fig. 136. ***Geranium caespitosum***

flowers regularly in pairs; leaves thin, the lobes narrow. **Geranium richardsonii** F. & T. (for Sir John Richardson), WHITE GERANIUM. Aspen thickets and mountain meadows, montane and subalpine. On the western slope, a more robust plant with pink flowers is common in moist meadows and roadside ditches, *G. viscosissimum* F. & T. var. *nervosum* (Rydb.) C. L. Hitchc.

3b. Plants with many stems; petals pink to deep purple; flowers not regularly in pairs; leaves thick, the lobes broad .... (4)

4a. Pedicels and usually parts of the stem and petioles glandular-viscid; petals broad, pink, pilose on the inner surface not more than one-fourth their length. **Geranium caespitosum** James, COMMON WILD GERANIUM, Fig. 136. Abundant on rocky slopes and dry meadows, foothills, montane. Var. *parryi* (Engelm.) W. A. Weber has the petioles of the lower leaves glandular-hairy, while var. *caespitosum* lacks glandular hairs below (*G. fremontii* of Ed. 4).

4b. Plants completely lacking glandular pubescence; petals narrower, pilose on the inner surface one-third to one-half their length; petals deep pink to purple. **Geranium atropurpureum** Heller. Pikes Peak region and southwestward.

GROSSULARIACEAE—CURRANT OR GOOSEBERRY FAMILY

The word currant is a corruption of *Corinth*, from whence Zante Currant, a small variety of grape, comes (raisins of Corinth). Wild currants are so-called because of their resemblance to these. Gooseberries are green, often spiny fruits with an entirely different flavor, and this group is often segregated as the genus *Grossularia*, from which the family gets its name.

1a. Spines or prickles absent from the twigs .... (2)
1b. Spines or prickles present .... (7)

2a. Flowers yellow; petals yellow or red .... (3)
2b. Flowers white or pink .... (4)

3a. Hypanthium 12-15 mm long, about twice as long as the sepals; sepals revolute or spreading in the fading flowers; young growth and leaves pilose. **Ribes odoratum** Wendl. Infrequent on the plains and along Boulder Creek, but probably more widely distributed than records indicate. The flowers of this and the next have a fragrance of cloves.

3b. Hypanthium less than 10 mm long and usually less than twice as long as the sepals; sepals erect and closed in fading flowers; young growth glabrous or nearly so. **Ribes aureum** Pursh, GOLDEN CURRANT, Fig. 139. Abundant in gulches along the foothills-plains margin.

4a. Hypanthium very shallowly developed above the ovary, open saucer-shaped; leaves 4 cm or more broad, resembling a maple leaf. **Ribes**

coloradense Cov., COLORADO CURRANT. Common in subalpine forests. The cluster of pink flowers arises from buds on the previous year's growth. In *Ribes wolfii*, a similar species of the western slope, the inflorescence of white flowers is terminal on the current year's growth.

4b. Hypanthium short- or long-tubular .... (5)

5a. Leaves obscurely lobed; plant glandular-pubescent and fragrant; flowers pink. ***Ribes cereum*** Dougl. (waxen), WAX CURRANT, Fig. 140. Abundant in gulches, canyons, hillsides, plains to upper montane. Berry translucent orange-red.
5b. Leaves deeply lobed about half-way to the midrib, not strongly glandular or fragrant; flowers white .... (6)

6a. Plant usually with some spines at the nodes; leaves lacking minute golden glands on the lower surface, but often hairy; leaves less than 4 cm broad, the lobes and teeth broad; flowers in short, few-flowered clusters. ***Ribes inerme*** Rydb. Berries black.
6b. Plant never with spines; leaves with minute golden glands on the lower surface; leaves large, the lobes and teeth acute; flowers in distinct racemes. ***Ribes americanum*** Mill. An endangered species, found only at Roxborough Park in the outer foothills. Berries black.

7a. Flowers 2 to 4 in a sessile cluster, the hypanthium tubular ...... (8)
7b. Flowers several in a raceme, each flower on a slender pedicel; hypanthium open, saucer-shaped .... (9)

Fig. 137. ***Ribes inerme***

Fig. 138. ***Ribes lacustre***

8a. Petals and sepals narrow-oblong; anthers red; style glabrous, white; sepals not reflexed. ***Ribes leptanthum*** Gray (slender-flowered). Chiefly in canyons west of the Continental Divide, but found occasionally in the southern part of the Front Range.

8b. Petals short and broad, much shorter than the usually reflexed sepals; anthers white; styles densely pilose toward their bases. ***Ribes inerme*** Rydb. (unarmed, a misnomer), COMMON GOOSEBERRY, Fig. 137. A common species of the foothill canyons.

9a. Leaves pubescent and glandular; spines 3 at a node but internodes usually unarmed. ***Ribes montigenum*** McClatchie (of mountains), SUBALPINE PRICKLY CURRANT. Common in wet forests, along streams, etc., subalpine.

9b. Leaves glabrous; spines single and internodes also spiny or bristly. ***Ribes lacustre*** (Pers.) Poir. (of lakes), PRICKLY CURRANT, Fig. 138. Found from Larimer County northward. Wet meadows, montane, subalpine.

HALORAGACEAE—WATER-MILFOIL FAMILY

A small family of mostly Australian species, some of which are shrubs. Aquatic species, although very unrepresentative of the family, are found across the Northern Hemisphere. Our only species is ***Myriophyllum exalbescens*** Fern., WATER-MILFOIL, Fig. 142. The leaves are pinnately divided with linear segments, and the flowering spikes resemble a cord knotted at intervals.

Fig. 139. ***Ribes aureum***   Fig. 140. ***Ribes cereum***

HIPPURIDACEAE—MARES-TAIL FAMILY

This family consists of a single species, *Hippuris vulgaris* L., Fig. 142, occurring around the world in the Northern Hemisphere. When emergent, the stems with their whorled leaves stand stiffly out of the water. Submerged forms have very lax leaves that might cause the plant to be mistaken for *Elodea*. Subalpine ponds.

HYDRANGEACEAE—HYDRANGEA FAMILY

One genus and species, *Jamesia americana* T. & G., WAXFLOWER, Fig. 141. A very common and attractive shrub in the foothill canyons, occasional in the subalpine. It is a very ancient plant, occurring as a fossil in the Oligocene beds of Creede. The opposite, crenate leaves, tomentose beneath, the peeling outer bark, and the waxy, white, slightly fragrant flowers, are characteristic. The genus name commemorates Edwin James, botanist for the Long expedition.

HYDROPHYLLACEAE—WATERLEAF FAMILY

The hydrophylls are probably best recognized by their inflorescences, which are tightly coiled into a helix when young, gradually uncoiling as the flowers open. The stamens are usually exserted on long, slender filaments. The family name derives from the succulent, watery stems and leaves of the genus *Hydrophyllum*, but many hydrophylls have rough-hairy foliage like the borages, a family which also has helicoid inflorescences but differs in having the fruit divided into four nutlets.

Fig. 141. *Jamesia americana*

1a. Flowers solitary or few; weak, much-branched annuals with pinnatifid leaves; fruit a berry. ***Ellisia nyctelea*** L. (*Nyctelea* is a pre-Linnaean
name for the genus, derived from the god, Bacchus), ELLISIA.
Shaded slopes, gulches on the mesas and in the lower foothills.
1b. Flowers numerous in balls or coiled spikes; perennials; leaves various
.... (2)

2a. Mesophytes with thin leaves, brittle stems, and watery juice; leaves
pinnately compounded into 5 to 9 leaflets or broad lobes; inflorescence
a ball-like cluster; plants growing on moist shaded streamsides.
Hydrophyllum fendleri (Gray) Heller (for August Fendler), WATERLEAF.
Abundant along streams on the mesas and lower foothills. The strongly
exserted stamens cause the flower-head to resemble a pin-cushion.
Flowers white. *Hydrophyllum capitatum* Dougl. *ex* Benth., with a ball of
lavender flowers overtopped by the leaves, is abundant on the western
slope as close as Rabbit Ears Pass.
2b. Xerophytes; leaves simple, few-lobed, or much-dissected; inflorescence of several distinct spikes; plants of open mesas, ravines, and
rock-slides .... (3)

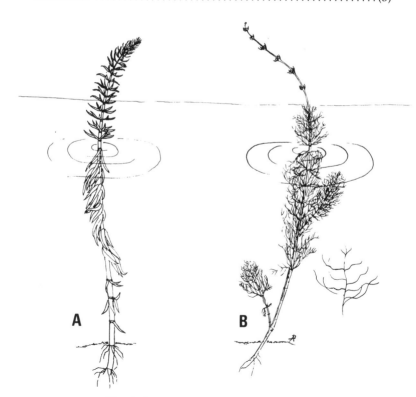

Fig. 142. A, ***Hippuris***; B, ***Myriophyllum***

3a. Leaves entire or with a few small lobes at the base; terminal leaflet much larger than the rest .... (6)
3b. Leaves pinnately lobed or dissected from base to apex, the terminal leaflet not larger than the rest .... (4)

4a. Inflorescence densely spicate; petals entire; upper stem leaves reduced in size; plants of subalpine meadows and rockslides. *Phacelia sericea* Hook. (silky), PURPLE FRINGE, Fig. 143. Flowers purple, the stamens exserted; leaves silky-pubescent.
4b. Inflorescence with several main branches; petals denticulate or fringed; upper stem leaves not reduced in size; glandular-pubescent plants of mesas and foothills .... (5)

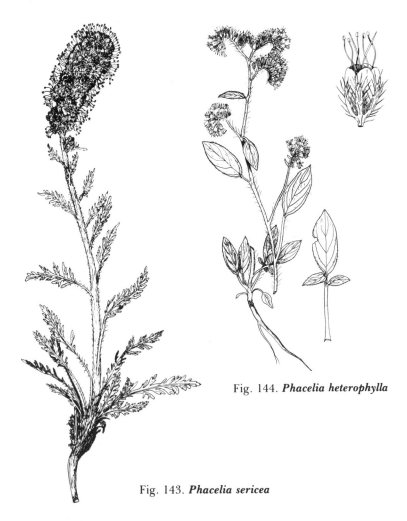

Fig. 144. *Phacelia heterophylla*

Fig. 143. *Phacelia sericea*

5a. Stamens included; corolla about 5 mm long, the lobes very small, pale blue-violet. ***Phacelia denticulata*** Osterh. Frequent in pine forests in the outer foothills.

5b. Stamens exserted; corolla with lobes well developed, white or pale violet. ***Phacelia neomexicana*** Thurber *ex* Torr. var. ***alba*** (Rydb.) Brand. Roadsides and disturbed places in the foothills.

6a. Flowers purplish; leaves simple; plants of subalpine meadows. ***Phacelia hastata*** Lehm., SCORPION-WEED.

6b. Flowers white; some leaves at least with basal lobes; plants mostly of mesas and foothills. ***Phacelia heterophylla*** Pursh (various-leaved), SCORPION-WEED, Fig. 144.

HYPERICACEAE—ST. JOHNSWORT FAMILY

Klamath Weed, *Hypericum perforatum* L., a European species that is not a nuisance in its homeland, came to the United States with the settlement of the Far West. Over a span of fifty years it cost Oregon and California millions of dollars in sheep poisoning losses. Two and one-third million acres of California land were infested, and in 1930 this plant was the cause of the worst financial losses on pasture and range lands in California. The plant sensitizes white animals to light, and death usually results from starvation following blindness or refusal to eat.

About 17,000 acres of land on Rocky Flats have been infested with this plant for many years but until recently the species did not move out of its original stands. Now it occurs high up in Boulder Canyon and in the Black Forest. At Rocky Flats the plant has been controlled, as elsewhere, by the introduction of a beetle, *Chrysolina quadrigemina* (Suffrian), for which *H. perforatum* is its sole food. This is a classic example of the value and possibilities of biological control of pests. While the plant has not been eliminated, it is kept in check by the beetles most of the time.

1a. Petals 7-15 mm long, with black dots near the margins; plants perennial .... (2)

1b. Petals 2-3.5 mm long, not black-dotted; annual. ***Hypericum majus*** (Gray) Britt. Drying pond shores and floodplains in the piedmont valleys. Uncommon.

2a. Leaves narrowly oblong; plants profusely branched; flowers very numerous in a broad, flat-topped cluster. ***Hypericum perforatum*** L., KLAMATH WEED.

2b. Leaves broadly elliptic; plants slender, sparingly branched; flowers few, in axillary cymes; inflorescence not flat-topped. ***Hypericum formosum*** H. B. K. (beautiful), Fig. 145. Wet meadows and streamsides, upper montane, subalpine. Flowers yellow in all species.

LABIATAE (LAMIACEAE)—MINT FAMILY

What would be left of the good life if we did not have this family? For scent, flavor and "that little something extra" in our foods we depend on mints: Rosemary, Lavender, Sage, Spearmint, Peppermint, Pennyroyal, Basil, Thyme, Hoarhound, Marjoram, Oregano, Savory! Citronella was once the only reliable insect-repellant. Coleus plants used to be in every home, before we learned about African Violets. Probably only the Umbelliferae comes close to supplying as many important culinary needs.

1a. Flowers in the axils of leaves, solitary or in clusters, not in terminal spikes or racemes .... (11)
1b. Flowers grouped in terminal spikes or racemes .... (2)

2a. Flowers 2 cm or more long, showy, in hemispherical terminal clusters subtended by a group of leaflike bracts. *Monarda fistulosa* L. var. *menthaefolia* (Graham) Fern., PINK BERGAMOT, Fig. 146. Abundant in gulches and along roadsides, mesas and foothills in midsummer. Flowers pink-purple.
2b. Flowers less than 2 cm long, in dense or often elongated spikes (3)

3a. Leaves entire or very shallowly crenate-serrate .... (4)
3b. Leaves regularly and distinctly serrate or crenate .... (6)

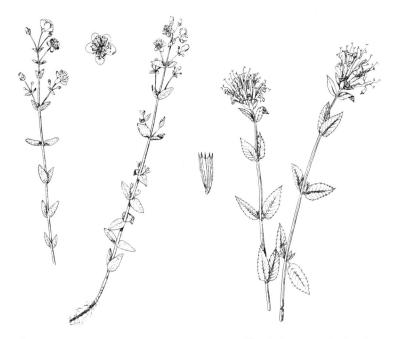

Fig. 145. *Hypericum formosum*   Fig. 146. *Monarda fistulosa*

4a. Spikes dense .... (5)

4b. Spikes or racemes very long and the flowers remote. *Salvia reflexa* Hornem. A common weedy annual on floodplains in the piedmont valleys, often in vacant lots in towns.

5a. Flowers bright blue; plant tall, up to a meter or more. *Salvia azurea* Lam. var. *grandiflora* Benth., BLUE SAGE. Native on the eastern plains, but locally abundant as an established adventive on outer foothills near Boulder.

5b. Flowers purple, subtended by broadly ovate, pointed, often purplish bracts; plant low, 10-20 cm high. *Prunella vulgaris* L., HEAL-ALL. Common in moist canyons and woodlands, foothills.

6a. Spikes containing numerous leaf-like, spine-tipped, serrate bracts; leaves with salient spine-tipped teeth. *Moldavica parviflora* (Nutt.) Britt. (small-flowered), DRAGONHEAD. A weedy species in disturbed ground, burned areas, etc., foothills, montane.

6b. Spikes without leaf-like serrate bracts; leaves serrate or crenate, not spine-toothed .... (7)

7a. Leaves heart-shaped, deeply crenate; plants with catnip odor. *Nepeta cataria* L., CATNIP. Common weed in gardens, sometimes established in gulches on the mesas. Flowers white.

7b. Leaves lanceolate to ovate, serrate .... (8)

8a. Flowers white, less than 0.5 cm long; plants with a spearmint odor. *Mentha spicata* L., SPEARMINT. Escaped from gardens and locally established.

8b. Flowers pink or purple, or if white, usually 1 cm long or more; plants without spearmint odor .... (9)

9a. Leaves woolly-pubescent, mostly basal; flowers white, in a much-interrupted branched inflorescence, each flower cluster subtended by a pair of broad, sharp-pointed bracts. *Salvia aethiopis* L. (of Ethiopia), SAGE. An introduced weed locally established between Longmont and Boulder.

9b. Leaves glabrous or finely pubescent; stems leafy; flowers white or purplish; inflorescence more or less continuous, the bracts not as above .... (10)

10a. Leaves glabrous, green above and pale below; calyx purplish and corolla blue-violet. *Agastache foeniculum* (Pursh) Kuntze, GIANT-HYSSOP. Infrequent in the foothills, vicinity of the Platte River Canyon.

10b. Leaves pubescent; calyx green; corollas pink to lavender. *Teucrium canadense* L. var. *occidentalis* (Gray) McClintock & Epling, GERMANDER. Irrigation ditches and swampy meadows on the plains and mesas.

11a. Calyx with a prominent transverse ridge on the upper side ... (12)
11b. Calyx lacking a transverse ridge on the upper side .... (13)

12a. Plant glandular-pubescent; leaves entire or nearly so; plants of dry mesa slopes. ***Scutellaria brittonii*** Porter (for N. L. Britton), SKULLCAP, Fig. 147. Common on the mesas. Flowers 2 cm or more long, in pairs, blue-purple.

12b. Plant glabrous or nearly so; leaves dentate; plants of swampy places on the plains and piedmont valleys. ***Scutellaria galericulata*** L. (helmeted), MARSH SKULLCAP.

13a. Flowers solitary in the leaf-axils (2 flowers at each node, since the leaves are opposite). ***Salvia reflexa*** Hornem., LANCE-LEAVED SAGE. A common weedy annual on floodplains in the piedmont valleys, often in vacant lots in and near towns.

13b. Flowers in clusters of more than one per leaf axil .... (14)

14a. Leaves deeply palmately cleft or lobed. ***Leonurus cardiaca*** L. (of the heart), MOTHERWORT. A weed in neglected sites, particularly in and around towns. Flowers white, densely white-woolly.

14b. Leaves entire or merely toothed, never deeply palmately cleft (15)

15a. Plant densely woolly-pubescent; leaves conspicuously veiny. ***Marrubium vulgare*** L., COMMON HOREHOUND. Very abundant in overgrazed pastures on the plains and mesas. Flowers in dense axillary clusters.

15b. Plant not densely woolly-pubescent .... (16)

16a. Leaves kidney-shaped, or round, or cordate, coarsely crenate-toothed .... (17)

Fig. 147. ***Scutellaria brittonii***

16b. Leaves longer than broad, ranging from entire to deeply serrate or pinnatifid, never coarsely crenate .... (19)

17a. Flowers few (2 to 6), in loose cymes; leaves rounded or kidney-shaped; plants creeping extensively. ***Glechoma hederacea*** L. (ivy-like), GROUND-IVY; GILL-OVER-THE-GROUND. A weed in lawns. Flowers blue-purple (*Nepeta hederacea* [L.] Trev.).
17b. Flowers numerous, in dense axillary clusters; leaves various; plants semi-erect .... (18)

18a. Upper stem leaves purple, usually distinctly petioled, not clasping the stem; plant densely pubescent. ***Lamium purpureum*** L., PURPLE DEAD-NETTLE. Sparingly introduced weed of cultivated ground.
18b. Upper stem leaves green, usually clasping the stem, only the lower leaves with distinct petioles; plant sparingly pubescent. ***Lamium amplexicaule*** L. (clasping), HENBIT. Sparingly introduced weed of cultivated ground.

19a. Leaves linear or elliptic, less than 1 cm long, or usually less than 3 mm wide; plants with a very strong odor .... (20)
19b. Leaves larger in both dimensions; plants without very strong odor .... (21)

20a. Annual; leaves narrowly linear. ***Hedeoma hispidum*** Pursh (with short, stiff hairs), ROUGH PENNYROYAL. Mesas and plains.
20b. Perennial; leaves, at least the lower, elliptic. ***Hedeoma drummondii*** Benth. (for Thomas Drummond), PENNYROYAL. Rimrock, canyons, and hogback ridges; mesas and foothills.

21a. Flowers 0.5 cm long or less .... (22)
21b. Flowers 1 cm or more long .... (24)

22a. Leaves with long salient teeth, or pinnately cleft; stamens hidden by the corolla-tube .... (23)
22b. Leaves merely shallowly and regularly serrate; stamens exserted. ***Mentha arvensis*** L., FIELD MINT. Irrigation ditches, sloughs, and streambanks, plains and piedmont valleys.

23a. Blades of lower and middle stem leaves tapering to petioles; roots rarely tuberous; nutlets with a smooth corky ridge. ***Lycopus americanus*** Muehl., WATER HOREHOUND. Swamps and streambanks, mostly in the piedmont valleys.
23b. Blades of lower and middle stem leaves sessile; roots tuberous; nutlet without corky ridge. ***Lycopus asper*** Greene (harsh), WATER HOREHOUND. Similar habitats (*L. lucidus* of manuals).

24a. Flowers white, cream-colored, or flesh-pink; floral bracts spine-tipped; foliage puberulent. ***Monarda pectinata*** Nutt. (comb-like), HORSE MINT. Common on the plains and mesas.
24b. Flowers deep pink or lavender; floral bracts not spine-tipped; foliage pilose. ***Stachys palustris*** L. (of marshes), HEDGE-NETTLE. Swampy streambanks and ditches on the plains and piedmont valleys.

LEGUMINOSAE (FABACEAE)—PEA FAMILY

Eric Partridge suggests that the word *legume* probably is derived from the Latin verb *legere* (stem, *leg* + suffix,-*umen*), "what one gathers or picks, thus a vegetable." In French, the word légume still refers to any vegetable, not only those we call legumes: peas, beans, soy beans, lima beans and pinto beans. A curious extension of the use of the word is also French, in which "les grosses légumes" means "the bigwigs."

Beside their food value, many species of *Astragalus* absorb large amounts of the poisonous element selenium and, when grazed, cause the ailments known as "blind staggers" or "alkali disease." Another disease, "loco," evidently is not caused by selenium although the toxic principle is not definitely known. Some *Astragalus* species and most *Oxytropis* species are "loco-weeds." The ability of plants to absorb minerals differentially from the soil opened up a new field, geobotanical prospecting, now used in the search for uranium and heavy metals, and for analyzing the extent of heavy-metal pollution in the environment.

1a. Woody plants (shrubs or trees) ....(2)
1b. Herbs ....(4)

2a. Flowers yellow; pod papery, greatly inflated. *Colutea*, BLADDER SENNA, page 226.
2b. Flowers white, lavender or purple ....(3)

3a. Leaves with thorns at the petiole base (stipular spines). *Robinia*, LOCUST, page 231.
3b. Leaves and stems lacking thorns. *Amorpha*, LEAD PLANT, page 223.

4a. Filaments all separate to the base or very nearly so; flowers never pink or purple ....(5)
4b. Stamens (some or all) united by their filaments; flowers variously colored ....(6)

5a. Flowers yellow; leaves with three leaflets. *Thermopsis*, GOLDEN BANNER, page 231.
5b. Flowers white; leaves odd-pinnately compound. *Sophora*, page 231.

6a. Leaves even-pinnately compound (the terminal leaflet missing), terminated by a tendril or bristle ....(7)
6b. Leaves odd-pinnately or digitately compound (terminal leaflet present), rarely simple, tendrils absent ....(8)

7a. Style slender, with a tuft of hairs near the apex. *Vicia*, VETCH, page 233.
7b. Style flattened, hairy along one side. *Lathyrus*, PEAVINE, page 227.

8a. Anthers of two forms, large and small; stamens 10, monadelphous (all united by their filaments); leaves digitately 5- or more-foliate. *Lupinus*, BLUEBONNET, page 228.
8b. Anthers all alike; stamens 10, diadelphous (9 united, one separate)

or 5 and monadelphous; leaves pinnately compound, or, if digitately compound, with less than 5 leaflets .... (9)

9a. Fruit a loment (constricted and jointed between the seeds), separating at maturity into one-seeded segments. ***Hedysarum***, page 227.
9b. Fruit a pod, dehiscent at maturity, not segmented .... (10)

10a. Foliage glandular-dotted .... (11)
10b. Foliage not glandular-dotted .... (13)

11a. Pod with hooked prickles (much like a small cocklebur). ***Glycyrrhiza***, WILD LIQUORICE, page 227.
11b. Pod not prickly .... (12)

12a. Leaves digitately 3- to 5-foliolate; ovule solitary. ***Psoralea,*** page 230.
12b. Leaves pinnately 5- to many-foliolate; ovules 2 or more in a pod. ***Dalea***, PRAIRIE-CLOVER, page 227.

13a. Leaf margins denticulate to serrate; leaves 3-foliolate .... (14)
13b. Leaf margins entire .... (16)

14a. Pod sickle-shaped or spirally coiled. ***Medicago***, ALFALFA; MEDIC, page 228.
14b. Pod straight or nearly so .... (15)

15a. Flowers in elongate, loose racemes; corolla yellow or white; foliage sweet-smelling when dry. ***Melilotus***, SWEET-CLOVER, page 228.
15b. Flowers in heads or short, dense spikes; corolla white, pink or purple; plants not aromatic when dry. ***Trifolium***, CLOVER, page 231.

16a. Climbing or trailing vine with underground tuberous roots; leaves with 5-9 broad leaflets. ***Apios***, GROUND-NUT, page 224.
16b. Erect or caespitose herbs .... (17)

17a. Flowers in umbels or capitate clusters .... (18)
17b. Flowers in racemes, spikes, or solitary .... (20)

18a. Flowers yellow. ***Lotus***, page 228.
18b. Flowers not yellow .... (19)

19a. Leaflets 3. ***Trifolium***, CLOVER, page 231.
19b. Leaflets numerous, pinnately arranged. ***Coronilla***, CROWN VETCH, page 227.

20a. Keel with an abruptly narrowed tip or beak; leaves chiefly basal. ***Oxytropis***, LOCO-WEED, page 229.
20b. Keel not beaked but rounded; plants usually, but not always, with leafy stems. ***Astragalus***, MILK VETCH, page 224.

AMORPHA. LEAD PLANT
1a. Tall shrub; leaflets about 2.5 cm long; pods usually 2-seeded; flowers

dark blue-purple. ***Amorpha fruticosa*** L. var. ***occidentalis*** (Abrams) Kearney & Peebles, LEAD PLANT. Common in gulches on the mesas, and along irrigation ditches in the piedmont valleys.

1b. Low shrub; leaflets 0.5-1.5 cm long; pod 1-seeded; flowers light lavender. ***Amorpha nana*** Nutt. (dwarf), SMALL-LEAVED FALSE INDIGO. Very rare and endangered, on mesa slopes in South Boulder and in the Black Forest. Several home-owners are actively protecting the few plants remaining on their property in town.

APIOS. GROUND-NUT

One species, ***Apios americana*** Medic. Extremely rare, in shade at the foot of cliffs on the floodplain of Boulder Creek, a relictual species of the midwestern woodlands; flowers reddish-purple.

ASTRAGALUS. MILK VETCH

1a. Leaflets 3 or 5 (rarely more), or leaves simple; densely matted dwarf plants of the mesas and foothills . . . . (20)
1b. Leaflets more numerous; plants not as above in every detail . . . (2)

2a. Flowering stems scapose, from a tuft of basal leaves; flowers pink or magenta; leaflets oval, silvery appressed-pubescent . . . . (19)
2b. Flowering stems leafy or at least with some leaves above the very base
. . . . (3)

3a. Pods fleshy, plum-shaped; plants prostrate; flowers white with blue- or purple-tipped keel. ***Astragalus crassicarpus*** Nutt. (thick-fruited), GROUND-PLUM. Common on mesas and plains in early spring.
3b. Pods neither fleshy nor plum-shaped; plants erect or spreading. (4)

4a. Leaves densely soft-hairy . . . . (5)
4b. Leaves glabrous or sparsely appressed-pubescent, not woolly to the touch . . . . (6)

5a. Plant tall, erect, leafy-stemmed; pods numerous, reflexed, stipitate. ***Astragalus drummondii*** Dougl. in Hook. (for Thomas Drummond). Abundant on mesas; flowers yellowish-white.
5b. Plants low, caespitose; leaves mostly near the base of the flowering stem; pods few, ascending, sessile. ***Astragalus parryi*** Gray (for C. C. Parry). In shade, dry gulches, foothills to upper montane.

6a. Pods stiffly erect (the lower flowers usually can be used to indicate the position the pods will assume) . . . . (7)
6b. Pods loosely spreading to reflexed . . . . (9)

7a. Stems 4 or more dm high, solitary or few; leaflets broadly elliptic. ***Astragalus canadensis*** L., CANADA MILK VETCH. Rare or infrequent, wooded gulches, lower foothills.
7b. Stems rarely over 3 dm high, clustered; leaflets narrowly elliptic; abundant species . . . . (8)

8a. Flower clusters longer than broad; calyx sparsely black-hairy; flowers purplish or white; plant without rhizomes. **Astragalus adsurgens** Pallas var. **robustior** Hook. Mesas and dry mountain slopes, foothills to upper montane.

8b. Flower clusters almost globose; calyx densely black-hairy; flowers usually lavender; plant with rhizomes. **Astragalus dasyglottis** Fisch. *ex* DC. (hairy-throated), PURPLE MILK VETCH. Frequent on the plains and mesas, forming patches *(A. agrestis* of Ed. 4).

9a. Pods papery-inflated, short-stipitate, mottled; leaflets narrowly linear. **Astragalus ceramicus** Sheld. var. **filifolius** (Gray) F. J. Hermann (like pottery). Sandy places, steep riverbanks, etc., on the plains.

9b. Plants not as above .... (10)

10a. Pods black-hairy. **Astragalus alpinus** L., ALPINE MILK VETCH. Forests, upper montane, subalpine.

10b. Pods smooth, or, if pubescent, the hairs light in color .... (11)

11a. Pod with two prominent longitudinal grooves along the upper suture. **Astragalus bisulcatus** (Hook.) Gray, TWO-GROOVED MILK VETCH. Abundant on the plains and mesas. Flowers usually pink or purple, sometimes white.

11b. Pod lacking longitudinal grooves .... (12)

12a. Pod with a long slender stipe 4-5 mm long that is evident without dissection of the calyx; pod over 3 cm long (2-4 cm in *A. racemosus*) .... (22)

12b. Pod without a long, slender stipe; pod less than 3 cm long .... (13)

13a. Pod flattened laterally, glabrous or nearly so; flowers white or merely tipped with pink or purple .... (14)

13b. Pod plump, pubescent; flowers pink or purple .... (15)

14a. Pods 15-20 mm long, sessile, somewhat rounded in cross-section, the valves convex; flower-clusters usually well-exserted beyond the foliage. **Astragalus miser** Dougl. *ex* Hook. var. **oblongifolius** (Rydb.) Cronquist. Mountain meadows and forest openings.

14b. Pods 8-15 mm long, with at least a short stipe, the valves flat; flower clusters little if at all exceeding the leaves. **Astragalus tenellus** Pursh (delicate), LOOSE-FLOWERED MILK VETCH. Montane and subalpine forests. Plants commonly blackening on drying.

15b. Pods very short, only 5-8 mm long .... (16)

15b. Pods 10-20 mm long .... (17)

16a. Leaflets narrowly oblong; plants exclusively of the plains. **Astragalus gracilis** Nutt. (slender). A plains species rarely found close to the mountains, but apparently frequent in the Denver area.

16b. Leaflets broad and circular; plants of the Platte River Valley, foothills. **Astragalus sparsiflorus** Gray, FRONT RANGE MILK VETCH.

17a. Plant erect, usually simple; flowers dark purple; pod densely appressed-pubescent with long hairs; subalpine. **Astragalus eucosmus** Robinson (elegant). Swampy borders of lakes and streams.

17b. Plant low, branched from the base and decumbent; flowers white or pale lavender; pod sparsely pubescent with short hairs; foothills (18)

18a. Leaflets very short and almost circular; pod broad and plump; flowers with pink-veined banner and purple-tipped keel. **Astragalus sparsiflorus** Gray var. **majusculus** Gray, FRONT RANGE MILK VETCH. Foothills, Platte River Valley.

18b. Leaflets oblong; pod narrow, elongate; flowers usually pinkish or lavender. **Astragalus flexuosus** (Dougl. *ex* Hook.) G. Don, WIRY MILK VETCH. Common in ravines and gulches, foothills and montane.

19a. Plants in dense tufts; flowering stems numerous, erect; pods not greatly inflated or bladder-like, but small (2-3 cm long) and woody at maturity. **Astragalus missouriensis** Nutt. Common on the plains, flowering in early spring. Largely replaced on the mesas by the next.

19b. Plants not in dense tufts, the stems usually solitary or a few together; flowering stems few, spreading; pods inflated or bladder-like at maturity, over 3 cm long. **Astragalus shortianus** Nutt. *ex* T. & G. (for Chas. Wilkins Short). A common early spring flower on the mesas. Flower deep pink.

20a. Leaves mostly simple; flower stalks exceeding the leaves. **Astragalus spatulatus** Sheld., TUFTED MILK VETCH. Rocky outcrops of the foothill hogbacks, Larimer County northward. Flowers pink, turning purple when dried.

20b. Leaves with three or more leaflets; flowers hidden among the leaves
. . . . (21)

21a. Leaves with three leaflets, very densely white-pubescent, not spine-tipped. **Astragalus tridactylicus** Gray (three-fingered). Common in early spring on the mesas, from Denver northward. Flowers pink.

21b. Leaves with 5 or more leaflets, spine-tipped, not very densely pubescent. **Astragalus kentrophyta** Gray var. **implexus** (Canby) Barneby. Infrequent in canyons of the foothills, flowering in summer. Flowers purplish.

22a. Pod triangular in cross-section, with a deep infolding along the lower side; plants of the plains. **Astragalus racemosus** Pursh.

22b. Pod not triangular in cross-section; plants of the foothills. **Astragalus aboriginorum** Rich., INDIAN MILK VETCH. Rare or infrequent, pine forests in the foothills.

COLUTEA. BLADDER SENNA

One species, **Colutea arborescens** L., a native of the Mediterranean region, escaped in Four-Mile Canyon near Boulder many years ago, and now spreading in the Boulder area.

CORONILLA. Crown Vetch

One species, ***Coronilla varia*** L., an introduced weed now becoming well established around Boulder. The pinkish flowers have a slender, purple-tipped keel.

DALEA. Prairie-clover

1a. Petals white. ***Dalea candida*** Willd. (shining white). Common on plains and mesas.
1b. Petals purple. ***Dalea purpurea*** Vent. Common on plains and mesas. *Dalea villosa* (Nutt.) Spreng., a similar species of sand hills east of our range, is densely hairy throughout.

GLYCYRRHIZA. Wild Liquorice

One species, ***Glycyrrhiza lepidota*** Pursh (scaly), Fig. 148. Abundant along irrigation ditches and sandy streambanks, plains and piedmont valleys. Flowers greenish-white. The cocklebur-like pods are unique in the family. A Mediterranean species is the source of liquorice.

HEDYSARUM

One species, ***Hedysarum boreale*** Nutt. (far-northern). Locally abundant on shale exposures on the mesas. Easily mistaken for *Astragalus* if fruits are not available. Flowers pink.

LATHYRUS. Peavine

1a. Flowers white. ***Lathyrus leucanthus*** Rydb., White-flowered Peavine.

Fig. 148. *Glycyrrhiza lepidota*

Forms dense colonies on slopes of gulches and canyons, mesas and foothills.

1b. Flowers purple, pink, or red .... (2)

2a. Flowers bright pink; leaflets 2; stem strongly winged. *Lathyrus latifolius* L., PERENNIAL SWEET PEA. Escaped from gardens and very common on urban fringes.

2b. Flowers blue, purple, or variegated pink and white; leaflets numerous; stem not strongly winged .... (3)

3a. Leaves silky-pubescent; flowers very fragrant. *Lathyrus polymorphus* Nutt. ssp. *incanus* (R. & S.) C. L. Hitchc., HOARY PEAVINE. Sandy soil on the plains.

3b. Leaves glabrous; flowers not very fragrant. *Lathyrus eucosmus* Butters & St. John (elegant), PURPLE PEAVINE. Gulches and canyons, plains and foothills.

LOTUS. BIRDFOOT TREFOIL

One species, *Lotus tenuis* Waldst. & Kit. (slender). Introduced and well established in a few places in the piedmont valleys.

LUPINUS. LUPINE

1a. Annual or biennial; racemes rarely overtopping the leaves; low plants. *Lupinus pusillus* Pursh (very small), LOW LUPINE. Sandy areas on the plains.

1b. Perennial; racemes exceeding the leaves; tall plants .... (2)

2a. Corolla blue, with a conspicuous dark spot on the standard. *Lupinus plattensis* Wats. (of the Platte River), NEBRASKA LUPINE. Common on the plains.

2b. Corolla blue, pink, or white, the standard not spotted. *Lupinus argenteus* Pursh (silvery), COMMON LUPINE, Fig. 149. Abundant and variable, mesas to subalpine.

MEDICAGO. ALFALFA; MEDIC

1a. Flowers yellow, in very small clusters; plants decumbent. *Medicago lupulina* L. (resembling hops), BLACK MEDIC. Common weed in lawns. Resembles a tiny yellow clover.

1b. Flowers purple to white, rarely with greenish-yellow color; heads large; plants usually erect. *Medicago sativa* L. (sown), ALFALFA. Cultivated for hay, and commonly escaped to roadsides and fields.

MELILOTUS. SWEET-CLOVER

1a. Flowers white. *Melilotus alba* Desr., WHITE SWEET-CLOVER. Extensively planted for forage, erosion control, and as a honey plant. Escaped to roadsides.

1b. Flowers yellow. *Melilotus officinalis* (L.) Lam. (of the shops). Range similar to the preceding.

OXYTROPIS. Loco-weed

1a. Pods pendulous; stipules only slightly adnate by their bases to the petioles; plants usually with leafy stems. ***Oxytropis deflexa*** (Pallas) DC. (bent downward). Dry lodgepole pine forests, subalpine.

1b. Pods erect or spreading, never pendulous; stipules adnate to the petiole; plants scapose or nearly so .... (2)

2a. Leaves having some of their leaflets in whorls. ***Oxytropis splendens*** Dougl., Showy Loco. Stony subalpine meadows. Flowers pink, the plant quite woolly-pubescent.

2b. Leaves strictly pinnate, the leaflets mostly paired .... (3)

3a. Fruiting calyx inflated and completely enclosing the ripe fruit; scapes less than 1.5 cm long, bearing only 1 to 4 flowers. ***Oxytropis multiceps*** Nutt. (many-headed), Tufted Loco. Open gravelly hilltops, foothills, montane. Flowers pink.

3b. Fruiting calyx not inflated and not completely enclosing the ripe fruit, or, if so, then the scapes much longer and bearing many flowers .... (4)

4a. Scapes short, bearing 1 to 4 flowers; dwarf alpine or subalpine plants .... (5)

4b. Scapes tall or bearing many flowers .... (6)

5a. Pod papery and inflated. ***Oxytropis podocarpa*** Gray (foot-like fruit). Rare, on high mountains, Grays Peak region.

5b. Pod not inflated, not papery, but leathery or woody at maturity. ***Oxytropis parryi*** Gray (for C. C. Parry). Montane to alpine, rather rare, our records being from gravelly benches of Clear Creek.

Fig. 149. *Lupinus argenteus*

6a. Plants sticky-glandular, at least on the calyx and bracts; rare species of the tundra. **Oxytropis viscida** Nutt. (sticky). Grays Peak region.

6b. Plants without sticky-glandular pubescence; lower elevations ... (7)

7a. Corolla purplish or red except in rare albino forms. **Oxytropis lambertii** Pursh (for A. B. Lambert), COLORADO LOCO, Fig. 150. The most common loco, from plains to subalpine. Hybridizes with *O. sericea* in the subalpine, producing plants intermediate in flower color.

7b. Corolla white or yellowish, the keel often purple-tinged, the whole corolla rarely purple-tinged .... (8)

8a. Flowers 12-15 mm long. **Oxytropis campestris** (L.) DC. var. **gracilis** (Nels.) Barneby. About a foot tall, with rather dense spikes of yellowish-white flowers. Could be confused with *O. sericea*, which has larger flowers. Montane, subalpine.

8b. Flowers 18-25 mm long. **Oxytropis sericea** Nutt. (silky). Common on mesas but largely absent from foothills and montane. Reappears in upper montane and subalpine, where it commonly hybridizes with *O. lambertii*. Hybrid individuals display flower colors from pink through various shades of pale violet, and usually retain the densely clumped habit of *O. sericea*.

PSORALEA

1a. Leaves all basal, overtopping the flower-clusters; plants with a deep-

Fig. 150. *Oxytropis lambertii*   Fig. 151. *Thermopsis divaricarpa*

seated potato-like root. ***Psoralea hypogaea*** Nutt. (underground). Locally abundant in sandy places on the plains.

1b. Plants with tall leafy stems, and otherwise not as above .... (2)

2a. Leaves white, pubescent. ***Psoralea argophylla*** Pursh (silvery-leaved). Locally abundant on the mesas, common farther out on the plains.

2b. Leaves green .... (3)

3a. Flowers white or cream-colored in dense racemes; leaflets linear. ***Psoralea lanceolata*** Pursh. Sandy places on the plains.

3b. Flowers blue or purple in loose racemes; leaflets elliptic. ***Psoralea tenuiflora*** Pursh (slender-flowered). Common on plains and mesas.

ROBINIA. Locust

1a. Flowers white, in a hanging raceme; pods smooth; tree. ***Robinia pseudoacacia*** L., Black Locust. Commonly cultivated as a street tree and around homesteads, persisting following abandonment of farms.

1b. Flowers purple, the short raceme not drooping; pods densely glandular-hirsute; shrub. ***Robinia neomexicana*** Gray. Native in foothills south of our area, but planted for windrows, escaping and locally established in some foothill canyons near Boulder and in the Black Forest.

SOPHORA

One species, ***Sophora nuttalliana*** B. L. Turner. Very common on the plains. Often mistaken for an *Astragalus*, but stamens are all separate. Flowers white; leaves silky-pubescent; pod constricted between the seeds.

THERMOPSIS. Golden Banner

1a. Pods stiffly erect, straight, densely pubescent. ***Thermopsis montana*** Nutt. Montane, and probably occurs rarely, if ever, east of the Continental Divide. Very common on the western slope.

1b. Pods strongly spreading or reflexed .... (2)

2a. Fruit spreading, moderately curved, somewhat pubescent. ***Thermopsis divaricarpa*** Nels. (with spreading pod), Fig. 151. Foothills to subalpine.

2b. Fruit reflexed, curved into half-circle or more, almost glabrous. ***Thermopsis rhombifolia*** (Nutt.) Rich. (rhombic-leaved). Sandy places on the plains. Blooms very early in the spring.

TRIFOLIUM. Clover

1a. Stems scapose, leaves chiefly basal; plants usually densely caespitose, restricted to tundra and subalpine slopes .... (2)

1b. Stems leafy, erect or creeping; plants not densely caespitose nor restricted to tundra and subalpine slopes .... (4)

2a. Flowers 1 to 3 per head. ***Trifolium nanum*** Torr. (dwarf), Fig. 152.

Common on tundra of the higher peaks. Flowers pink.

2b. Flowers numerous in each head .... (3)

3a. Flowers uniformly purple or rose-purple; stems few, leaflets broad; heads subtended by a papery involucre of fused bracts. ***Trifolium parryi*** Gray (for C. C. Parry). Common in moist subalpine meadows and on tundra.

3b. Flowers bicolored, the standard pale, the wings and keel pink- or purple-tipped. ***Trifolium dasyphyllum*** T. & G. (hairy-leaved), WHIPROOT CLOVER. Very common on alpine tundra.

4a. Heads subtended by an involucre of fused bracts; native species of upper montane and subalpine. ***Trifolium wormskjoldii*** Lehm. (for Morten Wormskjold, Danish botanist) (*T. fendleri* of Ed. 4).

4b. Heads not involucrate; introduced species .... (5)

5a. Calyx papery-inflated in fruit; flowers pink; creeping plants introduced on lawns and golf-courses. ***Trifolium fragiferum*** L. (bearing strawberries), STRAWBERRY CLOVER.

5b. Calyx not inflated in fruit; plants usually erect, or, if creeping, the flowers white .... (6)

6a. Flowers deep pink; plant hairy; heads terminal. ***Trifolium pratense*** L. (of meadows), RED CLOVER. Commonly escaped from cultivation.

6b. Flowers pale pink or white; plants sparsely hairy or glabrous ... (7)

Fig. 152. ***Trifolium nanum***   Fig. 153. ***Vicia americana***

7a. Stem erect or ascending; flowers pinkish; calyx pubescent in the sinuses between the teeth. ***Trifolium hybridum*** L. (hybrid; a misnomer), ALSIKE CLOVER (Alsike is a hamlet near Linnaeus' summer home).

7b. Stem creeping; flowers white; calyx glabrous or sparsely pubescent at the base. ***Trifolium repens*** L. (creeping), WHITE DUTCH CLOVER. Escaped from cultivation, but fully naturalized, especially in the mountains.

VICIA. VETCH

1a. Foliage densely villous; racemes many-flowered. ***Vicia villosa*** Roth. A Eurasian weed established in fields around Sedalia.

1b. Foliage not densely pubescent; racemes few-flowered ....(2)

2a. Flowers purple, pink, or blue. ***Vicia americana*** Muehl., Fig. 153. Common in spring on the plains and mesas.

2b. Flowers white, only purplish-tipped. ***Vicia exigua*** Nutt. Infrequent or rare, lower foothill slopes.

LENTIBULARIACEAE—BLADDERWORT FAMILY

A small family of mostly aquatic, often carnivorous plants. The bladderworts have flowers resembling the spurred ones of Butter-and-eggs and the submerged, finely divided leaves have some of the leaf-segments inflated to form a sac, open at one end, that acts as a trap for small aquatic animals such as *Paramecium*. Read F. E. Lloyd, *The Carnivorous Plants*, Chronica Botanica Co., 1943.

1a. Leaves pinnately divided, with a main rachis, the divisions usually well over 3 mm long. Corolla 10-12 mm broad, the spur conspicuous, long-pointed and curved. ***Utricularia vulgaris*** L., GREAT BLADDERWORT, Fig. 155. Ponds in the montane and subalpine.

1b. Leaves dichotomous, the divisions usually less than 3 mm long; corolla 5-6 mm broad, the spur almost lacking. ***Utricularia minor*** L., SMALL BLADDERWORT, Fig. 155. Rare or easily overlooked, similar habitats.

LINACEAE—FLAX FAMILY

The word linen comes from *Linum*, Flax, cultivated from ancient times as a source of fibre which is obtained by the process of retting (curing of the stems in water). *Linum* is also the source of Linseed Oil, a drying oil of a thousand uses. The seeds of flax are used medicinally. Flax blossoms open early in the morning and usually fall by mid-day. They come in yellow, copper, and one of the truest blues found in nature.

1a. Flowers yellow. ***Linum rigidum*** Pursh, YELLOW FLAX. Plains and outer foothills, Larimer County and eastward.

1b. Flowers blue ....(2)

2a. Plant perennial; stigmas only slightly longer than wide. ***Linum lewisii*** Pursh (for Meriwether Lewis), WILD FLAX, Fig. 154. Abundant from plains to upper montane. Petals blue, easily detached.

2b. Plant annual; stigmas considerably longer than wide. ***Linum usitatissimum*** L., (much-used), CULTIVATED FLAX. Occasional as a weed, piedmont valleys. Flowers blue.

LOASACEAE—LOASA FAMILY

The sandpaper surface of the leaves of *Mentzelia* is caused by some of the strangest plant hairs known. These multicellular hairs are "pagodaeform," broad-based, shaped like pagodas, each cell capped by a ring of stiff, curved hooks, which, unlike the corners of pagoda roofs, curve down, not up. There is hardly an article of clothing that will not carry away the leaves or fruits of *Mentzelia*. The flowers of *Mentzelia* are inconspicuous until they open wide at eventide, like the Night-blooming Cereus cactus which they resemble.

1a. Petals 2-5 mm long; capsule linear-cylindric, widest at the apex, less than 5 mm in diameter .... (2)

1b. Petals over 1 cm long; capsule broadly cylindric, broadest near the middle, over 5 mm in diameter .... (4)

2a. Seeds prismatic, truncate at the ends, grooved on three sides; bracts on the hypanthium ovate; flowers more or less crowded. ***Mentzelia dispersa*** Wats. (scattered). Frequent on dry slopes in the foothills.

2b. Seeds cuboidal, lacking grooves along the angles; bracts linear; flowers not crowded together .... (3)

3a. Seeds with large pointed papillae; bracts usually entire; petals

Fig. 154. ***Linum lewisii***

notched; capsules usually over 2 cm long. ***Mentzelia albicaulis*** Dougl. (white-stemmed). Common on the plains and mesas.

3b. Seeds with small rounded papillae; bracts toothed; petals obtuse; capsules usually less than 2 cm long. ***Mentzelia montana*** (Davidson) Davidson. Infrequent in the outer foothills and mesas.

4a. Bracts on or just below the hypanthium linear, not lobed; petals distinctly yellow . . . . (5)

4b. Bracts on or just below the hypanthium lobed, dentate or cleft; petals mostly white or cream-colored . . . . (6)

5a. All petals creamy-white or very pale yellow both inside and outside; mature seeds minutely punctate. ***Mentzelia multiflora*** (Nutt.) Gray, MANY-FLOWERED EVENING-STAR. Gravelly slopes in the outer foothill canyons.

5b. Petals in two series, the outer five white outside, lemon yellow inside, the inner five lemon yellow outside, golden yellow inside; mature seeds not punctate. ***Mentzelia speciosa*** Osterh. (handsome), YELLOW EVENING-STAR. Common on shale outcrops on the mesas, and in the foothill canyons. See Addenda.

6a. Petals 5-8 cm long. ***Mentzelia decapetala*** (Pursh) Urban & Gilg (ten-petaled), GIANT EVENING-STAR, Plate 14. Locally abundant on sandstone outcrops on the mesas and plains.

6b. Petals not over 4 cm long . . . . (7)

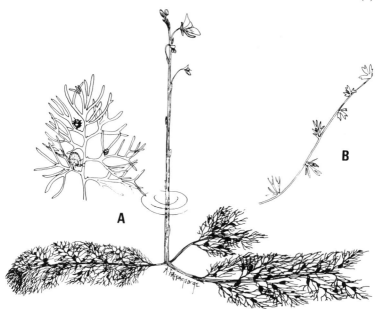

Fig. 155. A, ***Utricularia vulgaris***; B, ***U. minor***

7a. Petals 1.5-2.0 cm long. ***Mentzelia rusbyi*** Wooton (for Henry Rusby),
New Mexican Evening-star. Common in the intermountain valleys
west of the Front Range but occasional within the range of the next.

7b. Petals 2.5-4.0 cm long. ***Mentzelia nuda*** (Pursh) T. & G. Plains
Evening-star, Fig. 156. Abundant on the plains and piedmont
valleys in sandy soils.

Lythraceae—Loosestrife Family

A family with an ambiguous common name, because loosestrifes also
occur in the Primulaceae. Our species are inconspicuous nondescript
herbs with small rose-colored flowers. Two exotic species are worth
mentioning, however. *Lagerstroemia indica*, the Crepe-myrtle, is a striking
cultivar of the Gulf Coast with fringed and puckered petals with a narrow
claw; and *Lawsonia indica*, the Henna, was called by Mohammed "chief of
the flowers of this world and the next." However, no one has returned to
report the existence of this remarkable plant in the next world, and we do
not know whether hair dye or nail coloring is useful there. *Lawsonia* was
named for a surveyor-general of North Carolina who was burned by the
Indians in 1712.

Fig. 156. *Mentzelia nuda*

1a. Calyx narrow, cylindrical or tubular, with several prominent longitudinal ribs; petals usually conspicuous, rose-purple. ***Lythrum alatum*** Pursh, WINGED LOOSESTRIFE. Swamps and ditches, piedmont valleys and plains.

1b. Calyx broad, bell-shaped or top-shaped in flower, hemispheric or globose in fruit, not prominently ribbed; petals inconspicuous or lacking. ***Ammannia coccinea*** Rottb., SCARLET AMMANNIA. Drying shores of ponds on the plains, flowering in late summer.

MALVACEAE—MALLOW FAMILY

Everyone knows hollyhocks. Most old folks can remember making dolls with long dresses out of the flowers. Most mallow flowers are smaller copies of the Hollyhock. The main distinguishing feature of mallow flowers is the column of united stamen filaments forming a sheath around the gynoecium and standing in the midst of the flower like a fountain spraying out hundreds of tiny colored droplets, the anthers. Also, the leaves and stems are usually clothed with stellately-branched hairs. Although some species have a capsular fruit, most have a gynoecium resembling a wheel of cheese, with the carpels sloughing away at maturity as one-seeded disks (mericarps).

The confection, marshmallow, used to be based on the mucilaginous contents of the root of the Marsh Mallow, *Althaea officinalis*, which grows in marshes of western Europe and New England. Now there are synthetic sources. One of the important crops of man, cotton (*Gossypium*), is a mallow, as are the vegetable okra or gumbo, *Hibiscus esculentus*, and the ornamental shrub, Rose-of-Sharon (*Hibiscus syriacus*).

1a. Leaves very shallowly lobed, almost circular in outline, crenate-toothed; corolla pale pink or white ....(2)

1b. At least some of the leaves very deeply cleft or lobed; corolla white, deep orange, red, purple, or yellow ....(4)

2a. Petals twice as long as the calyx, about 1 cm long; carpels round-margined, smooth or only slightly reticulated on the back. ***Malva***

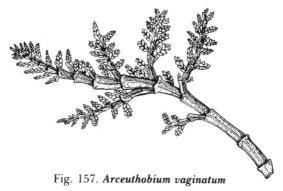

Fig. 157. *Arceuthobium vaginatum*

neglecta Wallr., CHEESEWEED, Fig. 158. A very common weed in lawns and gardens, growing from a very tenacious tap root and spreading horizontally to crowd out grass. The common name alludes to the shape of the ripe ovary, like a white wheel of cheese.

2b. Petals scarcely to barely exceeding the calyx; carpels acute-margined, rugose-reticulate .... (3)

3a. Claws of petals glabrous; calyx enlarged and widely spreading under the fruit, veiny-reticulate; carpels glabrous, with thin margins and denticulate angles. *Malva parviflora* L. Infrequent, in similar places.

3b. Claws of petals hairy; calyx barely enlarged, mostly closed over fruit, scarcely reticulate; carpels at first tomentulose, becoming glabrate, with acute wingless angles. *Malva rotundifolia* L. One record, from a garden in Boulder. The three above are all Eurasian weeds.

4a. Flowers white or cream-colored. *Sidalcea candida* Gray (shining-white), WHITE CHECKERMALLOW, Fig. 159. Wet subalpine meadows. Stems tall, solitary or a few together; upper leaves much more deeply dissected than the lower. On the western slope, from Routt County southwestward, a very handsome relative with tall stems and maple-like leaves, and very large white or rose-colored petals, is *Iliamna rivularis* (Dougl.) Greene.

4b. Flowers pink, purple, orange or yellow .... (5)

5a. Flowers orange-red, short-pedicelled, in dense, short racemes. *Sphaeralcea coccinea* (Pursh) Rydb. (scarlet), COPPER MALLOW, Fig. 160.

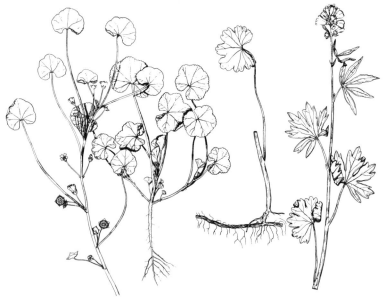

Fig. 158. *Malva neglecta*   Fig. 159. *Sidalcea candida*

Abundant along roadsides and on dry prairies and sagebrush lands, plains and mesas. Leaves deeply palmately dissected, stellate-pubescent. This plant is often so abundant as to line the roadside for miles.

5b. Flowers pink, purple or yellow, rather long-pedicelled, in few-flowered racemes or solitary in the leaf axils .... (6)

6a. All leaves of approximately the same shape and depth of lobing; plants with a carrot-like taproot; low, spreading or prostrate plant of sandy soil on the plains or a garden weed .... (7)

6b. Lower leaves deeply crenate but not nearly so deeply lobed or dissected as the upper leaves; root system branched, woody; tall, unbranched plants of wet montane and subalpine meadows. *Sidalcea neomexicana* Gray. Very common west of the Continental Divide, but apparently rare within our range.

7a. Corolla red-purple. *Callirhoë involucrata* (T. & G.) Gray, PURPLE POPPYMALLOW.Common on sandy soil on the plains.

7b. Corolla yellow with a purple-black "eye"; calyx conspicuously inflated in fruit with dark veins. *Hibiscus trionum* L., FLOWER-OF-AN-HOUR. A native of Africa, accidentally introduced here and becoming a fairly common weed at the base of the Front Range in gardens and on farms.

MENYANTHACEAE—BUCKBEAN FAMILY

One species, *Menyanthes trifoliata* L., BUCKBEAN or MARSH TREFOIL, Fig. 161, grows in subalpine ponds. The leaves and flower stalks rise above water level, and the very spongy stalks and rhizomes are rooted in the mud. The flowers are unusually attractive, with recurved white petals covered with a dense brush of crinkly white or pinkish hairs. Like the pond-lilies, it is a mystery why they occur in some ponds and not in others.

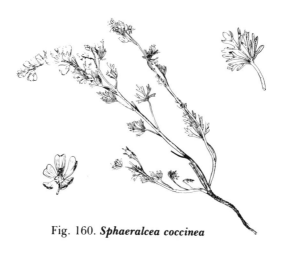

Fig. 160. *Sphaeralcea coccinea*

MORACEAE—MULBERRY FAMILY

One native genus and species, ***Humulus lupulus*** L. var. ***neomexicanus***
Nels. & Cockerell, WILD HOPS, Fig. 162. Clambering over shrubs and
rocky slopes, canyons and foothills, sometimes a weed in gardens. The
fruits are in pale papery clusters, conspicuous in fall. There is very little
difference between the wild hops and the cultivated ones used in
flavoring beer. The herbalist, Gerard, in 1633, wrote: "The manifold
vertues of Hops do manifestly argue the wholesomenesse of beere above
ale, for the hops rather make it a physickall drinke, to keepe the body in
health, than an ordinary drinke for the quenching of our thirst."

NYCTAGINACEAE—FOUR-O'CLOCK FAMILY

A small family characterized by the often tubular petal-like calyx,
inferior ovary forming a one-seeded often winged nutlet, opposite fleshy
leaves and umbellate flower clusters subtended by conspicuous, often
papery bracts. Few species occur in Colorado, but many species of Sand-
verbena bloom on the sandy deserts of the southwest. The cultivated
Garden Four-o'clock, *Mirabilis jalapa*, is a native of South America.

1a. Flower cluster surrounded by an involucre of several separate bracts;
flowers tubular, numerous in an umbellate cluster .... (2)

Fig. 161. *Menyanthes trifoliata*

1b. Flower cluster surrounded by a single bract or by a group of fused bracts; flowers rotate or campanulate, few in each cluster, very short-lived and ephemeral .... (3)

2a. Fruit with low, thickened ridges; flowers 2 cm or more long, white or pinkish. ***Abronia fragrans*** Nutt. *ex* Hook., SAND-VERBENA, Plate 21, Fig. 163. Sandy soil on the plains. Leaves opposite, thickish, ovate or oval.
2b. Fruit with papery wings; flower 2 cm long or less, greenish-white. ***Tripterocalyx micranthus*** (Torr.) Hook. (small-flowered), WING-FRUITED SAND-VERBENA. Sandy soil on the plains.

3a. Leaves linear or narrowly linear-lanceolate, usually glaucous. ***Oxybaphus linearis*** (Pursh) Robinson, NARROW-LEAVED UMBRELLA-WORT. Common on plains and mesas. Flowers pink.
3b. Leaves broader, not glaucous .... (4)

4a. Flowers 3-5 cm long, tubular-campanulate, very showy, magenta, each flower-cluster surrounded by a deep cup-shaped involucre. ***Mirabilis multiflora*** (Torr.) Gray (many-flowered), WILD FOUR-O'CLOCK,

Fig. 162. ***Humulus lupulus***

Fig. 163. ***Abronia fragrans***

Plate 23, Fig. 164. Pinon-juniper belt, barely entering our range on the south.

4b. Flowers smaller, rotate, the involucre shallow, saucer-shaped .... (5)

5a. All but the uppermost leaves distinctly petioled, ovate or cordate, glabrous. ***Oxybaphus nyctagineus*** (Michx.) Porter & Coulter (resembling the genus *Nyctago*, HEART-LEAVED UMBRELLA-WORT. Frequent as a weed in waste or cultivated ground.

5b. Leaves sessile or with very short and inconspicuous petioles, lance-ovate, hirsute. ***Oxybaphus hirsutus*** Sweet, HAIRY UMBRELLA-WORT. Frequent on mesas and open foothill slopes. Intermediates (probably hybrids) between this and *O. linearis* are frequent.

NYMPHAEACEAE—WATER-LILY FAMILY

The white or pink-flowered water-lilies belong to the genus *Nymphaea*. The sacred Lotus of the East is *Nelumbo*, cultivated in India for its edible rhizomes and fruit. A South American species, *Victoria amazonica*, has floating leaves up to 2 meters in diameter, strongly reinforced against buffeting of wave action and having an upturned rim. These leaves are claimed to support the weight of a child. In Scandinavian folklore there is a troll called "näck" who sits at the bottom of lakes and fishes for people, using the stem and flower of the Water-lily (the Näck-rose) as a lure.

One genus and species, ***Nuphar luteum*** Sibth. & Sm. ssp. ***polysepalum*** (Engelm.) Beal, YELLOW POND-LILY; SPATTERDOCK, Fig. 165. Occasional in subalpine ponds. Very sporadic in its occurrence.

Fig. 164. *Mirabilis multiflora*

OLEACEAE—OLIVE FAMILY

Our only genus is *Fraxinus*, the Ash, represented by the single species, **Fraxinus *pennsylvanica*** Marsh. var. *lanceolata* Sarg., the GREEN ASH. This is not native in Colorado but escapes from cultivation and in many places persists as if it were native. On the western slope our only native Ash, F. *anomala*, is "anomalous" because the leaves are usually simple!

ONAGRACEAE—EVENING-PRIMROSE FAMILY

Evening-primroses are unrelated to true primroses. This is the meaning of the hyphen between the words. Many are attractive, morning- and evening-flowering plants pollinated by night-flying long-tongued moths. The floral formula for most of them (4 sepals, 4 petals, 8 stamens, 4 united carpels in an inferior ovary) is unique, but because of their 4-merous pattern they are sometimes, especially those with small flowers, mistaken for crucifers. Hugo DeVries propounded the Mutation Theory in 1901 from studies on an Evening-primrose, *Oenothera*. The mutation theory stands today, despite the fact that the phenomena DeVries thought were mutations in *Oenothera* turned out to be the result of another genetic mechanism. It remained for others to demonstrate true mutations in other plants and animals. Horticulturally, the family is best known for *Fuchsia*, an Andean genus.

1a. Flowers with parts in twos; ovary spherical; leaves broadly ovate, long-petioled. *Circaea*, ENCHANTERS NIGHTSHADE, page 244.

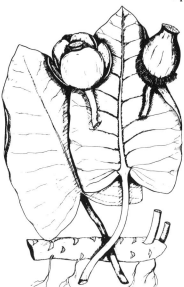

Fig. 165. *Nuphar luteum*

1b. Flowers with parts in fours; ovary more or less elongate; leaves narrower, short-petioled or sessile .... (2)

2a. Seeds with a tuft of hairs (coma) at one end; flowers pink or white, never yellow .... (3)
2b. Seeds without coma; flowers pink, white or yellow .... (4)

3a. Flowers large, the petals 1-2 cm long, entire, spreading; hypanthium not prolonged beyond the ovary. *Chamerion*, FIREWEED, page 244.
3b. Flowers smaller, the petals usually notched, ascending; hypanthium prolonged beyond the ovary. *Epilobium*, WILLOW-HERB, page 245.

4a. Fruit nut-like, indehiscent. *Gaura*, page 246.
4b. Fruit a dehiscent, usually elongate, capsule .... (5)

5a. Flowers minute; plants very delicate, with slender branches; ovary with 2 locules; hypanthium not prolonged beyond the ovary as a slender tube. *Gayophytum*, page 247.
5b. Flowers showy; plants moderately stout; ovary with 4 locules; hypanthium prolonged beyond the ovary as a slender tube ...... (6)

6a. Stigma deeply 4-lobed; flowers white, pink, or yellow, if yellow the plants either stemless or with a tall unbranched leafy stem. *Oenothera*, EVENING-PRIMROSE, page 247.
6b. Stigma disk-like or very shallowly 4-lobed; flowers yellow, the stems much branched, with small, serrulate leaves. *Calylophus*, page 244.

CALYLOPHUS

One species, *Calylophus serrulata* (Nutt.) Raven. Gravelly or sandy soil on the plains and mesas (*Oenothera serrulata* Nutt.).

CHAMERION. FIREWEED

1a. Racemes elongate, many-flowered, not leafy; styles hairy at the base, exceeding the stamens; leaves 5-20 cm long, veiny. *Chamerion angustifolium* (L.) Holub (narrow-leaved), FIREWEED, Fig. 166. Abundant along roadsides and in burned areas, upper montane and subalpine. Flowers pink.
1b. Racemes few-flowered, leafy; style glabrous, shorter than the stamens; leaves 2-6 cm long, glaucous, not veiny. *Chamerion latifolium* (L.) Holub (broad-leaved), ALPINE FIREWEED. Talus slopes and streamsides near timberline, locally abundant but not widespread. Flowers pink. This group has been called *Epilobium* in America, but belongs to a distinct group of mostly Eurasiatic species, which until recently went under the name of *Chamaenerion*.

CIRCAEA. ENCHANTERS NIGHTSHADE

One species, *Circaea alpina* L. Cool ravines in the foothills. Plant delicate, with opposite, denticulate leaves; flowers tiny, in a raceme; fruit covered with tiny hooked bristles.

EPILOBIUM. Willow-herb

To ensure proper identification, *Epilobium* should be collected with underground parts in order to determine the presence or absence of turions. Turions are compact overwintering tuberlike structures of thick overlapping fleshy scales persisting on the base of the next season's stems as dry brown structures. They must not be confused with scaly bulbous structures at the ends of stolons, or fleshy rosettes of leaves, or scaly branches that develop into leafy shoots. It is a technical point but well worth careful observation. Underground parts should be carefully washed; if the turions fall away their presence should be recorded.

1a. Annual; stems with peeling epidermis; leaves usually alternate. ***Epilobium paniculatum*** Nutt., Annual Willow-herb. Common weedy herb of disturbed roadsides in the mountains. Often mistaken for a crucifer or for *Gayophytum*.
1b. Perennial; epidermis not peeling; leaves mostly opposite .... (2)

2a. Turions present .... (3)
2b. Turions absent .... (5)

3a. Flowers large, the petals 5-10 mm long. ***Epilobium glandulosum*** Lehm., Northern Willow-herb. Swampy depressions, plains to upper montane.
3b. Flowers smaller, the petals 2-5 mm long .... (4)

Fig. 166. ***Chamerion angustifolium***

4a. Leaves lance-linear, not crowded, the margins often irregularly dentate. **Epilobium halleanum** Hausskn. Infrequent, Rocky Mountain National Park northwestward, subalpine forests.

4b. Leaves ovate with rounded bases, usually longer than the internodes, the margins usually entire. **Epilobium saximontanum** Hausskn. Common in subalpine forests.

5a. Leaves long and linear, not over 3 mm wide; tall plants of swampy areas. **Epilobium leptophyllum** Raf. (narrow-leaved). Rare in piedmont valleys, plains and mountain parks.

5b. Leaves broader and shorter .... (6)

6a. Tall, rank and weedy plants; plants producing leafy rosettes from base of old stems. **Epilobium adenocaulon** Hausskn. Very similar to *E. glandulosum* and in similar sites.

6b. Low, more delicate plants overwintering by branching scaly rhizomes which send out new shoots .... (7)

7a. Plants low and spreading, often in dense clumps, hardly over 20 cm tall, the stems often S-shaped; leaves 8-20 mm long .... (8)

7b. Plants erect, solitary or a few together, up to 40 cm or more tall, stems straight; leaves up to 50 mm long .... (9)

8a. Inflorescence nodding in bud; leaves oblong to narrowly ovate, thin, nearly entire; seeds smooth, 1 mm long. **Epilobium anagallidifolium** Lam., ALPINE WILLOW-HERB. Common along snow-melt streamlets in subalpine and alpine.

8b. Inflorescence erect in bud; leaves broadly ovate, thickish, more or less serrulate; seeds papillose, 1.5-2.0 mm long. **Epilobium clavatum** Trelease, BOULDERFIELD WILLOW-HERB. On rocky summits, Larimer County northwestward.

9a. Petals white or with pink tips, 3-4 mm long; seeds smooth; base of stem with several pairs of broad withered leaves at flowering time. **Epilobium lactiflorum** Hausskn. (milky-flowered). Wet meadows and streamsides, subalpine.

9b. Petals purplish, 5-7 mm long; seeds more or less papillose; base of stem with small and inconspicuous or no withered leaves. **Epilobium hornemannii** Hausskn. (for Jens W. Hornemann). Common in similar sites.

GAURA

1a. Plant less than one meter tall; anthers linear, 2-5 mm long; sepals 5-11 mm long; petals 3-10 mm long .... (2)

1b. Plant over a meter tall, with long naked spikes; anthers oval, 0.5-1.0 mm long; sepals 1.5-3.0 mm long; petals 1.5-2.0 mm long. **Gaura parviflora** Dougl. *ex* Hook. Tall weedy plant of roadsides on the mesas and plains.

2a. Stems erect, 40-70 cm tall; stem leaves 5-10 cm long; hypanthium

7-12 mm long; petals 8-10 mm long. *Gaura neomexicana* Wooton var. *coloradensis* (Rydb.) Munz. Rare, plains and outer foothills.

2b. Stems ascending or spreading, seldom over 30 cm tall; stem leaves 1-3.5 cm long; hypanthium 5-8 mm long; petals 3-6 mm long. *Gaura coccinea* Nutt., SCARLET GAURA. Dry sites on mesas and plains. Flowers white, turning pink in age.

GAYOPHYTUM

1a. Pedicels of mature capsules less than 3 mm long; petals less than 2 mm long . . . . (2)

1b. Pedicels of mature capsules 3 mm long or longer; petals 0.5-3.0 mm long . . . . (3)

2a. Branched only in the lower half; secondary branches few or none, the branching not dichotomous. *Gayophytum racemosum* T. & G. Gravelly soils throughout the forested mountains.

2b. Branched throughout or at least in the upper half; secondary branches evident. *Gayophytum diffusum* T. & G. ssp. *parviflorum* H. Lewis & Szweykowski. Similar habitats.

3a. Seeds crowded, overlapping, usually 2 rows in each locule; capsules terete . . . . (4)

3b. Seeds not crowded, in one row in each locule; capsules somewhat flattened or conspicuously torulose (constricted at intervals) (return to 2).

4a. Petals less than 1.5 mm long; pedicels equalling or longer than the capsules. *Gayophytum ramosissimum* T. & G. Similar habitats.

4b. Petals 1.5-3.0 mm long; pedicels equalling or shorter than the capsules. *Gayophytum diffusum* T. & G. ssp. *parviflorum*. Similar habitats.

OENOTHERA. EVENING-PRIMROSE

1a. Plants stemless; flowers very large, amid a cluster of basal leaves . . . . (2)

1b. Plants with leafy stems; flowers not as above . . . . (4)

2a. Flowers yellow; fruit sharply 4-winged, not warty . . . . (3)

2b. Flowers white, turning pink; capsule not strongly winged, but usually warty on the surface. *Oenothera caespitosa* Nutt. (in clumps), WHITE STEMLESS EVENING-PRIMROSE, Fig. 167. Abundant on plains, mesas, and canyonsides in the foothills.

3a. Petals 1.5-2.5 cm long; leaves usually narrow and deeply pinnatifid. *Oenothera flava* (Nels.) Munz (yellow). Mesas and plains. Flowers turning pink in age.

3b. Petals 4-6 cm long; leaves usually broad and very shallowly pinnatifid or almost entire. *Oenothera brachycarpa* Gray (short-fruited), YELLOW STEMLESS EVENING-PRIMROSE. Common on the mesas. Flowers turning orange-red in age.

4a. Flowers yellow; stems tall, usually simple, with broadly lanceolate leaves. ***Oenothera strigosa*** (Rydb.) Mack. & Bush (with appressed hairs), Common Evening-primrose. Tall, weedy plants of plains and foothills, flowering in late summer.

4b. Flowers white or pink .... (5)

5a. Leaves linear or narrowly lanceolate, entire or nearly so. ***Oenothera nuttallii*** Sweet (for Thomas Nuttall). Mesas and lower foothills.

5b. Leaves broader, deeply pinnatifid .... (6)

6a. Perennial from slender underground rhizomes; hypanthium with white hairs in the throat; petals 7-11 mm long; capsule 8-20 mm long. ***Oenothera coronopifolia*** T. & G. (with leaves like *Coronopus*, a mustard), Cut-leaf Evening-primrose. Dry slopes, plains to montane.

6b. Annual or winter annual; hypanthium not long-hairy in the throat; petals 15-40 mm long; capsule 20-40 mm long. ***Oenothera albicaulis*** Pursh (white-stemmed), Prairie Evening-primrose. Abundant on barren sandy soils on the plains.

Orobanchaceae—Broom-rape Family

By carefully digging around an *Orobanche*, the holdfast connecting this parasite to the host plant can usually be located. Our species of *Orobanche* are commonly parasitic on species of Compositae, including *Artemisia* and *Ambrosia*. The flowers remind one of Scrophulariaceae such as *Penstemon*.

1a. Flowers conspicuously long-peduncled, without accessory bractlets .... (2)

1b. Flowers sessile or on short peduncles; a pair of bractlets situated just below the calyx in addition to the normal subtending bract ... (3)

Fig. 167. ***Oenothera caespitosa***

2a. Pedicels 1 to 3, much longer than the short and inconspicuous main stem; calyx lobes slender, longer than the tube. ***Orobanche uniflora*** L., Fig. 168. Uncommon in montane and subalpine meadows.
2b. Pedicels 4 to 10 or more, not longer than the relatively long main stem; calyx-lobes broader, shorter than or equalling the tube. ***Orobanche fasciculata*** Nutt., Fig. 168. Common and usually associated with sagebrush, plains to montane.

3a. Corolla lobes acute; anthers woolly-hairy. ***Orobanche ludoviciana*** Nutt. Infrequent on hogbacks of the foothills near Fort Collins and probably elsewhere.
3b. Corolla lobes rounded; anthers glabrous, not woolly. ***Orobanche multifida*** Nutt., Fig. 168. Abundant on sand hills on the plains. Parasitic on *Ambrosia*.

OXALIDACEAE—WOOD-SORREL FAMILY

Oxalis plants, with their three-parted leaves with heart-shaped leaflets, are commonly sold as Irish shamrocks, but whether the original shamrock used by St. Patrick to symbolize the Doctrine of the Trinity

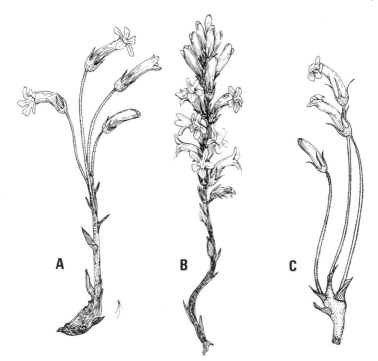

Fig. 168. A, ***Orobanche fasciculata***; B, ***O. multiflora***; C, ***O uniflora***

was an *Oxalis* or a *Trifolium* is debatable. The leaves of *Oxalis* contain oxalic acid and are pleasantly tart when chewed. Tubers of *Oxalis crenata* (the "oca" of crossword puzzles) have been an important foodstuff in Peru since ancient Inca times.

1a. Plants tall, usually simple, from an underground rhizome; stem and petioles with some septate (multicellular) hairs that become crinkled and show prominent reddish cross-walls; foliage green or sometimes deep red. ***Oxalis stricta*** L., WOOD-SORREL. Usually a garden weed.

1b. Stems low, branched from the base, without underground horizontal rhizomes; stem and petioles with straight or curved, simple hairs only, usually appressed to the stem; foliage distinctly glaucous. ***Oxalis dillenii*** Jacq., WOOD-SORREL, Fig. 169. The common native species of the plains and mesas. Flowers are yellow in both species.

PAPAVERACEAE—POPPY FAMILY

In poppy flowers the calyx is united from top to bottom. It does not open, but breaks away by a dehiscent line at its base when forced by the pressure of the expanding corolla, which is crumpled like a handkerchief in the bud. Open flowers therefore have no calyx. The unopened flower might be misinterpreted to be a fruit since the calyx may be crowned with style-like horns.

Fig. 169. ***Oxalis dillenii***   Fig. 170. ***Argemone polyanthemos***

1a. Petals white or scarlet, large (over 4 cm long) .... (2)
1b. Petals pale yellow or bright orange, smaller .... (4)

2a. Petals white; foliage spiny on the margins and veins; native plants of the mesas and plains .... (3)
2b. Petals scarlet with a purplish-black basal spot; foliage stiff-hairy but not spiny. ***Papaver orientale*** L., ORIENTAL POPPY. Escaped from cultivation and becoming established near towns and old homesteads.

3a. Leaves spiny but not pubescent; bristles on fruit comparatively few and stout. ***Argemone polyanthemos*** (Fedde) G. B. Ownbey (many-flowered), PRICKLY POPPY, Plate 31, Fig. 170. Abundant on the plains and mesas, flowering throughout the summer.
3b. Leaves minutely and densely pubescent in addition to being bristly; pods thickly covered by slender bristles. ***Argemone hispida*** Gray, PRICKLY POPPY. Similar habitats.

4a. Pod short and broad, goblet-shaped; alpine tundra plants with pale yellow, often almost white, flowers. ***Papaver kluanense*** D. Löve, ALPINE POPPY. Rare and endangered species, occurring in very small stands. A commonly cultivated relative, the Iceland Poppy, *Papaver croceum* Ledeb., with larger, bright orange flowers, sometimes persists as if wild around old mountain townsites.
4b. Pods elongate, linear, curved; introduced weeds along roadsides and in vacant lots in the outer valleys .... (5)

5a. Plant tall, the leaves with broad pinnate divisions; pod 15-20 cm long; petals yellow. ***Glaucium flavum*** Crantz, HORNED POPPY. Occasional weed in vacant lots, Boulder.
5b. Plant low, the leaves with many linear divisions; pod less than 10 cm long; petals orange. ***Eschscholtzia californica*** Cham., CALIFORNIA POPPY. Well-established as a roadside weed along the base of the mountains, native in the Pacific Coast states.

PLANTAGINACEAE—PLANTAIN FAMILY

The word plantain comes from Latin *planta*, the sole of the foot, and alludes to the usually broad spreading leaf. The tropical plantains, related to the Banana, bear no relation to our plantains but are monocots in the Musaceae. Some of our plantains are common dooryard weeds, and all are recognized by the cluster of basal leaves, and spikes of flowers with papery corollas, and a peculiar ovary that dehisces by a horizontal rift (circumscissilely).

1a. Leaves linear to filiform, rarely over 1 cm wide; plants annual (2)
1b. Leaves lanceolate to ovate, over 1 cm wide; plants perennial .. (3)

2a. Plants densely woolly-pubescent; lower floral bracts commonly exceeding the flowers. ***Plantago patagonica*** Jacq. (from Patagonia),

Fig. 171. A, ***Plantago patagonica***; B, ***P. elongata***; C, ***P. major***; D, ***P. lanceolata***

WOOLLY PLANTAIN, Fig. 171. Abundant on barren soils and overgrazed range, mesas and plains.
2b. Plants almost glabrous, none of the bracts exceeding the flowers. *Plantago elongata* Pursh, SLENDER PLANTAIN, Fig. 171. Locally abundant on alkali flats in the piedmont valleys, flowering in June.

3a. Leaf-blades broadly ovate, abruptly contracted to the petiole; seeds 6 to 20 in a capsule. *Plantago major* L., COMMON PLANTAIN, Fig. 171. Abundant weed in lawns.
3b. Leaf-blades lanceolate, if broader, then tapering to the petiole; seeds few (2 to 4) .... (4)

4a. Papery corollas with petals broad, 2 mm long, spreading and persistent, hiding the fruits; spikes short and broad at flowering time, the stamens with long filaments, forming a ring around the spike. *Plantago lanceolata* L., ENGLISH PLANTAIN, Fig. 171. An abundant weed in lawns and golf courses.
4b. Papery corollas with narrow petals, 1 mm long, never hiding the fruits; spikes usually elongate, at least in age, the stamens not as above .... (5)

5a. Leaf-base covered with reddish-brown wool; spikes over 5 cm long; leaves thick. *Plantago eriopoda* Torr. (woolly-footed), REDWOOL PLANTAIN. Wet places and alkali flats, piedmont valleys and mountain parks.
5b. Leaf-bases not woolly or only slightly so; spikes usually shorter; leaves not thick or fleshy. *Plantago tweedyi* Gray (for Frank Tweedy). Common in the mountains west of the Divide, one record in Rocky Mountain National Park east of the Divide.

POLEMONIACEAE—PHLOX FAMILY

The breeding behavior of two species of Trumpet Gilia, *Ipomopsis aggregata* and *I. candida* provides one of the most spectacular floral displays in the Front Range area. Along a wide zone of overlap, the southern scarlet-flowered species hybridizes with the northern cream-colored species. The resultant combinations and intermediate states of color and flower form present a bewildering array and a classic example of the phenomenon of introgressive hybridization, in which the genotype of one species infiltrates that of another. Outside the area of overlap, the parental species show relatively little evidence of this although careful study often shows that infiltration has in fact occurred. Read Edgar Anderson, *Introgressive Hybridization*, John Wiley & Sons, 1949.

1a. Leaves all simple, entire or palmately cleft to near the base (if pinnately cleft, then with sharp, pungent segments) .... (2)
1b. At least some of the basal leaves lobed or pinnatifid or pinnately compound but never prickly pointed .... (6)

2a. Leaves rigid, needle-like, in clusters at the nodes; plants of the plains and foothills .... (8)
2b. Leaves neither rigid nor needle-like nor clustered at the nodes, or if so, then plants of the alpine .... (3)

3a. Flowers showy, the corolla 1 cm or more wide; all leaves opposite. *Phlox*, page 258.
3b. Flowers small and inconspicuous, the corolla less than 5 mm wide; upper leaves usually alternate .... (4)

4a. True stem leaves lacking, the flower cluster subtended by a cup of leaflike bracts. *Gymnosteris*, page 256.
4b. True leaves present, scattered along the stem .... (5)

5a. Leaves elliptic, obtuse; flowers solitary in the leaf axils. *Microsteris,* page 257.
5b. Leaves lanceolate or linear, acute; flowers in dense clusters in the upper leaf axils. *Collomia*, page 254.

6a. Leaves pinnatifid into narrow segments but not distinctly compound (that is, the segments not stalked or abruptly narrowed to the base) .... (7)
6b. Leaves distinctly compound, with elliptic leaflets abruptly narrowed to the base. *Polemonium*, JACOBS LADDER; SKY PILOT, page 259.

7a. Flowers small, less than 1 cm long, in delicately branched inflorescences, the corolla tube funnelform, expanded into a wider throat above; leaves usually much reduced above the basal rosette. *Gilia*, page 256.
7b. Flowers 1 cm long or more, in racemes or branched inflorescences, if small then in dense spikes; corolla tube not differentiated, trumpet-shaped; stem usually quite leafy to the inflorescence. *Ipomopsis*, page 256.

8a. Annuals .... (9)
8b. Perennials, woody at the base .... (10)

9a. Flowers creamy white; stems very slender, the leaves appearing whorled, not at all prickly. *Linanthus*, page 257.
9b. Flowers blue or purplish; stems short, stiffish, the leaves stiff and prickly. *Navarretia*, page 257.

10a. Leaves alternate, clustered at the nodes on one side, sharp-pointed, rigid; flowers few. *Leptodactylon*, PRICKLY GILIA, page 257.
10b. Leaves appearing whorled, with linear but not pungent divisions; flowers in terminal clusters. *Linanthastrum*, page 257.

COLLOMIA

One species, *Collomia linearis* Nutt., Fig. 172. Common on dry hillsides, mesas to montane. Flowers pink.

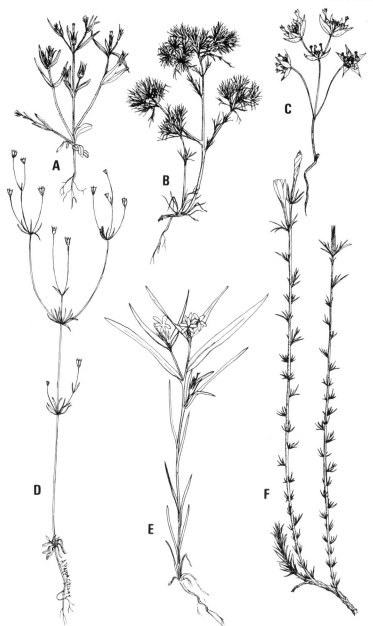

Fig. 172. A, *Microsteris*; B, *Navarretia*; C, *Gymnosteris*; D, *Linanthus*; E, *Collomia*; F, *Leptodactylon*

GILIA

1a. Annual; stamens included; flowers few, in a sparsely-branched inflorescence. **Gilia ophthalmoides** Brand ssp. **clokeyi** (Mason) A. & V. Grant. Common on dry hillsides on the mesas and foothills.

1b. Biennial; stamens exserted; flowers numerous, in a much-branched panicle. **Gilia pinnatifida** Nutt. var. **calcarea** Brand. Common on gravelly slopes or ridges, foothills to montane.

GYMNOSTERIS

One species, **Gymnosteris parvula** (Rydb.) Heller, Fig. 172. An inconspicuous and ephemeral spring flower on sagebrush hillsides in the foothill ridges near Fort Collins.

IPOMOPSIS. Trumpet Gilia

1a. Corollas with long tubes .... (2)

1b. Corollas short-tubular; flowers crowded into a dense spike of axillary flower-clusters. **Ipomopsis spicata** (Nutt.) V. Grant, Spike Gilia. Flowers cream-colored; plant sticky-glandular. A common early spring flower on dry slopes, mesas and foothills.

2a. Annual, corolla less than 3 cm long; capsule much longer than the calyx; plants of the plains. **Ipomopsis laxiflora** (Coult.) V. Grant (loose-flowered). Sandy places on the plains. A related species with

Fig. 173. *Ipomopsis aggregata*

much larger flowers, *I. longiflora* (Torr.) V. Grant, is also common on the plains but probably does not reach the Front Range area. The flowers are white in both species.

2b. Biennial with a basal rosette of leaves; corolla over 3 cm long; capsule not longer than the calyx; plants of foothills and mountains
. . . . (3)

3a. Flowers scarlet. *Ipomopsis aggregata* (Pursh) V. Grant, SCARLET GILIA, Fig. 173. Common in the foothills from Denver southward. Some red-flowered plants are found sporadically northward, but mostly replaced by the next. Hybrid swarms of the two occur where they overlap, producing plants with intermediate colors.

3b. Flowers cream-colored. *Ipomopsis candida* (Rydb.) W. A. Weber. Common in the foothills north from Palmer Lake. Pure populations occur between Boulder and Fort Collins, with little pink showing in the petals.

LEPTODACTYLON. PRICKLY GILIA

1a. Plants forming a dense low cushion; flowers 4-merous. *Leptodactylon caespitosum* Nutt. Plains, vicinity of Pawnee Buttes.

1b. Plants loosely caespitose, the stems more or less elongate; flowers 5-merous. *Leptodactylon pungens* (Torr.) Nutt. *ex* Rydb. (prickly), Fig. 172. Open ground of mesas and foothills.

LINANTHASTRUM

One species, *Linanthastrum nuttallii* (Gray) Ewan. Abundant west of the Divide from Rocky Mountain National Park south and west. A very showy roadside plant, especially on Rabbit Ears Pass.

LINANTHUS

One species, *Linanthus harknessii* (Curran) Greene var. *septentrionalis* (Jeps.) Bailey, Fig. 172. An extremely delicate, almost invisible annual of dry meadows on the western slope, in our range only in the western edge of Rocky Mountain National Park.

MICROSTERIS

One species, *Microsteris gracilis* (Dougl.) Greene, Fig. 172. A common but inconspicuous weedy annual of the mesas and foothills in early summer.

NAVARRETIA

One species, *Navarretia minima* Nutt., Fig. 172, native on the western slope, but evidently accidentally introduced and thriving around cattle wallows on the mesas near Boulder. On the western slope a similar species with yellow flowers occurs, *N. breweri* (Gray) Greene. The leaf tips are sharp enough to give one splinters.

PHLOX

1a. Plants cushion-like, densely caespitose; leaves crowded .... (4)
1b. Plants loosely branched; leaves not crowded .... (2)

2a. Flowers white; plants of sand-hills on the plains. ***Phlox andicola*** (Britt.) E. Nels. Abundant on the plains near Hudson.
2b. Flowers pink or lavender, rarely white; plants of the foothills and mesas .... (3)

3a. Leaves short and broad; plants in dense clumps. ***Phlox multiflora*** Nels. Abundant on slopes in the foothills.
3b. Leaves elongate, linear; stems solitary or a few together. ***Phlox longifolia*** Nutt. Mesas mostly from Denver southward.

4a. Leaves densely woolly, less than 5 mm long, scale-like and closely overlapping. ***Phlox bryoides*** Nutt. (moss-like), Moss PHLOX. Common on hogbacks and mesas from Fort Collins northward. West of the Divide in Middle Park, a close relative, *Phlox hoodii* Rich. occurs, with narrow leaves, not strongly overlapping, and without the woolly pubescence.
4b. Leaves ciliate-margined but not woolly, usually 1 cm long; alpine .... (5)

5a. Densely cushioned; leaves short (5 mm), erect; flowers white, the tube 7 mm, the lobes 3 mm long. ***Phlox condensata*** (Gray) E. Nels. Alpine tundra, mostly south of Clear Creek.
5b. Loosely cushioned; leaves spreading, over 1 cm long, green; flowers usually colored, the tube 11-12 mm, the lobes 5 mm long. ***Phlox sibirica*** L. ssp. ***pulvinata*** (Wherry) W. A. Weber. Abundant on alpine tundra throughout the range.

Fig. 174. ***Polemonium viscosum***

POLEMONIUM. Jacobs Ladder; Sky Pilot

1a. Corolla shallowly bell-shaped; leaflets opposite, leaves mostly cauline
. . . . (2)
1b. Corolla funnelform; leaflets whorled; leaves chiefly basal . . . . . . (4)

2a. Stems tall, leafy, solitary or a few together . . . . (3)
2b. Stems low (less than 3 dm high), several to many in tufts. **Polemonium delicatum** Rydb., Jacobs Ladder. Moist subalpine forests, very common. This and several other species have a strong skunk-like odor.

3a. Plants with a slender rhizome; leaflets narrow, almost glabrous; inflorescence longer than broad. **Polemonium caeruleum** L. ssp. **amygdalinum** (Wherry) Munz (blue; with almond odor), Western Jacobs Ladder. Swampy streamsides, subalpine and montane.

3b. Plants with a woody caudex; leaflets broad, pubescent; inflorescence broad, flat-topped. **Polemonium foliosissimum** Gray (very leafy), Leafy Jacobs Ladder. Streamsides and canyon slopes, foothills and montane.

4a. Corolla blue or purple, very rarely white (in occasional individuals); flowers in a terminal capitate cluster. **Polemonium viscosum** Nutt. (sticky), Sky Pilot, Plate 26, Fig. 174. Common on alpine tundra slopes. There are several races which differ in flower color and type of odor. One of the most distinctive is *P. grayanum* Rydb. with pale blue flowers and long-hairy calyx.
4b. Corolla cream-colored; flowers in several loose terminal and axillary clusters. **Polemonium brandegei** (Gray) Greene (for T. S. Brandegee). Rocky tundra and cliff-sides, subalpine·and alpine.

POLYGONACEAE—BUCKWHEAT FAMILY

This family contains two important food plants, Buckwheat (*Fagopyrum esculentum*) and Rhubarb (*Rheum rhaponticum*). Rhubarb is known as an escape around old mountain homesites. The stems are edible, but the leaves may cause lethal poisoning from oxalic acid. The pleasant flavor of the petioles comes from malic acid. Buckwheat is a photosensitizer like *Hypericum*, and cattle eating too much of it can develop a lethal sunburn.

1a. Herbaceous or woody vines. **Fallopia**, page 263.
1b. Plants erect or prostrate but not twining vines . . . . (2)

2a. Very dwarf plants of wet gravels in alpine tundra, resembling seedlings, red-tinged, with only a few pairs of small oval leaves and minute axillary flowers. **Koenigia**, page 263.
2b. Not as above . . . . (3)

3a. Flower clusters subtended by campanulate, turbinate or cylindric involucres of fused bracts. **Eriogonum**, page 261.

3b. Flower clusters not subtended by involucres .... (4)

4a. Stems and leaves with small hooked spines; leaves sagittate. ***Truellum***, TEARTHUMB, page 267.
4b. Stems and leaves not as above .... (5)

5a. Sepals 4 or 6, the outer ones spreading or reflexed, remaining small, the inner sepals usually erect and enlarged in fruit ..... (6)
5b. Sepals 5, the outer ones not smaller, usually petal-like, white or bright pink .... (8)

6a. Leaf-blades lanceolate to ovate, never basally lobed; coarse weedy plants. ***Rumex***, DOCK, page 266.
6b. Leaf-blades rounded-reniform or basally lobed; low, relatively delicate plants .... (7)

7a. Leaves with basal hastate lobes; flowers mostly unisexual. ***Acetosella***, SHEEP SORREL, page 260.
7b. Leaves rounded-reniform; flowers mostly perfect. ***Oxyria,*** ALPINE SORREL, page 264.

8a. Huge weedy herbs forming thickets; stems zigzag, leaves broadly ovate, truncate at the base; flowers in axillary panicles. ***Reynoutria***, page 266.
8b. Not as above .... (9)

9a. Leaves with a hinge-like joint at the point of attachment of blade and sheath; flowers in axillary clusters; bracts of the inflorescence with well-developed blades. ***Polygonum***, KNOTWEED, page 265.
9b. Leaves without a joint at the point of attachment of blade and sheath; flowers in terminal or axillary spike-like racemes; bracts of the inflorescence reduced to sheaths .... (10)

10a. Rootstock thickened and bulb-like; basal leaves well developed and stem leaves reduced; plants alpine and subalpine. ***Bistorta***, BISTORT, page 260.
10b. Rootstock, if any, not bulb-like; basal leaves none; plants of various altitudes. ***Persicaria***, page 264.

ACETOSELLA. SHEEP SORREL

One species, ***Acetosella vulgaris*** (Koch) Fourr. An abundant weed in disturbed areas and sites of recent fires. The plants turn red when mature. The flowers are tiny and in diffuse panicles (*Rumex acetosella* of Ed. 4).

BISTORTA. BISTORT

1a. Raceme narrowly cylindric, viviparous (bearing reproductive blackish bulblets in place of some of the lower flowers), 5-8 mm wide. ***Bistorta vivipara*** (L.) S. Gray, Fig. 175. Common in subalpine meadows and alpine tundra. *Bistorta* is a small genus of mountain plants found in western North America and Eurasia. This species is circumpolar.

1b. Raceme broadly cylindric or ovoid, not viviparous, 10-20 mm wide, flowers conspicuous, white or pinkish. ***Bistorta bistortoides*** (Pursh) Small, Fig. 176. One of the most common and conspicuous wild flowers of subalpine meadows, the spikes of white flowers often dominating the landscape.

ERIOGONUM. FALSE BUCKWHEAT

1a. Flowers in dense, many-flowered umbellate clusters subtended by a whorl of leaf-like bracts; stems scapose and unbranched below the inflorescence .... (2)
1b. Flowers in open or loose, few-flowered cymes; bracts not very leaf-like nor whorled .... (5)

2a. Perianth silky-pubescent on the outside .... (3)
2b. Perianth glabrous on the outside .... (4)

3a. Inflorescence consisting of a single tight cluster of flowers. ***Eriogonum flavum*** Nutt. var. ***xanthum*** (Small) Stokes. Common on alpine tundra. Variety *flavum* occurs on rocky buttes on the eastern plains. This is a nice example of an alpine race evidently derived from a wide-ranging species of lower altitudes.

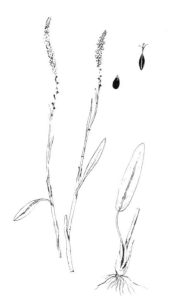

Fig. 175. ***Bistorta vivipara***   Fig. 176. ***Bistorta bistortoides***

3b. Inflorescence of several umbellate clusters in a branched group. ***Eriogonum jamesii*** Benth. var. ***flavescens*** Wats. (for Edwin James; yellowish). In the Boulder area this species has bright yellow flowers, but in most other places the flowers are cream-colored (var. *jamesii*). Common on mesas and in the lower foothills.

4a. Flowers bright yellow. ***Eriogonum umbellatum*** Torr., SULPHUR-FLOWER, Plate 22, Fig. 177. Abundant on dry, rocky hillsides, foothills to subalpine, richly diversified into local races.

4b. Flowers cream-colored, becoming rose-colored in age. ***Eriogonum subalpinum*** Greene. Dry hillsides, rocky meadows, subalpine. Often found with the preceding but never intergrading with it in our area. Because of intergradation north of Colorado, it has been considered a race of *E. umbellatum* (var. *major* Hook.).

5a. Stem and leaves green, stiffly pubescent; basal leaves numerous, in a rosette, but stem leaves reduced; fruits winged. ***Eriogonum alatum*** Torr., WINGED ERIOGONUM, Fig. 178. Pine forests and open slopes on the mesas and foothills. Very different in appearance from most eriogonums, having a tall, stout, leafless flowering stem up to a meter tall, the flowers inconspicuous, greenish-yellow.

5b. Stems and/or leaves white-tomentose, at least on one surface; stems leafy, at least below; fruits not winged .... (6)

6a. Leaves oval or round, chiefly near the base of the stem; peduncles usually reflexed. ***Eriogonum cernuum*** Nutt., NODDING ERIOGONUM.

Fig. 177. ***Eriogonum umbellatum***　　　Fig. 178. ***Eriogonum alatum***

Annual, with a delicate, much-branched inflorescence. Mesas and foothills, common from Denver southward.

6b. Leaves lanceolate or linear; stems leafy throughout or only below. (7)

7a. Annual or biennial; stem simple below the inflorescence, leafy throughout. ***Eriogonum annuum*** Nutt. A tall eriogonum with a broad, flat-topped flower-cluster, common on mesas and plains. Appears white at a distance.

7b. Perennial; stem branched below as well as above, leafy below only
· (8)

8a. Flowers yellow. ***Eriogonum brevicaule*** Nutt. (short-stemmed). Infrequent and apparently confined to shales on the mesas. Abundant in Middle Park on the western slope.

8b. Flowers white or rose-colored · (9)

9a. Flowering stem long and naked below the branches, smooth; leaves mostly basal, elongate and broadly linear-oblong; flowers 3-4 mm long. ***Eriogonum lonchophyllum*** T. & G. Mainly a species of the western slope, but locally abundant near Morrison. Plants forming hemispherical sprays.

9b. Flowering stem not much longer than the leafy stem portion, appressed cobwebby-pubescent; flowers 2 mm long. ***Eriogonum effusum*** Nutt. (spread out), BUSHY ERIOGONUM. Abundant on the plains and mesas; stem somewhat woody.

FALLOPIA. BLACK BINDWEED

1a. Woody perennial vine forming massive growths over fences and walls; flowers in large panicles, white, the sepals strongly winged; leaves not conspicuously cordate-hastate. ***Fallopia aubertii*** (L. Henry) Holub. Originally described from Tibet and western China in 1907, this species has spread from a few cultivated plants and is established in the Boulder-Denver area.

1b. Herbaceous annual vines with acuminate, cordate-hastate leaves and simple racemes · (2)

2a. Outer sepals keeled but hardly winged in fruit; achene granular, dull. ***Fallopia convolvulus*** (L.) A. Löve, BLACK BINDWEED. A common weed of disturbed sites in and around towns (*Bilderdykia* of Ed. 4).

2b. Outer sepals winged in fruit (the keel projecting outward as a membrane; achene smooth and shining. ***Fallopia scandens*** (L.) Holub, CLIMBING FALSE BUCKWHEAT. Known from a few old records near Denver and Colorado Springs.

KOENIGIA

One species, ***Koenigia islandica*** L. (of Iceland). Infrequent but locally abundant in frost scars, in wet gravel on alpine tundra, the only true annual plant in the alpine flora. This entire plant is only a few millimeters high. Circumpolar.

OXYRIA. Alpine Sorrel

One species, ***Oxyria digyna*** (L.) Hill (with two carpels), Fig. 179. Rock crevices in the alpine tundra, rarely in compensating environments in the subalpine. Resembling a dwarf *Rumex*, but easily distinguished by the kidney-shaped leaves.

PERSICARIA. Smartweed

1a. Plants aquatic or subaquatic; inflorescences all terminal or nearly so; flowers bright pink or red .... (2)

1b. Plants terrestrial although sometimes found in very wet places, never floating; inflorescence of axillary and terminal racemes or spikes; flowers pale pink or white .... (3)

2a. Leaf-blades obtuse or acute, commonly widest near the middle; spikes of flowers seldom more than 3 cm long, usually more than 10 mm wide. ***Persicaria amphibia*** (L.) S. Gray, Water Smartweed. Floating on ponds or growing in mud on pond margins. A single plant may exhibit branches with smooth floating leaves like *Potamogeton* and erect terrestrial branches with pubescent, erect leaves. Plains to montane (*Polygonum amphibium* L.).

2b. Leaf-blades acuminate, commonly widest near the base; inflorescence 3-10 cm long, seldom more and usually less than 10 mm wide. ***Persicaria coccinea*** (Muehl.) Greene, Scarlet Smartweed. Similar sites, on the plains (*Polygonum coccineum* Muehl.).

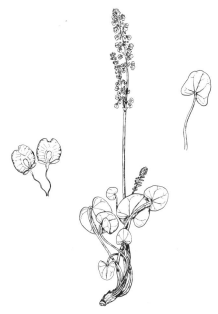

Fig. 179. *Oxyria digyna*

3a. Sheaths with marginal bristles .... (4)
3b. Sheaths without marginal bristles .... (5)

4a. Perianth greenish, glandular-dotted; racemes very slender ..... (6)
4b. Perianth pink, not glandular-dotted; racemes dense, thick. ***Persicaria maculata*** (Raf.) S. Gray, LADY'S THUMB. Wet places, piedmont valleys. The leaves commonly have a dark spot in the center, the "Lady's thumbprint" (*Polygonum persicaria* L.).

5a. Peduncle with granular yellow glands; perianth usually white or cream-colored; inflorescence commonly elongate, nodding or drooping. ***Persicaria lapathifolia*** (L.) S. Gray (dock-leaved). Frequent in wet places, piedmont valleys (*Polygonum lapathifolium* L.).
5b. Peduncle with stalked red-purple glands; perianth usually pink; inflorescence commonly erect, short and stout. ***Persicaria pensylvanica*** (L.) Gomez. Frequent in wet places, piedmont valleys (*Polygonum pensylvanicum* L.).

6a. Sheaths swollen, filled with cleistogamous flowers; achenes minutely granular-papillose, dull. ***Persicaria hydropiper*** (L.) Opiz (water-pepper). Swamps and streamsides, piedmont valleys (*Polygonum hydropiper* L.).
6b. Sheaths hugging the stem, not plump from hidden cleistogamous flowers; achenes smooth, with a high luster. ***Persicaria punctata*** (Ell.) Small, DOTTED SMARTWEED. Similar sites, but probably less common than the last.

POLYGONUM. KNOTWEED

1a. Fruit shiny; native species .... (3)
1b. Fruit dull, minutely roughened; weedy species in disturbed soil, gardens, and waste ground particularly in the piedmont valleys and plains .... (2)

2a. Plants tall, erect, much-branched; leaves narrow, acuminate, early deciduous; flowers greenish with yellowish perianth margins, the upper bract-like leaves greatly reduced, often not longer than the flowers. ***Polygonum ramosissimum*** Michx. (much-branched), BUSHY KNOTWEED. Common on borders of drying ponds and along roadsides on the plains.
2b. Plants usually prostrate or only ascending; leaves oblong, up to 5 mm wide and about a centimeter long; flowers with white perianth margins, the upper leaves not conspicuously smaller than the lower ones. ***Polygonum aviculare*** L. (of the bird-keeper = chicken-coop), DEVILS SHOESTRINGS. Abundant in cultivated ground everywhere (*P. rurivagum* of Ed. 4). A very complex species or group of species, too little studied here to justify division at the present time.

3a. Leaves broad and short, often almost circular; plants prostrate, often rooted in mud or wet sand in seepage areas or streamsides. ***Polygonum minimum*** Wats. Rare, Rocky Mountain National Park.

3b. Leaves lanceolate or linear, or ranging to narrowly elliptic; plants erect, growing in open gravelly sites and roadsides .... (4)

4a. Fruiting perianth reflexed, the pedicel bent downward .... (5)
4b. Fruiting perianth remaining erect, the pedicel not reflexed. ***Polygonum sawatchense*** Small, SAWATCH KNOTWEED. Common on dry slopes, mesas and foothills.

5a. Perianth 1.5-2.5 mm long; leaves narrowly linear. ***Polygonum engelmannii*** Greene (for George Engelmann). Dry slopes in the foothill canyons.
5b. Perianth 3-5 mm long; leaves variable, from narrowly linear to elliptic. ***Polygonum douglasii*** Greene (for David Douglas). Common on dry slopes and in open forests, foothills to subalpine.

REYNOUTRIA. JAPANESE BUCKWHEAT

One species, ***Reynoutria japonica*** Houtt. Occasionally cultivated in gardens but frequently escaping and forming dense thickets of rank growth, piedmont valleys (*Polygonum cuspidatum* Sieb. & Zucc.).

RUMEX. DOCK

1a. Fruiting calyx 1-3 cm broad, pink. ***Rumex venosus*** Pursh, VEINY DOCK; WILD "BEGONIA," Plate 6, Fig. 180. Fleshy-leaved species of sandy areas and roadsides on the plains.
1b. Fruiting calyx 0.5 cm or less broad .... (2)

2a. Inner sepals entire or nearly so .... (3)
2b. Inner sepals dentate or denticulate .... (6)

Fig. 180. ***Rumex venosus***

3a. Stems erect or ascending with well-developed axillary shoots. ***Rumex salicifolius*** Weinm. ssp. ***triangulivalvis*** Danser, WILLOW DOCK. The most common dock along roadsides in the foothills and montane.

3b. Stems erect but lacking axillary shoots .... (4)

4a. Nut-like callosities present on at least one of the three inner sepals; leaf-margins ruffled. ***Rumex crispus*** L., CURLY DOCK. Abundant weed in gardens and waste ground, piedmont valleys and plains.

4b. Nut-like callosities lacking .... (5)

5a. Plant with a vertical taproot. ***Rumex occidentalis*** Wats., WESTERN DOCK. Upper montane and subalpine, along the larger streams.

5b. Plant with a stout horizontal rhizome. ***Rumex densiflorus*** Osterh. Boggy places, mostly subalpine, but occasionally in the middle foothills. Difficult to separate from the last without the underground parts.

6a. Plants with broad ovate leaves with cordate or truncate base. ***Rumex obtusifolius*** L., BITTER DOCK. Introduced weed, in shade along streams in the piedmont valleys.

6b. Plants with long, relatively narrow leaves, usually narrowed to the petiole .... (7)

7a. Low spreading annual; inner sepals almost completely dissected into slender teeth. ***Rumex maritimus*** L. var. ***fueginus*** (Phil.) Dusén, GOLDEN DOCK. Sandy shores of ponds from plains to montane.

7b. Tall perennial; inner sepals with shallow teeth. ***Rumex stenophyllus*** Ledeb. Pond margins on the plains, a relatively recent introduction.

TRUELLUM. TEARTHUMB

One species, ***Truellum sagittatum*** (L.) Sojak. Very rare. An eastern North American species known in Colorado from one collection near Colorado Springs, in wet meadows (*Tracaulon* of Ed. 4).

PORTULACACEAE—PURSLANE FAMILY

This small family makes up for its size in the beauty of its cultivated members. The Moss-rose, *Portulaca grandiflora*, is one of the hardiest ever-blooming plants of hot, sunny gardens in our area, and many species of *Lewisia*, named after Meriwether Lewis of the Lewis and Clark Expedition, were at one time nearly exterminated in the Pacific Northwest by root-diggers for the rock garden trade. *Lewisia rediviva*, the Bitterroot, is the State flower of Montana.

1a. Plants prostrate-spreading, much-branched, matted, with fleshy spatulate leaves and inconspicuous yellow flowers. ***Portulaca oleracea*** L. (like a garden vegetable), COMMON PURSLANE. Abundant introduced weed of gardens and waste ground.

1b. Plants erect or stemless, without spreading prostrate branches; flowers pink, red, or white; native plants .... (2)

2a. Stems stolon-bearing at the base, with several pairs of opposite leaves; plants of wet streamsides. ***Crunocallis chamissoi*** (Ledeb.) Rydb. (for A. von Chamisso), WATER SPRING BEAUTY. Petals white, with pink streaks. Foothills to subalpine (*Montia chamissoi* of Ed. 4).

2b. Stems low or lacking, leaves chiefly basal, or flowering stems with a very few leaves; plants of drier habitats .... (3)

3a. Plants with a cluster of basal leaves from a stout taproot .... (4)

3b. Plant with one basal leaf and/or a pair of stem leaves; plant arising from a deep-seated round corm .... (6)

4a. Inflorescence an open cyme on a stalk longer than the linear basal leaves; plants of mesas, plains and lower foothills. ***Talinum parviflorum*** Nutt. (small-flowered), FAME-FLOWER.

4b. Inflorescence not exceeding the leaves; plants subalpine or alpine .... (5)

5a. Leaves broadly spatulate, obtuse, in very dense tufts; flower white or pink with red veins. ***Claytonia megarhiza*** (Gray) Parry (big-rooted), ALPINE SPRING BEAUTY. Fig. 181. Among rocks, tundra of the higher peaks, a member of an Asiatic group of alpine *Claytonia* species.

5b. Leaves linear, in small tufts; flowers deep solid red or pink, rarely white. ***Lewisia pygmaea*** (Gray) Robinson, PIGMY BITTERROOT. Gravelly soil, subalpine and alpine. The true Bitterroot, *L. rediviva* Pursh, a very showy species with petals over 1 cm long, is abundant just outside our area in Middle Park around Granby.

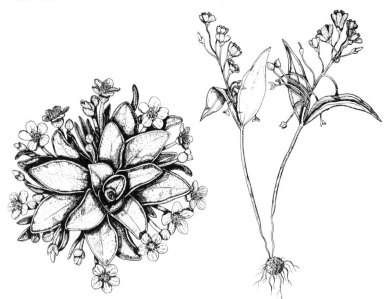

Fig. 181. ***Claytonia megarhiza***   Fig. 182. ***Claytonia lanceolata***

6a. Stem leaves narrowly lanceolate or lance-linear; plants usually with a basal leaf. **Claytonia rosea** Rydb., SPRING BEAUTY. The earliest spring flower under pines on the mesas and lower foothills.

6b. Stem leaves broadly ovate-lanceolate; plants without a basal leaf. **Claytonia lanceolata** Pursh, SPRING BEAUTY, Fig. 182. Subalpine in our area and relatively infrequent, but the common species of the plateaus of western Colorado.

PRIMULACEAE—PRIMROSE FAMILY

Primroses, or cowslips, have been cultivated in gardens since Elizabethan times and still are among the choicest of rock garden plants. The showiest come from the mountains of Asia; our red mountain primroses are close cousins of these. *Cyclamen*, known here as a potted plant, grows wild in Europe, and *Soldanella*, a unique genus with deeply fringed bell-shaped corollas, is a treasure of the Alps. Our own *Dodecatheon*, the Shooting Star, used to be called the American Cyclamen. The elite primrose of Colorado, however, is *Primula egaliksensis*, found only in an area of a few acres in South Park near Jefferson, the only locality in North America outside of the Arctic where it occurs from Greenland to Alaska.

1a. Plants leafy-stemmed .... (2)
1b. Plants bearing leaves at the base of the stem only .... (5)

2a. Stems not over 10 cm high; flowers pink or white .... (3)
2b. Stems several dm high; flowers yellow .... (4)

3a. Leaves opposite; petals lacking, the sepals petaloid. **Glaux maritima** L., SEA-MILKWORT, Fig. 185. Alkaline ground on the plains. Leaves oblong, 6-12 mm long, entire, sessile, the flowers sessile in the axils of the leaves.

3b. Leaves alternate; corolla shorter than the sepals, 4- to 5-cleft, often persisting as a withered cap over the circumscissile capsule. **Centunculus minimus** L., CHAFFWEED. Very rare, in wet places near Colorado Springs.

4a. Flowers 1 cm or more broad, solitary in the leaf-axils. **Lysimachia ciliata** L., FRINGED LOOSESTRIFE. Common in sloughs and along irrigation ditches, piedmont valleys. See Addenda.

4b. Flowers small, in dense spikes in the leaf-axils. **Lysimachia thyrsiflora** L. (with flowers in a thyrsus), TUFTED LOOSESTRIFE. Rare, in swamps, vicinity of Estes Park.

5a. Corolla-lobes reflexed; stamens exserted, the anthers appearing united, forming a beak-like projection. **Dodecatheon pulchellum** (Raf.) Merrill, SHOOTING-STAR, Fig. 183. Very abundant along streams, foothills to subalpine. Extremely variable as to size of flowers, a response of the plants to different amounts of moisture and sunlight.

5b. Corolla-lobes erect or spreading; stamens included, separate and distinct .... (6)

6a. Leaves white-mealy beneath. ***Primula incana*** Jones (hoary), BIRDS-EYE PRIMROSE. Wet subalpine meadows, Pikes Peak region. Quite common in the South Park, west of our range. Flowers lilac. A related species, *P. egaliksensis* Wormskj. occurs with *P. incana* in South Park. It has green, not whitened leaves and much smaller flowers (not over 5 mm diam).

6b. Leaves green on both sides .... (7)

7a. Flowers white or tinged with pink; corolla-tube shorter than the calyx; flowers usually minute .... (9)

Fig. 183. ***Dodecatheon pulchellum***   Fig. 184. ***Primula parryi***

Fig. 185. A, *Androsace filiformis*; B, *A. septentrionalis*; C, *A. occidentalis*;
D, *A. chamaejasme*; E, E´, *Glaux* growth forms

7b. Flowers deep pink or violet, showy; corolla-tube equalling or exceeding the calyx .... (8)

8a. Plants small (3-10) cm high); leaves small; flowers solitary or few. ***Primula angustifolia*** Torr., ALPINE PRIMROSE. High subalpine meadows and alpine tundra.
8b. Plants large (1.5-4.0 dm high); leaves large; flowers numerous, very showy, rather foul-scented. ***Primula parryi*** Gray, PARRY PRIMROSE, Fig. 184. Streambanks and bogs, subalpine.

9a. Perennial; flowers in a dense cluster, almost sessile; capsule few-seeded. ***Androsace chamaejasme*** Host. ssp. ***carinata*** (Torr.) Hultén, ROCK-JASMINE, Fig. 185. Flowers white with yellow center, becoming rose-colored in age. Plants tiny, only a few cm tall, locally abundant on high alpine tundra.
9b. Annual; flowers with long pedicels; capsule many-seeded .. (10)

10a. Bracts at base of umbel broad (lance-ovate to obovate). ***Androsace occidentalis*** Pursh, WESTERN ROCK PRIMROSE, Fig. 185. Open grassy slopes in the foothills and mesas.
10b. Bracts at base of umbel narrow (lanceolate to subulate) ......(11)

11a. Calyx strongly 5-keeled; leaves not distinctly petioled. ***Androsace septentrionalis*** L. (northern), ROCK PRIMROSE, Fig. 185. Extremely common throughout the mountains, in forested or open sites, extremely variable in size and length of pedicels and peduncles.
11b. Calyx not keeled; leaves abruptly narrowed to a distinct petiole. ***Androsace filiformis*** Retz, Fig. 185. Wet places in the subalpine.

RANUNCULACEAE—BUTTERCUP FAMILY

The petals of buttercups have a high, almost mirror-like gloss. Children test this quality by holding up a flower to another's chin and asking, "Do you like butter?" The basal part of the petal, however, is dull. Lyman Benson explains in *Plant Taxonomy, Methods and Principles*, that these qualities constitute a device for pollination by rainwater. The stigmas of buttercups are not well situated to be brushed by bees, but bees leave much pollen lying around on the petals. The glossy part of the petal is water-repellent, while the dull part is not. If rain or dew falls on the petal, the water will rise only as far as the top of the matte area, draining off between the petals above that point. This water level is usually about the same level as the stigmas. Pollen thus floats on the water film and is deposited on the stigmas as the water level recedes.

1a. Flowers bilaterally symmetrical .... (2)
1b. Flowers radially symmetrical .... (3)

2a. Uppermost sepal prolonged into a conspicuous spur. ***Delphinium***, LARKSPUR, page 278.
2b. Uppermost sepal forming a hood which arches over the flower. ***Aconitum***, MONKSHOOD, page 274.

3a. Carpels one-seeded, becoming achenes .... (4)
3b. Carpels few- to many-seeded, becoming either follicles or fleshy berry-like fruits .... (10)

4a. Tiny annual plants with linear basal leaves; fruiting receptacle many times longer than wide; petals spurred. *Myosurus*, Mousetail, page 279.
4b. Plant not as above; receptacle rarely more than 5 times as long as wide; petals, when present, not spurred .... (5)

5a. Petals and sepals distinctly different, the petals usually yellow (white in one submerged aquatic species) .... (6)
5b. Petals and sepals alike, or absent, or only one or the other present, usually white or colored, but not yellow .... (7)

6a. Achene with a long straight beak and with two pouch-like enlargements at the base; small annuals with linear-dissected leaves, growing on alkaline flats. *Ceratocephala*, page 276.
6b. Achene with a short, often curved beak, or beakless, lacking basal pouches. *Ranunculus*, Buttercup, page 279.

7a. Perianth segments small, less conspicuous than the stamens. *Thalictrum*, Meadow Rue, page 285.
7b. Perianth segments large and showy, petal-like .... (8)

8a. Perianth segments 5 or more, overlapping; upper stem leaves in a whorl below the inflorescence, sometimes forming an involucre (9)
8b. Perianth segments commonly 4, not overlapping; leaves not whorled beneath the inflorescence; styles becoming long and feathery at maturity. *Clematis*, Virgins Bower, page 276.

9a. Flowers appearing before the leaves; perianth parts more than 2 cm long; styles becoming long and feathery at maturity. *Pulsatilla*, Pasque Flower, page 279.
9b. Flowers appearing after the leaves; perianth parts about 1 cm long; styles not greatly elongated in fruit. *Anemone*, Wind-flower, page 274.

10a. Leaves compound .... (11)
10b. Leaves deeply lobed or cleft, never compound .... (12)

11a. Petals spurred; carpels 3-5, becoming follicles. *Aquilegia*, Columbine, page 276.
11b. Petals not spurred; carpel one, berry-like, red or rarely ivorywhite. *Actaea*, Baneberry, page 274.

12a. Leaves chiefly basal, kidney-shaped or rounded heart-shaped, not lobed. *Caltha*, Marsh-marigold, page 276.
12b. Plant leafy-stemmed; leaves palmately lobed. *Trollius*, Globeflower, page 286.

ACONITUM. Monkshood

One species, *Aconitum columbianum* Nutt. (of the Columbia River), Fig. 186. Forest openings, montane and subalpine. Flowers usually blue-purple, but a greenish-white form (f. *ochroleucum* St. John) occurs sporadically in the normal populations.

ACTAEA. Baneberry

One species, *Actaea rubra* (Ait.) Willd. ssp. *arguta* (Nutt. *ex* T. & G.) Hultén, Fig. 187. Deep shaded forests, montane. The racemes of red "berries" are conspicuous in late summer. The occasional white-fruited plant is a genetic variation of the same species and is not the White Baneberry of the eastern U.S.

ANEMONE. Windflower

1a. Achenes densely woolly; flowers 1-2 cm broad; leaves deeply cleft
     into narrow divisions .... (2)
1b. Achenes smooth or pubescent, not woolly; flowers 2.5-3.0 cm broad;
     leaves cleft into rather broad divisions .... (3)

2a. Perianth segments usually colored; receptacle globose; stem leaves
     gradually narrowing to short, indistinct petioles. *Anemone multifida*

Fig. 186. *Aconitum columbianum*   Fig. 187. *Actaea rubra*

Poir. var. ***globosa*** (Nutt.) T. & G., GLOBEFLOWER, Fig. 188. Upper montane and subalpine, the common summer-blooming anemone of the mountains. Flowers usually dull red.

2b. Perianth segments white; receptacle cylindrical; stem leaves abruptly narrowed to distinct petioles. ***Anemone cylindrica*** Gray, THIMBLE-WEED. Mesas and lower foothills. The elongate, woolly, thimble-shaped fruit is characteristic.

3a. Basal leaves three-parted, with broad, shallowly-lobed segments; plant less than 1 dm high, glabrous and glossy. ***Anemone parviflora*** Michx. Rare on cool subalpine rocky slopes, reported from Thunder Pass in Rocky Mountain National Park.

3b. Basal leaves cleft into 5 or more divisions; plant over 1 dm high, hairy .... (4)

4a. Flowers lemon-yellow to creamy-white; achenes glabrous; plant of subalpine meadows. ***Anemone narcissiflora*** L. ssp. ***zephyra*** (Nels.) Löve, Löve & Kapoor, SUBALPINE ANEMONE. The only anemone which regularly bears more than one flower on a stem. Subalpine meadows, not common. Easily confused with *Trollius*, but recognized by the whorl of leaves below the flower cluster.

4b. Flowers white; achenes appressed-pubescent; plants of piedmont valleys and plains. ***Anemone canadensis*** L., MEADOW ANEMONE. Occasional in ditches and moist places.

Fig. 188. ***Anemone multifida***   Fig. 189. ***Aquilegia caerulea***

AQUILEGIA. Columbine

1a. Sepals blue or purplish, rarely white .... (2)
1b. Sepals yellow or red .... (3)

2a. Plant exceeding 2 dm; flowers more than 2 cm across; spurs elongate, at least 1 cm long, straight; follicles over 1 cm long. *Aquilegia caerulea* James (blue), Colorado Blue Columbine, Fig. 189. Very common, montane, subalpine. The Colorado State flower. Spurless flowers occasionally are found (var. *daileyae* Eastw.), Plate 19.
2b. Plant less than 1 dm tall; flowers not exceeding 1.5 cm across; spur extremely short, curved; follicles about 1 cm long. *Aquilegia saximontana* Rydb. (Rocky Mountain), Dwarf Columbine. Rare, subalpine and alpine, on cliffs and rocky slopes.

3a. Sepals yellow. *Aquilegia chrysantha* Gray, Yellow Columbine. Montane, in Pikes Peak region and southward.
3b. Sepals red. *Aquilegia elegantula* Greene, Red Columbine. Common in southern and western Colorado, but probably not found east of the Continental Divide except in southern Colorado. Common in the vicinity of Grand Lake, montane. Hybridizes with *A. caerulea* where the two occur together. *A. pubescens* Coville, a long-spurred red- and-yellow species native in California and commonly grown in gardens, occurs locally as an introduction along the road to Caribou.

CALTHA. Marsh-marigold

One species, *Caltha leptosepala* DC. (with slender sepals), Fig. 190. Abundant in wet ground, subalpine. This characteristic plant of snowmelt basins belongs to a group of white-flowered species of the mountains of South America and Australia, possibly better placed in the genus *Psychrophila*.

CERATOCEPHALA

One species, *Ceratocephala testiculata* (Crantz) Roth (resembling testicles, referring to the achene). A weed of Asia Minor, naturalized locally in the Boulder area and doubtless elsewhere in the piedmont valleys. Very abundant in early springtime on the desert soils of the western slope.

CLEMATIS. Virgins Bower

1a. Flowers white, in cymose clusters; perianth segments less than 1 cm long; plants dioecious. *Clematis ligusticifolia* Nutt. (privet-leaved), Western Virgins Bower. River bottoms and fencerows along ditches, piedmont valleys. The masses of feathery fruits are conspicuous in late summer.
1b. Flowers blue, purple, or yellow; perianth segments over 1 cm long; flowers perfect .... (2)

2a. Flowers yellow. *Clematis orientalis* L. (oriental). An Asiatic species which is locally established, dating from mining times, in the Clear Creek Valley around Idaho Springs and Georgetown.

2b. Flowers blue or purple .... (3)

3a. Bushy herbs with urn-shaped, nodding flowers; sepals thick and leathery, deep purple inside .... (5)

3b. Trailing herbs or vines with lax, open flowers; sepals light blue-lavender, thin-textured .... (4)

4a. Leaves with 3 leaflets, the leaflets large, not cleft. **Clematis occidentalis** (Hornem.) DC. var. **grosseserrata** (Rydb.) Pringle, Blue Clematis, Fig. 191. Climbing on trees, foothills to subalpine *(C. columbiana* of Ed. 4). The nomenclature of this and the next species has evidently been as mixed up as the babies in a Gilbert and Sullivan operetta.

4b. Leaves biternately compound, the leaflets small, deeply cleft and lobed. **Clematis columbiana** (Nutt.) T. & G., Rocky Mountain Clematis, Plate 32. A miniature relative of the preceding, rarely becoming an extensive climbing vine, and easily distinguished by the doubly compound leaves. Extremely similar to its European counterpart, *Clematis alpina*. Unfortunately we can no longer call our plant *Clematis pseudoalpina* because the name was based on the same plant as the older name, *C. columbiana*.

Fig. 190. *Caltha leptosepala*

5a. Stems erect; leaves with linear leaflets; flowers narrowly turbinate, not conspicuously bordered with white hairs. ***Clematis hirsutissima*** Pursh (very hairy), Sugarbowls. Common on grassy slopes, foothills and montane.

5b. Stems sprawling; leaves with ovate leaflets; flowers broadly conical, the recurved sepals conspicuously bordered with white hairs. ***Clematis scottii*** Porter (for John Scott). Common south from Colorado Springs.

DELPHINIUM. Larkspur

1a. Flowers white; plants of mesas and plains. ***Delphinium virescens*** Nutt. (greenish), Plains Larkspur. Common in late spring.

1b. Flowers blue or purple .... (2)

2a. Roots small and tuber-like, often clustered, very easily detached from the stem; plants low, rarely up to 40 cm tall; spring-flowering plants of mesas and ponderosa pine forests. ***Delphinium nelsonii*** Greene (for Aven Nelson), Fig. 192. A small larkspur with very few stem leaves; mesas and foothills.

2b. Plants over 45 cm tall, with a woody fibrous, or long-tapering rootstock; summer-flowering .... (3)

3a. Stems pubescent; leaflets either less than 2 mm broad or more than 10 mm broad .... (4)

3b. Stems glabrous or nearly so; leaflets about 4 mm broad. ***Delphinium ramosum*** Rydb. (branched). Montane and subalpine. Midsummer.

4a. Stems densely pubescent, often purplish; basal leaves numerous, the lobes narrow. ***Delphinium geyeri*** Greene (for Carl Geyer). Common on shales of mesas, sparingly in the foothills. Very poisonous to livestock.

Fig. 191. *Clematis occidentalis*

4b. Stems sparsely pubescent; basal leaves few; leaf-lobes about 10 mm wide. ***Delphinium barbeyi*** Huth (for William Barbey). Subalpine, flowering in midsummer.

MYOSURUS. Mousetail

One species, ***Myosurus minimus*** L. (very small). Plains and mesas, on muddy shores of small pools that dry out in early summer. Not rare, but so inconspicuous as to escape casual notice.

PULSATILLA. Pasque Flower

One species, ***Pulsatilla patens*** (L.) Miller ssp. ***multifida*** (Pritzel) Zamels, Plate 7, Fig. 193. One of the first early spring flowers on the mesas and foothills, but found at higher altitudes later in the season, even under timberline trees. Flowers lavender, the sepals soft-hairy outside.

RANUNCULUS. Buttercup

1a. Flowers white; plant a submerged aquatic with finely dissected

Fig. 192. ***Delphinium nelsonii***   Fig. 193. ***Pulsatilla patens***

leaves; achenes roughly transversely ridged. ***Ranunculus trichophyllus*** Chaix, Water Crowfoot, Fig. 194. Common in ponds and streams, plains to subalpine (*R. aquatilis* of Ed. 4).

1b. Flowers yellow; plants not aquatic, or, if so, without the above characteristics .... (2)

2a. Plants aquatic or semiaquatic (less than 1 dm high), stoloniferous and rooting at the nodes .... (3)
2b. Plants terrestrial, or, if semiaquatic, then not stoloniferous nor rooting at the nodes (except in one introduced species, *R. repens*, but then the plants more than 1 dm high) .... (6)

3a. Leaves linear. ***Ranunculus reptans*** L., Spearwort. Muddy shores of ponds and streams, upper montane and subalpine. The combination of linear leaves and stolons is diagnostic (*R. flammula* var. *reptans* of Ed. 4).
3b. Leaves broad .... (4)

4a. Leaves round or oval, crenate-toothed, heart-shaped at the base. ***Ranunculus cymbalaria*** Pursh (for the genus *Cymbalaria* which has similar leaves), Shore Buttercup, Fig. 195. Muddy shores of ponds and streams, piedmont valleys and plains.
4b. Leaves deeply lobed .... (5)

5a. Leaves broadly 3-lobed, the lobes sometimes shallowly notched; submerged leaves not much different from the floating ones. ***Ranunculus hyperboreus*** R. Br. ssp. ***intertextus*** (Greene) Kapoor & Löve (far-northern; interwoven), Floating Buttercup. In small ponds, subalpine (*R. natans* of Ed. 4).
5b. Leaves deeply 3-lobed, the lobes again deeply lobed; submerged leaves usually finely dissected. ***Ranunculus gmelinii*** DC. var. ***hookeri***

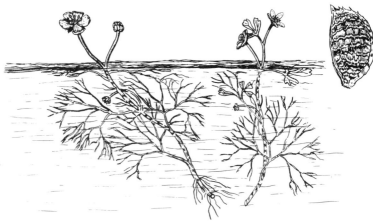

Fig. 194. *Ranunculus trichophyllus*

(D. Don) Benson (for J. G. Gmelin; for J. D. Hooker), WATER CROWFOOT, Fig. 196. Ponds and slow streams, chiefly on the plains.

6a. Plant very harshly pubescent; stem stout; leaves ternately compound or lobed, with broad divisions. ***Ranunculus macounii*** Britt. Along irrigation ditches and sloughs, piedmont valleys and plains.
6b. Plant glabrous or pubescent, never harshly so; leaves various .... (7)

7a. Carpel wall prominently veined, thin, and usually fragile at maturity; leaves biternately compound. ***Ranunculus ranunculinus*** (Nutt.) Rydb. (like *Ranunculus*, this species formerly in *Cyrtorhyncha*), NUTTALL BUTTERCUP. Moist, rocky canyonsides, foothills, infrequent or rare. The petals and sepals fall away very early.
7b. Carpel wall not veined but thick and firm; leaves various, not as above .... (8)

8a. Leaves entire (both the stem and basal leaves). ***Ranunculus alismae-folius*** Geyer var. ***montanus*** Wats., PLANTAINLEAF BUTTERCUP. Common in wet subalpine meadows.
8b. At least some of the leaves lobed or divided .... (9)

9a. Leaves 3-lobed, the lateral lobes often shallowly notched; very tiny plants growing in moss on alpine tundra. ***Ranunculus pygmaeus*** Wahl., PYGMY BUTTERCUP. Extremely rare, on tundra of the higher peaks. Easily overlooked because of its small size (1 cm or less tall). The

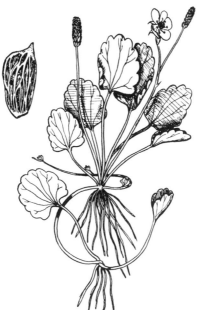

Fig. 195. ***Ranunculus cymbalaria***

plant is usually imbedded in moss.

9b. Leaves divided into more than 3 lobes; or taller plants .... (10)

10a. Style and achene-beak very short or absent; achene corky-keeled; rather fleshy annual. **Ranunculus sceleratus** L. var. **multifidus** Nutt. (cursed; dissected), BLISTER BUTTERCUP, Fig. 197. Introduced weed, found in very wet places such as around watering troughs, springs, and irrigation ditches.

10b. Style and achene-beak present; achenes not corky-keeled .... (11)

11a. Sepals usually tinged on the back with purple or lavender; leaves quite variable on the same plant; foliage glabrous or with spreading pubescence; plants of the foothills and mountains .... (13)

11b. Sepals not tinged on the back with purple or lavender; leaves all regularly palmately lobed or divided; foliage with appressed pubescence; weedy species or native on the plains .... (12)

12a. Stems rooting at the nodes. **Ranunculus repens** L., CREEPING BUTTERCUP. Introduced weed, frequent in pastures and along roadsides. The double-flowered buttercup of gardens is a horticultural variety of this.

12b. Stems not rooting at the nodes. **Ranunculus acriformis** Gray, SHARP BUTTERCUP. Infrequent on the plains, chiefly around sloughs.

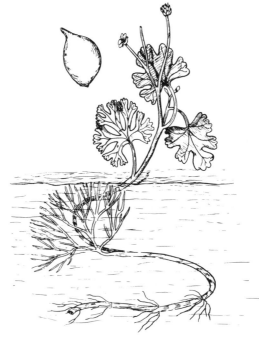

Fig. 196. **Ranunculus gmelinii**

13a. Leaves very finely dissected into thread-like divisions; flowers very showy; plants of high tundra. **Ranunculus adoneus** Gray (resembling the genus *Adonis*), Snow Buttercup, Fig. 198. Commonly found around melting snowbanks, one of the few strictly alpine buttercups.

13b. Leaves with broader divisions; flowers relatively small; plants of plains to subalpine or alpine .... (14)

14a. Receptacle at maturity longer than wide; achenes not stalked or winged at the base .... (15)

14b. Receptacle at maturity not elongated; achenes with a broad thin stalk or winged base. **Ranunculus glaberrimus** Hook. var. **ellipticus** Greene (very smooth; elliptic), Sagebrush Buttercup, Fig. 199. Open hillsides in the lower foothills, on sites which are moist in early spring. One of the earliest spring flowers, and easily overlooked.

15a. Achenes pubescent .... (17)
15b. Achenes glabrous .... (16)

16a. Some or all of the basal leaves merely crenate-dentate, not divided or parted. **Ranunculus abortivus** L. ssp. **acrolasius** (Fern.) Kapoor (abortive, i.e. with tiny petals; hairy at the top), Small-flowered Crowfoot. Infrequent, wooded streambanks in the foothills.

16b. Most of the basal leaves cleft to the middle or below. **Ranunculus eschscholtzii** Schlecht. (for J. F. Eschscholtz), Subalpine Buttercup, Fig. 200. In shade, moist forest floors, subalpine. A rare alpine relative of this, *R. gelidus* Kar. & Kar. ssp. *grayi* (Britt.) Hultén has been found on Grays Peak. *R. gelidus* has very regularly dissected, somewhat fleshy leaves, and flower stalks which hardly exceed the

Fig. 197. **Ranunculus sceleratus**

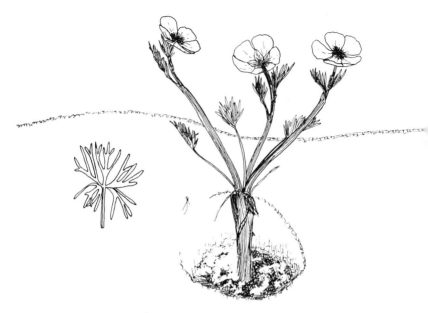

Fig. 198. **Ranunculus adoneus**

Fig. 199. **Ranunculus glaberrimus**

length of the basal leaves. In our region, *R. eschscholtzii* is usually taller, with irregularly dissected leaves.

17a. Most of the basal leaves cleft to near the base. ***Ranunculus pedatifidus*** Smith, Birdfoot Buttercup. Pond borders, wet meadows, subalpine.
17b. Blades of the basal leaves, or most of them, merely crenate or shallowly lobed .... (18)

18a. Petals large (averaging 1 cm long). ***Ranunculus cardiophyllus*** Hook., Heart-leaved Buttercup. Margins of ponds, wet meadows, upper montane and subalpine. Both flowers and fruit should be available for certain identification of this species and the ones preceding and following in the key.
18b. Petals small (averaging 5 mm or less). ***Ranunculus inamoenus*** Greene (unattractive). Meadows and pond borders, upper montane, subalpine.

THALICTRUM. Meadow-rue

1a. Plant very tall, stout, deep green; leaflets 3-lobed, the lobes usually entire; inflorescence a showy pyramidal panicle; achenes not flattened. ***Thalictrum dasycarpum*** F. & L. (hairy-fruited), Purple Meadow-rue.

Fig. 200. ***Ranunculus eschscholtzii***   Fig. 201. ***Thalictrum alpinum***

A tall, handsome plant, abundant in late spring along irrigation ditches in the piedmont valleys. Plants are sometimes over 2 meters tall.

1b. Plant delicate, slender; leaflets 3-lobed, the lobes usually lobed again; achenes flattened .... (2)

2a. Stems very low, less than 20 cm high, the leaves chiefly basal; flowers perfect, in a simple raceme; rare plant of peat bogs and tundra, alpine and subalpine. *Thalictrum alpinum* L., ALPINE MEADOW-RUE, Fig. 201. A distinctive meadow-rue because of its extremely small size and perfect flowers in a simple raceme.

2b. Stem tall and leafy; flowers in panicles, perfect or unisexual (flowers of each sex, however, may be present on the same stem) (3)

3a. Upper edge of carpel straight or concave; lower edge deeply convex; lateral parallel veins of carpel not prominent, but mature carpel with oblique veins. *Thalictrum sparsiflorum* Trel., FEW-FLOWERED MEADOW-RUE. Forests and shaded ravines, montane, subalpine.

3b. Upper and lower edges of carpels convex; lateral parallel veins of carpel prominent. *Thalictrum fendleri* Engelm. (for August Fendler). In similar habitats to the preceding, and difficult to distinguish from it except with mature fruit.

TROLLIUS. GLOBEFLOWER

One species, *Trollius laxus* Salisb. Common in moist forest openings and marshy places, subalpine, often in snowmelt basins along with *Caltha leptosepala*. A curious instance of a species found in low-altitude swamps in New England and at high altitudes in the Rockies. Although ours was originally thought to differ by having pure white flowers (var. *albiflorus* Gray) the eastern and western population both have cream-colored flowers and are hardly distinguishable.

RESEDACEAE—MIGNONETTE FAMILY

The word **reseda**, according to the Roman naturalist, Pliny (A. D. 23-79), is the imperative of the ancient verb *resedare*, to quiet, heal. The inhabitants of ancient Rimini used the plant to cure boils and inflammations with a magic incantation beginning, "Reseda, morbos, reseda" ("Reseda, cure the sickness"). This small family contains a favorite old-fashioned garden plant, *Reseda odorata*, cultivated for its exquisite fragrance. *Reseda luteola*, the Dyer's Woad, was a commercial dye plant yielding a yellow color. This species occurred around Denver in the 1880's but evidently did not persist there. *Reseda* flowers are peculiar in that the stamens and the gynoecium are mounted together on a common stalk called an androgynophore and the stamens are clustered on one side of the flower rather than being evenly distributed around the gynoecium.

One genus and species, *Reseda lutea* L. (yellow), WILD MIGNONETTE.

An introduced weed, locally abundant on the Pierre and Niobrara shales just north of Boulder. Curiously, it has been known to occur here since 1938, but has never spread beyond the area of the shale outcrops, probably bound to a particular ecological situation.

RHAMNACEAE—BUCKTHORN FAMILY

This family is characterized by the shrubby habit, leaves with three principal veins, with the remainder closely parallel and pinnate, and flowers in which the stamens are *opposite* the petals. Few families have this condition (see Primulaceae and Portulacaceae).

Our only genus, *Ceanothus*, is most diversified in California with over 40 species including some extremely beautiful and decorative shrubs used horticulturally (California Lilac). *Rhamnus purshiana* of the Pacific Northwest yielded the bark called *cascara sagrada*, used medicinally as a tonic and laxative. *Rhamnus cathartica* is a common cultivated ornamental shrub in our area.

1a. Plants sprawling, with thorn-like branchlets; leaves less than 2 cm long, entire or nearly so. ***Ceanothus fendleri*** Gray (for August Fendler), BUCKBRUSH. Dry hillsides, foothills. Flowers white.
1b. Plants without thorn-like branchlets; leaves 3 cm or more long, toothed .... (2)

2a. Leaves averaging 5 cm long or more, leathery, shining, sticky and balsam-scented, inrolled when dry. ***Ceanothus velutinus*** Dougl. (velvety), STICKY-LAUREL, Fig. 202. Frequent on mountainsides in the

Fig. 202. *Ceanothus velutinus*

foothills and drier parts of the subalpine zone. Flowers white.

2b. Leaves averaging 3 cm long or less, thin, dull, merely pubescent, not strongly balsam-scented. ***Ceanothus herbaceus*** Raf., Redroot; New Jersey Tea. Locally frequent on the mesas, where it belongs to the element of midwest prairie relicts. It hybridizes locally with *C. fendleri* in some outer foothill canyons, producing populations intermediate in leaf size and thorniness. This form was described by Rydberg as *C. subsericeus*.

Rosaceae—Rose Family

The flowers of most members of the rose family are astonishingly similar, the main differences, besides size and color, being in the number and structure of the carpels. All rosaceous flowers have an hypanthium or fused cup formed by the bases of the calyx, corolla and stamens. There is often a confusing "extra" set of calyx-like parts alternating with the real sepals. For want of an understanding we give them a name—bracteoles. They also occur in the mallows. In a family that provides so many edible fruits, it is odd to find that the edible part is formed in many ways from quite different floral parts: hypanthium (Apple, Pear), carpel wall (Cherry, Plum), receptacle (Strawberry), the whole carpel group (Raspberry), and carpel plus receptacle (Blackberries).

1a. Shrubs or small trees . . . . (2)
1b. Herbs, sometimes woody at the very base . . . . (13)

2a. Leaves compound . . . . (3)
2b. Leaves simple . . . . (6)

3a. Leaflets serrate, pinnately arranged; flowers white or pink . . . (4)
3b. Leaflets entire, pinnately arranged but crowded so that they appear palmate; flowers yellow. ***Pentaphylloides***, Shrubby Cinquefoil, page 293.

4a. Leaflets 11 to 15; small tree with umbel-like flower clusters and orange-red berries; thorns or prickles absent. ***Sorbus***, Mountain-ash, page 302.
4b. Leaflets 5 to 7; shrubs with thorns or prickles . . . . (5)

5a. Leaves strongly glaucous beneath; flowers white; fruit a "raspberry." ***Rubus***, Raspberry, page 300.
5b. Leaves green, often pale but not whitened beneath; flowers pink; fruit a "hip." ***Rosa***, Rose, page 300.

6a. Leaves oblanceolate, 3-lobed at the apex. ***Purshia***, Bitterbrush, page 299.
6b. Leaves not as above . . . . (7)

7a. Fruit a drupe (cherry or plum); leaves and twigs glabrous, the leaves finely serrulate, never lobed. ***Prunus***, Plum; Cherry, page 299.

7b. Fruit not a drupe; leaves and twigs either pubescent, or the leaves coarsely serrate, or lobed .... (8)

8a. Leaves palmately lobed, often faintly so .... (9)
8b. Leaves simple or shallowly pinnately lobed .... (11)

9a. Twigs with stout thorns. *Crataegus,* HAWTHORN, page 292.
9b. Twigs unarmed .... (10)

10a. Flowers large, solitary or in few-flowered cymes; fruit an aggregate of fleshy achenes (raspberry). *Rubus,* RASPBERRY, page 300.
10b. Flowers small, in umbellate cymes; fruit composed of a cluster of 2 or more papery carpels. *Physocarpus,* NINEBARK, page 295.

11a. Flowers in terminal, many-flowered, pyramidal clusters; leaves less than 2 cm long. *Holodiscus,* OCEAN-SPRAY, page 293.
11b. Flowers axillary or in few-flowered clusters; some leaves at least 2 cm long .... (12)

12a. Leaves tapering to the base; style becoming long and feathery in fruit; leaves permanently and densely pubescent beneath. *Cercocarpus,* MOUNTAIN-MAHOGANY, page 291.
12b. Leaves abruptly rounded at the base; petiole distinct; fruit a pome (apple type), without an elongate style; leaves often losing much of their pubescence at maturity. *Amelanchier,* JUNEBERRY; SHADBUSH; SERVICEBERRY, page 290. (Note: the common Apple Tree, *Malus domestica* Borkh., occasionally escaped from cultivation, will key down here also.)

13a. Leaves ternately cleft into many linear divisions. *Chamaerhodos,* page 292.
13b. Leaves simple, or digitately or pinnately compound .... (14)

14a. Leaves simple, crenate, whitened beneath; matted alpine plants. *Dryas,* MOUNTAIN AVENS, page 292.
14b. Leaves compound .... (15)

15a. Receptacle fleshy at maturity; plants reproducing by stolons; leaves with 3 leaflets. *Fragaria,* STRAWBERRY, page 293.
15b. Receptacle dry at maturity; plants without the above combination of characters .... (16)

16a. Fruit an aggregation of fleshy achenes (a raspberry); leaves long-petioled, with 3 leaflets; plant with stolons; very rare, foothills near Boulder. *Rubus pubescens* Raf.
16b. Plant not as above .... (17)

17a. Calyx covered with hooked prickles. *Agrimonia,* AGRIMONY, page 290.
17b. Calyx smooth or variously pubescent, not prickly .... (18)

18a. Style withering and falling from the achene at maturity ...... (20)
18b. Style persistent on the achene, frequently elongated .... (19)

19a. Style jointed, the lower part persistent and with a terminal hook; leaves pinnately compound with few leaflets, the uppermost one usually larger; flowers erect, yellow, white, or rose. *Geum*, Avens, page 293.
19b. Style continuous, the lower part without a hook; leaves with many narrow leaflets .... (24)

20a. Dwarf alpine mat-plant with thick, green, glabrous, trifoliolate leaves; leaflets few-toothed at apex; petals shorter than sepals. *Sibbaldia*, page 302.
20b. Not as above; if dwarf, the leaves thin, or regularly toothed, or pubescent .... (21)

21a. Flowers in tight many-flowered heads or spikes. *Sanguisorba*, Burnet, page 302.
21b. Flowers in more open clusters .... (22)

22a. Plant spreading by long stolons; leaves with 7 to 30 leaflets, pinnately compound, silky-tomentose beneath. *Argentina*, Silverweed, page 291.
22b. Plants not stoloniferous, or if so, then with palmately compound leaves .... (23)

23a. Style attached to near top of ovary; leaves either palmately or narrowly pinnately compound. *Potentilla*, Five-finger, page 295.
23b. Style attached near the base of the ovary; leaves pinnately compound with broadly oval leaflets. *Drymocallis*, page 292.

24a. Petals yellow; flowers erect. *Acomastylis*, Alpine Avens, below.
24b. Petals pinkish-white; flowers nodding. *Erythrocoma*, page 293.

ACOMASTYLIS. Alpine Avens

One species, *Acomastylis rossii* (R. Br.) Greene ssp. *turbinata* (Rydb.) W. A. Weber (for Capt. James C. Ross), Fig. 209. Very abundant on rocky tundra, forming a dense, tight turf in areas with relatively little winter snow cover. *Acomastylis* is responsible for the deep red autumn color on the tundra, contrasting with the golden bronze of *Kobresia*. *Acomastylis* is essentially an Asiatic genus (*Geum rossii* of Ed. 4).

AGRIMONIA. Agrimony

One species, *Agrimonia striata* Michx. Frequent in canyon bottoms in the foothills. Leaves pinnately compound, flowers yellow, in racemes.

AMELANCHIER. Juneberry; Shadbush; Serviceberry

1a. Plant entirely glabrous (even the buds and young twigs). *Amelanchier pumila* Nutt. (dwarf), Smooth Shadbush. Upper montane, subalpine.

1b. At least the young twigs pubescent ....(2)

2a. Leaves permanently soft-hairy beneath; plants of the mesas. ***Amelanchier utahensis*** Koehne, Utah Shadbush. Principally a plant of southern and western Colorado, but found on the fringe of mesas along the eastern Front Range.

2b. Leaves glabrate in age; plants of foothills and mountains. ***Amelanchier alnifolia*** Nutt. (alder-leaved), Common Shadbush, Fig. 203. Common shrub or small tree, foothills to subalpine.

ARGENTINA. Silverweed.

One species, ***Argentina anserina*** (L.) Rydb. Mountain meadows, occasionally also as a weed, montane and subalpine. The bicolored pinnate leaves and long red stolons are diagnostic (*Potentilla anserina* of Ed. 4).

CERCOCARPUS. Mountain-mahogany

One species, ***Cercocarpus montanus*** Raf., Fig. 204. Common in the chaparral belt on mesas and lower foothills. Style long and plumose in fruit, spirally twisted when dry, a "self-planter."

Fig. 203. *Amelanchier alnifolia*   Fig. 204. *Cercocarpus montanus*

CHAMAERHODOS

One species, ***Chamaerhodos erecta*** (L.) Bunge ssp. ***nuttallii*** (Pickering *ex* T. & G.) Hultén. Rare or infrequent on gravelly hillsides, foothills, montane. A small Asiatic genus, with our species occurring from Siberia to the Rocky Mountains.

CRATAEGUS. Hawthorn

1a. Leaves and stems somewhat pubescent, dull. ***Crataegus succulenta*** Link, Western Hawthorn. Common shrub on canyonsides, lower foothills, and mesas. Apparently hybridizes with the next.

1b. Leaves and stems glabrous, shining. ***Crataegus erythropoda*** Ashe (red-stemmed), Hawthorn. Common shrub on canyonsides, lower foothills and mesas.

DRYAS. Mountain Avens

One species, ***Dryas octopetala*** L. ssp. ***hookeriana*** (Juz.) Hultén, Fig. 205. Locally abundant on tundra. Petals white, usually about 8. Styles long, silky at maturity. The subspecies is recognized by presence of short, dark tack-shaped glandular hairs on the midrib underneath. The species proper lacks these and has instead plumose hairs scattered along the midrib. A few plants from Trail Ridge have both types on the same leaf.

DRYMOCALLIS

1a. Petals white or cream-colored, scarcely longer than the sepals. ***Drymocallis arguta*** (Pursh) Rydb., Sticky Cinquefoil. Montane and

Fig. 205. ***Dryas octopetala***

subalpine meadows. Taller than the next, with very glandular upper foliage and stems (*Potentilla arguta* of Ed. 4).

1b. Petals bright yellow, usually longer than the sepals. ***Drymocallis fissa*** (Nutt.) Rydb., Plate 24. Abundant from foothills to subalpine, flowering in late spring (*Potentilla fissa* of Ed. 4).

ERYTHROCOMA

One species, ***Erythrocoma triflora*** (Pursh) Greene. THREE-FLOWERED AVENS. Common in meadows and aspen groves, montane and subalpine (*Geum triflorum* of Ed. 4).

FRAGARIA. STRAWBERRY

1a. Hairs of the scapes (and commonly of the petioles) appressed or ascending; leaves commonly somewhat glaucous, thickish; leaflets obovate-oblong to nearly spatulate, long-cuneate at the base, few-toothed, mainly toward the apex; fruit deeply pitted, the carpels partly buried in the flesh. ***Fragaria ovalis*** (Lehm.) Rydb. Common on dry forested mountainsides, foothills to subalpine.

1b. Hairs of the scapes and petioles spreading or somewhat reflexed; leaves thin, not glaucous; leaflets rhombic-ovate or obovate, short-cuneate at the base, toothed to well below the middle; fruit shallowly pitted, the carpels on the surface. ***Fragaria americana*** (Porter) Britt. Similar habitats but much less abundant than the preceding.

GEUM. AVENS

1a. Petals yellow; sepals purplish, reflexed after blossoming . . . . (2)

1b. Petals pale violet; sepals green, not reflexed after blossoming. ***Geum rivale*** L. (of brooksides), PURPLE AVENS. Swamps and low grounds, subalpine.

2a. Lower section of style glabrous or sparsely pubescent at base, not glandular; terminal leaf segment not greatly enlarged. ***Geum aleppicum*** Jacq. (of Aleppo, Syria), YELLOW AVENS. Ravines and canyonsides, mesas to montane.

2b. Lower section of style glandular-puberulent; terminal leaf-segment usually greatly enlarged. ***Geum macrophyllum*** Willdenow, LARGE-LEAVED AVENS. Abundant in moist places, foothills to subalpine. The terminal leaflet is fan-shaped in the typical form, but narrower and incised in ssp. ***perincisum*** (Rydb.) Hultén.

HOLODISCUS. OCEAN SPRAY

One species, ***Holodiscus dumosus*** (Nutt.) Heller (bushy), Fig. 206. Locally abundant on canyonsides in the foothills, especially in the Clear Creek drainage.

PENTAPHYLLOIDES. SHRUBBY CINQUEFOIL

One species, ***Pentaphylloides floribunda*** (Pursh) A. Löve, Fig. 207.

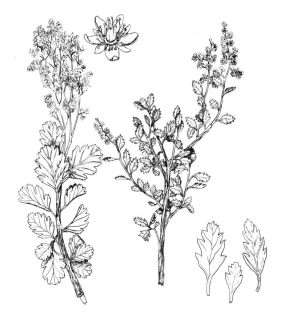

Fig. 206. **Holodiscus dumosus**

Fig. 207. **Pentaphylloides floribunda**

Abundant in wet meadows and on pond shores, montane, subalpine
(*Potentilla fruticosa* of manuals).

PHYSOCARPUS. Ninebark

1a. Leaves mostly wedge-shaped at the base, the blades 3-8 cm long, with
3 principal lobes; mature fruits up to 1 cm long. ***Physocarpus opulifolius***
(L.) Maxim. (with leaves like *Viburnum opulus*). Uncommon in the
foothills.

1b. Leaves truncate or even somewhat heart-shaped at the base, the
blades small (2-3 cm long), with a tendency to be 5-lobed; mature
fruits not much more than 5 mm long. ***Physocarpus monogynus*** (Torr.)
Coult. (with one ovary; a misnomer), Fig. 208. A very common shrub of
bushy hillsides; foothills to subalpine. The leaves resemble those of
currants but the flowers are in umbel-like clusters.

POTENTILLA. Cinquefoil; Five-finger

Our species are very complicated biologically. Several common
species hybridize, and their progeny reproduce asexually, giving rise to
large, relatively stable hybrid colonies. The alpine species are in great
need of careful research involving comparison with their Arctic and
Asiatic relatives. The key, therefore, should be considered very tentative.

1a. Short-lived annuals or biennials, mostly weeds .... (2)
1b. Perennials; native plants .... (4)

Fig. 208. ***Physocarpus monogynus***

2a. Leaves all pinnately compound, with 5 or more leaflets; achene with a swelling on the side. ***Potentilla paradoxa*** Nutt. (strange), BUSHY CINQUE-FOIL. Bottomlands and pond shores, plains and piedmont valleys.

2b. Some or all of the leaves with 3 leaflets (trifoliolate) .... (3)

3a. Upper leaves trifoliolate, the lower pinnately compound. ***Potentilla rivalis*** Nutt. (of brooksides), RIVER CINQUEFOIL. Bottomlands and lake shores, plains and piedmont valleys.

3b. All the leaves trifoliolate. ***Potentilla norvegica*** L., NORWAY CINQUE-FOIL. Common weed in disturbed soil (*P. monspeliensis* L.).

4a. Leaves with three leaflets .... (5)

4b. Leaves with more than three leaflets (the lower sometimes quite small) .... (7)

5a. Plants less than 10 cm high; flowering scapes unbranched, with only a few small bracts and 1 to 3 flowers. ***Potentilla ledebouriana*** A. Porsild, ALPINE CINQUEFOIL. Rocky tundra.

5b. Plants over 10 cm high; flowering scapes with a few spreading branches, several well-developed leaflike bracts and several flower clusters .... (6)

6a. Petioles with crinkled tomentum and some longer straight hairs. ***Potentilla hookeriana*** Lehm. Rare, on tundra of the Mt. Evans-Hoosier Pass area and middle ranges.

6b. Petioles with uniform tomentum and no straight hairs. ***Potentilla nivea*** L., SNOW CINQUEFOIL. Common on tundra. Externally very similar to *P. ledebouriana* when dwarfed, but that has some straight hairs on petioles.

Fig. 209. *Acomastylis rossii*

7a. Leaves digitately 5- to 9-foliolate, sometimes with an additional pair of leaflets on the petiole .... (8)
7b. Leaves distinctly odd-pinnately compound .... (15)

8a. Plants with long leafy stolons, creeping along the ground. ***Potentilla anglica*** Laicharding. An introduced weed locally established along Boulder Creek east of Boulder.
8b. Plants lacking stolons; caespitose perennials .... (9)

9a. Basal leaves with an additional pair of leaflets on the petiole. (10)
9b. Basal leaves without additional leaflets, strictly digitate .... (12)

10a. Leaflets glaucous, broad, not very deeply incised, the basal pair very close to the other three. ***Potentilla diversifolia*** Lehm., Fig. 210. Very common in subalpine meadows.
10b. Leaflets not glaucous, very deeply incised, the segments narrow; basal pair of leaflets usually remote from the others .... (11)

11a. Leaflets densely silky-pubescent, the leaflets somewhat rounded at the apex; leaflets usually five, but occasionally with a few smaller ones below. ***Potentilla rubricaulis*** Lehm. Common on tundra.
11b. Leaflets green, very sparingly pubescent, sharply pointed; leaves usually distinctly pinnate. ***Potentilla ovina*** Macoun (of sheep). Similar alpine habitats.

Fig. 210. ***Potentilla diversifolia***   Fig. 211. ***Prunus americana***

12a. Depressed-spreading alpine and subalpine plants; leaves with 5 leaflets, silvery-hairy on both sides. ***Potentilla concinna*** Rich. This is a catch-all of what may be depauperate plants of *P. gracilis* var. *pulcherrima* or forms of *P. nivea* with 5 leaflets.

12b. Plants erect, or over 1 dm high ....(13)

13a. Leaves bicolored, soft white-tomentose beneath, green above. ***Potentilla gracilis*** Dougl. *ex* Hook. var. ***pulcherrima*** (Lehm.) Fern. (slender; very handsome), SOFT CINQUEFOIL. Very common in subalpine meadows. Assumed hybrids of this with *P. hippiana* combine the bicolored leaves and pinnate arrangement of the two species. The hybrids are also very abundant.

13b. Leaves green on both sides ....(14)

14a. Low, suberect plants less than 3 dm tall; flowers few, on slender stems; leaves mostly basal, often somewhat glaucous. ***Potentilla diversifolia*** Lehm., Fig. 210. Moist situations, subalpine and alpine.

14b. Tall plants 3 dm or more high; flowers numerous in a flat-topped inflorescence; stems stout, leafy, very variable in pubescence. ***Potentilla gracilis*** Dougl. var. ***glabrata*** (Lehm.) C. L. Hitchc.

15a. Style short, no longer than the mature achene, glandular-thickened below; plant never subscapose, rarely densely woolly-pubescent.

Fig. 212. ***Prunus virginiana***

Potentilla pensylvanica L., PRAIRIE CINQUEFOIL. Meadows, montane and subalpine.

15b. Style long, exceeding the mature achene, filiform; plant either subscapose or densely woolly-pubescent ....(16)

16a. Leaves green or greenish, the leaflets deeply lobed or dissected, never tomentose; plants subscapose ....(17)
16b. Leaves whitish-silky or tomentose on both sides; plant leafy-stemmed. *Potentilla hippiana* Lehm. (for C. F. Hipp), WOOLLY CINQUEFOIL. Very common, from mesas to subalpine. Plants with the leaves green above may be hybrids between this and *P. gracilis.* Such plants are often found where the two species grow together.

17a. Leaves bipinnately compound with narrowly elliptical segments; flowering stems numerous with many flowers; plants of moist meadows and ditches, montane and subalpine. *Potentilla plattensis* Nutt.
17b. Leaves pinnately compound with cuneate segments; flowering stems few, not richly floriferous ....(18)

18a. Plants with only a few stems from a slightly woody base; alpine tundra plants. *Potentilla ovina* Macoun.
18b. Plants forming massive tussocks with much dead basal stem and leaf material, growing on cliffs in the foothills. *Potentilla rupincola* Osterh. An endangered species, known only from cliffs near Virginia Dale, north of Fort Collins.

PRUNUS. CHERRY; PLUM

1a. Short lateral twigs modified to form blunt thorns; fruit large, the pit or stone flattened. *Prunus americana* Marsh., WILD PLUM, Fig. 211. Forms dense thickets in gulches or canyonsides, mesas and foothills.
1b. Lateral twigs not modified; fruit small, the stone not flattened (2)

2a. Flowers and fruits in racemes. *Prunus virginiana* L. var. *melanocarpa* (Nels.) Sarg., CHOKE CHERRY, Fig. 212. Gulches and canyonsides, plains to foothills.
2b. Flowers in axillary clusters ....(3)

3a. Tall shrub or small tree; leaves tapering to an acuminate tip; fruits bright red. *Prunus pensylvanica* L., WILD RED CHERRY; PIN CHERRY. Infrequent, ravines in the foothills.
3b. Low shrub; leaves oblanceolate, acute or obtuse at the apex; fruits purple or maroon. *Prunus besseyi* Bailey (for C. E. Bessey), SAND CHERRY. Sandy soil on the plains, sparingly on the mesas.

PURSHIA. BITTERBRUSH; ANTELOPE-BRUSH

One species, *Purshia tridentata* (Pursh) DC. (three-toothed), Fig. 213. Chaparral belt on the mesas and foothills, and on rocky montane south slopes. An important browse food for game animals.

ROSA. ROSE

1a. Floral stems bristly to apex or nearly so, more rarely with thorns, very
rarely without armature; sepals about 3 mm wide at base ....(2)

1b. Floral stems with thorns and occasionally with intermixed bristles,
rarely without armature; sepals about 2 mm wide at the base.
Rosa woodsii Lindl. (for Joseph Woods). Common throughout the
mountains.

2a. Leaflets obovate-cuneate to cuneate, often pubescent below and
above; inflorescence usually 5- or more-flowered. ***Rosa arkansana***
Porter (of the Arkansas River). Plains and lower foothills.

2b. Leaflets ovate, occasionally pubescent below; inflorescence 1- to 3-
flowered; mostly absent from the plains. ***Rosa acicularis*** Lindl. (with
needle-like prickles). The roses are biologically very complex and
they may hybridize. For this reason many individuals will not key
satisfactorily.

RUBUS. RASPBERRY; BLACKBERRY

1a. Plant herbaceous; leaves trifoliolate. ***Rubus pubescens*** Raf. (hairy),
DWARF RASPBERRY. Very rare, in cool ravines in the foothills near
Boulder. The plant reproduces by stolons, and superficially resembles
a strawberry plant.

1b. Plant shrubby ....(2)

2a. Leaves simple ....(3)

2b. Leaves compound ....(4)

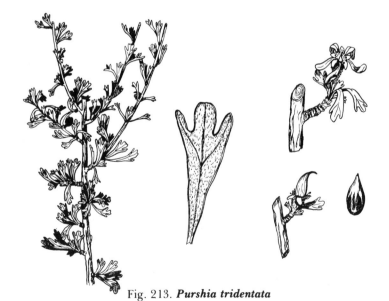

Fig. 213. ***Purshia tridentata***

3a. Leaves 3-6 cm wide, the lobes rounded. ***Rubus deliciosus*** James, Boulder Raspberry, Fig. 214. Common shrub of the mesas and foothills. Flowers white, about 4 cm across. The scientific name is a misnomer; the fruit is anything but delicious.

3b. Leaves 10-20 cm wide, the lobes acute. ***Rubus parviflorus*** Nutt. (small-flowered; a misnomer), Thimbleberry, Fig. 215. In cool ravines, foothills to subalpine. Flowers white.

4a. Leaves evergreen, green on both sides; stems with stout recurved thorns. ***Rubus laciniatus*** Willd., Evergreen Blackberry. A horticultural plant escaped and established in canyons near Boulder. It can be a nuisance because of the impenetrable thickets it forms.

4b. Leaves deciduous, white beneath; stems with slender straight prickles. ***Rubus idaeus*** L. ssp. ***melanolasius*** (Dieck) Focke (of Mt. Ida; black-hairy), Wild Raspberry. Cool moist hillsides and gulches, foothills to subalpine. The Black Raspberry, *R. occidentalis* L., has been found near Boulder as an escape. It has glaucous stems and purplish-black berries.

Fig. 215. ***Rubus parviflorus***

Fig. 214. ***Rubus deliciosus***

SANGUISORBA. Burnet

One species, ***Sanguisorba minor*** Scop. A perennial weed of Europe, established mostly south of Colorado Springs but known in the Denver area from an old collection. The tight flowering heads and the pinnately compound leaves with serrate, petioled leaflets, characterize the species.

SIBBALDIA

One species, ***Sibbaldia procumbens*** L. (lying on the ground). Gravelly or rocky slopes, particularly near patches of late-lying snow, subalpine and alpine.

SORBUS. Mountain-ash

One species, ***Sorbus scopulina*** Greene, Fig. 216. Cool ravines, foothills to subalpine, rare or infrequent. Its close relative, the European Rowan Tree, *S. aucuparia* L. is cultivated here for its orange berries, taken avidly by robins and cedar waxwings.

Rubiaceae—Madder Family

The Madder Family gets its name from Madder (*Rubia tinctorum*), cultivated since ancient times for a red dye obtained from its roots. It is a

Fig. 216. ***Sorbus scopulina***

large, mostly tropical family. Our little genus *Galium* is a pale shadow of the many useful and handsome ornamental trees and shrubs belonging to the group. Familiar members of the family are Coffee (*Coffea arabica*), Quinine (*Cinchona* spp.) and Ipecac (*Cephaelis* spp.). The name "Bedstraw" derives from the fact that masses of the light-weight stems of *Galium* form a springy "ticking" because the hook-like hairs on the corners of the stems and leaves catch on each other and prevent the stack from matting down.

Galium, our only genus, is unmistakeable with its combination of square stems, retrorse prickles on the stems and leaves, tiny white 4-merous flowers and "double," usually hairy or spiny fruits that separate at maturity into one-seeded ball-like nutlets (mericarps).

1a. Reclining or sprawling annual; leaves and stems harshly hispid; leaves 6 to 8 in a whorl . . . . (2)
1b. Erect, although sometimes weak, perennials; leaves and stems not excessively hispid; leaves 6 or fewer in a whorl . . . . (3)

2a. Flowers greenish-yellow, 1-1.5 mm in diameter; fruits 1.5-2.8 mm long (top to bottom); stem nodes glabrous or slightly hairy; leaves about 3 mm broad. **Galium spurium** L., FALSE CLEAVERS. In shade of shrubs on canyon slopes and shrubby roadsides. This species is very similar to the next, and has only recently been proven to occur in America. It seems to be more common here than the next. See Addenda.
2b. Flowers white, 2 mm in diameter; fruits 2.8-4 mm long; stem nodes usually tomentose; leaves about 5 mm broad. **Galium aparine** L. (old generic name, meaning to scratch or cling), GOOSEGRASS; CLEAVERS. Common on the mesas and foothills.

3a. Leaves 3-nerved; flowers numerous, in a showy terminal cymose panicle; robust plants of open places. **Galium boreale** L. ssp. **septentrionale** (R. & S.) Hara, Fig. 217. Leaves usually four at a node. Dry slopes, roadsides, from the foothill canyons to subalpine.
3b. Leaves one-nerved; flowers inconspicuous, in few-flowered axillary clusters; weak plants of forests and swamps . . . . (4)

4a. Leaves 6 at a node, abruptly sharp-pointed; inflorescence consisting of 3-flowered cymes; fruit very bristly; woodland species. **Galium triflorum** Michx. (3-flowered), FRAGRANT BEDSTRAW. Shady forests and canyon slopes. The dried foliage is sweet smelling.
4b. Leaves 2 or 4 at a node, blunt-tipped; flowers solitary or few, not in 3-flowered cymes; fruit almost or quite glabrous; species of very wet ground. **Galium trifidum** L. (3-cleft), SMALL BEDSTRAW. Lake shores and bogs, upper montane and subalpine.

Other species: *Galium bifolium* S. Wats., a little erect annual with opposite leaves (often with a second smaller pair creating a whorl of four) and bristly fruits, is abundant in forests from Rabbit Ears Pass westward into Routt County. *Galium coloradoensis* W. F. Wright, is a xerophytic bushy perennial occurring in the canyons of arid western Colorado. It has unisexual plants, somewhat woody bases, and fruits with long stiff hairs.

Salicaceae—Willow Family

Willows are very difficult to identify because the important characters are ephemeral. One needs young leaves, mature leaves, flowering catkins, fruiting catkins and stipules. These parts appear, mature and fall at different times of year and in order to see them all one must tag a bush or tree and return to it several times. Most of us do not have the patience, hence the difficulty of telling which willow is which. Much of the variability of willows is developmental; at least in our region we have hardly any real evidence of interspecific hybridization although this is common in higher latitudes. Anyone in search of a productive hobby would do well to study willows.

1a. Buds with several overlapping scales, resinous; bracts lacerate (jagged-edged); stamens numerous in each flower; flowers on broad cup-shaped disks; aments (catkins) pendulous. *Populus,* Cottonwood; Aspen, page 304.

1b. Bud enclosed by a single scale, not resinous; bracts entire or denticulate; stamens few, 2 to 5; flowers not borne on disks; catkins usually erect. *Salix,* Willow, page 306.

POPULUS. Cottonwood; Aspen; Poplar

1a. Petiole flattened perpendicular to the plane of the leaf; leaves little or no longer than broad .... (2)

1b. Petioles not flattened as above; leaves mostly at least one-third longer than broad .... (3)

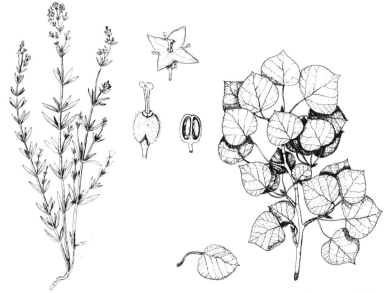

Fig. 217. **Galium boreale**   Fig. 218. **Populus tremuloides**

2a. Leaves broadly ovate to suborbicular, 3-8 cm in diameter, finely serrate; bark smooth, white or greenish; buds conical; stigmas 2, filiform. ***Populus tremuloides*** Michx. (resembling the European species, *P. tremula*), QUAKING ASPEN, Fig. 218. Foothills to subalpine.

2b. Leaves deltoid, 5-10 cm long, coarsely serrate; bark furrowed; buds ovoid; stigmas 3 to 4, broad. ***Populus sargentii*** Dode (for C. S. Sargent), PLAINS COTTONWOOD, Fig. 219. Floodplains, piedmont valleys, and plains. Commonly cultivated as a shade tree.

3a. Leaves ovate to ovate-lanceolate, lighter below; terminal bud 2-2.5 cm long, very resinous-sticky. ***Populus balsamifera*** L., BALSAM POPLAR, Infrequent, upper montane, subalpine.

3b. Leaves lanceolate to ovate-lanceolate, green on both sides; terminal bud less than 2 cm long, slender (may or may not be sticky) .... (4)

4a. Leaves with an abruptly acuminate apex; blade ovate-lanceolate to rhombic-lanceolate, never narrowly lanceolate; petiole at least half the length of the blade; buds 6- to 7-scaled, non-aromatic, not sticky. ***Populus X acuminata*** Rydb. Evidently a first-generation hybrid between *P. sargentii* and *P. angustifolia*, occurring in the lower canyons where the ranges of these overlap, and reproducing by suckers and branch rooting.

4b. Leaves with merely an acute apex; blade usually lanceolate, but sometimes quite broad; petiole a third the length of the blade or shorter; bud 5-scaled, aromatic, rather sticky. ***Populus angustifolia*** James, NARROWLEAF COTTONWOOD, Fig. 220. Floodplains and streambanks, foothills to montane. The most abundant wild cottonwood, with the exception of Aspen.

Fig. 219. ***Populus sargentii***   Fig. 220. ***Populus angustifolia***

SALIX. Willow

1a. Leaves linear, many times longer than wide; plants exclusively of wet, sandy places on the plains and along the foothills creeks .... (2)
1b. Leaves broader .... (3)

2a. Leaves permanently pubescent on both sides, mostly entire but sometimes remotely denticulate. *Salix exigua* Nutt. (little), Sandbar Willow. Along ditches, riverbanks, plains, piedmont valleys and foothill canyons. Very variable in pubescence, depending somewhat on the age of the leaves.
2b. Leaves glabrous or nearly so at maturity, at least on the upper surface, remotely dentate. *Salix interior* Rowlee (inland), Sandbar Willow. Very similar to the last, and in similar habitats.

3a. Depressed, prostrate-creeping, strictly alpine plants less than 10 cm high .... (4)
3b. Taller plants, sometimes dwarfed by grazing or alpine conditions, but hardly ever creeping or less than 10 cm high .... (6)

4a. Apex of most leaves obtuse, the blades glaucous and reticulate beneath. *Salix nivalis* Hook., Snow Willow, Fig. 221. A tiny alpine mat plant, easily overlooked. Very closely related to the Arctic *S. reticulata* L. and considered by some to be a race of it.
4b. Apex of most leaves acute, the blades not reticulate beneath. (5)

5a. Catkins 2-4 cm long, many-flowered; leaves 2-4 cm long, paler beneath; old leaves not persistent; scales dark brown. *Salix arctica* Pallas. Common on upper subalpine and alpine slopes.
5b. Catkins 0.7-2.0 cm long, few-flowered; leaves 1-1.2 cm long, green and shining on both surfaces; old leaves more or less persistent; scales black. *Salix cascadensis* Cockerell. Rare in alpine tundra.

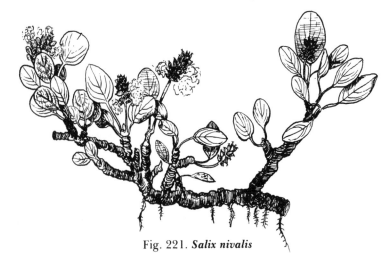

Fig. 221. *Salix nivalis*

6a. Capsules hairy. (The key treats only carpellate plants, since it is often extremely difficult to distinguish species from staminate catkins alone, which often appear before the leaves. Unknown staminate materials usually can be matched up with the corresponding carpellate plants in the field by vegetative comparison.) .... (7)
6b. Capsules glabrous .... (17)

7a. Twigs pruinose (with a white waxy coat) .... (8)
7b. Twigs not pruinose .... (9)

8a. Catkins subglobose, numerous, 10 (rarely up to 20) mm long, on pubescent leafy peduncles 5-10 mm long; leaves silky-pubescent on both sides, or glabrate, more or less glaucous beneath. *Salix geyeriana* Anderss. (for Carl A. Geyer, early western explorer). Montane and subalpine.
8b. Catkins longer, dense, 10-50 mm long, usually sessile or nearly so, bracteate at the base; leaves sparingly pubescent above, glaucescent and silky-hairy beneath. *Salix subcoerulea* Piper, BLUE WILLOW. Upper montane, subalpine.

9a. Capsules on long pedicels 2-3 (-5) mm long. *Salix depressa* L. ssp. *rostrata* (Anderss.) Hiitonen. Streambanks and lake shores, foothills to subalpine (*S. bebbiana* of Ed. 4).
9b. Capsules short-pedicellate or sessile .... (10)

10a. Catkins sessile or nearly so .... (11)
10b. Catkins on leafy peduncles or terminating leafy branches, sometimes sessile when immature .... (13)

11a. Leaves glabrous or sparsely pubescent above, variously pubescent beneath .... (12)
11b. Leaves glabrous above, glabrous and glaucous beneath (except young leaves, which can be sparsely hairy on both sides.) *Salix phylicifolia* L. ssp. *planifolia* (Pursh) Hiitonen, PLANELEAF WILLOW. Abundant in subalpine bogs and streamsides, and lower tundra slopes (*S. planifolia* of Ed. 4).

12a. Leaves dark green and sparsely pubescent above, glaucous and silky-hairy beneath. *Salix subcoerulea* Piper.
12b. Leaves dark green and glabrous above, thinly pubescent beneath, the pubescence consisting in part of reddish hairs. *Salix scouleriana* Barr. (for Dr. John Scouler). The only willow of our area which grows in forests away from the vicinity of streams.

13a. Low shrubs 0.5-2.0 m high; leaves entire .... (14)
13b. Shrubs 3-5 m high; leaves entire to sub-entire or serrulate ... (15)

14a. Petiole 3-10 (-15) mm long, usually yellowish; pedicel 0.5-1.0 (-2.0) mm long. *Salix glauca* L. An abundant timberline willow.
14b. Petiole 1-3 mm long, reddish; pedicel 0-0.25 (-0.5) mm long. *Salix brachycarpa* Nutt. Common in subalpine meadows and along

streams and evidently going up into the alpine, where it occurs along with the previous species.

15a. Leaves obovate or oblanceolate, dark green and glabrate above, glaucous, strongly reticulate and often thinly pubescent beneath, the pubescence consisting in part of reddish hairs; capsules tomentose; pedicels 1-2 mm long. *Salix scouleriana* Barr.

15b. Leaves elliptic-oblong or oblong-lanceolate, dull green and minutely downy above, pale and sparsely hairy beneath; capsules puberulent
.... (16)

16a. Catkins 2-6 (-8) cm long; capsules 6-8 mm long; mature leaves usually obovate. *Salix depressa* L. ssp. *rostrata* (Anderss.) Hiitonen. Streambanks and lake shores, foothills to subalpine (*S. bebbiana* of Ed. 4).

16b. Catkins 1-2 cm long; capsules 3-6 mm long; mature leaves narrowly oblanceolate. *Salix petiolaris* J. E. Smith. Frequent in vicinity of Estes Park. Similar to *S. geyeriana* in leaf form, but never with glaucous bloom on the twigs.

17a. Trees, 3-12 m tall .... (18)

17b. Erect shrubs, 0.3-6.0 m tall .... (21)

18a. Branches pendulous. *Salix babylonica* L., WEEPING WILLOW. Commonly cultivated, and persisting after abandonment.

18b. Branches not pendulous .... (19)

19a. Leaves with a few raised glands at the base of the blade; branchlets very brittle, easily broken by bending the base toward the main stem. *Salix fragilis* L., CRACK WILLOW. Cultivated and established along streams in the piedmont valleys.

19b. Leaves without raised glands; branchlets not excessively brittle at the base .... (20)

20a. Branchlets greenish; leaves not very different beneath, abruptly slender-acuminate. Native species. *Salix amygdaloides* Anderss., PEACH-LEAVED WILLOW. Common along streams in the piedmont valleys and plains.

20b. Branchlets golden-yellow; leaves whiter beneath, short-acuminate. *Salix alba* L. var. *vitellina* (L.) Koch, GOLDEN OSIER. Common cultivar on ranches on the plains and piedmont valleys, strikingly colored in winter condition.

21a. Leaves commonly opposite as well as alternate. *Salix purpurea* L., BASKET WILLOW. A cultivated species that has long been established along streams and in and around Colorado Springs.

21b. Leaves never opposite .... (22)

22a. Leaves pubescent on both sides or at least on one side at maturity
.... (23)

22b. Leaves glabrous on both sides at maturity .... (24)

23a. Branchlets with a glaucous bloom; leaves long and narrow **Salix irrorata** Anderss. (moist with dew), BLUESTEM WILLOW. Common in canyons in the foothills.

23b. Branchlets without a bloom; leaves usually broadly lanceolate or broader. **Salix wolfii** Bebb (for John Wolf). Upper montane and sub-alpine, especially west of the Continental Divide.

24a. Leaves not glaucous beneath .... (25)
24b. Leaves glaucous beneath .... (27)

25a. Catkins short and stout, not over 3 cm long; capsule thick-walled, 7-9 mm long. **Salix serissima** (Bailey) Fern. (very late), AUTUMN WILLOW. Extremely rare, known in Colorado from only one locality, near the old Longs Peak Inn.

25b. Catkins 3-10 cm long; capsule thin-walled, 5-7 mm long .... (26)

26a. Leaves with long-acuminate tips, lanceolate, margins glandular-serrate, 6-15 (-20) cm long, 1.5-3 (-4) cm wide. **Salix caudata** (Nutt.) Heller (tailed). Montane and subalpine.

26b. Leaves with short-acuminate tips, generally smaller. **Salix boothii** Dorn. Foothills and montane (*S. pseudocordata* of Ed. 4).

27a. Leaves with entire margins. **Salix ligulifolia** (Ball) Ball. Foothills and montane.

27b. Leaves with serrulate or serrate margins .... (28)

28a. Styles 0.3-0.5 mm long; scales tawny or reddish-brown; twigs slender .... (29)

28b. Styles 0.8-1.5 mm long; scales dark brown to black; twigs thickish. **Salix monticola** Bebb. Foothills to subalpine (including *S. padophylla*).

29a. Twigs, budscales and petioles yellowish (reddish on the sunny side), glabrous; capsules on pedicels 1-2.5 mm long. **Salix lutea** Nutt. Foothills and montane.

29b. Twigs reddish-brown to dark brown, sometimes pubescent; capsules with pedicels 2-4 mm long. **Salix ligulifolia** (Ball) Ball. Foothills and montane.

SANTALACEAE—SANDALWOOD FAMILY

Comandra is what we call a hemiparasite. It has pale green leaves but at the same time is parasitic, attached to the roots of other plants and deriving some nutrition from them. Our little herbaceous species is unlike the majority of the Santalaceae, which are usually shrubs or trees, some parasitic on other trees, others on the roots of grasses! Most of them are, or were, found in Australia and southeast Asia. One of the earliest conservation tragedies was the wholesale extermination, in the 18th and 19th centuries, of the fragrant wild sandalwoods of Australia and new Caledonia by exploiters for the perfumery, incense, and fine woodcarving trades. Sandalwoods are cultivated for these purposes in India.

Fig. 222. A, *Comandra*; B, *Anemopsis*

One species, **Comandra umbellata** (L.) Nutt., BASTARD TOADFLAX, Fig. 222. A common spring flower on the mesas and plains. Roots blue in cross-section, a very unusual color in such organs. Hemiparasite on many different plants. Presumably the leaves were thought to resemble those of the Toadflax, *Linaria vulgaris*, hence the common name.

SAURURACEAE—LIZARD-TAIL FAMILY

One genus and species, **Anemopsis californica** Hook., YERBA MANSA, Fig. 222. Occasional in marshes in the piedmont valleys, perhaps introduced with the seed of irrigated crops, but completely naturalized in the Denver-Boulder area. The appearance of an *Anemone*-like flower is created by a ring of large creamy-white bracts subtending the short dense spike of inconspicuous flowers. The Saururaceae is a very small family of virtual living fossils. Its four genera occur in eastern Asia and in the relictual Tertiary forest areas of eastern United States and California.

SAXIFRAGACEAE—SAXIFRAGE FAMILY

Because so many saxifrages are rock garden plants and grow, in nature, in rocky crevices, I assumed that the name alluded to the ability of these plants to break up rocks. Gérard, on the contrary, wrote in *The Herbal* (1633): "This name *Saxifraga* or Saxifrage, hath of late been imposed upon sundry plants farre different in the shapes, places of growing, and temperature, but all agreeing in this one facultie of expelling or driving the stone out of the Kidneies, though not all by one meane or manner of operation." Saxifrages are much more important horticulturally than they ever might have been in medicine. The fleshy-leaved *Bergenia* of the Himalaya and Siberia, and the deep red Coral Bells, *Heuchera sanguinea*, native in our Southwest, are favorite rock garden plants.

1a. Leaves entire, oval or kidney-shaped, all (or all but one) basal; stamens 5, alternating with clusters of sterile stamens; flower white, solitary on a long stalk. **Parnassia**, GRASS-OF-PARNASSUS, page 313.
1b. Plants without the above combination of characteristics. . . . . (2)

2a. Leaves deeply palmately lobed or even divided into narrow leaflets
. . . . (3)
2b. Leaves entire, toothed, or shallowly lobed, never compound. (4)

3a. Petals entire or merely notched; •leaves deeply 3- or 5-lobed. **Saxifraga**, SAXIFRAGE, page 313.
3b. Petals deeply and irregularly cleft into slender, pointed divisions; leaves very deeply lobed, some of them compound. **Lithophragma**, page 312.

4a. Flowers deep rose-pink, in dense, short panicles; densely matted plants with crenate, kidney-shaped leaves. **Telesonix**, page 318.
4b. Flowers white, pink, or the petals absent; plants otherwise . . . . . . (5)

5a. Leaves as broad as long, pentagonal in outline .... (6)
5b. Leaves various, sometimes broad but not pentagonal .... (7)

6a. Flowers in a simple raceme, the flowers remote from each other; petals usually lobed or dissected. *Mitella*, Bishops Cap, page 313.
6b. Flowers in narrow panicles, usually crowded; petals entire. *Heuchera*, Alum-root, page 312.

7a. Petals lacking; flowers in a terminal bracteate cluster; plants very weak, from slender stolons, the leaves about 1 cm wide, round-cordate and crenately-toothed or lobed. *Chrysosplenium*, Golden Carpet, page 312.
7b. Petals present, or plants otherwise not as above. *Saxifraga*, Saxifrage, page 313.

CHRYSOSPLENIUM. Golden Carpet

One species, *Chrysosplenium tetrandrum* Fries, Fig. 224. An extremely rare plant found in moss along cold mountain streamlets.

HEUCHERA. Alum-root

1a. Flowers large, about 1 cm long, zygomorphic and very oblique at the mouth, the base of the hypanthium swollen on one side. *Heuchera richardsonii* R. Br. (for Sir John Richardson), Rough Alum-root. Rare, found only in the Black Forest region. Flowers greenish; foliage and stem hirsute.
1b. Flowers small, most often less than 5 mm long, regular or nearly so
.... (2)

2a. Stamens exserted. *Heuchera bracteata* (Torr.) Ser., Bracted Alum-root. On cliffs and rock ledges, foothills to subalpine. The leaves have very sharp teeth, in contrast to the blunt lobes of *H. parvifolia*, with which *H. bracteata* often grows and sometimes hybridizes.
2b. Stamens included .... (3)

3a. Flowers rather deeply campanulate, the sepals usually much exceeding the open-campanulate or hemispheric hypanthium; beaks of the ovary prominent. *Heuchera hallii* Gray (for Elihu Hall). Foothills, montane, Pikes Peak region southward.
3b. Flowers flat-campanulate, the sepals only slightly exceeding the flat saucer-shaped hypanthium; beaks of the ovary broad and flat, often imbedded in a surrounding disk, becoming somewhat prominent in fruit. *Heuchera parvifolia* Nutt. (small-leaved), Common Alum-root, Fig. 226. Common on cliffs and rock outcrops from mesas to the lower tundra. The dwarf alpine form is var. *nivalis* (Rosend.) Löve, Löve & Kapoor.

LITHOPHRAGMA

1a. Petals pinkish, usually about 5-cleft; upper part of stem bearing purple bulblets; entire plant often tinged with purple; leaves glabrous or nearly so. *Lithophragma glabrum* Nutt. Rare, subalpine.

1b. Petals white, about 3-cleft; bulblets lacking; entire plant green; leaves pubescent. **Lithophragma parviflorum** (Hook.) T. & G. One record, Rocky Mountain National Park.

MITELLA. Bishops Cap

1a. Stamens opposite the greenish, pinnatifid petals; leaves rather distinctly lobed, the lobes coarsely toothed. **Mitella pentandra** Hook (five-stamened). Common in deep shade, subalpine forests.
1b. Stamens alternating with the 3-parted or entire petals: leaves scarcely lobed; the teeth very shallow and blunt. **Mitella stauropetala** Piper var. **stenopetala** (Piper) Rosend. (with cross-shaped, narrow petals). Infrequent, subalpine.

PARNASSIA. Grass-of-Parnassus

1a. Flower stalk with a bract, usually above the level of the basal leaves; petals large, 5- to 13-nerved .... (2)
1b. Flower stalk bractless; petals small (about equalling the sepals), 1- to 3- nerved. **Parnassia kotzebuei** Chamisso (for Otto von Kotzebue, Russian explorer), Fig. 223. Very rare and local, on rocky ledges on the tundra.

2a. Leaves ovate, lanceolate or elliptic. **Parnassia parviflora** DC. (small-flowered), Fig. 223. Infrequent in subalpine bogs.
2b. Leaves cordate or kidney-shaped. **Parnassia fimbriata** Banks (fringed), Fig. 223. Common in subalpine bogs and streamsides.

SAXIFRAGA. Saxifrage

1a. Stem with only basal leaves; flowers numerous, in loose or compact spikes or panicles .... (2)
1b. Stem leafy (the stem leaves, however, sometimes considerably reduced); flowers solitary or in few- (1-10)-flowered racemes or spikes .... (5)

2a. Petals lacking, the flowers replaced by small green bulblets; leaves about 1 cm long, few-toothed at the tip. **Saxifraga foliolosa** R. Br., Fig. 224. Extremely rare, Mt. Evans, alpine.
2b. Petals present; leaves usually more than 2 cm long, more regularly toothed .... (3)

3a. Leaves circular in outline, cordate at base, coarsely saw-toothed; petioles long and slender; panicle loose. **Saxifraga odontoloma** Piper (toothed edge), Brook Saxifrage, Fig. 226. Common along streams in subalpine forests.
3b. Leaves lanceolate or broader, variously toothed or entire, tapering to a short, broad petiole; panicle dense, spike-like .... (4)

4a. Leaves short, rhomboid; spikes usually simple; plants of open ground, never wet meadows or streamsides. **Saxifraga rhomboidea** Greene, Fig. 224. Common from mesas to alpine.

Fig. 223. A, *Parnassia parviflora*; B, *P. kotzebuei*; C, *P. fimbriata*

4b. Leaves elongate, narrowly oblanceolate; spikes often compound; plants of wet meadows and streamsides. ***Saxifraga oregana*** Howell var. ***montanensis*** (Small) C. L. Hitchcock.

5a. Leaves deeply and narrowly 3-cleft. ***Saxifraga caespitosa*** L., MATTED SAXIFRAGE, Fig. 225. Tundra of the highest peaks. Forming dense mats, the flowering stems a few cm high. Flowers less than 1 cm across, the petals white.

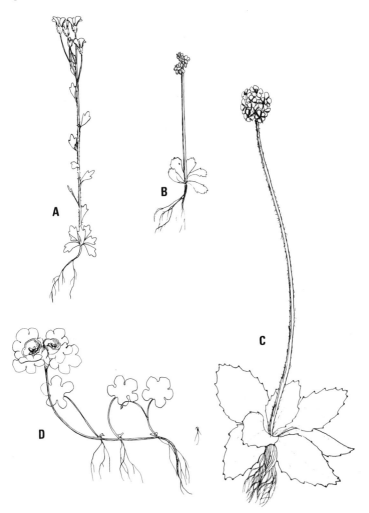

Fig. 224. A, ***Saxifraga adscendens***; B, ***S. foliolosa***; C, ***S. rhomboidea***; D, ***Chrysosplenium***

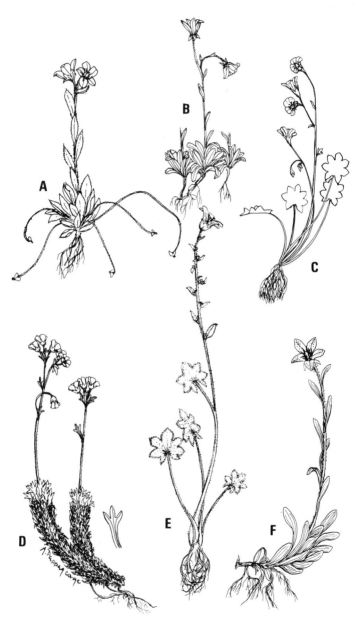

Fig. 225. A, *Saxifraga flagellaris*; B, *S. serpyllifolia*; C, *S. hyperborea*; D, *S. caespitosa*; E, *S. cernua*; F. *S. hirculus*

5b. Leaves entire or variously lobed but never with 3 narrow divisions
....(6)

6a. Plants forming dense mats; leaves awl-shaped, rigid; flowers white, in loose, few-flowered panicles. **Saxifraga bronchialis** L. ssp. **austromontana** (Wieg.) Piper (for the wind-pipe, reason obscure), SPOTTED SAXIFRAGE, Fig. 226. Petals white, with tiny purple or orange spots. On rocks, foothills to alpine. The plants suggest a very large moss or a very small evergreen.
6b. Plants not forming mats; leaves not rigid; flowers white or yellow, solitary or in few-flowered racemes ....(7)

7a. Leaves toothed or lobed, flowers white ....(8)
7b. Leaves entire, spatulate, flowers yellow ....(11)

8a. All but the relatively large terminal flower replaced by reddish bulblets; plants more or less glandular-pubescent. **Saxifraga cernua** L., NODDING SAXIFRAGE, Fig. 225. Frequent along snow-runoff rivulets, alpine and upper subalpine.
8b. Bulblets absent; all flowers normal ....(9)

9a. Leaves palmately lobed, with long petioles ....(10)
9b. Leaves spatulate, few-toothed at apex, sessile in a basal rosette, a few reduced ones up the stem. **Saxifraga adscendens** L. ssp. **oregonensis** (Raf.) Bacigalupi, Fig. 224. Rare and inconspicuous, subalpine and alpine.

10a. Inflorescence strict, the pedicels erect; hypanthium narrowly campanulate; calyx lobes usually shorter than the hypanthium; glandular hairs on the pedicel short, straight. **Saxifraga hyperborea** R. Br. ssp. **debilis** (Engelm.) Löve, Löve & Kapoor, PYGMY SAXIFRAGE, Fig. 225. Subalpine and alpine, usually in shaded hollows under boulders.
10b. Inflorescence with spreading pedicels; hypanthium broadly campanulate; calyx-lobes equalling or exceeding the hypanthium; glandular hairs on the pedicels long and crinkly. **Saxifraga rivularis** L. Edges of alpine rivulets.

11a. Lower leaves arranged in a basal rosette; plants of rocky tundra (12)
11b. Lower leaves not arranged in a basal rosette; bog plants. **Saxifraga hirculus** L. ssp. **propinqua** (R. Br.) Löve & Löve (goat; neighboring), ARCTIC SAXIFRAGE. Infrequent in subalpine and alpine bogs and drainage basins.

12a. Slender stolons present; plant very glandular-pubescent; leaves ciliate-margined. **Saxifraga flagellaris** Willd. ssp. **platysepala** (Trautv.) Porsild, WHIPLASH SAXIFRAGE, Fig. 225. Locally abundant on rocky alpine ridges.
12b. Stolons absent; plants almost glabrous; leaf margins not ciliate. **Saxifraga serpyllifolia** Pursh ssp. **chrysantha** (Gray) W. A. Weber, Fig. 225. Rocky alpine ridges. Has a tendency to form thin mats when well developed.

TELESONIX

One species, *Telesonix jamesii* (Torr.) Raf., Plate 28, Fig. 226. Abundant on talus slopes along the Cog Railway near Windy Point on Pikes Peak, at one site in Rocky Mountain National Park, and on granite tors in the Platte River drainage.

SCROPHULARIACEAE—FIGWORT FAMILY

The showy tubular bilabiate flowers of the scrophs show diverse adaptations to insect pollination. In *Penstemon* (*penicillum* = brush) one of the stamens lacks anthers and instead has a tuft of often golden hairs possibly attractive to insects, or at least offering a claw-hold. Scarlet penstemons are hummingbird-pollinated. The corolla of *Castilleja* is so dingy that the floral bracts and calyx are highly colored as attractants, and the corolla is so narrow as well that the stamens can hardly fit unless staggered, a challenge neatly met by attaching them at different points and elongating the anther-sacs. Some scrophs, such as *Pedicularis*, have developed such complicated flowers that potential pollinators either cannot reach the nectar or become so impatient that they bite a hole through the base of the corolla, bypassing the stamens and style completely and cancelling the whole adaption!

1a. Anther-bearing stamens 5; corolla nearly regular, rotate, yellow; tall, coarse herbs. *Verbascum*, MULLEIN, page 330.
1b. Anther-bearing stamens 4 or 2; corolla usually somewhat or quite irregular; flowers variously colored ....(2)

2a. Fleshy-leaved plants rooted in mud and either stoloniferous or prostrate and rooting at the nodes; flowers white, not strikingly irregular ....(3)
2b. Plants not as above in all details ....(4)

3a. Leaves orbicular; plants prostrate, rooting at the nodes; flowers solitary in the leaf-axils. *Bacopa*, WATER-HYSSOP, page 321.
3b. Leaves narrowly spatulate or linear; plants erect, but spreading by short stolons; flowers in a basal cluster, the pedicels about 1 cm long. *Limosella*, MUDWORT, page 325.

4a. Corolla distinctly spurred. *Linaria*, TOADFLAX, page 325.
4b. Corolla not spurred but sometimes somewhat swollen or sac-like at the base ....(5)

5a. Upper lip of the strongly 2-lipped corolla helmet-shaped, keeled, or deeply concave; stamens always either 4 or 2 ....(6)
5b. Upper lip of the corolla not helmet-shaped, keeled, or deeply concave; stamens 5, 4, 2; sterile stamens often present ....(10)

6a. Anther cells equal, parallel; stamens 4 ....(7)
6b. Anther cells unequal, separated; bracts often highly colored ....(9)

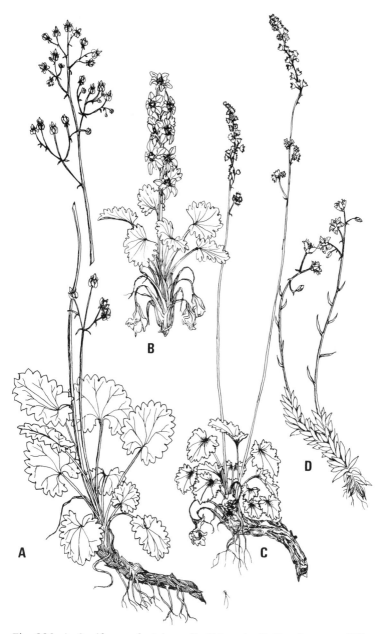

Fig. 226. A, **Saxifraga odontoloma**; B, **Telesonix**; C, **Heuchera parvifolia**; D. **Saxifraga bronchialis**

7a. Corolla 4-5 cm long, tubular-bell-shaped, pendulous with a gaping mouth, spotted. *Digitalis*, FOXGLOVE, page 324.
7b. Corolla not as above .... (8)

8a. Leaves opposite, merely toothed; calyx 4-toothed, becoming bladder-like and veiny, completely enclosing the fruit and not filled by it. *Rhinanthus*, YELLOW RATTLE, page 330.
8b. Leaves alternate or basal, pinnatifid in all but two species; calyx cleft on one or both sides, becoming distended but neither bladder-like nor completely enclosing the fruit. *Pedicularis*, LOUSEWORT, page 326.

9a. Bracts highly colored or white; upper corolla lip (galea) very much longer than the small, 3-toothed or 3-keeled lower lip; plants perennial. *Castilleja*, PAINTBRUSH, page 321.
9b. Bracts green or purplish; upper corolla lip not or little surpassing the inflated, saccate lower lip; plants annual. *Orthocarpus*, OWL-CLOVER, page 326.

10a. Corolla distinctly hump-backed; dainty annuals with minute blue-and-white flowers; stamens with anthers 4. *Collinsia*, BABY-BLUE-EYES; BLUE-EYED MARY, page 324.
10b. Corolla not hump-backed; otherwise not as above .... (11)

11a. Stamens 5, four of these anther-bearing and the fifth sterile ... (12)
11b. Stamens 4 or fewer, without any rudiment of a fifth stamen ... (14)

12a. Sterile stamen represented by a scale on the upper inside of the corolla throat; corolla greenish, somewhat urn-shaped, broad and open with little distinction of tube and throat. *Scrophularia*, FIGWORT, page 330.
12b. Sterile stamen an elongate, often bearded filament not much shorter than the anther-bearing stamens; corolla large, colored or white. (13)

13a. Calyx deeply 5-parted or divided; corolla not flattened; plants of various habitats, not restricted to tundra. *Penstemon*, BEARD-TONGUE, page 329.
13b. Calyx obtusely 5-lobed; corolla strongly flattened; low plants of tundra. *Chionophila*, SNOW-LOVER, page 324.

14a. Anther-bearing stamens 2 .... (15)
14b. Anther-bearing stamens 4 .... (18)

15a. Leaves chiefly basal, the stem leaves alternate; corolla very irregular, cleft nearly to the base, or absent; flowers in a dense spike. *Besseya*, page 321.
15b. Leaves chiefly cauline, opposite; corolla irregular but not as above; flowers axillary or in terminal spikes .... (16)

16a. Corolla 4-lobed, nearly regular, rotate, not deeply tubular, usually blue. *Veronica*, SPEEDWELL, page 333.
16b. Corolla 2-lipped, irregular and deeply tubular, not blue .... (17)

17a. Corolla whitish with a yellow tube; foliage and branches glandular-pubescent, sticky. *Gratiola*, HEDGE-HYSSOP, page 325.
17b. Corolla white to pinkish, lacking any yellow; plant glabrous. *Lindernia*, FALSE PIMPERNEL, page 325.

18a. Corolla green with maroon or purplish tint, inconspicuous; stems four-angled, leaves triangular-ovate, dentate. *Scrophularia*, FIGWORT, page 330.
18b. Corolla colored, usually showy, pink or yellow; stems not four-angled, leaves various . . . . (19)

19a. Flowers yellow (pink in one rare species); calyx strongly ribbed and angular. *Mimulus*, MONKEY-FLOWER, page 325.
19b. Flowers pink; calyx not strongly ribbed or angular. *Agalinis*, page 321.

AGALINIS

One species, *Agalinis tenuifolia* (Vahl) Raf. (narrow-leaved), Fig. 227. Rare, in sandy soil or wet meadows on the piedmont valleys and plains. The large pink flowers seem out of proportion to the slender stems and small leaves (*Gerardia tenuifolia* Vahl).

BACOPA. WATER-HYSSOP

One species, *Bacopa rotundifolia* (Michx.) Wettst., Fig. 227. Drying shores of seasonal pools and reservoirs, piedmont valleys and plains.

BESSEYA

1a. Leaves oval or subcordate; plants restricted to tundra; stems less than 1 dm high. *Besseya alpina* (Gray) Rydb., ALPINE BESSEYA, Fig. 227.
1b. Leaves oblong; plants of foothills and montane; stems 1 or more dm high. *Besseya plantaginea* (Benth.) Rydb. (resembling plantains), FOOTHILLS BESSEYA.

CASTILLEJA. PAINTBRUSH

1a. Galea several times longer than the short lower lip, and usually at least two-thirds as long as the corolla-tube; bracts in most species tinged with scarlet, crimson or rose . . . . (2)
1b. Galea less than 3 times as long as the lower lip, rarely half as long as the corolla tube; bracts in most species tinged with yellow or brown. (5)

2a. Calyx very deeply slit down the lower side, merely toothed or lobed on the upper side; plant tall, 4-10 dm high; leaves very narrow. *Castilleja linariaefolia* Benth. *in* DC. (with leaves like *Linaria*), WYOMING PAINTBRUSH. Openings and meadows, lodgepole pine forests, montane.
2b. Calyx about equally cleft above and below . . . . (3)

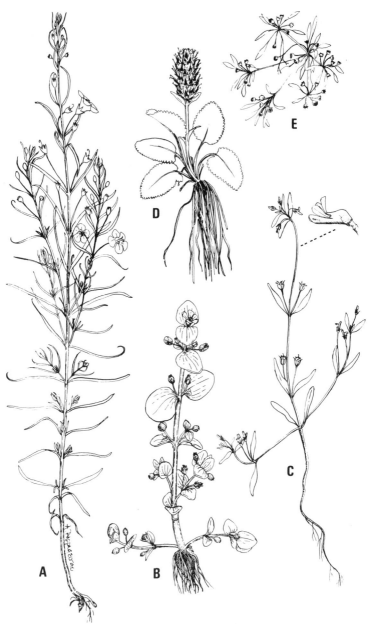

Fig. 227. A, *Agalinis*; B, *Bacopa*; C, *Collinsia*; D, *Besseya alpina*; E, *Limosella*

3a. Stems tomentose or canescent; leaves and bracts entire; bracts brilliant red-orange. ***Castilleja integra*** Gray (entire), Orange Paintbrush. Mesas and hogback ridges, most common from Denver southward. Common also in the high meadows of Middle and South Park.

3b. Stems glabrous or pubescent, but neither tomentose nor canescent; leaves and bracts entire or usually cleft; bracts red, old rose, purplish, or rarely white .... (4)

4a. Bracts usually entire and obtuse, or, if 3-lobed, with a broad middle lobe; bracts usually old-rose, sometimes white; subalpine and alpine. ***Castilleja rhexifolia*** Rydb. (with leaves like *Rhexia*). A very beautiful species of subalpine meadows, occasional above timberline. Hybridization with *C. sulphurea* appears to be responsible for much color variation.

4b. Bracts usually 3-cleft with lanceolate lobes, or, if entire, very acute; middle altitudes. ***Castilleja miniata*** Dougl. (vermilion), Scarlet Paintbrush, Fig. 228. Probably the most common and variable paintbrush, most common in the montane but present in subalpine and foothills.

5a. Leaves entire; bracts also entire or slightly 3-lobed .... (6)

5b. Leaves pinnately divided, at least the upper ones .... (7)

6a. Plant 0.5-2.0 dm high, densely villous above; characteristically found on tundra or near it. ***Castilleja occidentalis*** Torr., Western Yellow Paintbrush.

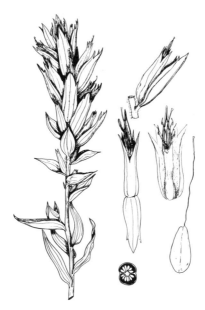

Fig. 228. ***Castilleja miniata***

6b. Plant 2-4 dm high, slightly if at all villous in the inflorescence; wet, usually shaded meadows or forest glades, subalpine. ***Castilleja sulphurea*** Rydb., YELLOW PAINTBRUSH.

7a. Corolla 1.5-3.0 cm long, slightly exceeding the calyx; plants restricted to tundra. ***Castilleja puberula*** Rydb. (minutely pubescent), ALPINE PAINTBRUSH. Flowers yellowish; foliage, especially in the inflorescence, woolly-pubescent.

7b. Corolla 4-5 cm long, almost twice as long as the calyx; plants of mesas and plains, flowering in early spring. ***Castilleja sessiliflora*** Pursh, PLAINS PAINTBRUSH. Very common on mesas and plains in early spring. The base of the greenish-yellow or whitish corolla is filled with sweet nectar.

CHIONOPHILA. SNOW-LOVER

One species, ***Chionophila jamesii*** Benth. (for Edwin James), Fig. 229. Alpine tundra, not common. The foliage turns brown or black in drying.

COLLINSIA. BABY-BLUE-EYES; BLUE-EYED MARY

One species, ***Collinsia parviflora*** Lindl. (small-flowered), Fig. 227. Common but inconspicuous and delicate annual, in shaded gulches and slopes, mesas and lower foothills. The foliage is usually strongly purplish-tinged.

DIGITALIS. FOXGLOVE

One species, ***Digitalis purpurea*** L. Originally escaped from cultivation at an old homestead and established locally in a canyon near Eldorado Springs. One of the most important plants known to medicine.

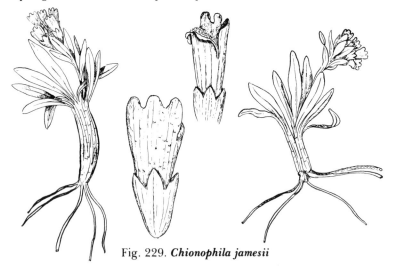

Fig. 229. *Chionophila jamesii*

GRATIOLA. HEDGE-HYSSOP

One species, *Gratiola neglecta* Torr. (overlooked). Frequent in mud of lake shores and drying springs, on the mesas and plains.

LIMOSELLA. MUDWORT

One species, *Limosella aquatica* L., Fig. 227. Infrequent, on drying shores of seasonal pools, from plains to subalpine.

LINARIA. TOADFLAX

1a. Flowers yellow, with an orange palate; flowers over 1 cm long; introduced weed .... (2)
1b. Corolla blue, less than 0.5 cm long; native species. *Linaria canadensis* (L.) Dum., BLUE TOADFLAX. Uncommon on grassy slopes of plains and mesas.

2a. Leaves linear. *Linaria vulgaris* Mill., BUTTER-AND-EGGS. Locally abundant in the foothill canyons, particularly around old dwellings and mine-dumps.
2b. Leaves ovate. *Linaria dalmatica* L. var. *macedonica* Fenzl. A recently established weed now rampant in many of the semi-arid areas of Colorado. Originally native in southeastern Europe.

LINDERNIA. FALSE PIMPERNEL

One species, *Lindernia anagallidea* (Michx.) Pennell (resembling *Anagallis*, the Pimpernel). Muddy shores or seasonal pools, piedmont valleys and plains.

MIMULUS. MONKEY-FLOWER

1a. Flowers rarely produced; delicate annuals with sac-like petioles containing a disciform vegetative propagulum falling free in the petiole upon withering of the leaf blade. *Mimulus gemmiparus* W. A. Weber. Very rare, on seeping granite outcrops, Rocky Mountain National Park. The flowers are yellow, but rarely found.
1b. Flowers always present; petioles not modified .... (2)

2a. Corolla pink or red. *Mimulus rubellus* Gray, LITTLE RED MIMULUS. Rare, on mossy cliffs beside waterfalls, subalpine. Flowers very tiny.
2b. Corolla yellow .... (3)

3a. Calyx-teeth equal or nearly so. *Mimulus floribundus* Dougl., MANY-FLOWERED MIMULUS. Wet banks, seepage areas, foothills to montane. Extremely variable in size of both leaves and flowers.
3b. Calyx-teeth unequal, the uppermost tooth larger than the others. (4)

4a. Corolla throat open; flowers axillary, in a loose, few-flowered raceme, or solitary; stems low, mostly creeping or trailing. *Mimulus glabratus* H.B.K., SMOOTH MIMULUS. Swamps and irrigation ditches, piedmont valleys and plains.

4b. Corolla throat partly or nearly closed by the prominent palate; flowers commonly more numerous, in a distinct raceme, or sometimes few-flowered .... (5)

5a. Flowers in distinct racemes; pedicels usually shorter than the corollas; rhizomes rarely fleshy or yellow. *Mimulus guttatus* DC. (spotted), COMMON YELLOW MONKEY-FLOWER, Fig. 230. The most common mimulus in this area, from foothills to subalpine, in shade along streambanks.

5b. Flowers mostly 1 to 3, rarely 5 in the raceme; pedicels usually longer than the corollas; stems arising from a mass of fleshy yellow rhizomes. *Mimulus tilingii* Regel, SUBALPINE MIMULUS.

ORTHOCARPUS. OWL-CLOVER

One species, *Orthocarpus luteus* Nutt., YELLOW OWL-CLOVER. Common on dry hillsides, from mesas to subalpine.

PEDICULARIS. LOUSEWORT

1a. Leaves crenulate .... (7)

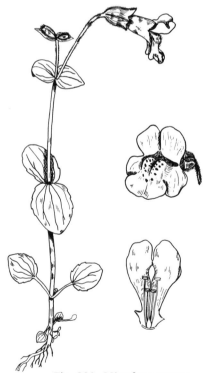

Fig. 230. *Mimulus guttatus*

1b. Leaves deeply pinnately lobed or incised ....(2)

2a. Corolla yellow or yellowish or white ....(3)
2b. Corolla pink or purplish ....(6)

3a. Leaves simple, but shallowly or deeply pinnatifid, the leaflets joined
together by the common winged rachis; plants usually less than 2 dm
high ....(4)
3b. Leaves divided into separate leaflets; plants always over 2 dm high
....(5)

4a. Upper lip of corolla (galea) terminating in a prominent sickle-
shaped beak; leaves with very narrow linear lobes; plants of subalpine and alpine slopes. *Pedicularis parryi* Gray (for C. C. Parry),
Fig. 231.
4b. Upper lip of corolla without a prominent sickle-shaped beak; leaves
with broad lobes; plants of the pine forests, foothills. *Pedicularis
canadensis* L. ssp. *fluviatilis* (Heller) W. A. Weber (Canadian; of
watercourses), LOUSEWORT. Scattered in mesic canyons and woodland along the base of the mountains, an eastern North American
species with this local race in Colorado and New Mexico.

5a. Corolla 3.0-3.5 cm long; lower lip almost reaching the tip of the
galea. *Pedicularis grayi* Nels., GRAYS LOUSEWORT. Subalpine forests.
Plants up to a meter tall, the flowers streaked with reddish (*P.
procera* Gray).

Fig. 231. *Pedicularis parryi*

5b. Corolla less than 3 cm long; lower lip not reaching the tip of the galea. *Pedicularis bracteosa* Benth. var. *paysoniana* (Pennell) Cronquist (for Edwin Payson). More common than the preceding, in similar habitats. Plants seldom more than a meter tall, the flowers not streaked with reddish.

6a. Beak of galea short and straight; inflorence woolly-pubescent, the flowers crowded in a short spike. *Pedicularis sudetica* Willd. ssp. *scopulorum* (Gray) Hultén, ROCKY MOUNTAIN LOUSEWORT. Swampy meadows and lake shores, subalpine, rather rare. Flowers pink.

6b. Beak of galea long and curved, the flower resembling an elephant's head; inflorescence glabrous or nearly so, the flowers in an elongated spike. *Pedicularis groenlandica* Retz (of Greenland), ELEPHANTELLA, Fig. 232. Abundant in wet meadows, montane, subalpine. Flowers deep pink or purplish.

7a. Flowers white; leaves glabrous. *Pedicularis racemosa* Dougl. ssp. *alba* Pennell, CURLED LOUSEWORT, Fig. 233. Abundant and often dominant understory in subalpine spruce forests.

7b. Flowers pink or rose-colored; leaves or stems pubescent. *Pedicularis crenulata* Benth., PURPLE LOUSEWORT. Wet meadows, montane, subalpine.

Fig. 232. *Pedicularis groenlandica*   Fig. 233. *Pedicularis racemosa*

PENSTEMON. Beard-tongue

1a. Flowers white; stems sticky-glandular above; plants of the plains. *Penstemon albidus* Nutt., White Penstemon. Barely entering this area from the Great Plains.

1b. Flowers blue, pink, purple, or red (white with purple-tinge in a form of *P. whippleanus*); stems not sticky-glandular above; plants of various altitudes .... (2)

2a. Flowers scarlet (fire-cracker red). *Penstemon barbatus* (Cav.) Roth (bearded), Fig. 234. Canyonsides in the southern part of the range. Abundant in the arid canyon country of the west slope.

2b. Flowers not scarlet .... (3)

3a. Plant 5-10 cm high, dwarfed, weak, and somewhat trailing, with about 3 pairs of thickish, oval leaves; flowers few (2 to 5) in a terminal cluster; very rare plants of rocky alpine talus slopes. *Penstemon harbourii* Gray (for J. P. Harbour), Scree Penstemon, Plate 30. Frequent on the east slope of Grays Peak.

3b. Taller plants with erect stems, otherwise not as above .... (4)

4a. Leaves strongly glaucous, thick and fleshy .... (5)
4b. Leaves not strongly glaucous .... (6)

5a. Corolla pink or magenta when fresh; leaves usually broad at the base, clasping the stem; racemes one-sided. *Penstemon secundiflorus* Benth., One-sided Penstemon, Fig. 234. Abundant in spring, on mesas and foothills.

5b. Corolla sky-blue when fresh; leaves usually narrow, lanceolate or lance-linear, only the uppermost sometimes clasping and broad; racemes not strongly one-sided. *Penstemon angustifolius* Pursh, Narrow-leaved Penstemon. Common on the plains.

6a. Flowers dull purple or white, in loose nodding clusters; basal leaves ovate. *Penstemon whippleanus* Gray (for A. W. Whipple). Common on moraines and gravelly subalpine slopes. The white-flowered form varies in its frequency from place to place, in some areas occurring in about equal proportion to the normal purple-flowered form.

6b. Flowers blue or pink, never dull purple; otherwise not as above. (7)

7a. Flowers 2 cm or more long, the corolla-tube abruptly expanded. (8)
7b. Flowers smaller, or the corolla-tube not abruptly expanded .... (10)

8a. Stems tall, with a one-sided terminal raceme; flowers not crowded; anthers perfectly glabrous. *Penstemon virgatus* Gray ssp. *asa-grayi* Crosswhite. Common summer-flowering penstemon on mesas and foothills.

8b. Stems relatively low; raceme often one-sided but flowers crowded; anthers sparingly short-hirsute (this sometimes hard to see) .... (9)

9a. Leaves linear or narrowly oblanceolate; plant less than 15 cm tall;

raceme few-flowered; Pikes Peak region to Grays Peak. **Penstemon hallii** Gray (for Elihu Hall). Meadows at or above timberline. Flowers deep pink.
9b. Leaves broader; plant usually over 15 cm tall; raceme many-flowered; generally distributed, montane and subalpine. **Penstemon alpinus** Torr., ALPINE PENSTEMON. A common and very showy penstemon of gravelly slopes and roadsides from the foothills to subalpine. Flowers usually blue, but pink forms sometimes are found.

10a. Leaves entire; flowers in very dense terminal clusters; corolla obscurely 2-lipped .... (11)
10b. Leaves obscurely serrulate or denticulate; flowers in loose clusters, the corolla obviously 2-lipped .... (12)

11a. Corolla 6-10 mm long, more or less declined; anther sacs rotund, mostly 0.5 mm long or less. **Penstemon procerus** Dougl. (stretched out), SMALL-FLOWERED PENSTEMON. Subalpine meadows, uncommon.
11b. Corolla 10 mm or more long, horizontal; anther sacs longer than broad, mostly more than 0.5 mm long. **Penstemon rydbergii** Nels. Similar habitats.

12a. Flowers deep blue-violet; leaves very obscurely and weakly toothed or almost entire; stems numerous, forming dense clumps. **Penstemon virens** Pennell (green). The abundant small-flowered penstemon of the foothills and montane.
12b. Flowers pale; leaves regularly and finely serrate-denticulate to almost entire; stems slender, few. **Penstemon gracilis** Nutt., SLENDER PENSTEMON. Rather rare, on the mesas.

RHINANTHUS. YELLOW RATTLE

One species, **Rhinanthus minor** L. Uncommon in subalpine meadows. The large papery calyx is distinctive.

SCROPHULARIA. FIGWORT

One species, **Scrophularia lanceolata** Pursh. Gulches and brushy hillsides, mesas and foothills. A tall herb with coarsely serrate leaves and the greenish or copper-colored flowers. The "fig" in FIGWORT refers to an old name for hemorrhoids, which the plant was supposed to cure.

VERBASCUM. MULLEIN

1a. Foliage very densely woolly-pubescent; flowers in dense terminal spikes or spikelike racemes .... (2)
1b. Foliage sparingly pubescent or glabrate; leaves coarsely toothed; flowers in loose racemes. **Verbascum blattaria** L. (ancient name for a moth), MOTH MULLEIN, Fig. 235. Introduced along rights-of-way and spreading to overgrazed range on the mesas and piedmont valleys. A sterile hybrid between this and *V. thapsus* was found once along the Boulder-Denver turnpike. It was twice as tall as either parent and had great numbers of racemes from a stout main stem. It never appeared

Fig. 234. A, *Penstemon secundiflorus*; B, *P. whippleanus*; C, *P. barbatus*

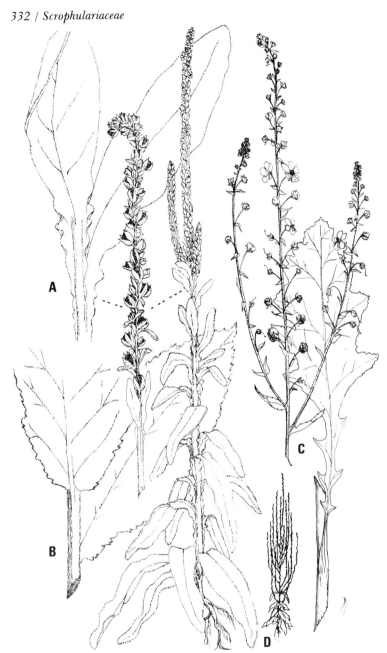

Fig. 235. A, *Verbascum thapsus*; B, *V. phlomoides*; C, *V. blattaria*; D, *V. X pterocaulon*

again, having produced no seeds. The hybrid is called *Verbascum X pterocaulon* Franchet, Fig. 235.

2a. Leaves decurrent on the stem, entire. **Verbascum thapsus** L. (from Thapsus, a Sicilian peninsula), GREAT MULLEIN, Fig. 235. Very common and conspicuous roadside weed in disturbed, overgrazed or burned areas, often growing to a height of two meters or more.
2b. Leaves not decurrent but often with clasping bases, crenate. **Verbascum phlomoides** L. (resembling the mint, *Phlomis*), Fig. 235. A European species recently discovered as a weed in the outer foothills near Golden and very likely established elsewhere.

VERONICA. SPEEDWELL

1a. Flowers racemose in the axils of the leaves .... (2)
1b. Flowers either in terminal spikes or racemes, or solitary in the leaf-axils .... (3)

2a. Leaves sessile and clasping the stem, or the lowermost short-petioled, serrulate or entire. **Veronica anagallis-aquatica** L. (water-pimpernel), WATER SPEEDWELL, Fig. 236. Uncommon in swampy areas on the plains and piedmont valleys.
2b. Leaves all short-petioled, serrate. **Veronica americana** (Raf.) Schwein., AMERICAN BROOKLIME, Fig. 236. Common in muddy places along water-courses, plains and piedmont valleys.

3a. Plants annual; flowers solitary in the leaf-axils .... (4)
3b. Plants perennial with creeping rhizomes; flowers in racemes ... (6)

4a. Flowers sessile in the leaf-axils; capsule nearly orbicular in outline, emarginate. **Veronica peregrina** L. ssp. **xalapensis** (H. B. K.) Pennell (wandering; from Xalapa, Mexico), PURSLANE SPEEDWELL, Fig. 236. A common low weed in cultivated or disturbed ground, mesas to subalpine.
4b. Flowers on arching pedicels; capsule much broader than high, obcordate .... (5)

5a. Plant erect; corolla 2-4 mm wide. **Veronica biloba** L., Fig 236. A newly established weed in disturbed ground near Boulder.
5b. Plant decumbent and trailing; corolla 5-11 mm wide. **Veronica persica** Poir. (Persian), BIRDS-EYE. Occasional weed in gardens and waste ground.

6a. Leaves all sessile; plant erect; capsule elliptic, emarginate; foliage blackening in drying; subalpine. **Veronica wormskjoldii** R. & S., ALPINE SPEEDWELL, Fig. 236. Subalpine meadows and tundra. Flowers dark blue.
6b. Lower leaves petioled; plant decumbent; capsule orbicular to obcordate; foliage drying green. **Veronica serpyllifolia** L. ssp. **humifusa** (Dicks.) Syme, THYME-LEAVED SPEEDWELL. Muddy ground, montane and subalpine.

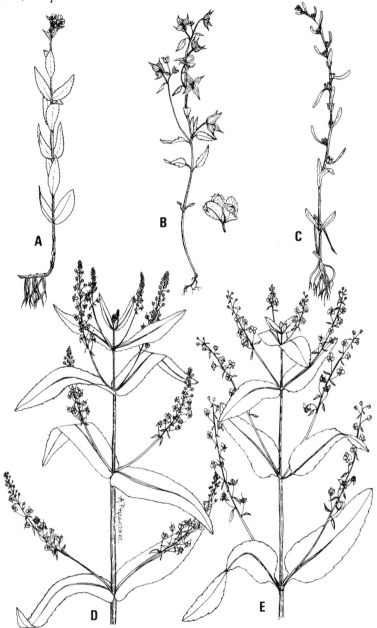

Fig. 236. A, *Veronica wormskjoldii*; B, *V. biloba*; C, *V. peregrina;* D, *V. anagallis-aquatica*; E, *V. americana*

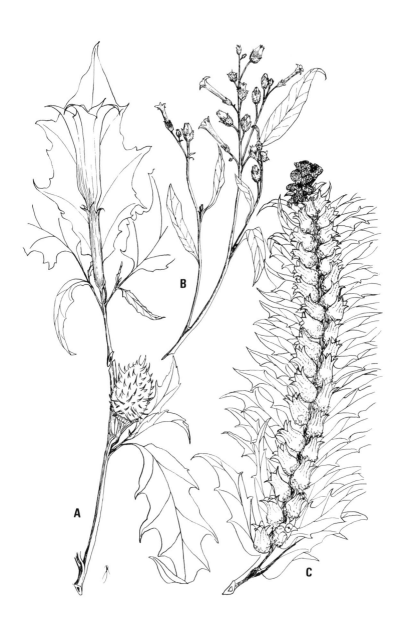

Fig. 237. A, *Datura*; B, *Nicotiana*; C, *Hyoscyamus*

SIMAROUBACEAE—QUASSIA FAMILY

Our only species is the introduced Tree-of-heaven, ***Ailanthus altissima*** (Mill.) Swingle, a Chinese tree cultivated for its attractive leaves, rapid growth, ornamental fruits, and as a host for a domesticated silkworm. In America it has become a symbol of ultimate urbanization. This is the tree alluded to in the title of the novel, *A Tree Grows in Brooklyn*. Its exceptional hardiness under the most extreme urban conditions symbolized the stamina of the novel's protagonists. Cities along our urban corridor now have the Tree-of-heaven entrenched in back yards and vacant lots just as it is in New York. Its foliage has an unpleasant odor, the branches are weak and contain a disproportionate amount of pith, but in autumn the great masses of oblong, twisted samaras are very attractive with tints of red and brown.

SOLANACEAE—POTATO FAMILY

More than most families, the Solanaceae has affected for good or ill the course of history. Many species are gifts to Western civilization from the American Indian. The white potato, *Solanum tuberosum*, went from Incan Peru to Europe where it became the major crop in Ireland. A catastrophic fungal blight destroyed the potato farming there, and thousands of Irish migrated to Boston and New York. Sir Walter Raleigh introduced tobacco into British society with well-known results. The tomato, *Lycopersicon esculentum*, was a native American, thought poisonous not too long ago. Eggplant, *Solanum melongena*, native in southern Asia, is as important in Greek cooking as in Indian. Mexican foods would not be the same without the multitude of races of chile and bell peppers, *Capsicum frutescens*. The drug, atropine, used for dilating eyes, comes from *Atropa belladonna*, and in Delibes' grand opera, Lakme, the heroine commits suicide by eating the flower of *Datura*. In our gardens, *Petunia violacea* continues to brighten the patio long into autumn. Read Charles Heiser's fascinating account of the family in his book, *Nightshades, the Paradoxial Plants*, W. H. Freeman Co., 1969.

1a. Flowers less than 2 cm long or wide; fruit a berry .... (2)
1b. Flowers 2.5 cm or more long; fruit a dry capsule .... (12)

2a. Stems and foliage spiny .... (3)
2b. Stems and foliage not spiny .... (5)

3a. Flowers yellow; leaves deeply lobed. ***Solanum rostratum*** Dunal (beaked), BUFFALO-BUR, Fig. 238. Common weed in cultivated ground on the plains.
3b. Flowers purple, violet or white .... (4)

4a. Flowers purple; leaves and stems whitened by a scurfy scaly pubescence. ***Solanum elaeagnifolium*** Cav. (with leaves like *Elaeagnus*), SILVER-LEAVED NIGHTSHADE. Established weed along roadsides and railroad tracks, more common in southeastern Colorado.

Fig. 238. A, **Physalis lobata**; B, **Solanum triflorum**; C, **S. rostratum**

4b. Flowers white; leaves and stems green. **Solanum carolinense** L.
(of Carolina), Horse-nettle. Recently discovered as a weed in the
Boulder area.

5a. Leaf-blades deeply pinnatifid with acute, triangular segments.
Solanum triflorum Nutt. (three-flowered), Cut-leaved Nightshade,
Fig. 238. A weed in cultivated ground on the plains. Flowers white,
with yellow stamens.
5b. Leaf-blades entire, or, if lobed, not as above .... (6)

6a. Flowers white; fruit not enclosed at maturity by an inflated calyx. (7)
6b. Flowers yellow or purple; fruit enclosed at maturity by the inflated calyx (*Physalis*, Ground-cherry) .... (9)

7a. Plants annual .... (8)
7b. Plants perennial from small, potato-like underground tubers.
Solanum jamesii Torr. (for Edwin James), Wild Potato. Rare or
infrequent in the piedmont valleys, usually in somewhat disturbed
places, not appearing as if native.

8a. Leaves thin; plants glabrous or nearly so; calyx remaining small, not
covering part of the berry at maturity. **Solanum americanum** Mill.,
Nightshade. Weed of disturbed soil, piedmont valleys.
8b. Leaves thick; plants hirsute or glandular-villous; calyx enlarged at
maturity, covering lower half of berry. **Solanum sarachoides** Sendtn.
(resembling the genus *Saracha*), Nightshade. Similar habitats.

9a. Corolla rotate, purple or pale violet-pink. **Physalis lobata** Torr.
(lobed), Purple-flowered Ground-cherry, Fig. 238. Common in
sandy soil on the plains, also roadsides and cultivated ground.
9b. Corolla campanulate, yellow with a brown or purplish center ... (10)

10a. Flowering peduncles usually 3-8 mm long; corolla limb often reflexed when fully opened. **Physalis hederaefolia** Gray (ivy-leaved),
Ground-cherry. Mesas and plains.
10b. Flowering peduncles usually 10-15 mm long; corolla limb usually
not reflexed when fully open .... (11)

11a. Pubescence villous; hairs jointed. **Physalis heterophylla** Nees (various-leaved), Ground-cherry. Plains and piedmont valleys.
11b. Pubescence not villous. **Physalis virginiana** Mill., Ground-cherry.
Similar habitats.

12a. Flowers white, trumpet-shaped, in loose clusters or solitary ... (13)
12b. Flowers with a network of purple veins, in a one-sided spike; capsule circumscissile, in two rows along the stem, the calyx much enlarged at maturity. **Hyoscyamus niger** L., Henbane, Fig. 237. Introduced, established along lower Boulder Creek and doubtless elsewhere.

13a. Huge bushy glabrous herbs; corolla 4 cm or more long, open funnel-shaped; fruit a dry, spiny capsule. **Datura stramonium** L. (Stramon-

ium: an old generic name), JIMSON WEED, Fig. 237. Floodplains of the larger creeks, on the plains and piedmont valleys; blossoming in August.

13b. Sparingly branched herbs with glandular or sticky pubescence; corolla narrow, tubular; fruit not as above. *Nicotiana attenuata* Torr., WILD TOBACCO, Fig. 237. Infrequent in the piedmont valleys.

TAMARICACEAE—TAMARISK FAMILY

One genus and species, *Tamarix pentandra* Pallas (5-stamened), SALT CEDAR, Fig. 239. Escaped from cultivation and very much at home on bottomlands and sandbars of the rivers of the plains. A very attractive, slender-branched shrub or small tree with minute, scale-like bluish-green leaves and panicles of pink or white flowers. *Tamarix* and certain other plants that grow in low alkaline areas are able, by means of salt-excreting glands, to get rid of surplus salts, sometimes in such quantity that the salt may be gathered by humans. *Tamarix* is a *phreatophyte*, that is, a plant capable of reaching the water table. Phreatophytes are so successful in using water that they can actually lower the water table and therefore are a real problem in areas of water impoundment such as the Colorado River Basin.

ULMACEAE—ELM FAMILY

One native genus and species, *Celtis reticulata* Torr. (netted, alluding to the prominent veins), HACKBERRY, Fig. 239. Canyons and arroyos, outer foothills and plains. The trees are often stunted and misshapen, with the leaves infested with galls, but the tree is extremely hardy. Plants of this family have the leaves oblique (i.e. with one side extending farther down the petiole than the other). In *Celtis* the fruit is a hard-textured berry persisting through the winter. In elms, *Ulmus* spp., the fruit is a samara—a single flat one-seeded fruit with a circular wing. The Chinese Elm, *U. pumila* L. is a small-leaved species very hardy here but not a very desirable tree because of its structural weakness and suckering habits.

UMBELLIFERAE (APIACEAE)—PARSLEY FAMILY

The umbellifers are recognized by the usually ternately compound leaves with a sheathing petiole (this is what the edible part of celery is), the umbellate flower clusters, the fruits that separate at maturity into two one-seeded units (think of caraway seeds), and a generally pungent specific odor or taste. Many important herbs belong here: Dill (*Anethum graveolens*), Carrot (*Daucus carota*), Cumin (*Cuminum cyminum*), Coriander (*Coriandrum sativum*), Fennel (*Foeniculum vulgare*), Parsley (*Petroselinum hortense*), Celery (*Apium graveolens*), Anise (*Pimpinella anisum*), Parsnip (*Pastinaca sativa*), Caraway (*Carum carvi*), and Myrrh (*Myrrhis odorata*). But beware of chewing the leaves, stalks, roots or seeds of any umbel whose identity is doubtful! Two of the most poisonous plants in our region are

Fig. 239. A, *Tamarix*; B, *Celtis*

Conium, Poison Hemlock, and *Cicuta*, Water Hemlock. Cases of fatal or near-fatal poisoning are reported every season. Learn to recognize these species before using wild umbels for food.

1a. Leaves palmately cleft into 5 to 9 simple, toothed segments; fruit covered with hooked bristles. **Sanicula**, BLACK SNAKEROOT, page 348.
1b. Leaves various; fruit not bearing hooked bristles .... (2)

2a. Flowers yellow .... (3)
2b. Flowers white or pinkish .... (8)

3a. Flowering stem leafless, the leaves all coming off the top of the root or caudex .... (4)
3b. Flowering stem bearing one or more leaves (in early-flowering plants of *Musineon* the stem is so short as to appear leafless, but it elongates rapidly after the flowers begin to appear, although most of it may remain underground) .... (5)

4a. Tiny plants, less than 5 cm high, restricted to tundra. **Oreoxis**, ALPINE PARSLEY, page 347.
4b. Taller plants, at least 15 cm high; plants of the foothills. **Aletes**, page 343.

5a. Leaves pinnately compound with leaflets over 1 cm wide. **Pastinaca**, PARSNIP, page 348.
5b. Leaves palmately or ternately compound, if pinnate the leaflets narrow .... (6)

6a. Leaves prostrate on the ground, veiny; flowering stem shorter than the leaves (except in later fruiting stages); leaf rachis winged. **Musineon**, page 347.
6b. Leaves erect, not veiny; flowering stem taller than the leaves; leaf rachis not winged .... (7)

7a. Ultimate leaf-divisions linear, not narrowed at each end, stiff and wiry; fruit wingless. **Harbouria**, WHISK-BROOM PARSLEY, page 346.
7b. Ultimate leaf-divisions variable but usually narrowed at each end, not stiff and wiry. **Pseudocymopterus**, YELLOW MOUNTAIN PARSLEY, page 348.

8a. Low, early spring plants of mesas and plains; flowering stems hardly exceeding the basal leaves .... (9)
8b. Tall plants with well-defined stems; flowering stems much exceeding the basal leaves .... (10)

9a. Fruit with both lateral and dorsal wings developed, not strongly flattened dorsally. **Cymopterus**, page 345.
9b. Fruits lacking dorsal wings, the lateral wings prominent (thus the mericarps flat and thin-edged). **Lomatium**, page 346.

10a. Leaves usually simple, palmately cleft, the larger ones sometimes

divided into 3 or 5 leaflets. **Heracleum**, Cow Parsnip, page 346.
10b. Leaves variously compound, not as above . . . .(11)

11a. Leaves once pinnately compound; plants of wet places . . . .(12)
11b. Leaves repeatedly divided, ternately compound, or twice pinnately compound . . . .(14)

12a. Main umbels with a ring of linear or lanceolate bracts at the base.
 . . . .(13)
12b. Main umbels naked at the base. **Oxypolis**, Cowbane, page 348.

13a. Stems tall, up to a meter high, the branches few, strongly ascending; leaves with 3 to 9 simply serrate leaflets, all leaves similar. **Sium**, Water Parsnip, page 349.
13b. Stems low, less than a half meter high, with numerous spreading branches; leaves with 9 to 19 leaflets, the upper leaves usually much more deeply cleft than the lower. **Berula**, page 345.

14a. Fruits 4-5 times longer than wide; fruits and roots with an anise odor when crushed. **Osmorhiza**, Sweet Cicely, page 347.
14b. Fruits short, almost as wide as long; fruits and roots lacking anise odor . . . .(15)

15a. Tall, coarse plants, the ultimate leaf-divisions 1 cm or more broad; leaves generally not more than twice pinnately compound . . . .(16)
15b. Slender plants, or, if tall and coarse, the ultimate leaf-divisions less than 0.5 cm wide; leaves generally very finely dissected, fern-like . . . .(17)

16a. Leaf-divisions lanceolate; ribs of fruit prominent but not forming wings; roots tuberous, clustered; plants of sloughs and ditches on the plains. **Cicuta**, Water Hemlock, page 345.
16b. Leaf divisions ovate; ribs of fruit forming wings; plant with a taproot; foothills and mountains. **Angelica**, page 343.

17a. Fruits covered with hooked bristles; umbels subtended by a conspicuous ring of leaflike bracts, sometimes equalling the umbel rays. **Daucus**, Wild Carrot, page 345.
17b. Fruits not bristly; umbels subtended by very inconspicuous small bracts or none . . . .(18)

18a. Weeds of irrigation ditches or cultivated ground . . . .(19)
18b. Plants of natural mountain habitats (forests and subalpine stream-sides) . . . .(20)

19a. Stems spotted with purple; tall plants with hollow stems over a meter tall, and huge fern-like basal leaves. **Conium**, Poison Hemlock, page 345.
19b. Stems not spotted with purple; plants not over a meter tall, smaller in all details; fruit with characteristic caraway odor. **Carum**, Caraway, page 345.

20a. Leaflets linear, 1-3 mm wide. *Ligusticum*, LOVAGE, page 346.
20b. Leaflets ovate, oblong or lanceolate, 5-40 mm broad ....(21)

21a. Fruits oval, strongly flattened dorsally; plant less than 1 meter tall, unbranched. *Conioselinum*, HEMLOCK PARSLEY, page 345.
21b. Fruits oblong, not flattened dorsally; plants over a meter tall, freely branched. *Ligusticum*, LOVAGE, page 346.

ALETES

1a. Lateral leaflets with linear or narrowly elliptic lobes, minutely spine-tipped and rigid; plant with strong anise odor. *Aletes anisatus* (Gray) Theobald & Tseng. Steep gravelly slopes, Platte River Canyon to Pikes Peak.
1b. Lateral leaflets with ovate, flaring lobes; plants lacking anise odor. *Aletes acaulis* (Torr.) C. & R. (stemless), MOUNTAIN CARAWAY, Fig. 240. Common on fixed rock ledges in foothills canyons.

ANGELICA

1a. Coarse, stout herbs of streambanks in the foothills and montane; plants over 2 meters high with very large umbels. *Angelica ampla* Nels., GIANT ANGELICA.
1b. Lower herbs less than 2 meters high; subalpine meadows and lower tundra slopes. *Angelica grayi* C. & R. (for Asa Gray). These species are very easily distinguished; when in doubt, the seed is free in the pericarp and the oil tubes numerous in cross-section in *A. ampla*, but seed fused to the pericarp and oil tubes few in *A. grayi*.

Fig. 240. *Aletes acaulis*

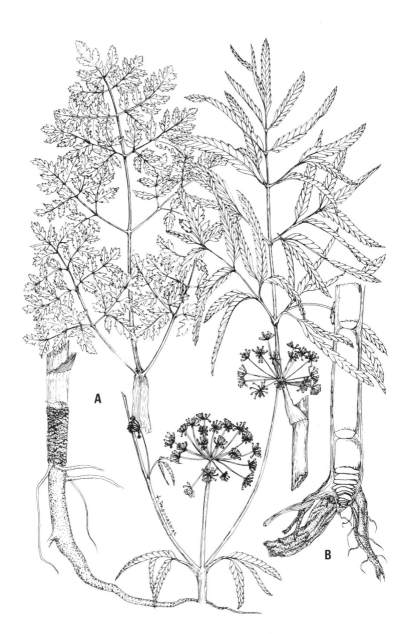

Fig. 241. A, *Conium*; B, *Cicuta*

BERULA
One species, ***Berula erecta*** (Huds.) Coville. Sloughs in the piedmont valleys.

CARUM. Caraway
One species, ***Carum carvi*** L. A common weed, particularly around villages in the montane zone. Evidently the climate is not right for this in the piedmont valleys, where *Conium*, the somewhat similar Poison Hemlock, is abundant.

CICUTA. Water Hemlock
One species, ***Cicuta douglasii*** (DC.) C. & R. (for David Douglas), Fig. 241. The fascicled tuberous roots, and the partitioned stem cross-section just above the roots, are diagnostic. This plant is so deadly that convulsions may result only minutes after ingesting it.

CONIOSELINUM. Hemlock Parsley
One species, ***Conioselinum scopulorum*** (Gray) C. & R. Frequent in wet meadows and roadside ditches, montane and subalpine. A low herb with usually one or two stem leaves and little branching, never tall and rank like its close relative *Ligusticum porteri*.

CONIUM. Poison Hemlock
One species, ***Conium maculatum*** L., Fig. 241. An abundant tall, rank weed in towns, especially near irrigation ditches and wet ground. The plant produces a rosette of fern-like leaves the first year, and can be easily hoed out in that stage. The second year it sends up a flower stalk up to 3 meters high. Children have been poisoned by using the hollow stems for whistles. Every effort should be made to eliminate this from our area because of the potential danger of poisoning. This is the plant a decoction of which Socrates drank.

CYMOPTERUS
1a. Flowers pink; leaves glaucous-bluish; bracts with papery margins. ***Cymopterus montanus*** Nutt. Common early spring flower on dry shale outcrops, plains and mesas.
1b. Flowers white; leaves glossy green; bracts without papery margins. ***Cymopterus acaulis*** (Pursh) Raf. (stemless). Common in early spring, on sandstone or sandy substrates on the plains and mesas.

DAUCUS. Carrot
One species, ***Daucus carota*** L., Wild Carrot; Queen Anne's Lace. Introduced weed or garden escape, established along roadsides in the piedmont valleys. The first blooming flower of the umbel (very center) is often deep purple.

HARBOURIA. Whisk-broom Parsley

One species, **Harbouria trachypleura** (Gray) C. & R. (rough-ribbed), Plate 1, Fig. 242. On open slopes from the mesas to warm south exposures in the montane. This is a monotypic genus (consisting of this single species) and is endemic on the eastern slope of the Front Range.

HERACLEUM. Cow Parsnip

One species, **Heracleum sphondylium** L. ssp. **montanum** (Schleich. *ex* Gaud.) Briquet (old name for *Heracleum*), Fig. 243. Plant of giant proportions, growing in swampy thickets along streams, foothills and montane (*H. lanatum* of Ed. 4).

LIGUSTICUM. Lovage

1a. Leaflets linear, 1-3 mm broad; low, slender plant less than 0.5 meters high. **Ligusticum filicinum** Wats. var. **tenuifolium** (Wats.) Math. & Const., Fern-leaved Lovage. Frequent in meadows and moist grassy slopes, subalpine.

1b. Leaflets ovate, oblong or lanceolate, 5-40 mm wide; tall, rank plants over a meter tall. **Ligusticum porteri** C. & R. (for T. C. Porter). Very common in forested ravines and aspen groves, foothills and montane.

LOMATIUM

One species, **Lomatium orientale** C. & R. (eastern), Salt-and-pepper. The most abundant early spring parsley on grassy mesa slopes. *Lomatium* is a very large genus of about 80 species ranging through the western U. S. The initials C. & R. stand for Coulter and Rose, who monographed the family in 1888. Mathias and Constance revised the group in 1944-45.

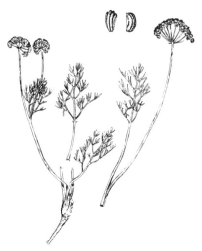

Fig. 242. *Harbouria trachypleura*

MUSINEON

One species, ***Musineon divaricatum*** (Pursh) Nutt. (spreading out). Common early spring flower, particularly on shales, on the mesas.

OREOXIS. Alpine Parsley

1a. Leaves less than 5 cm long (unless in deep shade), the side pinnae less than 5 mm long. ***Oreoxis alpina*** (Gray) C. & R. Abundant on tundra throughout our range, but replaced on Pikes Peak by the next.

1b. Leaves 5-8 cm long, the side pinnae 5-10 mm long. ***Oreoxis humilis*** Raf. Endemic on the tundra of Pikes Peak, a larger plant in all respects than the last.

OSMORHIZA. Sweet Cicely

1a. Bracts present at ·base of umbels; styles 2-3 mm long. ***Osmorhiza longistylis*** (Torr.) DC. Rare in cool canyons in the outer foothills.

1b. Bracts at base of umbels absent; styles 0.5 mm long or less. (2)

2a. Fruit less than 12 mm long, blunt or rounded at the tip. ***Osmorhiza depauperata*** Phil. Very common in forested slopes and ravines, foothills to subalpine.

2b. Fruits over 12 mm long, distinctly pointed, the styles about 1 mm long. ***Osmorhiza chilensis*** H. & A. (Chilean). Infrequent in similar situations.

Fig. 243. ***Heracleum sphondylium***

OXYPOLIS. Cowbane

One species, *Oxypolis fendleri* (Gray) Heller (for August Fendler). Fig. 244. Swamps and streamsides, montane and subalpine.

PASTINACA. Parsnip

One species, **Pastinaca sativa** L. (cultivated). Escaped from cultivation and well established locally in the piedmont valleys.

PSEUDOCYMOPTERUS. Yellow Mountain Parsley

One species, *Pseudocymopterus montanus* (Gray) C. & R. Abundant in aspen groves and subalpine meadows. Extremely variable in leaf width and one of the most commonly misidentified umbels because it changes so in appearance from early to late stages of maturity.

SANICULA. Black Snakeroot

One species, **Sanicula marilandica** L. (of Maryland). Locally abundant in cool moist canyons of the outer foothills. This is one of the Eastern Woodland-prairie relict species stranded in the mesic canyons of the foothills after the connection with eastern populations was broken by the present development of the High Plains climate.

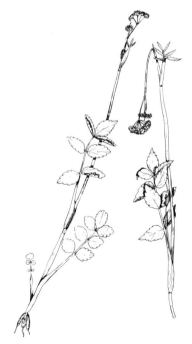

Fig. 244. *Oxypolis fendleri*

SIUM. WATER PARSNIP
One species, *Sium suave* Walt. (fragrant). Very common in swampy ground on the western slope but rarely collected in the montane zone in our area.

URTICACEAE—NETTLE FAMILY

Nettles "sting" by means of epidermal hairs that are filled with an irritant substance, including acetylcholine and histamine. The hairs are silicified at the tip, thus are brittle and break when brushed against. The irritation is brief but severe in humans. Hunting dogs are prone to more serious systemic disorders. This family contains a major fibre plant, Ramie (*Boehmeria nivea*), a native of Asia.

1a. Leaves opposite, sharply serrate; plants with stinging hairs. *Urtica dioica* L. ssp. *gracilis* (Ait.) Selander (unisexual; slender), STINGING NETTLE, Fig. 245. A tall coarse herb found chiefly along irrigation ditches and streams in the lower foothills and piedmont valleys.
1b. Leaves alternate, entire; plants without stinging hairs. *Parietaria pensylvanica* Muehl., PELLITORY, Fig. 245. Small, weak herb found in shade of trees or rocks, plains and foothills.

VALERIANACEAE—VALERIAN FAMILY

Although the valerians are a small family, they are very conspicuous in moist forests and meadows in late summer. Because of their compound leaves and umbel-like flower clusters they are often mistaken for Umbelliferae but actually they are more closely related to Compositae. Two features clearly mark our species: the corolla with a small gibbosity at the base on one side, and the plumose parachute formed by the calyx, which unrolls when the fruits are mature (see Fig. 246).

1a. Plants with thick, fleshy, vertical taproots; leaves and leaflets thick, narrow; venation almost parallel; inflorescence very open even at flowering time; flowers unisexual. *Valeriana edulis* Nutt. *ex* T. & G. (edible), Fig. 246. Rather dry, gravelly hillsides and meadows, montane, subalpine.
1b. Plants with creeping rhizomes; leaves and leaflets thin, broad; venation distinctly pinnate; inflorescence a dense compound cyme, becoming more open at fruiting time; flowers perfect or apparently so ....(2)

2a. Corolla shallowly cup-shaped, without a definite cylindrical tube and not noticeably swollen at the base. *Valeriana occidentalis* Heller (western). Wet meadows and streamsides, montane and subalpine; more common on the western slope.
2b. Corolla funnel-shaped or trumpet-shaped, with a definite cylindrical tube and usually swollen at the base on one side ....(3)

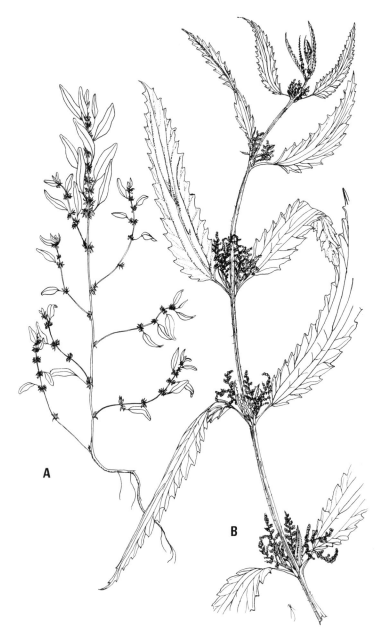

Fig. 245. A, *Parietaria*; B, *Urtica*

Fig. 246. A, *Valeriana edulis*; B, *V. capitata*; flowers and fruits

3a. Basal leaves lanceolate, oblanceolate or obovate, cuneate at base and gradually narrowed to a wide petiolar base. ***Valeriana capitata*** Pallas *ex* Link ssp. *acutiloba* (Rydb.) F. G. Meyer, Fig. 246. Abundant in mountain meadows and forest openings, subalpine.
3b. Basal leaves broadly ovate, rounded or subcordate at the base, the petiole slender and sharply defined. ***Valeriana arizonica*** Gray. Barely entering our range near Cripple Creek, but the common species south into New Mexico.

VERBENACEAE—VERVAIN FAMILY

Our verbenas might be mistaken for mints, but the foliage lacks any minty odor. The stems are often square, however, and the flowers mintlike. Verbenas are cultivated for their handsome flower clusters. This family includes teakwood (*Tectona grandis*), one of the finest of timbers for furniture and, in the days of wooden ships, shipbuilding. Teakwood was especially sought for armored vessels because, unlike oak, the wood did not corrode the iron. Oddly enough, the wood sinks in water unless dried for two years. Trees were girdled and left standing that long before harvesting.

1a. Flowers white or pale pinkish-lavender, in globose or short-cylindric tight heads; plants trailing and rooting at the nodes. ***Phyla cuneifolia*** (Torr.) Greene (with cuneate leaves), FOG-FRUIT, Fig. 247. Pond shores and marshy sites, plains and piedmont valleys.
1b. Flowers pink, blue or purple (rarely white in occasional individuals); flowers in elongate spikes, at least in age; plants erect or prostrate but not rooting at the nodes .... (2)

2a. Flowers showy, lavender; corolla-tube much exceeding the calyx; leaves very deeply pinnatifid. ***Verbena ambrosifolia*** Rydb. (with leaves like *Ambrosia*), Fig. 247. A handsome species of the plains and mesas, similar to some of the cultivated ones.
2b. Flowers small, blue or purple; corolla tube scarcely longer than the calyx; leaves merely toothed or very shallowly pinnatifid .... (3)

3a. Floral bracts leaflike, equalling or exceeding the flowers; plant usually prostrate. ***Verbena bracteata*** Lag. & Rodr., Fig. 247. A common roadside weed on the mesas and plains.
3b. Floral bracts shorter than the flowers, not leaflike; tall, erect plants .... (4)

4a. Spikes slender, acute at the apex; leaves deep green; flowers dark blue or purple. ***Verbena hastata*** L., BLUE VERVAIN, Fig. 247. Swamps and irrigation ditches, piedmont valleys and plains, flowering in late summer.
4b. Spikes stout, blunt at the apex; leaves light green, whitened by appressed pubescence; flowers lavender. ***Verbena stricta*** Vent. (erect), WOOLLY VERVAIN. Plains and mesas, usually in badly overgrazed sites.

Fig. 247. A, **Verbena hastata**; B, **V. ambrosifolia**; C, **V. bracteata**; D, **Phyla**

VIOLACEAE—VIOLET FAMILY

Many violets produce attractive and sweet-smelling flowers, but these often do not produce seeds. The effective seed-producing flowers are cleistogamous, that is, they never open, lack attractive floral parts, and are subterranean or emerge only after fruit is matured. They are obviously self-pollinated in such instances. Many violets are adapted for dispersal of the seeds by ants, and to aid the ant in grasping the seed there may be a small irregularly shaped growth on the side of the seed (a caruncle). This relationship between ants and plants is called *myrmecophily.*

1a. Leaves sessile, linear-lanceolate, simple, entire, not basal; lower-most petal not spurred (not true violets). ***Hybanthus verticillatus*** (Ort.) Baill. (whorled), GREEN VIOLET, Fig. 249. Mostly found on shale outcrops on the mesas.
1b. Leaves not as above, often chiefly basal, lowermost petal spurred (true violets) . . . . (2)

2a. Plants stemless (but sometimes stolon-bearing), the leaves arising directly from the rhizome; flowers borne on the leafless stalk (scape); petals never yellow . . . . (3)
2b. Plants with leafy stems (sometimes very short); flowers axillary; petals violet, white, or yellow . . . . (7)

3a. Leaves greatly dissected. ***Viola pedatifida*** G. Don, BIRDFOOT VIOLET, Fig. 249. Infrequent on the mesas, flowering in early spring.
3b. Leaves entire or merely toothed . . . . (4)

4a. Rhizomes slender (1-2 mm thick); plants usually bearing stolons; petals pale violet or white (deeper colored in one very rare species), less than 10 mm long . . . . (5)
4b. Rhizome thick (5 mm or more); plants without stolons; petals blue or purple, usually more than 10 mm long. ***Viola nephrophylla*** Greene (kidney-leaved), BLUE VIOLET. The common violet on bottomlands of the plains and piedmont valleys.

5a. Petals lilac or violet; spur large, 5 mm or more long; leaves minutely hairy on the upper surface. ***Viola selkirkii*** Pursh (for Thomas Douglas, Earl of Selkirk), GREAT-SPURRED VIOLET. Extremely rare, vicinity of Devils Head, and Rocky Mountain National Park.
5b. Petals white or very pale lilac, with purple veins; spur small; leaves glabrous above . . . . (6)

6a. Rhizomes thin, filiform, with long runners from the upper part; leaves somewhat acute; petals usually very pale violet with darker veins. ***Viola epipsela*** Ledeb. ssp. ***repens*** (Turcz.) Becker, SWAMP VIOLET. Common in woodland bogs, pond shores and willow streamsides, subalpine. Underground parts should be taken for sure identification (*V. pallens* of Ed. 4).
6b. Rhizomes comparatively thick, ascending, lacking runners; leaves broad-cordate, rounded at the top; flowers white with violet stripes.

Viola renifolia Gray var. *brainerdii* (Greene) Fernald. Similar sites, but evidently not as common.

7a. Annuals; stipules large, leaf-like, palmately divided; petals pale bluish-violet. *Viola kitaibeliana* R. & S. (for Paul Kitaibel), HEARTS-EASE; FIELD PANSY, Fig. 249. Frequent in rocky gulches on the mesas, blossoming in early spring.

7b. Perennials; stipules entire or nearly so .... (8)

8a. Petals yellow .... (9)
8b. Petals violet, blue, or white with purple veins . ... (10)

9a. Leaves with pointed apex, tapering or merely rounded at the base; petals often tinged on the back with purple or brown. *Viola nuttallii* Pursh (for Thomas Nuttall), Fig. 249. The most common spring-flowering violet on the plains, mesas, and foothills. Blooms later in the subalpine.

9b. Leaves almost orbicular, narrowly cordate at the base; petals not tinged on the back with purple or brown. *Viola biflora* L., TWIN-FLOWER VIOLET. Rare, in cold ravines in a few foothill localities, and in shade of great boulders in alpine cirque basins. The only other North American localities for this species outside of Colorado are in Alaska.

10a. Petals blue or violet; plants quite small; stems short, often obscure; leaves seldom distinctly cordate. *Viola adunca* Smith (hooked), MOUNTAIN BLUE VIOLET, Fig. 248. The most abundant summer-blooming violet in the montane and subalpine. The small subalpine race is ssp. *bellidifolia* (Greene) Harrington.

Fig. 248. *Viola adunca*

Fig. 249. A, *Viola kitaibeliana*; B, *V. pedatifida*; C, *V. nuttallii*; D, *Hybanthus*

10b. Petals white, often with purple veins; stems several cm tall, the leaves cordate. ***Viola canadensis*** L. (including *V. rugulosa* Greene), Fig. 250. An extremely variable violet of gulches and streamsides from foothills to alpine, varying in pubescence, leaf size and shape, presence and absence of stolons, flower size and amount of purple coloration, but evidently impossible to divide into well-separated races.

VISCACEAE—DWARF-MISTLETOE FAMILY

The dwarf-mistletoes are important parasites on coniferous trees in western North and Central America. Almost every tree species has its own distinctive species or race of *Arceuthobium*. The mistletoes are extremely reduced plants. The flowers, leaves, branches and root system are so simplified and condensed that to the layman the species look almost identical. The seeds are explosively shot from the fruits at high speed (27 meters/sec) for distances up to 15 meters. They are sticky and adhere to pine needles. When the needles become wet from rain the seeds slide down to the branch where they germinate by a penetrating holdfast. Many mistletoes produce characteristic "witches brooms" on the branches of trees. See Hawksworth & Wiens, *Biology and Classification of Dwarf Mistletoes (Arceuthobium).* USDA Agric. Handbook No. 401, 1972.

1a. Flowers blooming in late summer (Aug.-Sept.); parasitic on limber pine. ***Arceuthobium campylopodum*** Engelm.(curved-foot). See Addenda.
1b. Flowers blooming in spring (May-June); parasitic on Ponderosa Pine, Lodgepole Pine, or Douglas-fir . . . . (2)

2a. Secondary branches several at each node, forming whorls; parasitic on Lodgepole Pine. ***Arceuthobium americanum*** Nutt.
2b. Secondary branches few at each node and in a flattened or fan-like arrangement . . . . (3)

Fig. 250. ***Viola canadensis***

3a. Plants yellowish, robust; stems more than 2 mm in diameter at base, 2-15 cm long; parasitic on Ponderosa Pine. ***Arceuthobium vaginatum*** Willd. (sheathed), Fig. 157.

3b. Plants greenish, slender; stems not more than 1 mm in diameter at base, nor over 3.5 cm long; parasitic on Douglas-fir. ***Arceuthobium douglasii*** Engelm. (for David Douglas).

Vitaceae—Grape Family

The Mediterranean region has been called the cradle of civilization. Around its eastern end, in what we call the Near East, man first developed agriculture between 8000 and 7000 B.C. He probably would not have reached the pinnacle without wine, so it has always seemed to me that it was at least a remarkable coincidence that the Mediterranean area offered, side by side, the three basic necessities for oenophiles—the grape, *Vitis vinifera*, the goat (for the wine-skins) and the cork oak, *Quercus suber*. The Garden of Eden must have been a reality, but I suspect that it was the grape rather than the apple that got Adam and Eve into all that trouble!

1a. Leaves simple, cordate with shallow palmate lobing. ***Vitis riparia*** Michx. (of streamsides), WILD GRAPE. Gulches and canyons of the outer foothills.

1b. Leaves palmately compound .... (2)

Fig. 251. *Parthenocissus inserta*   Fig. 252. *Tribulus terrestris*

2a. Tendrils ending in adhesive disks; leaves dull above. ***Parthenocissus quinquefolia*** (L.) Planch., Virginia Creeper, Woodbine. Widely cultivated and covering stone buildings, sometimes established in and around towns.

2b. Tendrils lacking adhesive disks or with very few; leaves shiny above. ***Parthenocissus inserta*** (Kerner) Fritsch, Fig. 251. Native in gulches and canyons on the mesas and outer foothills.

Zygophyllaceae—Caltrop Family

One species, ***Tribulus terrestris*** L., Puncture-vine, Fig. 252. Prostrate-spreading weed with small, pinnately-compound leaves and yellow flowers, common in sandy soil along roadsides and ruderal sites on the plains and piedmont valleys. The fruits break up into 4 or 5 hard, spiny segments (mericarps), which are capable of puncturing bicycle tires.

Class Monocotyledoneae
Monocots

AGAVACEAE—AGAVE FAMILY

One species, *Yucca glauca* Nutt., SPANISH BAYONET, Fig. 290. Abundant on the plains and mesas, especially where the soil is too poor to support grassland. This genus is noted for one of the most interesting cases on record of the phenomenon of symbiosis involving plants and insects. *Yucca* is visited by a night-flying moth, *Pronuba*. Alighting on the flower, the moth first stabs the ovary and lays an egg inside. Then it mounts a stamen and collects a mass of pollen from the anther. It is not possible to pollinate *Yucca* by merely brushing the stigma with pollen accidentally, for the stigmatic surface is deeply seated in the bottom of the funnel-shaped style. As if understanding the problem, the moth proceeds to stuff the wad of pollen deep in the funnel, thus assuring pollination,

Fig. 253. *Alisma plantago-aquatica*
360

and consequently ample food for the developing larva inside. Pollination results in the production of hundreds of seeds, so that neither actor in the drama loses anything and each achieves posterity.

ALISMATACEAE—WATER-PLANTAIN FAMILY

1a. Leaves sagittate; flowers in whorls of 3 along a central axis; carpels in a tight ball ....(2)
1b. Leaves oval; flowers in a diffusely-branched panicle, the ultimate branches bearing flowers in umbels; carpels in a ring. *Alisma plantago-aquatica* L. ssp. *brevipes* (Greene) Samuelsson, WATER-PLANTAIN, Fig. 253. Common in mud along irrigation ditches and pond shores on the plains and piedmont valleys. Submerged leaves are usually narrower.

2a. Beak of achene horizontal or nearly so (at right angles to the long axis). *Sagittaria latifolia* Willd., ARROWHEAD, Fig. 254. Frequent in mud along irrigation ditches and pond shores, as above.
2b. Beak of achene erect or nearly so (parallel to the long axis). *Sagittaria cuneata* Sheld. (wedge-shaped), ARROWHEAD, Fig. 254. Similar habitats.

ALLIACEAE—ONION FAMILY

Usually included in the Lily family, the onions, for reasons other than their distinctive odors, stand alone because of their umbellate flower clusters and papery spathe-like bract, as well as numerous other technical features. In this family we find the culinary Leek, *Allium porrum*; Garlic, *Allium sativum*; commercial Onion strains, *Allium cepa*, and Chives, *Allium schoenoprasum*. *Allium* is a particularly diversified genus in the arid West and in southwest Asia and contributes many showy species to rock garden culture.

1a. Leaves hollow, terete. *Allium schoenoprasum* L. var. *sibiricum* (L.) Hartman (Greek name for a Leek), WILD CHIVES. Infrequent in wet meadows, subalpine, on the fringes of our range in North Park and Larimer County.
1b. Leaves not hollow (but may be flat or terete) ....(2)

2a. Umbel nodding. *Allium cernuum* Roth, NODDING ONION. Common on grassy slopes from mesas to subalpine. Flowers pink, the petals rounded, not spreading.
2b. Umbel erect ....(3)

3a. Outer bulb-scales membranous, not fibrous; plant 3-5 dm tall from a stout, elongated bulb. *Allium brevistylum* Wats. (short-styled). In wet places around Grand Lake and probably within our range.
3b. Outer bulb-scales persisting as a network of coarse fibers; plant rarely over 3 dm tall ....(4)

4a. Leaves usually 2 per stem; tips of inner perianth segments spreading; flowers usually white. **Allium textile** Nels. & Macbr. (woven), WILD ONION. Common on the plains and mesas.

4b. Leaves 3 or more per stem; tips of inner perianth segments erect; flowers usually pink. **Allium geyeri** Wats. (for Carl A. Geyer), WILD ONION, Fig. 296. Common from the foothills to the tundra, dwarfed at very high altitudes.

ARACEAE—ARUM FAMILY

Typically the Arum family includes plants with the inflorescence spike (spadix) enveloped by a large, often colored bract (spathe). Aroids include many of our most ornamental house plants (*Dieffenbachia, Monstera, Anthurium, Philodendron* and *Calla*). The Jack-in-the-Pulpit and

Fig. 254. **Sagittaria cuneata** (left), **S. latifolia** (right)

Skunk-cabbage of the eastern U.S. also belong in this family. Our single species is different in that it lacks an obvious spathe although in this instance the spathe simulates a continuation of the stem.

One genus and species, ***Acorus calamus*** L. (from ancient Greek name for a reed), SWEET-FLAG, Fig. 255. The leaves are long and sword-like, as in cat-tails, but have a distinctive sweet odor when crushed. Formerly found up and down the piedmont valleys, it is now almost extinct following urbanization and draining of watercourses. Stands still occur near and in Fort Collins.

ASPARAGACEAE—ASPARAGUS FAMILY

One species, ***Asparagus officinalis*** L., abundantly escaped along irrigation ditches in the piedmont valleys. The young shoots, which we eat, are extraordinarily different in appearance from the older, mature ones. The succulent shoots possess triangular scale leaves which are soon lost as the shoot elongates and branches to form an intricate fern-like growth in which the filiform green "leaves" are modified shoots and not true leaves at all. In summer the plants bear bright red berries. The potted "Asparagus Fern" is *Asparagus sprengeri* Regel, a broad-"leaved" plant, and the one used by florists is *A. plumosus* Baker. The family is Mediterranean, and the wild species of that area are tough, thorny bushes making impenetrable thickets.

Fig. 255. ***Acorus calamus***

COMMELINACEAE—SPIDERWORT FAMILY

The genus from which the family takes its name is a homely little weed common in city back yards in the eastern U.S. and northern Europe, called the Dayflower. The flowers last only through one day, then simply melt into a slimy residue. Linnaeus explained the name he gave the plant: "*Commelina* has flowers with three petals, two of which are showy [blue], while the third [white] is not conspicuous: [named] from the two botanists called Commelin: for the third died before accomplishing anything in botany."

One genus and species, ***Tradescantia occidentalis*** (Britt.) Smyth (western), SPIDERWORT, Fig. 256. Very common in spring and early summer on rocky slopes of the lower foothills and mesas. Flowers blue-purple, very rarely pink.

CYPERACEAE—SEDGE FAMILY

The word "sedge" is derived as far back as Middle English *segge* and Teutonic *seg*, and is related to the modern German *Säge*, meaning saw. Many sedges have sharp cutting edges on the leaves, and some of them are actually minutely saw-toothed. Relatively few sedges are of major economic importance, but *Cyperus papyrus* was famous from antiquity. Gérard wrote: "Paper Reed hath many large flaggie leaves somewhat triangular and smooth, not much unlike those of Cats-taile, rising

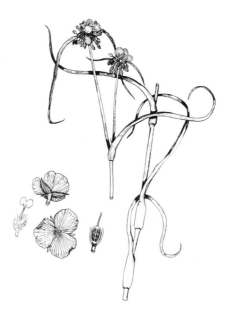

Fig. 256. ***Tradescantia occidentalis***

immediately from a tuft or roots compact of many strings, amongst the which it shooteth up two or three naked stalkes, square, and rising some six or seven cubits high above the water; at the top whereof there stands a tuft or bundle of chaffie threads set in comely order, resembling a tuft of flowers, but barren and void of seed. . . . This kinde of Reed which I have Englished Paper Reed, or Paper Plant, is the same (as I do reade) that Paper was made of in Aegypt, before the invention of paper made of linen clouts was found out. It is thought by men of great learning and understanding in the Scriptures, and set downe by them for truth, that this plant is the same Reed mentioned in the second chapter of Exodus, whereof was made that basket or cradle, which was dawbed within and without with slime of that countrey, called *Bitumen indicum*, wherein *Moses* was put being committed to the water, when *Pharoah* gave commandment that all the male children of the Hebrewes should be drowned." The Umbrella Sedge, cultivated in greenhouses and around ornamental ponds, is *Cyperus umbellatus*, a relative of Papyrus.

1a. Flower cluster resembling a powderpuff or tassel, the perianth consisting of long white silky hairs. **Eriophorum,** Cotton-grass, page 382.
1b. Flower cluster not as above .... (2)

2a. Floral bracts (scales) in two distinct rows, the spike flattened ... (3)
2b. Floral bracts arranged in ascending spirals, the spikes not distinctly flattened .... (4)

3a. Annuals, the culms not thickened at the base. **Cyperus,** Galingale, page 380.
3b. Perennials, the culms with thickened corm-like bases. **Mariscus**, page 383.

4a. Flowers perfect (all alike and never grouped into different types of spikes on the same plant); gynoecium merely subtended by a scale-like bract .... (5)
4b. Flowers unisexual, the plants and spikes either entirely staminate or entirely carpellate, or with both staminate and carpellate flowers in the same spike; gynoecium enclosed in a sac-like structure (called a perigynium) .... (8)

5a. Spike solitary, terminal; leaf-blades lacking. **Eleocharis,** Spike-rush, page 380.
5b. Spikes more than one, or if solitary, not terminal but protruding from the side of the stem .... (6)

6a. Spikes terminal, numerous. **Scirpus,** Bulrush; Tule, page 383.
6b. Spikes protruding sideways from the side of the stem .... (7)

7a. Plants less than 10 cm high; spike solitary, only 3 mm long. **Hemicarpha**, page 382.
7b. Plants half a meter to several meters high; spikes a centimeter or more long. **Scirpus**, page 383.

8a. Perigynium split down the middle throughout its length with over-lapping margins (like the open sheath of a grass). ***Kobresia***, page 382.

8b. Perigynium completely closed except at the apex where the style protrudes (like the closed sheath of a grass). ***Carex***, page 366.

CAREX. Sedge (revised by Miriam F. Colson)

Note: In this key the word "scale" means the bract of a single flower, while the word "bract" means the leaf subtending an entire spike of flowers.

1a. Spikes one to a culm (careful observation needed here; several species may *appear* to have one spike but on close examination show more than one rachis) . . . . **Key A**, page 366.

1b. Spikes more than one to a culm, although sometimes crowded so as to appear single (careful examination will reveal separate rachises or branches of the inflorescence) . . . . (2)

2a. Spikes in a ball-like cluster, the individual spikes not easily detected by manipulation, only by dissection; scales brown, never black . . . . **Key B**, page 368.

2b. Spikes either separate or clustered but always distinguishable without dissection . . . . (3)

3a. Spikes sessile, never black unless perigynia wing-margined or very sharp-edged, usually with staminate and carpellate flowers in the same spike, terminal spike never markedly different from the rest . . . . **Key C**, page 368.

3b. Spikes pedunculate (at least the lowermost one) or black, or with markedly different staminate terminal spikes . . . . **Key D**, page 375.

KEY A

1a. Plants in dense clumps, not rhizomatous; leaf blades always narrow and filiform . . . . (2)

1b. Plants with obvious rhizomes, the culms solitary or a few together; leaf blades up to 3 mm wide . . . . (7)

2a. Spike short and broad, shiny brown or black, the terminal staminate portion inconspicuous, or the spike broadly triangular with conspicuous staminate flowers at the apex . . . . (3)

2b. Spike elongate, narrow, often pale, with a distinct elongate narrow staminate portion, only a few carpellate flowers at the base, bulging when mature . . . . (5)

3a. Spikes globose or triangular, stigmas 2; perigynia not stipitate. ***Carex capitata*** L. ssp. ***arctogena*** (H. Smith) Boecher. Rare or local on alpine summits.

3b. Spikes not globose, stigmas 2 or 3; perigynia stipitate . . . . (4)

4a. Plants less than 10 cm tall; spikes less than 1 cm long; stigmas 2 or 3; tip of perigynium dark. **Carex nardina** Fries ssp. **hepburnii** (Boott) Löve, Löve and Kapoor (resembling the grass, *Nardus*; for James Hepburn). On the highest tundra ridges, often on very dry sites.

4b. Plants usually over 10 cm tall; spikes up to 15 mm long; stigmas 3; tip of perigynium hyaline. **Carex pyrenaica** Wahlenb. (of the Pyrenees). Common in snowmelt areas, alpine and subalpine.

5a. Leaf-blades 1.5-2.0 mm wide; culms stout, often rough above; lowest scale awned. **Carex oreocharis** Holm (mountain-loving). Dry grasslands, mesas to montane and subalpine. The spike is thick and very smooth owing to the broad overlapping and clasping scales.

5b. Leaf-blades 0.25-0.5 mm wide; culms filiform, smooth or nearly so above; lowest scale usually not awned .... (6)

6a. Perigynia rounded on the angles, truncately short-beaked, puberulent above; carpellate scales with broad hyaline margins; basal sheaths usually shredded and filamentose; style exserted. **Carex filifolia** Nutt. Dry grasslands, plains to montane.

6b. Perigynia more sharply triangular, slender-beaked, the body slightly puberulent or glabrous at base of beak; margins of scales not as strongly hyaline; basal sheaths not shredded; style not much exserted. **Carex elynoides** Holm (resembling *Elyna* = *Kobresia*). Subalpine and alpine, very abundant and easily confused with *Kobresia myosuroides*.

7a. Spike dioecious, subtended by a dark scale-like bract. **Carex parryana** Dewey ssp. **hallii** (Olney) Murray (for C. C. Parry; Elihu Hall). Open gravelly meadows, subalpine. This species may have 1 to 3 very small lateral carpellate spikes (see 10a in **Key D**).

7b. Spike with both staminate and carpellate flowers, bractless .... (8)

8a. Perigynia few, yellowish, narrow and pointed, sharply reflexed. **Carex microglochin** Wahlenb. (little arrow), Fig. 257. Subalpine willow-bogs, often with *Sphagnum* moss.

8b. Perigynia not as above .... (9)

9a. Spike broad and densely-flowered with numerous perigynia; scales dark brown or black .... (10)

9b. Spike few-flowered, with only a few perigynia; scales pale or reddish-brown .... (11)

10a. Perigynia reflexed at maturity, narrow and stipitate; leaves 1.5-2.0 mm wide. **Carex nigricans** C. A. Meyer (blackish). Common on wet streamsides, subalpine and alpine.

10b. Perigynia erect at maturity, broadly ovate; leaves less than 1 mm wide. **Carex engelmannii** Bailey· (for George Engelmann). Rare, alpine tundra.

11a. Leaves straight, up to 1 mm wide; perigynium beak with two flaring broad hyaline tips. **Carex obtusata** Lilj. Dry slopes, montane and alpine.

11b. Leaves drying and curling at the tip, up to 3 mm wide; perigynium beak without teeth .... (12)

12a. Spike closely-flowered with 6 to 15 perigynia; staminate and carpellate flowers close together with no exposed rachis. **Carex rupestris** All. ssp. **drummondiana** (Dewey) Holub (of rocks; for Thomas Drummond). Alpine and upper subalpine slopes.

12b. Spike loosely-flowered with 1 to 3 perigynia; staminate and carpellate flowers separated, exposing the rachis between the flowers. **Carex geyeri** Boott (for Carl Andreas Geyer), ELK SEDGE, Fig. 257. Very common in open spruce-fir forests, sometimes in Douglas-fir, foothills to subalpine.

KEY B

1a. Flowering culm exceeding the leaves; leaves about 2 mm wide, mostly stiffly erect, not withered and curled at the tips. **Carex vernacula** Bailey (indigenous). Rare, alpine tundra.

1b. Flowering culms hardly exceeding the leaves; leaves usually narrower, with a strong tendency to wither and curl at the tips ... (2)

2a. Spikes forming a broadly conical cluster, the basal scales preventing the head from becoming spherical; perigynia narrowly ovate or lanceolate. **Carex incurviformis** Mack. Frost scars and wet gravels, alpine.

2b. Spikes forming a shaggy, globose cluster, the lower spikes spreading downward; perigynia broad, almost or quite orbicular. **Carex perglobosa** Mack. (quite round), Fig. 257. Alpine scree slopes.

KEY C

1a. Spikes few-flowered, green, scattered along the culm, the perigynia conspicuous, usually spreading .... (2)

1b. Spikes many-flowered in definite spikes rather than short, few-flowered clusters .... (6)

2a. Flowering culms very slender and weak, commonly nodding or reclining .... (3)

2b. Flowering culms more or less stiffly erect .... (4)

3a. Perigynia with slender beaks half as long as the body; leaves 2-5 mm wide. **Carex deweyana** Schwein. (for Chester Dewey). Moist foothill and montane ravines.

3b. Perigynia with short conical beaks; leaves not more than 2 mm wide. **Carex disperma** Dewey (two-seeded). Moist forests and thickets, montane and subalpine.

4a. Perigynia ascending, the inner faces not exposed; terminal spike with inconspicuous apical staminate portion (androgynous). **Carex occidentalis** Bailey (western). Foothills and montane.

4b. Perigynia widely spreading, exposing the very flat inner sides;

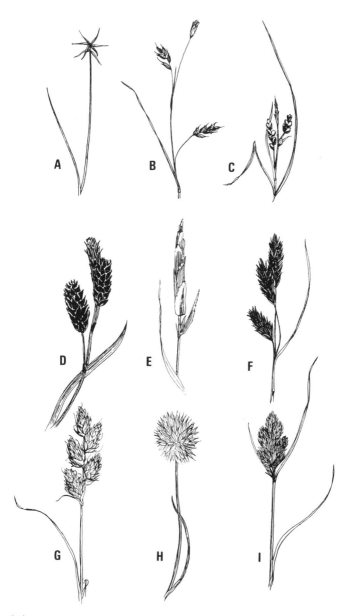

Fig. 257. A, *Carex microglochin*; B, *C. capillaris*; C, *C. aurea*; D, *C. scopulorum*; E, *C. geyeri*; F, *C. misandra*; G, *C. brevior*; H, *C. perglobosa*; I, *C. athrostachya*

terminal spike with several staminate scales sheathing the peduncle at its base (gynaecandrous) .... (5)

5a. Perigynium beak one-fourth to one-third the length of the body, shallowly bidentate with short, broad teeth. ***Carex interior*** Bailey. Moist meadows and forest openings, foothills to subalpine.

5b. Perigynium beak from more than half to about the length of the body, deeply and sharply bidentate. ***Carex angustior*** Mack. (narrower). Similar habitats.

6a. Culms arising singly or a few together from long-creeping rhizomes .... (7)

6b. Culms caespitose or the rhizomes short, with short internodes, never long-creeping .... (15)

7a. Perigynia wing-margined, the beaks deeply bidentate. ***Carex foenea*** Willd. (hay-like). Common on dry, gravelly sites, foothills to subalpine.

7b. Perigynia not wing-margined or winged only at the junction of the beak and body, the beaks obliquely cut dorsally, becoming only slightly bidentate .... (8)

8a. Plants dioecious or nearly so .... (9)

8b. Plants not dioecious; at least the terminal spike androgynous (the staminate flowers at the top of the spike; the persistent, whitish filaments can be seen with a lens) .... (11)

9a. Carpellate scales clasping the perigynia, usually completely concealing them; leaf sheaths dark brown or black. ***Carex praegracilis*** Boott (very slender). Wet meadows and roadsides, plains and foothills.

9b. Scales not clasping the perigynia; leaf sheath light brown .... (10)

10a. Perigynium winged at the junction of the beak and body, very small, not longer than 3 mm; beaks very short. ***Carex simulata*** Mack. (imitative). Wet meadows and swamps, foothills to subalpine.

10b. Perigynium not at all winged, 3.5-4 mm long; beak as long as the body. ***Carex douglasii*** Boott (for David Douglas). Dry plains, foothills and lower montane.

11a. Inflorescence suborbicular, 1-2.5 cm wide; perigynium beak nearly as long as the body. ***Carex douglasii*** Boott (for David Douglas). Dry plains, foothills and lower montane. This species is usually dioecious (see 10b above).

11b. Inflorescence linear-oblong, 5-10 mm wide .... (12)

12a. Upper leaf-sheaths green-striate ventrally except near the mouth. ***Carex sartwellii*** Dewey (for Henry Parker Sartwell). Infrequent, marshes and bogs.

12b. Upper leaf-sheaths hyaline ventrally .... (13)

13a. Lower leaf-sheaths dark brown or black; carpellate scales clasping the perigynia at the base. ***Carex praegracilis*** Boott (very slender). Wet meadows and roadsides, plains and foothills. This species is often dioecious (see 9a above).

13b. Lower leaf-sheaths light brown; carpellate scales not as above. (14)

14a. Scales dark brown; perigynium winged at the junction of the beak and the body, abruptly narrowed to a very short beak. **Carex simulata** Mack. (imitative). Wet meadows and swamps, foothills to subalpine. This species is often dioecious (see 10a above).

14b. Scales chestnut to light brown; perigynium not at all winged, contracted to a beak one-fourth to one-third the length of the body. **Carex stenophylla** Wahlenb. ssp. **eleocharis** (Bailey) Hultén (narrow-leaved; like *Eleocharis*). Grassy slopes, montane and subalpine.

15a. Spikes androgynous (the staminate flowers at the top of the spike; the persistent whitish filaments can be seen with a lens) . . . . (16)

15b. Spikes gynaecandrous (the staminate flowers at the base of the spike) . . . . (19)

16a. Perigynium tapering into a beak almost from the base; inflorescence thick, up to 2 cm wide, the spikes stiffly spreading, like a pin-cushion. **Carex stipata** Muehl. (crowded), Fig. 258. Wet places, piedmont valleys.

16b. Perigynium abruptly contracted into a beak; inflorescence slender, 5-10 mm wide, the spikes ascending . . . . (17)

17a. Leaves 3-4 mm wide, short and stiffly erect, the sheaths transversely wrinkled on the thin ventral side; inflorescence with many spikes, sometimes up to 1 cm wide. **Carex vulpinoidea** Michx. (fox-tail). Open wet meadows in the piedmont valleys.

17b. Leaves 1-3 mm wide, weak and lax, the sheaths not transversely wrinkled; inflorescence 5-7 mm wide, with not more than ten spikes. . . . . (18)

18a. Perigynia ovate, dark glossy-brown, widely margined, the vivid green margins conspicuously serrulate above the middle, rather abruptly long-beaked, the beaks conspicuously bidentate; scales lustrous, dark chestnut-brown; inflorescence stiff. **Carex hoodii** Boott (for Sir Samuel Hood). Common in western Colorado, but only one record in our area, from Rocky Mountain National Park.

18b. Perigynia elliptic, greenish-straw-colored to brown-centered, the margins narrow, usually less serrulate, the beaks shorter, shallowly bidentate; scales greenish-brown; inflorescence lax. **Carex occidentalis** Bailey (western). Forested streamsides in the foothills and montane.

19a. Bract of the lowest spike longer than the inflorescence . . . . . (20)

19b. Bract of the lowest spike shorter than the inflorescence or the inflorescence bractless . . . . (21)

20a. Lower 2 to 4 bracts longer than the inflorescence; scales greenish-white; perigynia subulate-lanceolate. **Carex sychnocephala** Carey (many-headed). Wet places, subalpine, rare.

20b. Only the lowest bract longer than the inflorescence; scales brown;

perigynia ovate. **Carex athrostachya** Olney (crowded-spike), Fig. 257. Wet meadows, montane, subalpine.

21a. Perigynia not wing-margined, plano-convex and thin edged. (22)
21b. Perigynia wing-margined to the base, thin and scale-like or plano-convex ....(26)

22a. Scales hyaline with green center (may be light brownish-tinged at maturity) ....(23)
22b. Scales medium- to dark brown or black ....(24)

23a. Perigynia distinctly beaked (the beaks 0.5 mm long or more), serrulate, loosely spreading; spikes few-flowered (5 to 10 perigynia); leaves green, 1.0-2.5 mm wide. **Carex brunnescens** (Pers.) Poir. (brownish). Habitat same as the next.
23b. Perigynia apiculate to very short-beaked (the beaks usually 0.25 mm long or less), appressed-ascending; spikes many-flowered (9 to 20 perigynia); leaves glaucous, 2-4 mm wide. **Carex canescens** L. Marshes and lake shores, montane, subalpine.

24a. Scales black; perigynia partly black; inflorescence broadly triangular-conic, the spikes very close. **Carex illota** Bailey (dirty). Wet subalpine and alpine meadows.
24b. Scales medium to dark brown; perigynia yellow-brown; inflorescence not triangular-conic, the spikes distinct ....(25)

25a. Spikes 3 or 4; perigynia 2.0-3.5 mm long, beaks smooth. **Carex lachenalii** Schkuhr (for Werner de Lachenal). Alpine and upper subalpine.
25b. Spikes 4 or 5; perigynia 1.5-2.5 mm long, beaks often slightly serrulate. **Carex praeceptorum** Mack. (for Professors Peck and Nelson). Upper subalpine and alpine, tundra and grassy slopes.

26a. Beaks flat and serrulate to the tip ....(27)
26b. Beaks terete (at least the tip) not flat and serrulate ....(31)

27a. Scales shorter than the perigynia, noticeably narrower above and largely exposing them ....(28)
27b. Scales almost equalling the perigynia, nearly the same width above and nearly concealing them ....(30)

28a. Perigynia orbicular, 3.5-5.5 mm long, 2.5-3.5 mm wide. **Carex brevior** (Dewey) Mack. (shorter), Fig. 257. Mesas and foothill valleys.
28b. Perigynia lanceolate to ovate, 4.0-8.0 mm long ....(29)

29a. Perigynia lanceolate to narrowly ovate-lanceolate, greenish-white to straw-colored, nerved on both faces. **Carex scoparia** Schkuhr (sweeper= broom-like). Infrequent, swampy places in piedmont valleys.
29b. Perigynia ovate, olive-green to brownish, nerveless on the faces. **Carex egglestonii** Mack. (for W. W. Eggleston). Montane and subalpine.

Fig. 258. A, *Carex ebenea*; B, *C. microptera*; C, *C. stipata*; D, *C. utriculata*; E, *C. hystricina*; F, *C. lanuginosa*; G, *C. chalciolepis*; H, *C. aquatilis*

30a. Perigynia broadest above the middle, finely nerved ventrally; spikes aggregated, usually into a definite head; spikes subtended by several very pale, hyaline, papery staminate scales, contrasting with the darker carpellate ones above. **Carex arapahoensis** Clokey (for Arapahoe Peak). Infrequent, alpine and subalpine.

30b. Perigynia usually broadest below the middle, nerveless ventrally; spikes in a somewhat moniliform inflorescence or nearly approximate; staminate scales not markedly different from the carpellate ones above. **Carex xerantica** Bailey (arid). Ponderosa pine woodlands of the mesas and montane.

31a. Perigynium very flat and scale-like, only distended over the achene ....(32)
31b. Perigynium plano-convex or concavo-convex, often spongy at the base and/or up the sides ....(35)

32a. Spikes predominantly green and brown, the brown scales usually contrasting with the green perigynia ....(33)
32b. Spikes predominantly brown to blackish-brown, the perigynia themselves partly brown and contributing to the generally dark appearance of the spikes ....(34)

33a. Spikes clearly separate and distinguishable; perigynia appressed, the inflorescence thus tapered to the apex and base; scales dark chestnut to blackish-brown. **Carex festivella** Mack. (diminutive of festiva=gay, compared to *Carex festiva*). Meadows and open slopes, montane and subalpine.
33b. Spikes congested and often scarcely distinguishable; perigynia spreading-ascending, the tips conspicuous in the heads, which are more "bristly" as a result; scales dull brown. **Carex microptera** Mack. (small-wing), Fig. 258. More common than the above, similar habitats.

34a. Perigynia lanceolate, 5-7 mm long; scales dark brown or black. **Carex ebenea** Rydb. (black), Fig. 258. Subalpine and alpine, common.
34b. Perigynia ovate, 4-6 mm long; scales black. **Carex haydeniana** Olney (for F.V. Hayden). Alpine tundra.

35a. Scales shorter and narrower than the perigynia ....(36)
35b. Scales about the same width and length as the perigynia; beaks may protrude slightly ....(38)

36a. Perigynia ovate-lanceolate to narrowly lanceolate, 2.5-3.5 mm long, 1.0-1.3 mm wide. **Carex limnophila** Hermann (pond-loving). Banks of streams and lakes, foothills to montane.
36b. Perigynia ovate, 3.5-5.0 mm long, 1.5-2.5 mm wide ....(37)

37a. Perigynia spreading at maturity, inflorescence looking bristly; base of perigynia spongy and the margins often filled with spongy tissue; scales with the hyaline margins very narrow or obsolete. **Carex pachystachya** Cham. *ex* Steud. (thick-spiked). Montane meadows and open woods.

37b. Perigynia ascending, perigynia not spongy; scales with conspicuous white-hyaline margins. *Carex macloviana* Urv. (from an island in the Falkland Islands). Montane and subalpine.

38a. Spikes separated along the culm so as to barely overlap the base of one with the apex of the next, the spikes thus forming a slender, nodding graceful group (moniliform—like a string of beads). *Carex praticola* Rydb. (of prairies). Subalpine meadows, infrequent.
38b. Spikes more densely aggregated; culms stiff ....(39)

39a. Perigynia lanceolate, 5-7 mm long; plants of foothills and lower mountains. *Carex petasata* Dewey (with a traveling cap on, that is, ready for a journey).
39b. Perigynia ovate, 4-5 mm long; common subalpine and alpine. *Carex phaeocephala* Piper (brown-headed).

KEY D

1a. Perigynia pubescent on the faces, not merely ciliate-margined .. (2)
1b. Perigynia faces glabrous ....(8)

2a. Tall plants of bogs and wet meadows; staminate spikes 1 or 2, clearly different from the 2 to 4 elongate carpellate ones distributed along the culm. *Carex lanuginosa* Michx. (woolly), Fig. 258. Swampy meadows and pond shores, montane and subalpine.
2b. Low, spreading matted plants of dry forested areas or otherwise not as above ....(3)

3a. Fertile culms with all spikes sessile or very short-peduncled .... (4)
3b. Fertile culms with staminate spike and upper carpellate spikes approximate, with other carpellate spikes widely separated, nearly basal, long-peduncled, appearing as separate culms ....(5)

4a. Perigynium body (excluding stipitate base and beak) oval-obovoid, much longer than wide; scales about half the length of the mature perigynia bodies. *Carex peckii* E. C. Howe (for Charles E. Peck). Foothill streamsides.
4b. Perigynium (excluding stipitate base and beak) suborbicular or suborbicular-obovoid or very short-oval, about as long as wide; scales longer than the mature perigynia bodies. *Carex heliophila* Mack. (sun-loving). The earliest-flowering *Carex* on the mesas and outer foothills.

5a. Bract of lowest non-basal carpellate spike squamiform, shorter than the culm, the spike sometimes bractless. *Carex geophila* Mack. (ground-loving). Dry wooded slopes in the foothills.
5b. Bract of lowest non-basal carpellate spike leaf-like, normally exceeding the culm ....(6)

6a. Upper carpellate spikes 1- to 3-flowered; perigynia beaks obliquely cut, in age shallowly bidentate, margins little if at all ciliate-serrulate.

Carex pityophila Mack. (pine-loving). Rare on dry pine lands and in sagebrush-grass parks.

6b. Upper carpellate spikes normally several- to many-(3 to 20)-flowered; perigynia beaks shallowly to deeply bidentate, the margins ciliate-serrulate ....(7)

7a. Perigynia 2.5-3.25 mm long, the beaks 0.25-0.75 mm long, shallowly bidentate. **Carex brevipes** Boott (short-stem). Subalpine up to timber-line.

7b. Perigynia 3.5-4.5 mm long, the beaks more than 1 mm long, deeply bidentate. **Carex rossii** Boott (for Capt. J. C. Ross). Ponderosa pine forests on the mesas and foothills up to dry subalpine forests.

8a. Lower scales leaflike, party enveloping and much longer than the perigynia; terminal spike androgynous; leaves as long or longer than the culms ....(9)

8b. Lower scales not leaflike; terminal spike not androgynous; leaves shorter than the culms ....(10)

9a. Perigynia 5-6 mm long, the upper third of the body empty, the beaks stout, 2-3 mm long, smooth-margined. **Carex backii** Boott (for Sir George Back). Dry woods of foothills and montane.

9b. Perigynia 4-5 mm long, the upper part of the body filled by the achene, the beaks 0.5-1 mm long, more or less serrulate on the margins. **Carex saximontana** Mack. (Rocky Mountain). Pine forests and thickets, montane and foothills canyons.

10a. Fertile culm with a single staminate spike and 1 to 3 small, one- or few-flowered carpellate spikes immediately below it, often so close as to appear to be part of the same spike; some flowering culms entirely staminate or carpellate or with a single unisexual spike (see 7a, **Key A.**) **Carex parryana** Dewey ssp. **hallii** (Olney) Murray (for C. C. Parry; Elihu Hall). Open gravelly meadows, subalpine.

10b. Fertile culm with several staminate or carpellate spikes, the carpellate usually many-flowered ....(11)

11a. Scales green, pale brown or pale reddish-brown, never purple-black; inflorescence never appearing purple-black ....(12)

11b. Scales dark reddish-brown or purple-black, sometimes with a green or lighter midrib, the inflorescence appearing very dark ....(19)

12a. Perigynia beakless, very round at the apex, ribbed, may be golden yellow, orange or brown at maturity. **Carex aurea** Nutt. (golden), Fig. 257. Common in wet places, foothills to subalpine. The ripe perigynia fall easily from the spike. The separation of this species from Carex hassei Bailey depends mostly on the ribs being coarse and the perigynia turning orange. Since not all perigynia do turn golden or orange, and the obscurity or coarseness of ribs varies even in perigynia that have turned color, no attempt has been made in this key to differentiate between these two species, if in fact, two species are represented in our area.

12b. Perigynia strongly beaked and/or tapered to the apex ...... (13)

13a. Carpellate spikes hanging from slender peduncles ....(14)
13b. Carpellate spikes on erect peduncles (lower spikes may droop when over-mature) ....(17)

14a. Tall robust plants of montane and foothills regions; perigynia beaks long and conspicuous; scales with long filiform tip .... (15)
14b. Slender short plants of subalpine and alpine regions; perigynia beaks short; scales not as above ....(16)

15a. Perigynia very strongly many-ribbed. **Carex hystricina** Muehl. (porcupine), Fig. 258. Foothill streambanks.
15b. Perigynia nerveless except for two prominent lateral ribs. **Carex sprengelii** Dewey (for Kurt Sprengel). Rare, along streams in the foothill and montane canyons.

16a. Lowest bract long-sheathing, that is, with a portion sheathing the stem between the blade and the node of attachment; perigynia nerveless except for the two marginal nerves. **Carex capillaris** L., Fig. 257. Subalpine and alpine streamsides and willow-bogs.
16b. Lowest bract not sheathing; perigynia conspicuously few-nerved. **Carex magellanica** Lam. ssp. **irrigua** (Wahlenb.) Hiit. (from Straits of Magellan; of wet places). Lake shores and willow-bogs, subalpine (*C. paupercula* Michx.).

17a. Spikes in a close terminal cluster; leaf-sheaths pubescent; perigynium abruptly short-beaked. **Carex torreyi** Tuck. (for John Torrey). Extremely rare, rocks in mesa or outer foothill canyons.
17b. Spikes scattered along the culm; leaf-sheaths not pubescent; perigynium large, strongly nerved, with long beak ....(18)

18a. Leaves conspicuously septate-nodulose, 4-15 mm wide; lower leaf-sheaths not fragile, not becoming filamentose; rhizomes with long, horizontal stolons; culms mostly thick and spongy at the base, bluntly triangular below the spikes, smooth; perigynia ascending to squarrose at maturity, rather abruptly beaked. **Carex utriculata** Boott (like a small skin bag), Fig. 258. Abundant, forming zones on shores of ponds, montane and subalpine (*Carex rostrata* of manuals, not of Stokes).
18b. Leaves not conspicuously septate-nodulose, 2-7 mm wide; lower leaf-sheaths fragile, becoming strongly filamentose; rhizomes without horizontal stolons; culms rarely spongy-based, sharply triangular and rough below the spikes; perigynia appressed or ascending, gradually long-beaked. **Carex vesicaria** L. (bladder-like). Occasional, very wet habitats, montane and subalpine. Occasionally forms a sterile hybrid (the achenes are undeveloped) with *C. utriculata*.

19a. Principal bract at base of the lowest spike long-sheathing, that is, with a portion sheathing the stem between the blade and the node of attachment. **Carex misandra** R. Br. (man-hater, because of the few staminate flowers), Fig. 257. Tundra slopes and basins.

19b. Principal bract lacking a distinct sheathing portion .... (20)

20a. Terminal spike staminate (occasionally a few perigynia at the base of the spike) .... (21)
20b. Terminal spike gynaecandrous or spikes all alike .... (26)

21a. Carpellate spikes nodding on slender peduncles. **Carex magellanica** Lam. ssp. *irrigua* (Wahlenb.) Hultén (from Straits of Magellan; of wet places). Lake shores and willow-bogs, subalpine (*C. paupercula* Michx.).
21b. Carpellate spikes erect .... (22)

22a. Carpellate spikes entirely purple-black or the perigynia at least strongly purple-tinged or purple-spotted .... (23)
22b. Carpellate spikes green-and-black, the perigynia green, contrasting with the darker scales .... (24)

23a. Perigynium shining, with a slender beak, the spikes usually widely spaced; culms solitary or a few together from elongate rhizomes. **Carex saxatilis** L. ssp. *laxa* (Trautv.) Kalela (of rocks; not stiff). Pond shores and willow-bogs, subalpine (*C. physocarpa* Presl).
23b. Perigynium dull purple or green-and-purple mottled, irregular-inflated and nearly beakless; culms forming dense mats or tussocks; the rhizomes producing many stems. **Carex scopulorum** Holm (of rocks), Fig. 257. Abundant in wet basins, subalpine and alpine.

24a. Culms aphyllopodic; perigynia lightly few-nerved dorsally; scales and perigynia early deciduous. **Carex emoryi** Dewey (for Major W. H. Emory). Swampy meadows or springy places, often edging irrigation ditches, plains and piedmont valleys. One of the early species, the rachis usually is completely free of carpellate scales and fruit by mid-June.
24b. Culms phyllopodic; perigynia nerveless or strongly many-ribbed on both faces; scales and perigynia not early deciduous .... (25)

25a. Leaves short, broad, spreading, conspicuously glaucous; spikes plump; perigynia nerved on the faces. **Carex nebraskensis** Dewey. Streamsides, springs and meadows, often alkaline, plains to subalpine. This species may be from 1.0 dm to 17 dm high.
25b. Leaves long and lax, erect, somewhat glaucous when young; spikes slender and elongate; perigynia nerveless on the faces. **Carex aquatilis** Wahlenb., Fig. 258. Lake shores, alpine and subalpine. The dwarfed alpine race with short spikes is ssp. *stans* (Drej.) Hultén. The stouter, coarser variety, uncommon in our area, is var. *altior* (Rydb.) Fern.

26a. Spikes slender, not more than 5 mm wide, scattered along the culm, never forming a dense cluster .... (27)
26b. Spikes often up to 1 cm wide or more, in a rather dense terminal cluster .... (29)

27a. Spikes gracefully nodding from slender peduncles, all spikes gynaecandrous; lowest bract long-sheathing; plants tall, often more than 4 dm
high. ***Carex bella*** Bailey (handsome). Aspen groves and open hillsides,
subalpine.
27b. Spikes erect, only the terminal spike gynaecandrous; lowest bract
not sheathing; plants usually shorter than above ....(28)

28a. Perigynia finely many-nerved; fertile culms aphyllopodic; beaks
minute, 0.2 mm long. ***Carex buxbaumii*** Wahlenb. (for Johann
Christian Buxbaum). Rare, upper montane, subalpine.
28b. Perigynia not nerved; fertile culms phyllopodic; beaks short, 0.5 mm
long. ***Carex norvegica*** Retz ssp. ***stevenii*** (Holm) Murray. Upper
montane forest openings. *Carex norvegica* ssp. *norvegica*, with a more
compact inflorescence, is a shorter plant of the alpine tundra.

29a. Spikes short and plump, in a more or less dense terminal cluster;
all spikes sessile ....(30)
29b. Spikes either spaced apart or conspicuously nodding or at least
twice as long as broad ....(32)

30a. Plants usually less than 2 dm tall, the spikes pointed; perigynia
with narrow, sloping shoulders and much purple pigmentation on the
faces. ***Carex nelsonii*** Mack. (for Aven Nelson). Snowmelt areas, alpine.
30b. Plants usually more than 2 dm tall, the spikes almost globose. (31)

31a. Perigynia ciliate-scabrous-margined, base substipitate; scales blunt,
midrib obsolete; culms erect. ***Carex nova*** Bailey (new). Common in
subalpine and alpine wet spring-slopes.
31b. Perigynia smooth-margined, the base rounded, not stipitate; scales
acuminate with more or less prominent midrib; culms slender,
generally flexuous. ***Carex pelocarpa*** Hermann (dark-fruit). Occasional,
alpine and subalpine slopes and meadows.

32a. Spikes nodding ....(33)
32b. Spikes erect ....(34)

33a. Upper carpellate scales exceeding the perigynia (usually conspicuously so), dark copper-brown; lowest peduncle less than half the
length of the spike; apex of perigynium-body acute. ***Carex chalciolepis***
Holm (bronze-scaled), Fig. 258. Abundant, alpine and subalpine
slopes.
33b. Upper carpellate scales usually exceeded by the perigynia, dark red
to blackish-brown, fading with age; lowest peduncle 1-2 times the
length of the spike; apex of perigynium-body obtuse. ***Carex atrata*** L.
(blackened). Rare, subalpine meadows and rocky alpine slopes. There
is no agreement among botanists that the true *C. atrata* L. occurs in
North America; however, our plant, which Hermann calls *C.
heteroneura* W. Boott var. *brevisquama* Hermann, compares favorably
with the European *C. atrata*. Therefore this species is being included
in this key under the name *C. atrata* L. until further comparative
studies can be made.

34a. Scales conspicuously white-hyaline at the apex, nearly equalling or wider than the perigynia. ***Carex albonigra*** Mack. (white-black, referring to the white-margined scales). Alpine tundra.

34b. Scales not white hyaline or only slightly so, shorter and narrower than the perigynia .... (35)

35a. Perigynia slightly and irregularly inflated, narrowly elliptic, upper margins forming two sides of a triangle. ***Carex atrosquama*** Mack. (black-scaled). Open meadows, subalpine and lower alpine.

35b. Perigynia flat, not inflated, broadly ovate to orbicular, upper margins forming the arc of a circle. ***Carex epapillosa*** Mack. (not papillose). Meadows and margins of lakes, subalpine, alpine.

CYPERUS. GALINGALE

1a. Styles 2; achenes lenticular; scales reddish-brown, often quite dark. ***Cyperus rivularis*** Kunth (of streams). Rare on gravel bars in streams, piedmont valleys.

1b. Styles 3; achenes trigonous, plump; scales usually yellowish-brown, never dark purple-brown .... (2)

2a. Rachis of the spike not winged .... (3)

2b. Rachis winged with a pair of inner hyaline appendages at each node. ***Cyperus erythrorhizos*** Muehl. (red-rooted). Sandy or muddy pond margins in the piedmont valleys.

3a. Scales strongly ribbed, with acuminate or awned, strongly recurved tips. ***Cyperus inflexus*** Muehl. (incurved). Sandy or muddy streambanks and pond margins in the piedmont valleys.

3b. Scales not at all ribbed, neither long-acuminate nor awned, the tips pointing forward. ***Cyperus acuminatus*** Torr. & Hook. Rare, in similar habitats.

ELEOCHARIS. SPIKE-RUSH

1a. Stems less than 10 cm high, slender and filiform (less than 1 mm wide), or if taller then the achene with very fine horizontal crossbars and longitudinal ribs .... (2)

1b. Stems over 10 cm high, or with thicker stems, erect and stiffish; achenes not as above .... (3)

2a. Culms tiny (1-5 cm tall), in dense mats; achene without crossbars or ribs, with pitted surface. ***Eleocharis coloradoensis*** (Britt.) Gilly var. ***anachaeta*** (Torr.) Svenson. On drying mudflats, piedmont valleys.

2b. Culms usually taller, very weak; fruit with cross-bars and ribs. ***Eleocharis acicularis*** (L.) R. & S. (needle-like), Fig. 259. Very common in wet places from plains to subalpine.

3a. Plant annual, growing in a tuft or clump, easily uprooted .... (4)

3b. Perennial with creeping rhizomes; stems arising singly or a few together, difficult to collect with underground parts .... (5)

4a. Achenes shining black. ***Eleocharis atropurpurea*** (Retz) Kunth (black-purple). Rare, piedmont valleys and plains. Found once at Greeley.
4b. Achenes shining brown or greenish. ***Eleocharis obtusa*** (Willd.) Schultes var. ***detonsa*** (Gray) Drap. & Mohl. Lake shores in the piedmont valleys (*E. engelmannii* Steud.).

5a. Styles 2; fruit biconvex. ***Eleocharis macrostachya*** Britt. (large-spiked), Fig. 260. Very common in wet places, plains to subalpine.
5b. Styles 3; fruit three-sided .... (6)

6a. Stems flattened; plants of the piedmont valleys. ***Eleocharis elliptica*** Kunth var. ***compressa*** (Sull.) Drap. & Mohl. Infrequent in wet places (*E. compressa* Sull.).
6b. Stems not flattened; plants of subalpine meadows. ***Eleocharis quinqueflora*** (F. X. Hartm.) D. Schwartz (five-flowered). Common in boggy meadows (*E. pauciflora* of Ed. 4).

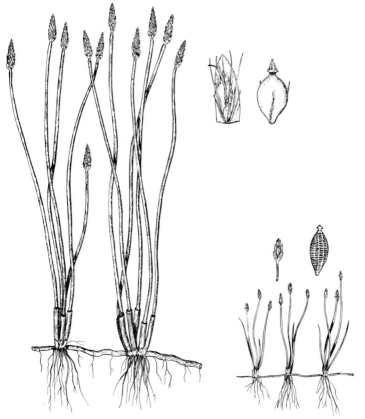

Fig. 260. ***Eleocharis macrostachya***   Fig. 259. ***Eleocharis acicularis***

ERIOPHORUM. COTTON-GRASS

1a. Leaves 1-3 mm wide; cottony bristles 1-1.5 cm long; main bract of inflorescence 1-1.5 cm long, erect. ***Eriophorum gracile*** Koch (slender). Very rare in montane and subalpine bogs.

1b. Leaves 3-6 mm wide; cottony bristles 2 cm or more long; main bract of inflorescence over 2 cm long, leaflike, often spreading. ***Eriophorum angustifolium*** Honck. (narrow-leaved), Fig. 261. Frequent in montane and subalpine bogs, by far the more common species.

HEMICARPHA

One species, ***Hemicarpha micrantha*** (Vahl) Pax. A rare plant of muddy shores and streambanks in the piedmont valleys, late summer. Easily recognized by its small size and almost leafless stems with a single tiny spike standing out laterally near the top of the stem.

KOBRESIA

Note: In *Kobresia* the perigynium often encloses a staminate and a carpellate floret; these flower pairs are here referred to as spikelets. Groups of spikelets on distinct major axes are called spikes.

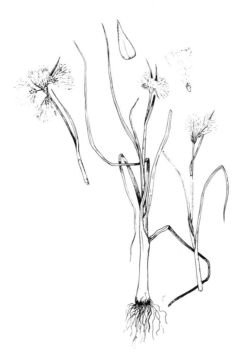

Fig. 261. ***Eriophorum angustifolium***

1a. Spikelets consisting of one staminate and one carpellate floret. (2)
1b. Spikelets unisexual, 1-flowered, the upper ones staminate, the lower carpellate; spikes several, the lower ones quite distinct. **Kobresia simpliciuscula** (Wahlenb.) Mack. In moist gravelly tundra.

2a. Spike 1-3 cm x 2-3 mm; scales 2-3 mm long; perigynia 3-3.5 x 1.25 mm; plants very densely caespitose, forming hummocks; flowering culms very slender. **Kobresia myosuroides** (Vill.) Fiori & Paol. The climax dominant on mature soils of alpine tundra. In the autumn the tundra slopes are colored a rich bronze-yellow-brown by the drying foliage of this species. Extremely similar to *Carex elynoides* and distinguished with certainty only by the closed perigynium of the latter.
2b. Spike 1-2 cm x 4-5 mm; scales 4-5 mm long; perigynia 5.5 x 1.25 mm; forming dense clumps but hardly ever forming large stands. **Kobresia sibirica** Turcz. Moist tundra, solifluction slopes and gravelly alpine lake shores (*K. macrocarpa* of Ed. 4).

MARISCUS (*Scirpus*, in part, of Ed. 4)
1a. Scales 2-2.5 mm long, with a prominent spreading or recurved tip; spikes in a sessile cluster. **Mariscus fendlerianus** (Boeckel.) Koyama (for August Fendler). Cliffs and outcrops in the foothill canyons.
1b. Scales 3 mm long or more, the tip inconspicuous, often incurved; several spikes exserted on peduncles of varying lengths, suggesting an umbel. **Mariscus schweinitzii** (Torr.) Koyama (for L. D. de Schweinitz). Dry slopes on the mesas and hogbacks, often in sandy soil.

SCIRPUS. BULRUSH; TULE
1a. Inflorescence subtended by 2 or more leaf-like bracts; stem leaves well developed; stems always triangular, never round in cross-section
. . . . (2)
1b. Inflorescence subtended by a single bract which appears to be a continuation of the stem; stem leaves poorly developed or absent; stems triangular or round in cross-section . . . . (4)

2a. Spikelets few (3 to 10), each 1 cm or more long, sessile or nearly so, pale brown. **Scirpus paludosus** Nels. (of marshes), ALKALI BULRUSH. Margins of temporary reservoirs and sloughs on the plains and piedmont valleys.
2b. Spikelets numerous, averaging less than 0.5 cm long, grouped into dense spherical, stalked clusters, green or deep brown . . . . (3)

3a. Leaf-sheaths green, drying brown; perianth-bristles barbed only above the middle; styles 3. **Scirpus pallidus** (Britt.) Fern. (pale). Common along irrigation ditches and in sloughs, plains and piedmont valleys.
3b. Leaf-sheaths usually red-tinged; bristles barbed nearly to the base; styles 2 or 3. **Scirpus microcarpus** Presl. In similar habitats (*S. rubrotinctus* Fern.).

4a. Stems slender, triangular in cross-section; spikelets sessile, solitary
    or few. ***Scirpus americanus*** Pers., THREE-SQUARE, Fig. 262. Common in
    sloughs, plains and piedmont valleys.
4b. Stems stout, round in cross-section; spikelets numerous, on peduncles
    . . . . (5)

5a. Scales 2.5-3.0 mm long, scarcely exceeding the achenes; inflorescence
    open, the primary branches up to 6 cm long and nearly all the spikes
    peduncled. ***Scirpus lacustris*** L. ssp. ***validus*** (Vahl) Koyama (stout),
    TULE; GREAT BULRUSH. Very wet places, piedmont valleys and plains.
5b. Scales about 4 mm long, definitely exceeding the achenes; inflores-
    cence compact, composed at least in part of a subsessile cluster of
    spikelets and with or without additional spikelet clusters on short
    peduncles 1-4 cm long. ***Scirpus acutus*** Muehl. Habitat similar to the
    last.

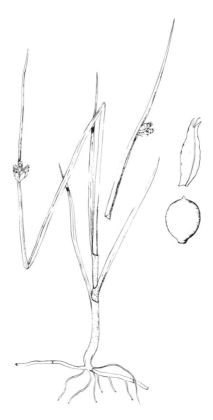

Fig. 262. ***Scirpus americanus***

GRAMINEAE (POACEAE)—GRASS FAMILY

The grass family is usually considered a difficult group, and the terminology used for their floral parts is unique. Once one understands the fundamental structure of the grass spikelet, which actually is very simple, the grasses become a fascinating and not too difficult subject. Every voting citizen should know the dominant grasses, because they tell a great deal about the condition of the range by their presence, absence or abundance. There is good grass literature available for every level of competence. See the bibliography under Chase, Gould, Heiser, Hitchcock, and Pohl.

1a. Plants dioecious (spikelets entirely staminate or carpellate, on different plants and usually conspicuously different in appearance; plants of each sex usually occur nearby) . . . . **Key A**, page 386.
1b. Plants not dioecious (most grasses belong to this category) . . . . (2)

2a. Plants prostrate on the ground and radially spreading, with long naked internodes and dense fascicles of short, stiff leaves with pale thickened margins; spikelets hidden in the leaf clusters. *Munroa*, FALSE BUFFALO-GRASS, page 412.
2b. Plants not as above . . . . (3)

3a. Spikelets consisting of hard burs with sharp, hooked spines. *Cenchrus*, SAND BUR, page 402.
3b. Spikelets not bur-like . . . . (4)

4a. Spikelets sessile, alternating on either side of a flattened rachis. (5)
4b. Spikelets not alternating on either side of a flattened rachis . . (6)

5a. Each spikelet cluster nested in a group of long white hairs. *Hilaria*, GALLETA-GRASS, page 409.
5b. Spikelet clusters not subtended by a group of white hairs. . . . . **Key B**, page 386.

6a. Foliage and stem harshly retrorse-scabrous (saw-grass); glumes lacking, the spikelet with a single lemma and palea. *Leersia*, RICE CUT-GRASS, page 410.
6b. Foliage not as above; spikelets with glumes . . . . (7)

7a. Spikelets sessile on one side of the rachis, the spikes often resembling little flags . . . . **Key C**, page 387.
7b. Spikelets not sessile on one side of the rachis, not flagged . . . . (8)

8a. Spikelets disarticulating below the glumes (falling in one piece), glumes and lemmas flat or curved, never keeled (the spikelet tends to be terete, without a right and left side) . . . . (9)
8b. Spikelets usually disarticulating above the glumes and between the florets (shattering at maturity and leaving the glumes attached to the pedicel), the glumes and lemmas strongly curved or keeled (the spikelet tends to lie flat, with a right and left side) . . . . (10)

9a. Spikelets in pairs, one sessile and bisexual, the other pediceled and staminate or reduced to a mere pedicel ...... **Key D**, page 388.
9b. Spikelets not in pairs ....**Key E**, page 388.

10a. Spikelets with a single floret .... **Key F**, page 389.
10b. Spikelets with at least two florets ....(11)

11a. Glumes as long as the lowest floret, usually as long as the whole spikelet, the awn, when present, attached on the back of the lemma or appearing so .... **Key G**, page 391.
11b. Both glumes shorter than the lowermost floret; awn, when present, attached to the tip of the lemma or arising from between the teeth of a bifid lemma apex .... **Key H**, page 392.

KEY A (Dioecious Grasses)

1a. Spikelets of each sex superficially alike ....(2)
1b. Spikelets of each sex so different as to suggest unrelated genera. (4)

2a. Florets numerous in the spikelet (5 to 15); lemmas 5- to 11-nerved; plants of low, mostly alkaline areas on the plains. *Distichlis*, SALT GRASS, page 405.
2b. Florets relatively few in the spikelet (3 to 7); lemmas 3- to 5-nerved; plants of well-drained mountain soils ....(3)

3a. Leaf-tip boat-shaped. *Poa fendleriana*, page 417.
3b. Leaf-tip not boat-shaped. *Leucopoa kingii*, page 410.

4a. Male spikelets one-sided (flagged); female spikelet a bony nutlike structure hidden in the foliage. *Buchloë*, BUFFALO-GRASS, page 402.
4b. Male spikelets not one-sided, awnless; female spikelets with long slender awns. *Scleropogon*, BURRO-GRASS, page 420.

KEY B (Wheat and Barley Group)

1a. Spikelets so arranged as to form a perfect cylinder, the rachis bent so as to accomodate them; spikelets rough and long-awned, the rachis shattering at maturity. *Aegilops*, GOAT-GRASS, page 394.
1b. Spikelets loose, not forming a solid cylinder ....(2)

2a. Spikelets solitary at each node of the rachis ....(3)
2b. Spikelets 2 or more at some or all of the nodes (count the glumes; there are two for each spikelet) ....(6)

3a. Spikelets placed edgewise to the rachis; first glume lacking, its function undertaken by the rachis. *Lolium*, DARNEL, page 410.
3b. Spikelets placed with the flat side next to the rachis; both glumes present ....(4)

4a. Annual plants cultivated for grain, occasionally "volunteering" for one season in fallow soil ....(5)

4b. Perennials, wild or cultivated as soil binders or forage grasses. *Agropyron*, WHEAT-GRASS, page 394.

5a. Glumes subulate, one-nerved. *Secale*, RYE, page 420.
5b. Glumes broad, 3-nerved. *Triticum*, WHEAT, page 424.

6a. Spikelets each bearing a single floret; spikelets clustered, 3 at each node, the two lateral ones pedicelled and rudimentary, except in cultivated ("six-row") barley. *Hordeum*, BARLEY, page 409.
6b. Spikelets all essentially alike, with 2 or more florets each ...... (7)

7a. Glumes subulate, extending into long spreading awns; rachis of the inflorescence brittle and shattering at maturity. *Sitanion*, SQUIRRELTAIL, page 421.
7b. Glumes broad or narrow but not subulate or extended into long awns; rachis usually remaining intact at maturity, or, if shattering, then the awns less than 2 cm long .... (8)

8a. Only a few nodes bearing 2 spikelets, the spikelets mostly solitary; rhizomes present. *Agropyron*, WHEAT-GRASS, page 394.
8b. Most nodes bearing two or more spikelets; spikelets mostly paired at the nodes; rhizomes absent. *Elymus*, RYE-GRASS, page 406.

KEY C (Flagged Grasses)

1a. Spikes in a digitate cluster, like spokes of a wheel .... (2)
1b. Spikes arranged in a raceme or other type of cluster .... (3)

2a. Plants with above-ground scaly stolons. *Cynodon*, BERMUDA-GRASS, page 403.
2b. Plants lacking stolons, although tending to root at the decumbent lower nodes. *Digitaria*, CRAB-GRASS, page 405.

3a. Spikes pendent, hanging from one side of the culm. *Bouteloua*, GRAMA, page 399.
3b. Spikes erect or spreading but not pendent .... (4)

4a. Spikes distinctly brush-like, with the spikelets standing out at an angle from the rachis .... (5)
4b. Spikes not brush-like .... (7)

5a. Spikes less than 1 cm long; entire plants not over 5 cm tall, forming extensive turfs. *Buchloë*, BUFFALO-GRASS, page 402.
5b. Spikes over 1 cm long; taller plants .... (6)

6a. Spikes standing out from the culm at nearly right angles; low plants of dry grassland. *Bouteloua*, GRAMA, page 399.
6b. Spikes more or less appressed to the culm; coarse tall plants of wet ditches or seasonally wet alkali flats. *Spartina*, CORD-GRASS, page 421.

7a. Spikes very slender, forming long recurved arcs, the spikelets minute. **Schedonnardus**, TUMBLE-GRASS, page 420.
7b. Spikes not as above, the spikelets fairly large .... (8)

8a. Spikelets very broad, almost circular .... (9)
8b. Spikelets narrow, pointed .... (10)

9a. Spikelets with the glumes folded, the spikelet lying flat, with an open slit where the glumes meet. **Beckmannia**, SLOUGH-GRASS, page 399.
9b. Spikelets with the glumes flat, the spikelet in face view not bisected. **Paspalum**, page 413.

10a. Spikelets in two or three very dense clusters at the ends of a few main panicle branches. **Dactylis**, ORCHARD-GRASS, page 403.
10b. Spikelets in slender, straight, erect racemes. **Leptochloa**, SPRANGLE-TOP, page 410.

KEY D (Sorghum Group)

1a. Spikelets plump, spherical or nearly so, not more than twice as long as wide. **Sorghum**, page 421.
1b. Spikelets narrow (oblong or linear), more than twice as long as wide .... (2)

2a. Panicle of soft-hairy, golden-brown spikelets; pedicelled spikelet reduced to only a hairy pedicel. **Sorghastrum**, INDIAN-GRASS, page 421.
2b. Panicle of reddish or silvery spikelets; pedicellate spikelet well developed, staminate .... (3)

3a. Spikes slender, delicate, the racemes not in close groups but spaced along the slender rachis. **Schizachyrium**, LITTLE BLUESTEM, page 420.
3b. Spikes stout, in digitate or densely clustered terminal groups. (4)

4a. Spikes reddish, in a digitate cluster. **Andropogon**, TURKEYFOOT; BIG BLUESTEM, page 397.
4b. Spikes silvery-white, in a dense brush-like, not distinctly digitate terminal cluster. **Bothriochloa**, SILVER BEARD-GRASS, page 399.

KEY E (Panicum Group)

1a. Spikelets subtended by slender bristles that represent the pedicels of suppressed spikelets, the entire spike resembling a bottle-brush. **Setaria**, BRISTLE-GRASS, page 420.
1b. Spikelets not subtended by bristles although the lemmas may be slender-tipped .... (2)

2a. Spikelets long-pedicelled, in open panicles, the glumes or lemmas never awned .... (3)

2b. Spikelets short-pedicelled or sessile on the panicle branches, the glumes or lemmas usually awned. Coarse weedy grasses with broad leaves and narrowly pyramidal spikes. *Echinochloa*, BARNYARD-GRASS, page 406.

3a. Basal leaves on short shoots, distinctly different from those of the flowering culm, forming overwintering rosettes. *Dichanthelium*, page 405.

3b. Basal leaves similar to the culm leaves, not overwintering as rosettes. *Panicum*, page 413.

KEY F (One-flowered Spikelets)

1a. Panicle very dense and spike-like, forming a cylindric head, the lateral panicle branches suppressed or absent .... (2)
1b. Panicle loose or dense, occasionally spike-like, but lateral branches always well-developed although sometimes appressed to the rachis. (4)

2a. First glume with two awns, the second with a single awn. *Lycurus*, WOLFTAIL, page 410.
2b. Glumes with a single awn or awnless .... (3)

3a. Each glume with a short, stout awn, the keel ciliate; lemmas awnless or only mucronate. *Phleum*, TIMOTHY, page 414.
3b. Glumes awnless, the keels densely hairy; lemma with a dorsal awn. *Alopecurus*, FOXTAIL, page 397.

4a. Lemma with three awns. *Aristida*, THREE-AWN, page 397.
4b. Lemma with a simple awn or none .... (5)

5a. Lemma with an awn from the back (very delicate and appressed in a few species) .... (6)
5b. Lemma with a terminal awn or none .... (7)

6a. Lemma with a tuft of hairs at the base; palea about as long as the lemma. *Calamagrostis*, REED-GRASS, page 402.
6b. Lemma naked at the base; palea up to ⅔ as long as the lemma, or entirely lacking. *Agrostis*, BENT-GRASS, page 396.

7a. Lemma indurate, terete; callus well developed, often sharp-pointed .... (8)
7b. Lemma membranous or firm, not terete; callus not differentiated. .... (10)

8a. Awn plumose, less than 2 cm long; lemma prolonged beyond the base of the awn into a rounded, bifid tip; glumes rounded, often purplish; plants of peat hummocks in willow bogs, subalpine. *Ptilagrostis*, page 418.
8b. Awn usually naked, but if plumose, then more than 4 cm long; lemma not prolonged beyond the base of the awn; glumes pointed, straw-colored; plants of dry sites and forest floors .... (9)

9a. Awn persistent, bent and twisted; callus sharp-pointed. **Stipa**, NEEDLE-GRASS, page 422.
9b. Awn deciduous, only slightly twisted and bent; callus blunt. **Oryzopsis**, RICE-GRASS, page 412.

10a. Floret with a tuft of long hairs at the base, the hairs at least 1 mm long. ....(11)
10b. Floret without a tuft of hairs at the base, or the hairs very short. (12)

11a. Glumes awnless; spikelets mostly over 5 mm long; many hairs at base of floret. **Calamovilfa**, SAND-REED, page 402.
11b. Glumes awned; spikelets mostly less than 5 mm long; base of floret sparsely hairy. **Muhlenbergia**, MUHLY, page 411.

12a. Articulation below the glumes, the spikelets falling as units. (13)
12b. Articulation above the glumes, the florets falling out of the spikelets, leaving the glumes attached to the rachis ....(14)

13a. Glumes with awns 4 mm long or more; panicle very dense and compact. **Polypogon,** RABBITFOOT-GRASS, page 418.
13b. Glumes awnless; panicle loose and open. **Cinna**, WOOD-REED, page 403.

14a. Lemma awned from the apex, the awn over 1 mm long .....(15)
14b. Lemma awned from the back, or awnless, or with an awn-tip less than 1 mm long ....(16)

15a. Awn bent and twisted, plumose, **Ptilagrostis**, page 418.
15b. Awn straight, never plumose. **Muhlenbergia**, MUHLY, page 411.

16a. Nerves of the lemma densely silky-hairy. **Blepharoneuron,** PINE DROPSEED, page 399.
16b. Nerves of the lemma not silky-hairy, and if pubescent, not especially so on the nerves ....(17)

17a. Tall reed-grass over 2 meters high, in wet ditches on the plains, with dense spike-like pale inflorescences; lemma smooth and shining, hard, with a minute hairy scale on each side of the lemma base. **Phalaris,** REED CANARY-GRASS, page 413.
17b. Not as above ....(18)

18a. Palea lacking, or a minute nerveless scale. **Agrostis**, BENT-GRASS, page 396.
18b. Palea present, at least half as long as the lemma, 2-nerved ....(19)

19a. Glumes as long as the lemma ....(20)
19b. Glumes one or both shorter than the lemma ....(21)

20a. Dwarf tufted grasses without rhizomes; alpine and subalpine. **Podagrostis**, page 418.

20b. Taller leafy-stemmed plants with rhizomes or with the culms bent at the base and rooting at the decumbent nodes. *Agrostis*, BENT-GRASS, page 396.

21a. Grain falling free from the lemma and palea at maturity; seed loose in the seed-coat (when wetted); ligule mostly of hairs. *Sporobolus*, DROPSEED, page 422 (see also *Muhlenbergia asperifolia*).
21b. Grain remaining enclosed within the lemma and palea at maturity; seed fused to the seed-coat; ligule membranous ....(22)

22a. Panicle small and inconspicuous, hardly exceeding the enclosing culm leaves; leaves with a boat-shaped tip; rare alpine grass of permanently wet gravels. *Phippsia*, page 413.
22b. Panicle conspicuous, spike-like or open, exserted; leaves not boat-tipped. *Muhlenbergia*, MUHLY, page 411.

KEY G (Large-glumed Group)

1a. Florets of the spikelet unlike, one bisexual and the other(s) staminate, one awned, the other(s) not ....(2)
1b. Florets of the spikelet all essentially alike (the uppermost florets may be progressively smaller and less well developed) ....(4)

2a. Spikelets with two florets, one bisexual, the other staminate .... (3)
2b. Spikelets with two staminate florets alongside the single bisexual floret, all three falling attached to each other; foliage sweet-smelling, especially when dry. *Hierochloë*, SWEET-GRASS, page 409.

3a. Lower floret bisexual, awnless, the upper floret awned; velvety-hairy grass with pale whitish spikelets. *Holcus*, VELVET-GRASS, page 409.
3b. Lower floret staminate, with a bent and twisted awn; tall oat-like grass with smooth foliage. *Arrhenatherum*, TALL OAT-GRASS, page 398.

4a. Annual; spikelets very large, the glumes over 2 cm long; awns large and conspicuous except in some cultivated varieties. *Avena*, OATS, page 399.
4b. Perennial; spikelets smaller, the glumes usually less than 2 cm long; awn, when present, less than 1.5 cm long ....(5)

5a. Lemma awnless; plant less than a meter tall ....(6)
5b. Lemma awned (minutely in *Trisetum wolfii*, a tall plant usually over a meter tall) ....(7)

6a. Articulation below the glumes; glumes unlike, the first narrow, the second wider, broadest above the middle. *Sphenopholis*, WEDGE-GRASS, page 421.
6b. Articulation above the glumes, the glumes essentially similar. *Koeleria*, JUNE-GRASS, page 410.

7a. Lemma with a flattened, twisted awn arising from between the split apex. *Danthonia*, OAT-GRASS, page 404.

7b. Lemma with the awn arising from the back, the apex not split. (8)

8a. Spikelets large, the glumes over 8 mm long; awns large and conspicuous .... (9)
8b. Spikelets smaller, the glumes less than 8 mm long; awn, when present, less than 10 mm long .... (10)

9a. Leaf-blades flat or folded; spikelets with 3 to 6 florets; terminal florets exserted slightly beyond the glumes; culms usually well over 20 cm tall, the inflorescence well-exserted, golden-brown. *Avenochloa*, page 399.
9b. Leaf-blades involute; spikelets usually with 2 florets, these included between the glumes; culms less than 20 cm tall, the inflorescence not greatly overtopping the leaves, pale straw-colored. *Helictotrichon*, page 409.

10a. Lemma rounded on the back, awned from the middle or below. (11)
10b. Lemma folded, awned from well above the middle. *Trisetum*, page 423.

11a. Glumes longer than the florets; leaf-blades flat; callus hairs over 1 mm long; lemma awned from near the middle. *Vahlodea*, page 424.
11b. Glumes not exceeding the upper floret; leaf-blades usually folded; callus hairs less than 1 mm long; lemma awned from near the base (easily recognized even when dormant by the rigid tips to the clumped leaves, tested with the open palm). *Deschampsia*, TUFTED HAIR-GRASS, page 404.

KEY H (Short glumes, several florets)

1a. Rachilla with long silky hairs as long as the lemmas; tall reed-grasses of the plains and piedmont valleys with large tassel-like panicles. *Phragmites*, GIANT REED; CARRIZO, page 414.
1b. Rachilla glabrous or with short hairs (the callus of the lemma may be hairy); rarely tall enough to be called reed-like .... (2)

2a. Lemma 3-nerved; ligule composed mostly of hairs .... (3)
2b. Lemma 5- to many-nerved, the nerves usually not conspicuous; ligule membranous (except in *Distichlis*) .... (7)

3a. Annual weedy grass of disturbed sites; palea remaining attached to the rachis after the fall of the lemma and grain. *Eragrostis*, LOVE-GRASS, page 406.
3b. Perennial .... (4)

4a. Lemma glabrous, awnless .... (5)
4b. Lemma pubescent on the nerves or the callus, mucronate or awned at the tip .... (6)

5a. Lemma truncate; spikelets 2-flowered; plant semiaquatic, usually with the lower part of the stem in water. *Catabrosa*, BROOK-GRASS, page 402.

5b. Lemma acute or acuminate; spikelets 3- to many-flowered; plants of dry sites. *Eragrostis*, LOVE-GRASS, page 406.

6a. Panicle open, the branches slender and wavy; sand-dune plants with creeping rhizomes; lemmas acute, the glumes much shorter, collar smooth. *Redfieldia*, BLOWOUT-GRASS, page 420.

6b. Panicle narrow, the branches stiffly erect; bunchgrasses; lemmas rounded at apex, the glumes as long as the florets; collar hairy. *Tridens*, page 423.

7a. Lemma 8 mm or more long; sheaths closed .... (8)
7b. Lemma less than 8 mm long .... (10)

8a. Annual. *Bromus*, CHEAT-GRASS, page 401.
8b. Perennial .... (9)

9a. Spikelets flattened, the glumes and lemmas sharply folded. *Ceratochloa*, RESCUE-GRASS, page 403.
9b. Spikelets more or less terete, the lemmas rounded on the back. *Bromopsis*, BROME, page 400.

10a. Lemma awned, the awn 1 mm long or more .... (11)
10b. Lemma awnless or awn-pointed, with the point less than 1 mm long
.... (15)

11a. Spikelets in dense, rather one-sided clusters on a few main panicle branches. *Dactylis*, ORCHARD-GRASS, page 403.
11b. Spikelets not as above .... (12)

12a. Awn from a notched lemma-apex or from slightly back of the apex; spikelets often over 12 mm long; leaf-sheaths closed (the margins fused for most of their length) .... (13)
12b. Awn terminal; spikelets less than 12 mm long; sheaths open (the margins merely overlapping) .... (14)

13a. Callus with a prominent tuft of straight hairs. *Schizachne*, FALSE MELIC, page 420.
13b. Callus not hairy. *Bromopsis*, BROME, page 400.

14a. Annual; plants yellow-green, in age reddish-brown, flowering in early spring. *Vulpia*, SIX-WEEKS FESCUE, page 425.
14b. Perennial; plants not turning brown or flowering early. *Festuca*, FESCUE, page 407.

15a. Lemma tough and leathery; palea serrate; ligules mostly of hairs; plants dioecious. *Distichlis*, SALT-GRASS, page 405.
15b. Lemma membranous; palea not serrate; ligules membranous; plants bisexual or, in one genus only, dioecious .... (16)

16a. Culm usually bulbous at the base; lemmas of uppermost florets often rolled together to form a club-shaped nubbin; sheaths closed. *Melica*, ONION-GRASS, page 410.

16b. Culms not bulbous at the base; upper florets separate; sheaths mostly open (rarely closed) .... (17)

17a. Lemma with parallel nerves not converging at the tip (if projected); lemma apex broadly obtuse or truncate .... (18)

17b. Lemma with nerves converging toward the tip (if projected); lemma apex usually acute .... (20)

18a. Nerves faint; plants usually of low alkaline soils. *Puccinellia*, ALKALI-GRASS, page 420.

18b. Nerves prominent; plants of fresh-water marshes and wet places generally, avoiding alkaline soils .... (19)

19a. Leaf-sheaths closed; second glume one-nerved. *Glyceria*, MANNA-GRASS, page 408.

19b. Leaf-sheaths open; second glume 3-nerved. *Torreyochloa*, WEAK MANNA-GRASS, page 423.

20a. Lemmas and glumes folded (keeled) .... (21)

20b. Lemmas rounded on the back (glumes may be keeled) ..... (22)

21a. Leaf-tip boat-shaped, splitting apart when flattened. *Poa*, BLUE-GRASS, page 414.

21b. Leaf-tip not boat-shaped. *Koeleria*, JUNE-GRASS, page 410.

22a. Lemma less than 5 mm long; glumes usually folded; leaf-tip boat-shaped. *Poa*, BLUE-GRASS, page 414.

22b. Lemma 5 mm or more long; glumes not folded .... (23)

23a. Plant dioecious; stigmas hispidulous all around; tall broad-leaved glaucous plants of pine forests. *Leucopoa*, SPIKE FESCUE, page 410.

23b. Plant bisexual; stigmas plumose; plants not as above. *Festuca*, FESCUE, page 407.

AEGILOPS. GOAT-GRASS

One species, *Aegilops cylindrica* Host. An introduced weed, established locally in the piedmont valleys. The spike forms an unbroken cylinder. *Aegilops* is regarded as a possible ancestor of wheat.

AGROPYRON. WHEAT-GRASS

1a. Plants growing in clumps; creeping rhizomes absent (there are occasional exceptions to this in almost every species) .... (2)

1b. Plants forming sods; creeping rhizomes present (stems solitary or a few together)... (7)

2a. Spikelets appressed to the axis of the spike or at most the upper end curving away from the axis .... (3)

2b. Spikelets standing out stiffly at an angle from the axis .... (6)

3a. Awn of lemma straight or absent .... (4)
3b. Awn of lemma present and divergent .... (5)

4a. Tall plants up to 2-3 meters; florets 5 to 11; glumes truncate, much shorter than the lowest floret, the spikelets curving outward. ***Agropyron elongatum*** (Host.) P. Beauv. An Asiatic species introduced in the piedmont valleys. Similar to *A. intermedium* and evidently hybridizing with it.
4b. Smaller plants less than 1 meter high; florets 2 to 4; glumes acute, not much shorter than the lowest floret; spikelets appressed to the axis. ***Agropyron trachycaulum*** (Link) Malte (rough-stemmed), SLENDER WHEAT-GRASS. Common and with several races, plains to alpine (*A. latiglume* Scribn. & Smith, an alpine race).

5a. Glumes awnless or with a straight awn; plants erect. ***Agropyron trachycaulum*** var. ***glaucum*** (Pease & Moore) Malte. Montane and subalpine.
5b. Glumes and lemmas with long, curved awns; culms decumbent, spreading. ***Agropyron scribneri*** Vasey (for F. Lamson-Scribner). Exposed sites, upper subalpine and alpine.

6a. Glumes twisted, the margins very narrow; spikelets spreading at almost right angles to the rachis. ***Agropyron cristatum*** (L.) Gaertn., CRESTED WHEAT-GRASS. An Asiatic species commonly planted to stabilize soil.
6b. Glumes straight, the hyaline margin broad and conspicuous; spikelets spreading at a narrower angle. ***Agropyron desertorum*** (Fisch.) Schult. An Asiatic introduction in similar sites.

7a. Lemmas pubescent .... (8)
7b. Lemmas glabrous .... (10)

8a. Glumes tapering from the base; plants glaucous. ***Agropyron smithii*** Rydb. var. ***molle*** (Scribn. & Smith) Jones, WESTERN WHEAT-GRASS. Common on the plains and piedmont valleys.
8b. Glumes broadest near the middle; plants green, rarely glaucous. (9)

9a. Glumes and lemmas pointed, softly pubescent. ***Agropyron dasystachyum*** (Hook.) Scribn. (hairy-spike). Sandy soil, roadsides, mostly on the plains.
9b. Glumes and lemmas rounded or truncate, hirsute. ***Agropyron trichophorum*** (Link) Richt. (bearing hairs). An Asiatic species introduced for range cover.

10a. Lemmas with divergent awns; plant green. ***Agropyron albicans*** Scribn. & Smith var. ***griffithsii*** (Scribn. & Smith) Beetle. In shelter of rocks on the mesas. Often mistaken for *Agropyron spicatum*, Bluebunch Wheat-grass, but not strictly a bunch-grass.
10b. Lemmas with short, straight awns .... (11)

11a. Plants glaucous; glumes tapering from the base to a slender tip. **Agropyron smithii** Rydb., WESTERN WHEAT-GRASS.

11b. Plants green; glumes broadest near the middle. **Agropyron repens** (L.) Beauv., QUACK GRASS, Fig. 263. Abundant in wet ditches, a common weed in fields, gardens, and roadsides, very difficult to eradicate because of the deep, brittle rhizomes.

AGROSTIS. BENT-GRASS

1a. Plants with stolons or rhizomes; palea well developed, 2-nerved, at least half as long as the lemma .... (2)

1b. Plants forming tufts, lacking stolons or rhizomes; palea lacking or a short nerveless scale .... (3)

2a. Panicle narrow; stems decumbent and rooting at the nodes, often producing long above-ground stolons. **Agrostis palustris** Huds. (of swamps). Piedmont and foothill valleys.

2b. Panicle open; stems erect, with underground rhizomes. **Agrostis gigantea** Roth, RED-TOP. Commonly cultivated in pastures, and established in moist meadows, plains to subalpine.

3a. Leaves 2-10 mm wide; ligule 2-6 mm long; panicle narrow, some branches bearing spikelets to their bases. **Agrostis exarata** Trin.

Fig. 263. **Agropyron repens**

(plowed-out, alluding to the weedy character). Uncommon in disturbed meadows, montane.

3b. Leaves narrower, 1-3 mm wide and ligule shorter; panicle open or narrow .... (4)

4a. Panicle narrow, at last some of the lower branches spikelet-bearing near their bases; lemma always awnless. *Agrostis variabilis* Rydb. Subalpine and alpine.

4b. Panicle open, or when narrow the spikelets sometimes with awns. (5)

5a. Panicle very delicate, with very slender branches forking beyond their middles; plants relatively tall and slender. *Agrostis scabra* Willd., TICKLEGRASS. Common along roadsides, plains to subalpine. Panicles up to 30 cm long.

5b. Panicles less widely branched; plants low, often dwarf alpine bunch-grasses .... (6)

6a. Lemma with a short, straight, hardly exserted awn. *Agrostis bakeri* Rydb. Poorly understood and possibly a race of the next.

6b. Lemma with a conspicuous exserted and bent awn. *Agrostis borealis* Hartm. Alpine tundra.

ALOPECURUS. FOXTAIL

1a. Spikelets 5-6 mm long; basal leaves curled; introduced species. *Alopecurus pratensis* L., MEADOW FOXTAIL. Commonly used for re-seeding along highways, foothills.

1b. Spikelets 2-4 mm long; native species of wet meadows and shores. (2)

2a. Panicle 1-4 cm long, about 1 cm broad; glumes densely covered with long hairs. *Alopecurus alpinus* Smith. Wet meadows and shores, montane and subalpine.

2b. Panicle 3-7 cm long, 3-5 mm broad; glumes hairy on keel and nerves only. *Alopecurus aequalis* Sobol. Common in wet ditches and muddy shores, plains to subalpine.

ANDROPOGON. BIG BLUESTEM; TURKEYFOOT

1a. Awns 5 mm or less long; plant with elongate rhizomes; foliage glaucous. *Andropogon hallii* Hack. (for Elihu Hall), SAND BLUESTEM. Sand dunes on the plains, mostly east of our area.

1b. Awns 1-2 cm long; rhizomes short or lacking; foliage not strongly glaucous. *Andropogon gerardii* Vitm. (for Louis Gérard), BIG BLUESTEM. Common on the plains and mesas, a remnant of the old tall-grass prairie which once reached continuously from the midwest to the foot of the mountains.

ARISTIDA. THREE-AWN

1a. Annual; central awn spirally coiled at base; lateral awns ½ to ⅓ as long as central awn. *Aristida basiramea* Engelm. Rare, on sandstone ledges at White Rocks near Boulder, and on disturbed sandy ground at Rocky Flats. A close relative, *A. curtissii* (Gray) Nash, with the lateral awns much shorter than the central awns, has been found near Fort Collins.

1b. Perennial; central awn not spirally coiled; lateral awns nearly equal to central awn .... (2)

2a. Awns less than 4 cm long; leaf blades short, forming a distinctly curled basal cluster; second glume less than 18 mm long. *Aristida fendleriana* Steud. (for August Fendler), Fig. 264. Dry grasslands on the plains, mesas and foothills.

2b. Awns over 4 cm long; some leaf-blades about as long as culms, mostly straight. *Aristida longiseta* Steud. (long-awned), Red Three-awn. The more abundant species on plains, mesas and foothills.

ARRHENATHERUM. Tall Oat-grass

One species, *Arrhenatherum elatius* (L.) Mert. & Koch. Often planted for hay and forage, but locally established along roadsides.

Fig. 264. *Aristida fendleriana*   Fig. 265. *Beckmannia syzigachne*

AVENA. Oats

1a. Lemma with stiff, usually reddish brown hairs; awn bent and twisted. *Avena fatua* L. (useless), Wild Oats. A weed in grain fields and established along roadsides.

1b. Lemmas glabrous; awn straight or absent. *Avena fatua* L. var. *sativa* (L.) Hausskn., Cultivated Oats. Widely cultivated, and escaped to roadsides and horse trails.

AVENOCHLOA. Mountain-oat

One species, *Avenochloa hookeri* (Scribn.) Holub. Rare or only locally abundant, upper subalpine slopes and lower tundra. According to Soviet specialists, this species is identical to the Central Asiatic *A. asiatica* (Roshevic) Holub. *A. hookeri* is the older name.

BECKMANNIA. Slough-grass

One species, *Beckmannia syzigachne* (Steud.) Fern. (with scissors-like glumes), Fig. 265. Irrigation ditches and standing water of swamps, plains to montane. The disk-shaped spikelets, stacked like poker-chips, are unmistakeable.

BLEPHARONEURON. Pine Dropseed

One species, *Blepharoneuron tricholepis* (Torr.) Nash (hairy scale). Montane, especially in the white fir forests of southern Colorado.

BOTHRIOCHLOA. Silver Beard-grass

One species, *Bothriochloa saccharoides* Swartz, Silver Beard-grass. Native in southeastern Colorado, but invading our area along newly disturbed highway rights-of-way.

BOUTELOUA. Grama

1a. Spikelets arranged in dense one-sided spikes (brush-shaped); spikes 1 to 3, persisting after the fall of the florets .... (2)

1b. Spikelets not grouped in spikes, but racemosely arranged, pedulous or reflexed, 20 to 50 on an elongate rachis; each spikelet cluster falling at maturity as a unit. *Bouteloua curtipendula* (Michx.) Torr. (short, hanging), Side-oats Grama, Fig. 266. Abundant on the plains and mesas.

2a. Plants annual; spikes one to a culm. *Bouteloua simplex* Lag. (simple). Common in Colorado Springs, probably introduced there.

2b. Plants perennial; spikes usually two or more to a culm .... (3)

3a. Rachis prolonged beyond the spikelet cluster as a naked point; glumes with dark tubercles on the surface. *Bouteloua hirsuta* Lag., Hairy Grama. One of the dominant species on the shortgrass plains, less common on the mesas.

3b. Rachis not prolonged beyond the spikelet cluster; glumes without tubercles. ***Bouteloua gracilis*** (H.B.K.) Lag. (slender), Blue Grama, Fig. 267. Abundant on plains and mesas, the most common *Bouteloua* in this area.

BROMOPSIS. Perennial Brome (*Bromus* in part, of Ed. 4)

1a. Rhizomes present; awn of lemma not over 3 mm long .... (2)
1b. Rhizomes absent; awn often over 3 mm long .... (3)

2a. Lemma glabrous to scabrous; nodes and leaves usually glabrous; introduced plant of fields and roadsides. ***Bromopsis inermis*** (Leyss) Holub (unarmed), Smooth Brome. Piedmont valleys and plains, sparingly in the mountains.
2b. Lemma pubescent; nodes hairy; leaves usually pubescent. ***Bromopsis inermis*** ssp. ***pumpelliana*** (Scribn.) W. A. Weber. The native American counterpart of *B. inermis*, common in the mountains.

3a. First glume (i.e. the lower and shorter one) 1-nerved (with no lateral nerves) .... (4)
3b. First glume 3-nerved. ***Bromopsis porteri*** (Coult.) Holub (for T. C. Porter), Nodding Brome. Common, montane and subalpine.

4a. Lower culm leaves with spreading hairs on the sheaths. ***Bromopsis lanatipes*** (Shear) Holub (woolly-based). Common, especially along roadsides and trails, foothills and montane.

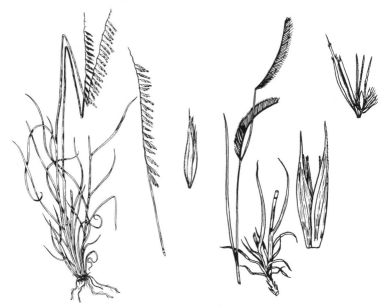

Fig. 266. ***Bouteloua curtipendula***   Fig. 267. ***Bouteloua gracilis***

4b. Lower culm leaves glabrous or nearly so. ***Bromopsis ciliata*** (L.) Holub, FRINGED BROME. Common in montane and subalpine (including *Bromopsis richardsonii*).

BROMUS. CHEAT-GRASS

1a. Lemma narrow, acuminate, tapering to the awn, the teeth of the bifid apex over 2 mm long; first glume 1-nerved ....(2)

1b. Lemma broad, not acuminate, abruptly awned, the teeth of the bifid apex rarely over 1 mm long; first glume 3- to 5-nerved ....(3)

2a. Awns 2-3 cm long; second glume over 1 cm long. ***Bromus sterilis*** L., POVERTY BROME. Vacant lots in and around towns or on overgrazed range.

2b. Awns less than 2 cm long; second glume shorter. ***Bromus tectorum*** L. (of roofs), CHEAT-GRASS, Fig. 269. Introduced weed becoming abundant wherever range is overgrazed or otherwise mismanaged. Often infected with a black smut-fungus that converts the grains to black dust (spores).

Fig. 269. ***Bromus tectorum***

Fig. 268. ***Buchloë dactyloides***

3a. Awns lacking or very short; lemmas very broad and inflated, the spikelets rattling when shaken together. ***Bromus brizaeformis*** F. & M. (like *Briza*), RATTLESNAKE GRASS. Common on mesas and foothills.
3b. Awns well-developed; lemmas not very broad nor conspicuously inflated .... (4)

4a. Foliage glabrous. ***Bromus secalinus*** L., CHESS. Introduced weed, uncommon.
4b. Foliage hairy. ***Bromus japonicus*** Thunberg, JAPANESE BROME. Abundant weed on the mesas and in the piedmont valleys.

BUCHLOË. BUFFALO-GRASS

One species, ***Buchloë dactyloides*** (Nutt.) Engelm. (resembling *Dactylis*), Fig. 268. Abundant on plains and mesas, where it forms continuous sods over large areas. Plants never more than 4 or 5 cm high. An excellent lawn grass for dry, non-irrigated sites.

CALAMAGROSTIS. REED-GRASS

1a. Awn of lemma bent, exserted beyond the glumes. ***Calamagrostis purpurascens*** R. Br., PURPLE REED-GRASS. Common on gravelly slide areas, subalpine.
1b. Awn of lemma straight, included within the glumes .... (2)

2a. Panicle loose and open; leaf-blades flat, 2-8 mm wide; callus hairs as long as the lemma. ***Calamagrostis canadensis*** (Michx.) P. Beauv., CANADIAN REED-GRASS. Wet shores of lakes and bogs, montane and subalpine.
2b. Panicle narrow; leaf-blades generally involute (especially when dry), 1.5-4.5 mm wide; callus hairs to about ¾ as long as the lemma. ***Calamagrostis inexpansa*** Gray, NORTHERN REED-GRASS. Subalpine swamps and bogs.

CALAMOVILFA. SAND-REED

One species, ***Calamovilfa longifolia*** (Hook.) Scribn., PRAIRIE SAND-REED. Sandy areas on the plains and piedmont valleys.

CATABROSA. BROOK-GRASS

One species, ***Catabrosa aquatica*** (L.) P. Beauv. A semiaquatic grass growing with the lower part of the stems in shallow water of oxbows and slow streams, montane and subalpine. One record from our area, Owl Canyon northwest of Fort Collins.

CENCHRUS. SAND BUR

One species, ***Cenchrus longispinus*** (Hackel in Kneucker) Fern., Fig. 270. Common in sandy soil of cultivated fields, roadsides and floodplains. The small burs are easily caught on stockings and pants-legs (*C. pauciflorus* of Ed. 4).

CERATOCHLOA. RESCUE-GRASS (*Bromus* in part, of Ed. 4).

1a. Lemma awnless or nearly so. ***Ceratochloa unioloides*** (Willd.) P. Beauv. (like *Uniola*), RESCUE-GRASS. Introduced weed, known from an old collection from Boulder (*Bromus catharticus* of manuals).

1b. Lemma with an awn over 3 mm long. ***Ceratochloa marginata*** (Nees ex Steud.) Jackson. Extensively used in reseeding depleted mountain range lands, common in montane and subalpine (*Bromus marginatus* of Ed. 4).

CINNA. WOOD-REED

One species, ***Cinna latifolia*** (Trev.) Griseb., DROOPING WOOD-REED. Infrequent in swampy woodlands, montane and subalpine.

CYNODON. BERMUDA-GRASS

One species, ***Cynodon dactylon*** (L.) Pers. A cultivated grass not hardy this far north, but surviving on ground that does not freeze in winter. A colony has persisted above heating tunnels on the University of Colorado campus for many years.

DACTYLIS. ORCHARD-GRASS

One species, ***Dactylis glomerata*** L. (in bunches), Fig. 272. A common introduced weed in lawns and fields, sometimes grown in pasture mixes. The clumps of succulent bluish-green, folded leaves form unsightly patches, overspreading bluegrass in lawns throughout our area. An important cause of hay fever.

Fig. 270. ***Cenchrus longispinus***

DANTHONIA. Oat-grass

1a. Lemma glabrous on the back, pilose on the margins only. *Danthonia intermedia* Vasey, Timber Danthonia. Grasslands, subalpine and alpine.

1b. Lemma pilose on the back, sometimes sparsely so .... (2)

2a. Glumes over 15 mm long; lemma over 9 mm long; flowering culms robust, over 1 mm wide; old leaf-sheaths persisting at the base of the plant. *Danthonia parryi* Scribn. (for C. C. Parry). Common on dry hillsides, upper montane and subalpine.

2b. Glumes less than 15 mm long; lemma less than 9 mm long; flowering culms slender, not over 1 mm wide; old leaf-sheaths not conspicuous. *Danthonia spicata* (L.) P. Beauv. (having a spike), Poverty Oat-grass. Locally abundant on the mesas and open pine forests in the foothills.

DESCHAMPSIA. Tufted Hairgrass

One species, *Deschampsia caespitosa* (L.) P. Beauv., Fig. 273. Wet meadows and pond margins, subalpine, one of the most valuable forage grasses in the mountains. There are two distinct races or species, differing in the size of the spikelets and the scabrousness of the peduncles. The

Fig. 271. *Digitaria sanguinalis*   Fig. 272. *Dactylis glomerata*

alpine one (*Deschampsia alpicola* Rydb.) has glabrous peduncles and large spikelets (4-7 mm).

DICHANTHELIUM (*Panicum* in part, of Ed. 4)

1a. Spikelet less than 2 mm long. ***Dichanthelium lanuginosum*** (Ell.) Gould. Rare, base of sandstone bluffs in the piedmont valleys near Boulder.
1b. Spikelets over 2 mm long. ***Dichanthelium oligosanthes*** (Schult.) Gould var. ***scribnerianum*** (Nash) Gould. Common in rocky places on the mesas and outer foothills.

DIGITARIA. CRAB-GRASS

1a. First glume minute but present; second glume about half the length of the sterile lemma; spikelet pedicels 3-winged, the edges of the wings scabrous; lower sheaths papillose-hairy. ***Digitaria sanguinalis*** (L.) Scop. (stanching blood, named from its supposed styptic properties), HAIRY CRAB-GRASS, Fig. 271. A common and annoying weed in gardens and lawns, spreading by adventitious roots arising at the lower nodes.
1b. First glume usually absent; second glume as long as the spikelet; spikelet pedicels merely 3-angled, the angles not scabrous; lower sheaths glabrous or with scattered hairs. ***Digitaria ischaemum*** (Schreb.) Muehl. (styptic), SMOOTH CRAB-GRASS. In similar habitats.

DISTICHLIS. SALT-GRASS

One species, ***Distichlis spicata*** (L.) Greene var. ***stricta*** (Torr.) Beetle. Common in alkaline swales, borrow-pits and margins of reservoirs on the plains and piedmont valleys.

Fig. 273. ***Deschampsia caespitosa***

ECHINOCHLOA. BARNYARD-GRASS

One species, **Echinochloa crus-galli** (L.) P. Beauv. (cockspur). Common weed in gardens, irrigation ditches and farmyards, piedmont valleys and plains. Very variable as to the length of the awns.

ELYMUS. WILD-RYE

1a. Awns either lacking or more than 1 cm long and widely divergent; plants usually robust, 60-200 cm tall; spikelets 2 to 5 (commonly 3 to 5) at a node .... (2)
1b. Awns, when present, usually less than 1 cm long, or if longer, not widely divergent; plants usually slender, 40-100 cm tall; spikelets 1 to 2 at a node .... (3)

2a. Lemma awnless or merely awn-pointed. **Elymus cinereus** Scribn. & Merr. (ash-colored), GIANT WILD-RYE. Plains and foothills, uncommon here but abundant and conspicuous on the western slope. Tall and robust, forming massive leafy clumps.
2b. Lemma with long, divergent awns. **Elymus canadensis** L., CANADA WILD-RYE. Common along roadsides, plains through lower foothills. Spikes often nodding.

3a. Leaf-blades 2-6 mm wide; glumes subulate or narrowly linear ... (4)
3b. Leaf-blades 8-15 mm wide; glumes lanceolate or linear. **Elymus glaucus** Buckley, BLUE WILD-RYE. Common in open woods, especially aspen groves, foothills and montane.

4a. Spike very slender; lemma with awn up to 15 mm long; rachis disarticulating at maturity. **X Agrohordeum macounii** (Vasey) Lepage, a hybrid involving *Hordeum jubatum* and *Agropyron* species, but the combination of characters corresponds to *Elymus*. Marshes in the piedmont valleys.
4b. Spike not extremely slender; awn of lemma rarely over 5 mm long; rachis not disarticulating at maturity. **Elymus ambiguus** Vasey & Scribn., COLORADO WILD-RYE. Dry rocky slopes in the outer foothills.

ERAGROSTIS. LOVE-GRASS

1a. Plants prostrate and rooting at the nodes; spikelets in dense clusters. **Eragrostis hypnoides** (Lam.) B.S.P. (like *Hypnum*, a creeping moss), CREEPING LOVE-GRASS. In wet sand, streambanks, plains and piedmont valleys.
1b. Plants not rooting at the nodes .... (2)

2a. Lemmas with raised "glands" along keel; some spikelets over 2.5 mm wide. **Eragrostis cilianensis** (All.) Lutati (of Ciliani, an Italian estate), STINKGRASS. Common weed in gardens and waste places in and around towns.
2b. Lemmas without such raised glands; spikelets seldom over 2 mm wide .... (3)

3a. Perennial; panicles purple, on tall, erect culms. ***Eragrostis trichodes*** (Nutt.) Wood (thread-like, referring to the panicle branches). Common along roadsides, Longmont area, probably introduced.

3b. Annual; panicles blackish, on spreading, often almost prostrate culms. ***Eragrostis diffusa*** Buckl., SPREADING LOVE-GRASS. Common weed. Two other species, *E. pilosa* and *E. pectinacea*, are difficult to distinguish from this, but have been reported for our area.

FESTUCA. FESCUE

1a. Leaf-blades flat, averaging over 3 mm wide ....(2)
1b. Leaf-blades involute, or, if flat, then less than 3 mm wide ..... (3)

2a. Panicle spike-like; plants dioecious; stigmas bearing branches on all sides; leaves without auricles; native in the mountains (see *Leucopoa kingii*, page 410).
2b. Panicle narrow but not spike-like; plants not dioecious; stigmas with branches on two sides only; auricles present on some leaves. ***Festuca pratensis*** Huds., MEADOW FESCUE. Pastures and hay-meadows, often in swampy areas and roadside ditches, plains.

3a. Ligule 2 to 4 mm long or longer; lemmas awnless or cuspidate. ***Festuca thurberi*** Vasey (for George Thurber), THURBER FESCUE. Montane and subalpine. A tall and handsome bunchgrass, sometimes forming pure stands on high subalpine ridges.
3b. Ligule shorter; lemma distinctly awned (except in *F. arizonica*) ...(4)

4a. Culms curved (decumbent) at the base, the new shoots breaking out through the side of the old leaf-sheath; basal leaf-sheaths reddish, fibrillose, the culms in loose tufts. ***Festuca rubra*** L., RED FESCUE. Meadows, plains to subalpine. Anthers 2-3 mm long.
4b. Culms erect, the new shoots not breaking out through the side of the old leaf-sheath; basal leaf-sheaths not reddish or fibrillose .... (5)

5a. Plants with creeping rhizomes; always growing in *Kobresia* stands on alpine tundra. ***Festuca halli*** (Vasey) Piper. Rare, Cameron Mountain.
5b. Plants caespitose, without rhizomes ....(6)

6a. Anthers to 1.5 mm long; lemma up to 4 mm long exclusive of the awn ....(7)
6b. Anthers 2.5-4.0 mm long; lemma up to 5-7 mm long excluding the awn, often inrolled and exposing the rachillas ....(8)

7a. Anthers 1.0-1.5 mm long; leaves glaucous; culms tall, about 2 to 3 times the height of the basal leaves; ligule 3 mm long; lemma 6.0-7.5 mm long including the awn. ***Festuca saximontana*** Rydb. Foothills and montane, in open forests and dry meadows.
7b. Anthers 0.7-0.8 mm long; leaves green; culms usually less than twice the height of the basal leaves; ligule minute or obsolete; lemma 3-4 mm long including awn ....(9)

8a. Awn 2-4 mm long; persistent papery basal leaf-sheaths less than 4 cm long; leaves seldom up to 30 cm long. ***Festuca idahoensis*** Elmer, IDAHO FESCUE. Infrequent, subalpine.

8b. Awn up to 1.5 mm long; persistent papery leaf-bases 5-10 cm long; leaves filiform, usually over 30 cm long. ***Festuca arizonica*** Vasey, ARIZONA FESCUE. Common in dry forests from the Black Forest southward.

9a. Culm minutely and densely pubescent just below the heads; spikelets tending to be reddish-brown, the cluster dense and somewhat onesided. ***Festuca baffinensis*** Polunin. Rare, on alpine tundra.

9b. Culm glabrous or slightly scabrous just below the heads; spikelets dark green, the cluster usually slender. ***Festuca brachyphylla*** Schult., Fig. 274. Very abundant in alpine tundra. Represented by several micro-races, some extremely slender and low.

GLYCERIA. MANNA-GRASS

1a. Spikelets linear, over 7 mm long; panicle narrow. ***Glyceria borealis*** (Nash) Batch., NORTHERN MANNA-GRASS. Margins of ponds, upper montane, subalpine.

1b. Spikelets ovate to oblong, less than 7 mm long; panicle open. (2)

2a. Leaf-blades narrow, 2-6 mm wide; first glume 0.5-0.9 mm long; culms usually less than a meter tall. ***Glyceria striata*** (Lam.) Hitchc., FOWL MANNA-GRASS. Swampy streamsides, mesas and foothills.

Fig. 274. ***Festuca brachyphylla***   Fig. 275. ***Hordeum jubatum***

2b. Leaf-blades wider; first glume 1 mm long or more; culms usually over a meter tall .... (3)

3a. First glume 1.5 mm long or more; spikelets 5-7 mm long or longer; panicle very compound. ***Glyceria maxima*** (Hartm.) Holmb. ssp. ***grandis*** (Wats.) Hultén, American Manna-grass. Swamps and irrigation ditches, plains and piedmont valleys (*G. grandis* of Ed. 2).

3b. First glume 1 mm long or less; panicle only moderately compound. ***Glyceria elata*** (Nash) Hitchc., Tall Manna-grass. Aspen thickets and pond borders, subalpine.

HELICTOTRICHON. Alpine Oat

One species, ***Helictotrichon mortonianum*** (Scribn.) Henr. (for J. Sterling Morton, Secretary of Agriculture). Alpine tundra. Our only representative of this Asiatic genus.

HIEROCHLOË. Sweet-grass

One species, ***Hierochloë hirta*** (Schrank) Borbas ssp. ***arctica*** (Presl) G. Weimarck. Common in swampy meadows and lower alpine slopes. Spikelets rich golden-brown. The plant is used, in Poland, to flavor vodka.

HILARIA. Galleta-grass

One genus and species, ***Hilaria jamesii*** (Torr.) Benth. Rare in our area but becoming common on mesas and plains from the Arkansas River southward.

HOLCUS. Velvet-grass

One species, ***Holcus lanatus*** L. A European grass locally established on wooded slopes above streams in the piedmont valleys in the Boulder area. The very soft quality of the foliage and heads is distinctive.

HORDEUM. Barley

1a. Plants perennial; awns slender; leaves lacking auricles .... (2)

1b. Plants annual, branching at the base; awns mostly stouter; leaves sometimes with auricles .... (3)

2a. Spike, including awns, as broad as long or nearly so; awns 2-5 cm long. ***Hordeum jubatum*** L. (having a mane), Foxtail Barley, Fig. 275. A very beautiful plant, abundant in wet ditches and meadows. At low altitudes the awns are pale yellowish, at high altitudes reddish.

2b. Spike, including awns, much longer than broad, the awns not more than 1 cm long. ***Hordeum brachyantherum*** Nevski (short-flowered), Meadow Barley. Plains to montane, roadsides and meadows.

3a. Leaf-blades with prominent auricles .... (4)

3b. Leaf-blades lacking auricles. ***Hordeum pusillum*** Nutt., Little Barley. Roadside weed in the piedmont valleys and plains.

4a. Rachis not disarticulating, the 3 spikelets sessile. ***Hordeum vulgare*** L., CULTIVATED BARLEY. Commonly escaped from cultivation, plains and piedmont valleys.

4b. Rachis disarticulating; lateral spikelets with pedicels. ***Hordeum glaucum*** Steud. Abundant street weed in Boulder and probably elsewhere.

KOELERIA. JUNE-GRASS

One species, ***Koeleria macrantha*** (Ledeb.) Schult. Very common on meadows and hillsides, foothills to subalpine. In blossom the panicle is open and very different in appearance from its fruiting aspect, a dense, contracted panicle. The nomenclature of this species (or possibly more than one species) is still rather confused (*K. gracilis* of Ed. 4).

LEERSIA. RICE CUT-GRASS

One species, ***Leersia oryzoides*** (L.) Sw. Streambanks and irrigation ditches in the piedmont valleys. Easily recognized by the harsh, minutely saw-toothed stems and flat spikelets lacking glumes. Common in the Boulder area and possibly introduced here through an old plant nursery.

LEPTOCHLOA. SPRANGLETOP

One species, ***Leptochloa fascicularis*** (Lam.) Gray. On drying mud-flats of ponds in the piedmont valleys. This was incorrectly listed in Ed. 4 as *L. dubia*.

LEUCOPOA. SPIKE FESCUE

One species, ***Leucopoa kingii*** (Wats.) W. A. Weber (for Clarence King). Common in pine forests, foothills and montane. Long thought to be a monotypic American genus (*Hesperochloa*), this species belongs to a small genus of Asiatic *Festuca*-like dioecious grasses.

LOLIUM. RYE-GRASS; DARNEL

1a. At least some of the lemmas awned. ***Lolium multiflorum*** Lam., ITALIAN RYE-GRASS. Common weed in lawns and along irrigation ditches in and near towns.

1b. Lemmas not awned, or merely awn-pointed. ***Lolium perenne*** L., PERENNIAL RYE-GRASS. Similar sites.

LYCURUS. WOLFTAIL

One species, ***Lycurus phleoides*** H.B.K. (resembling Timothy). Mesas and outer foothill hogbacks and lower canyons.

MELICA. ONION-GRASS

1a. Culms bulbous at the base; spikelets erect, not pendulous, purplish. ***Melica spectabilis*** Scribn. (showy), PURPLE ONIONGRASS. Mountain meadows, aspen groves in the upper montane and subalpine.

1b. Culms not bulbous at the base; spikelets nodding on slender pedicels, turned to one side of the stem, pale green. *Melica porteri* Scribn. (for T. C. Porter). On soil accumulations at base of cliffs in the outer foothills canyons from Clear Creek to Pikes Peak region.

MUHLENBERGIA. Muhly

1a. Panicle open at maturity, the branches long, naked at base; inflorescence over 4 cm wide, often as wide as long .... (2)

1b. Panicle narrow at maturity, the branches short, bearing spikelets to near the base; inflorescence less than 4 cm wide, much longer than wide
.... (4)

2a. Lemma awnless or mucronate; leaves not in a basal cluster; rhizomes present. *Muhlenbergia asperifolia* (N. & M.) Parodi (harsh-leaved), Alkali Muhly. Wet, usually alkaline depressions on the plains. The panicles are so finely branched as to have a gossamer appearance.

2b. Lemma awned from the tip; leaves mostly in basal clusters ..... (3)

3a. Leaf-blades stiff, sharp-pointed; creeping rhizomes present; awn of lemma 1 mm long. *Muhlenbergia pungens* Thurb. (sharp), Sandhill Muhly. Abundant in sandy places on the plains, at the extreme edge of our range.

3b. Leaf-blades not stiff nor sharp-pointed, curled; long rhizomes absent; awn of lemma at least 2 mm long. *Muhlenbergia torreyi* (Kunth) Hitchc. (for John Torrey), Ring Muhly. Common on the plains and less frequent on the mesas. The plant gets its common name from its manner of growth. As the clump grows, the inner portion dies, leaving a ring of living grass, sometimes several feet in diameter. *M. pungens* behaves in the same manner.

4a. Second glume 3-nerved, each nerve ending in a tooth. *Muhlenbergia montana* (Nutt.) Hitchc., Mountain Muhly. One of the very common bunch-grasses in gravelly soil on dry slopes, montane and subalpine.

4b. None of the glumes with more than a single tooth or awn, if any. (5)

5a. Lemma with many long hairs at the base, as long as the lemma itself. *Muhlenbergia andina* (Nutt.) Hitchc. (of the Northern Andes = Rocky Mountains), Foxtail Muhly. Rock outcrops in the foothill canyons, where water seeps along ledges.

5b. Lemma smooth, or with some short hairs at the base .... (6)

6a. Leaf-blades flat, 2-6 mm wide; glumes awned; hairs present at base of floret. *Muhlenbergia racemosa* (Michx.) B.S.P., Marsh Muhly. Grassy swales in the foothill canyons.

6b. Leaves involute to flat, less than 2 mm wide; glumes awnless; base of floret without hairs .... (7)

7a. Rhizomes present; culms not densely tufted. *Muhlenbergia richardsonis* (Trin.) Rydb. (for Sir John Richardson), Mat Muhly. Gravelly

or sandy soils, on open sites, montane.
7b. Rhizomes absent; culms often in dense tufts .... (8)

8a. Annuals; glumes obtuse, less than ½ the length of the lemma.
   Muhlenbergia filiformis (Thurb.) Rydb. (thread-like), SLENDER MUHLY.
   Swampy woodlands, meadows, and streamsides, subalpine.
8b. Perennials; glumes awn-pointed, at least ½ the length of the lemma.
   Muhlenbergia wrightii Vasey (for Charles Wright), SPIKE MUHLY.
   Rocky places, mesas, plains, and lower foothill canyons.

MUNROA. FALSE BUFFALO-GRASS

One species, ***Munroa squarrosa*** (Nutt.) Torr. (spreading-recurved). Frequent in sandy areas, along roadsides on the plains. Easily recognized by its matted form and very rigid, prickly-pointed leaves. In some areas a plant louse infests the foliage, resulting in the plant being covered by a loose cobwebby material.

ORYZOPSIS. RICEGRASS

1a. Lemma densely covered with long hairs; panicle wide-spreading at maturity. ***Oryzopsis hymenoides*** (R. & S.) Ricker (membranous, referring to the thin glumes), INDIAN RICEGRASS, Fig. 276. An attractive bunchgrass of shale or clay soil, plains and mesas. Occasionally first-generation hybrids are formed between this and species of *Stipa*, resulting in plants with intermediate characters.

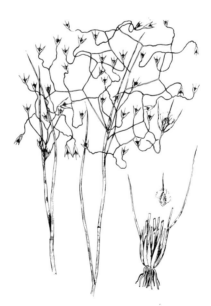

Fig. 276. ***Oryzopsis hymenoides***

1b. Lemma glabrous or covered with short, appressed hairs; panicle narrow at maturity .... (2)

2a. Spikelets 5-8 mm long, not including the awns; callus densely pubescent. ***Oryzopsis asperifolia*** Michx., ROUGH-LEAVED RICEGRASS. Infrequent in pine forests, foothills and montane.
2b. Spikelets 3-4 mm long, not including the awns; callus not densely pubescent .... (3)

3a. Panicle branches erect or appressed at maturity .... (4)
3b. Panicle branches spreading or reflexed at maturity. ***Oryzopsis micrantha*** (Trin. & Rupr.) Thurber, LITTLESEED RICEGRASS. Infrequent in the foothills, usually in deep shade.

4a. Awn less than 2 mm long or almost lacking. ***Oryzopsis pungens*** (Torr.) Hitchc. Ponderosa pine forests on the Arkansas Divide.
4b. Awn 5 mm or more long. ***Oryzopsis exigua*** Thurber, LITTLE RICEGRASS. Infrequent in open forests in the foothills.

PANICUM
1a. Weedy annual, low and spreading, with filiform panicle branches; sterile palea lacking. ***Panicum capillare*** L. var. ***occidentale*** Rydb., WITCHGRASS. Common late summer weed grass in cultivated fields and roadsides.
1b. Perennial; sterile palea present .... (2)

2a. Leaves over 5 mm wide; panicle 15-40 cm long; rhizomes present; tall plant up to a meter or more. ***Panicum virgatum*** L. (wand-like), SWITCHGRASS. Common on mesas and plains, flowering in late summer.
2b. Leaves less than 5 mm wide; panicle 3-6 cm long; rhizomes lacking; low plant, less than a half meter tall. ***Panicum perlongum*** Nash (elongate). Rare, in rocky places on the mesas.

PASPALUM
One species, ***Paspalum pubiflorum*** Rupr. *ex* Fourn. var. ***glabrum*** Vasey *ex* Scribn. A locally established weed in lawns in the Boulder area.

PHALARIS. REED CANARY-GRASS
One species, ***Phalaris arundinacea*** L. (reed-like). Abundant along irrigation ditches and in wet meadows, piedmont valleys.

PHIPPSIA
One species, ***Phippsia algida*** (Phipps) R. Br. An arctic-alpine grass with very special ecological requirements occurring in permanently wet gravels of melting snow-fields on the tundra. The culms are very low and spreading, 1-3 cm tall and the leaf-blades have a boat-shaped tip as in *Poa*.

PHLEUM. Timothy

1a. Panicle oblong or ovoid, less than 5 times as long as wide; base of culms not bulbous; upper sheaths inflated (loose). ***Phleum commutatum*** Gaudin, Alpine Timothy, Fig. 277. Subalpine meadows (*P. alpinum* of Ed. 4).

1b. Panicle cylindrical, over 6 times as long as wide; base of culms swollen or bulbous; sheaths not inflated. ***Phleum pratense*** L. (of meadows), Timothy, Fig. 278. Common along roadsides and trails, in meadows and pastures, plains to subalpine.

PHRAGMITES. Giant Reed; Carrizo

One species, ***Phragmites australis*** (Cav.) Trin. *ex* Steud. Introduced and established along irrigation ditches on the plains and piedmont valleys. The stout culms were used to make arrow-shafts (*P. communis* of Ed. 4).

POA. Blue-grass

1a. Annual ....(Annuae, **Key A**)
1b. Perennial ....(2)

2a. Rhizomes present, well developed, the plants not forming bunches
.... (Pratenses, **Key B**)

Fig. 277. ***Phleum commutatum***   Fig. 278. ***Phleum pratense***

2b. Rhizomes lacking; plants forming dense tight clumps (although occasionally the culms decumbent, rooting at the basal nodes) .... (3)

3a. Lemmas with a weft of cobwebby hairs at the base (the web sometimes scanty in *P. nemoralis* ssp. *interior*) .... (Palustres, **Key C**)
3b. Lemmas not cobwebby at the base (sometimes sparsely so in *P. pattersonii*) .... (4)

4a. Spikelets flattened; glumes and lemmas keeled. (Alpinae, **Key D**)
4b. Spikelets rounded, the glumes and lemmas not keeled or only obscurely keeled at the tip .... (Scabrellae, **Key E**)

KEY A. Annuae

One species, **Poa annua** L. An introduced weedy species found in poorly drained sites such as compacted ground along trails across wet meadows or clearings, and in lawns.

KEY B. Pratenses

1a. Culms flattened and 2-edged; nodes exposed and marked by a prominent black line. **Poa compressa** L., Canada Blue-grass. Common on dry hillsides. Although the eastern American plants are introduced from Europe, the western race appears to be native and to differ from the European type in several ways.
1b. Culms not flattened or two-edged .... (2)

2a. Panicle contracted, the branches stiffly ascending to erect. **Poa arida** Vasey, Plains Blue-grass. In low, often alkaline areas on the plains and piedmont valleys.
2b. Panicle open, the branches spreading or reflexed .... (3)

3a. Lemmas webbed at the base .... (4)
3b. Lemmas not webbed, sometimes pubescent .... (6)

4a. Ligule (on culm leaves) 1 mm long, truncate; lemmas 2-3 mm long .... (5)
4b. Ligule 2-4 mm long, obtuse or truncate; lemmas 3.5-5.5 mm long. **Poa arctica** R. Br. Frequent on alpine tundra (*P. grayana* Vasey, *P. longipila* Nash).

5a. Basal leaves bright green, 2-3 mm broad, flat or channeled, withering and disintegrating in a few years; spikelets mostly 3-flowered, the lowest lemma very cobwebby at base. **Poa pratensis** L., Kentucky Blue-grass. Introduced and widely used for lawns.
5b. Basal leaves glaucous, 0.8-2.0 mm broad, folded and somewhat revolute on the margin, remaining intact for several years; spikelets mostly 2-flowered, the lemma only slightly cobwebby. **Poa agassizensis** Boivin & D. Löve. The native counterpart of Kentucky Blue-grass, common in open forested land in the mountains.

6a. Lower sheaths minutely retrorse-pubescent and purplish; spikelets commonly purplish. **Poa nervosa** (Hook.) Vasey. Common, montane and subalpine.

6b. Lower sheaths smooth, green. **Poa arctica** R. Br.

KEY C. Palustres

1a. Lemmas glabrous except for sparse, silky pubescence on the keel, and for the web at the base. **Poa trivialis** L. Introduced from Europe and established in a few places around Boulder.

1b. Lemmas pubescent on the keel and marginal nerves, with a web at the base .... (2)

2a. Panicle nodding, open, with flexuous, capillary branches; blades short, flat, up to 4 mm wide; anthers 0.4-0.9 mm long .... (3)

2b. Panicle not nodding nor with flexuous branches .... (4)

3a. Glumes very unequal, the lower one often more or less subulate; lemmas 3-4 mm long, acuminate, the nerves pilose to glabrate. **Poa leptocoma** Trin. Springs and boggy forests, subalpine.

3b. Glumes subequal, the lower rarely much narrower than the upper; lemmas 2-3 mm long, acute, the nerves more densely pilose. **Poa reflexa** Vasey & Scribn. Similar habitats.

4a. Culms 5-12 dm high, loosely tufted; ligule 1.5 mm or longer; panicle pyramidal, 15-30 cm long .... (5)

4b. Culms 2-5 dm high, densely tufted; ligule 0.5-1.5 mm long; panicle 5-15 cm long, with short ascending branches; lemmas sometimes only scantily webbed. **Poa nemoralis** L. ssp. **interior** (Rydb.) Butters & Abbe. Common on dry road-cuts, rock outcrops and mountainsides, montane and subalpine. The short leaf-blades stand out stiffly at an angle from the stem.

5a. Ligule 1.5-3.0 mm long; leaf blades 3-7 mm wide; lemmas 3-5 mm long; anthers 1.8-3.0 mm long. **Poa tracyi** Vasey. Forest openings, montane and subalpine (*P. occidentalis* [Vasey] Rydb.). Easily known by the very broad leaves and tall stature.

5b. Ligule 3-5 mm long; leaf blades 1-3 mm wide; lemmas 2.5-3.0 mm long, more or less bronze-colored around the tip. **Poa palustris** L. Common in moist places, foothills to subalpine.

KEY D. Alpinae

1a. Lemma pubescent on the keel and marginal nerves .... (2)

1b. Lemma glabrous .... (5)

2a. Basal leaves short and broad, 2-4 mm wide; spikelets broad and broadly rounded or almost cordate at the base. **Poa alpina** L., Fig. 279. Common in dry gravelly trailsides or open slopes, alpine tundra.

2b. Leaves narrow and elongate; spikelets narrow, not broadly rounded at the base .... (3)

3a. Culms 25 cm or less tall; spikelets 2-3 mm long; panicles narrow and condensed; florets perfect; alpine and subalpine ....(4)

3b. Culms usually over 3 dm tall; spikelets 4-5 mm long in a thick, lax panicle, often unisexual; foothills to subalpine. ***Poa fendleriana*** (Steud.) Vasey, MUTTON-GRASS. Common in open forests and occasionally around timberline. The basal leaf-sheaths are long (4-6 cm), papery, and persist for several years.

4a. Leaves stiffly erect, the sheaths not elongate and papery; inflorescence slender, stiff, the branches usually clearly separate; plants forming tight, dense clumps. ***Poa glauca*** Vahl. Alpine and subalpine, on dry sites (*P. rupicola* Nash).

4b. Leaves gracefully curved, the sheaths elongate and papery, to 4-5 cm long, persistent; inflorescence dense but soft and lax; plants forming loose clumps, narrow at the base. ***Poa pattersonii*** Vasey. Wet gravels and frost scars, alpine.

5a. Dwarf alpine 3-10 cm high; spikelets 3-4 mm long; lemmas 2-3 mm long; leaves all alike. ***Poa lettermanii*** Vasey. On the highest peaks, usually above 3,500 meters.

5b. Taller, up to 30 cm high; spikelets 5-7.5 mm long; lemmas 4-4.5 mm long. Culm leaves with broad (2-3 mm) blades, the new basal leaves filiform. ***Poa epilis*** Scribn., SKYLINE BLUE-GRASS. Common on gravelly alpine ridges.

Fig. 279. ***Poa alpina***

KEY E. SCABRELLAE

1a. Lemmas more or less pubescent on the back, keel or nerves, at least toward the base .... (2)
1b. Lemmas merely scabrous or glabrous .... (4)

2a. Spring-flowering and tending to wither and dry by summertime; typically in small tufts with the slender culms much exceeding the basal leaves, and less than 3 dm high. Mesas and foothills. *Poa sandbergii* Vasey (for J. H. Sandberg).
2b. Summer-flowering and summer-active; middle to high altitudes. (3)

3a. Panicle narrow, the branches all strongly ascending. *Poa canbyi* (Scribn.) Piper. Common, mesas to subalpine.
3b. Panicle open, the lower branches at right angles to the axis. *Poa gracillima* Vasey. Subalpine, very likely here but not definitely verified.

4a. Ligule of upper leaves 3-6 mm long, acute or acuminate; sheaths and blades often scabrous, the blades usually folded or involute, bright or pale green; plants of meadows. *Poa nevadensis* Vasey. Moist meadows and bottoms, foothills and montane.
4b. Ligule 1-2 mm long, rounded or obtuse; sheaths smooth or slightly scabrous; plants of drier slopes .... (5)

5a. Blades tightly involute, greenish, 1-2 dm long; plants often in alkaline soils. *Poa juncifolia* Scribn., ALKALI BLUE-GRASS.
5b. Blades flat, usually glaucous, 2-5 dm long; plants in forest openings, never in alkaline flats. *Poa ampla* Merrill.

PODAGROSTIS

1a. Panicle narrow or somewhat open, 3-7 cm long; leaf-blades about 2 mm wide; rachilla prolonged beyond the palea as a minute prong. *Podagrostis thurberiana* (Hitchc.) Hultén (for George Thurber). Subalpine bogs and wet meadows (*Agrostis thurberiana* Hitchc.).
1b. Panicle very narrow, spike-like, 1-4 cm long; leaf-blades 1 mm wide or less; rachilla not prolonged. *Podagrostis humilis* (Vasey) Björkman. Alpine meadows and tundra (*Agrostis humilis* Vasey).

POLYPOGON. RABBITFOOT-GRASS

One species, *Polypogon monspeliensis* (L.) Desf. (of Montpellier). Swamps, roadside ditches, lake shores, on the plains.

PTILAGROSTIS

One species, *Ptilagrostis porteri* (Rydb.) W. A. Weber, Fig. 280. A rare species known in our area from Guanella Pass. It is very closely related to a Central Asiatic species, *P. mongolica*, Fig. 280, and was originally reported as that in 1862. It occurs only on peat hummocks in willow bogs.

Fig. 280. A, ***Ptilagrostis mongolica*** (specimen from USSR); B, ***P. porteri***

PUCCINELLIA. Alkali-grass

1a. Lower panicle branches becoming reflexed at maturity; lemma 1.5-2.0 mm long; first glume less than 1.5 mm long; ligule usually less than 1.5 mm long. *Puccinellia distans* (L.) Parl. (remote), Weeping Alkali-grass. Alkali flats and shores of reservoirs on the plains.

1b. Lower panicle branches spreading but rarely reflexed at maturity; lemma 2-3 mm long; first glume about 1.5 mm long; ligule usually more than 1.5 mm long. *Puccinellia airoides* (Nutt.) Wats. & Coult. (like *Aira*), Nuttall Alkali-grass. Habitats similar to the preceding (*P. nuttalliana* of manuals).

REDFIELDIA. Blowout-grass

One species, *Redfieldia flexuosa* (Thurb.) Vasey (wavy). Common on sandy soil or dunes, chiefly east of the range of this manual.

SCHEDONNARDUS. Tumble-grass

One species, *Schedonnardus paniculatus* (Nutt.) Trel. Frequent on the plains and mesas.

SCHIZACHNE. False Melic

One species, *Schizachne purpurascens* (Torr.) Swallen (purplish). Rare or infrequent, deep forests, foothills and montane.

SCHIZACHYRIUM. Little Bluestem

One species, *Schizachyrium scoparium* (Michx.) Nash (broom-like). Plains and mesas, less common in the outer foothills. The culms turn pink or reddish-brown in the autumn. A relictual species of the mid-grass prairie that once extended continuously to the base of the Rockies (*Andropogon scoparius* of Ed. 4).

SCLEROPOGON. Burro-grass

One species, *Scleropogon brevifolius* Phil. A shortgrass plains species barely entering our area from the south, on the north side of the Arkansas River between Pueblo and Canon City. Marked by the extreme difference between the male and female spikelets.

SECALE. Rye

One species, *Secale cereale* L. Cultivated on the plains and piedmont valleys and sown as a nurse crop on depleted soils. Escaping to roadsides.

SETARIA. Bristle-grass

1a. Bristles downwardly barbed; panicle branches distinct. *Setaria verticillata* (L.) P. Beauv. A weed in cultivated ground on the plains.

1b. Bristles upwardly barbed; panicle branches crowded into a dense spike ....(2)

2a. Fertile lemma strongly transversely wrinkled; 5 to 16 bristles below each spikelet; second glume not over ⅔ the length of the spikelet; spikelets yellow at maturity, about 3 mm long. *Setaria glauca* (L.) P. Beauv. Common weed in cultivated ground.

2b. Fertile lemma only faintly wrinkled; 1 to 3 bristles below each spikelet; second glume about as long as the spikelet; spikelets green at maturity, about 2.5 mm long. *Setaria viridis* (L.) P. Beauv. Common weed in cultivated ground.

SITANION. Squirreltail

1a. Lowermost floret of one or both spikelets at each rachis node sterile and reduced to a subulate or lanceolate structure, giving the appearance of extra glume segments. *Sitanion hystrix* (Nutt.) J. G. Smith. Common on disturbed ground, plains to subalpine.

1b. Lowermost floret of each spikelet fertile, not reduced. *Sitanion longifolium* J. G. Smith. Similar habitats, evidently the more abundant of the two.

SORGHASTRUM. Indian-grass

One species, *Sorghastrum avenaceum* (Michx.) Nash (like oats). Frequent in grasslands on the mesas and plains, a tall grass of late summer, with soft, reddish-gold panicles. A relictual mid-grass prairie species (*S. nutans* of Ed. 4).

SORGHUM. Johnson-grass

One species, *Sorghum halepense* (L.) Pers. (of Aleppo), cultivated for forage and escaping to roadsides. This species is perennial, whereas the cultivated *Sorghum vulgare* Pers. (broom-corm, sudan-grass, sorghum, kaffir-corn) is annual.

SPARTINA. Cord-grass

1a. Blades usually more than 5 mm wide, flat when fresh, at least at the base, the tip involute; plants very robust, more than a meter tall. *Spartina pectinata* Link (comb-like), Prairie Cord-grass. A tall grass of sloughs and irrigation ditches on the plains, with large, brush-like spikes, and long, curved leaves. Plant up to 2 or 3 meters tall.

1b. Blades less than 5 mm wide, rarely wider, involute or flat; plants slender and less than 1 meter tall. *Spartina gracilis* Trin. (slender), Alkali Cordgrass. Alkaline flats and sloughs, on the plains.

SPHENOPHOLIS. Wedge-grass

One species, *Sphenopholis obtusata* (Michx.) Scribn. (blunt), Prairie Wedge-grass. Sloughs and irrigation ditches and moist canyon-bottoms, plains to lower foothills. *S. intermedia* of Ed. 4 is now *S. obtusata* var. *major* (Torr.) Erdman.

SPOROBOLUS. Dropseed

1a. Spikelets over 3.5 mm long .... (3)
1b. Spikelets less than 3.5 mm long .... (2)

2a. Panicle branchlets appressed to main branches at maturity; second glume and lemma scabrously keeled; collar pilose well around to the back. *Sporobolus cryptandrus* (Torr.) Gray (with hidden flowers), Sand Dropseed. Abundant on sandy or adobe soil, plains and mesas. The culms are often strongly curved, partly enclosing the panicle.
2b. Panicle branchlets not appressed at maturity; second glume and lemma rounded and glabrous on the back; collar sometimes pilose on margins but glabrous on back. *Sporobolus airoides* (Torr.) Torr. (resembling *Aira*), Alkali Sacaton. Sandy or alkaline flats on the plains.

3a. Panicle open; glumes about equal. *Sporobolus heterolepis* (Gray) Gray (referring to the glumes, one broad, one narrow), Prairie Dropseed. Very rare, on the mesas.
3b. Panicle spike-like; glumes of different lengths. *Sporobolus asper* (Michx.) Kunth. Infrequent, piedmont valleys.

STIPA. Needle-grass

1a. Awn partly or completely plumose. *Stipa neomexicana* (Thurb.) Scribn., New Mexican Feather-grass. Frequent on the mesas and hogbacks.
1b. Awn not plumose, but may have appressed hairs .... (2)

2a. Awn usually over 7 cm long; lemma over 8 mm long; glumes over 15 mm long .... (3)
2b. Awns less than 7 cm long; lemma less than 7 mm long (if longer, then pubescent at apex); glumes less than 15 mm long .... (4)

3a. Lemma over 15 mm long; glumes over 3 cm long; leaves 3-5 mm wide. *Stipa spartea* Trin. (broom-like), Porcupine-grass. Rare, mesas and plains.
3b. Lemma less than 15 mm long; glumes less than 3 cm long; leaves 1-3 mm wide. *Stipa comata* Trin. & Rupr. (with tufts of hair), Needle-and-thread, Fig. 281. The most common *Stipa*, from plains to upper montane.

4a. Sheaths villous at the throat, one margin ciliate; lemma over 6 mm long .... (5)
4b. Sheaths not villous at the throat, margins not ciliate; lemma usually less than 6 mm long. *Stipa occidentalis* Thurber *ex* Wats. Common in open forests, foothills to subalpine (*S. columbiana* of Ed. 4). *Stipa lettermanii* Vasey is a doubtfully separable relative with short awns and small technical differences.

5a. Hairs at apex of lemma over 2 mm long; awn less than 2 cm long;

glumes 10-15 mm long. ***Stipa scribneri*** Vasey (for F. L. Scribner). Rare, on mesas and outer foothills.

5b. Hairs at apex of lemma less than 2 mm long; awns over 2 cm long; glumes 7-11 mm long ....(6)

6a. Lemma 6-8 mm long; ligules over 1.5 mm long; nerves of glumes not especially conspicuous; panicle usually dense. ***Stipa robusta*** (Vasey) Scribn., SLEEPYGRASS. Common on the mesas. The plant has a mild narcotic effect on grazing animals, hence the name.

6b. Lemma 5-6 mm long; ligules less than 1.5 mm long; nerves of glumes conspicuous, green when young; panicle usually looser. ***Stipa viridula*** Trin., GREEN NEEDLE-GRASS. Mesas and outer foothills.

TORREYOCHLOA

One species, ***Torreyochloa pauciflora*** (Presl) Church (few-flowered), WEAK MANNA-GRASS. Margins of subalpine ponds (*Glyceria pauciflora* of manuals).

TRIDENS

One species, ***Tridens elongatus*** (Buckl.) Nash. Locally abundant on an outer foothill slope near Lyons.

TRISETUM

1a. Awn minute, included within the glumes or sometimes lacking. ***Trisetum wolfii*** Vasey (for John Wolf). Infrequent, usually with the stems solitary and intermixed with other grasses, swamps and pond margins, subalpine. Once learned, this is easily recognized, but generally overlooked.

Fig. 281. ***Stipa comata***

1b. Awn large, exserted, divergent ....(2)

2a. Panicle dense, thick, often purple; culms densely pilose to nearly
tomentose below the panicle; upper subalpine and alpine. ***Trisetum
spicatum*** (L.) Richt. ssp. ***spicatum***, Fig. 282. Abundant and striking
species when typically developed, but intergrading with the next.
2b. Panicle slender, greenish-straw-colored, rarely with purple tints;
culms almost or clearly glabrous below the panicle; foothills to
subalpine ....(3)

3a. Panicle branches short, not lax. ***Trisetum spicatum*** ssp. ***majus*** Hultén.
Dry forested areas.
3b. Panicle branches elongate, loose. ***Trisetum spicatum*** ssp. ***montanum***
(Vasey) W. A. Weber. This is a very complicated group of which the
above are simply distinguishable nodes of variation. The complex has so
far defied taxonomic analysis. The characters noted above may occur in
other combinations than those given.

TRITICUM. Wheat

One species, ***Triticum aestivum*** L. (of summer). Many varieties are
cultivated, and plants frequently escape and survive for a season along
roadsides and trails of the plains and piedmont valleys.

VAHLODEA

One species, ***Vahlodea atropurpurea*** (Wahlenb.) E. Fries ssp. ***latifolia***
(Hook.) Porsild. Subalpine meadows and rocky gorges on soil of ledges.
The spikelets are usually dark purple, but a pale phase is occasionally
found.

Fig. 282. ***Trisetum spicatum***

VULPIA. Six-weeks Fescue

One species, *Vulpia octoflora* (Walt.) Rydb. Spikelets with 7 or more florets; leaves short, some less than 5 cm long. Common in disturbed soil and on dry slopes, plains and foothills (*Festuca octoflora* Walt.).

HYDROCHARITACEAE—FROGBIT FAMILY

The floral biology of *Elodea,* our only genus, can only be described as bizarre. The plant is submerged. How does pollination take place? The staminate flowers, formed under water, break away and float to the surface, liberating the pollen to the surface film of water. The carpellate flowers are produced on long thread-like stalks that remain attached to the main stem but grow to reach the water surface where the stigmas accidentally encounter the floating pollen.

We have, by conservative standards, one species, *Elodea canadensis* Rich. in Michx., which may be divided into three, including *E. longivaginata* St. John and *E. nuttallii* (Planch.) St. John. The characters used to separate them may or may not be variable, and the little material we have of the genus seems to belong to one of these species, but much more is needed to settle their identity.

IRIDACEAE—IRIS FAMILY

Irises need no introduction. Our wild species is so much like some of the cultivated types as to be instantly recognized. Recognition of the floral parts is not as easy. The perianth consists of three outer hanging "falls" and three inner erect or over-arching "standards." The three spreading flat structures that cover and hide the three stamens are the style branches. The folded-triangular grooved leaves of the equitant type are common to Iridaceae and Juncaceae. Other well-known Iridaceae in cultivation are the spring-blooming *Crocus* and *Gladiolus*.

1a. Flowers more than 5 cm wide; sepals spreading or reflexed; petals erect; fruit a cylindrical capsule. *Iris missouriensis* Nutt., Wild Iris, Fig. 283. Abundant in wet meadows, mesas to subalpine.

1b. Flowers less than 2 cm wide; all perianth segments alike and spreading; fruit a round berry or capsule. *Sisyrinchium montanum* Greene, Blue-eyed-grass. Common on grassy slopes, mesas to subalpine.

JUNCACEAE—RUSH FAMILY

The rushes form a neat little group whose diversity of small technical characters should appeal to the biometrically inclined. Vegetatively resembling both the grasses and sedges, they can always be recognized by their small brownish or greenish miniature lily flowers with all floral parts present. As in the sedges, some species display inflorescences on what seems to be the side of the stem, while the lowest bract stands erect and appears to continue the stem to the apex. Since this tendency occurs in several unrelated marsh plants (convergent evolution), one might speculate that this life form may present less resistance to wind than a terminal inflorescence and thus prevent "lodging" of the culms in areas of marshland swept by strong winds.

1a. Plants glabrous; leaf-sheaths with the margins overlapping but not fused; ovary usually more or less 3-loculed; ovules numerous. *Juncus*, RUSH, page 426.

1b. Plants with a few long soft hairs along the leaf-blades or sheaths; leaf-sheaths with the margins fused; ovary with one locule; ovules three. *Luzula*, WOOD-RUSH, page 431.

JUNCUS. RUSH

1a. Annual; inflorescence making up half the height of the plant or more .... (2)

1b. Perennial, or if appearing annual, the inflorescence making up less than half the height of the plant .... (3)

2a. Capsule oblong, 3.0-4.5 mm long; perianth 4-6 mm long. *Juncus bufonius* L., TOAD RUSH. Muddy pond shores, roadside depressions, plains to subalpine.

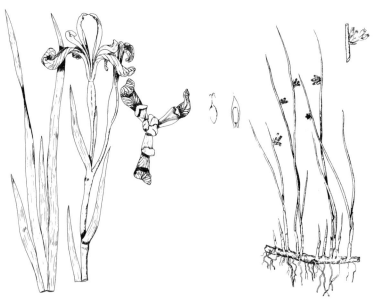

Fig. 283. *Iris missouriensis*   Fig. 284. *Juncus arcticus*

2b. Capsule subglobose, 2-3 mm long; perianth 3-4 mm long. *Juncus bufonius* L. var. *occidentalis* F. J. Hermann. Similar habitats, but rare.

3a. Lowest leaf of the inflorescence erect, terete, and appearing to be a continuation of the stem; inflorescence appearing to be lateral. (4)
3b. Lowest leaf of the inflorescence divergent, not appearing to be a continuation of the stem, *or if so, then the leaf grooved along the inner side;* inflorescence appearing terminal .... (8)

4a. Creeping rhizomes present; seeds with a short white "tail" at each end .... (5)
4b. Rhizomes absent; seed with a long white tail at each end .... (6)

5a. Stems with the flower cluster more than half-way up. *Juncus arcticus* Willd. ssp. *ater* (Rydb.) Hultén, Fig. 284. Abundant along streams, lake-shores and alkali flats, plains to subalpine (*J. balticus* Willd.).
5b. Stems with the flower clusters within a few centimeters of the ground, the portion of the stem above the flower cluster many times as long as that below it. *Juncus filiformis* L. Similar habitats, rare, but perhaps overlooked.

6a. Upper leaf-sheaths bristle-tipped, the blade lacking; capsule blunt and depressed at the tip. *Juncus drummondii* Mey. (for Thomas Drummond), Fig. 285. Very common alpine tundra plant, forming conspicuous tufts.
6b. Upper leaf-sheaths bearing blades .... (7)

7a. Capsule pointed at the tip. *Juncus parryi* Engelm. (for C. C. Parry). Wet places, subalpine.
7b. Capsule broad and depressed at the tip. *Juncus hallii* Engelm. (for Elihu Hall). Wet places, rare, subalpine.

8a. Leaves septate within (having papery cross-partitions visible when the leaf is slit lengthwise); leaves hollow, terete or folded like the leaves of *Iris* .... (9)
8b. Leaves not septate; leaf-blades flat or folded, never hollow or pulpy or folded V-shaped as in *Iris* .... (23)

9a. Inflorescence consisting of a solitary capitate cluster of from 1 to 5 flowers; leaves mostly shorter than 8 cm .... (10)
9b. Inflorescence consisting of several clusters of more than 5 flowers each; leaves over 8 cm long .... (12)

10a. Inflorescence terminal, without subtending bracts that are longer than the flowers, the flower cluster not appearing pushed to one side .... (11)
10b. Inflorescence with subtending bract longer than the flower cluster and standing erect, pushing the cluster to the side. *Juncus biglumis* L. Rare, in wet gravels and frost scars on the higher peaks. Bracts and perianth segments always very dark.

11a. Bracts and perianth uniformly dark reddish-brown; plants of wet gravel frost scars in the upper subalpine and tundra. *Juncus triglumis* L.
11b. Bracts paler, the perianth very pale or white; plants of subalpine peat bogs. *Juncus albescens* (Lange) Fernald.

12a. Leaf-blades like those of *Iris* (thick and pulpy and folded V-shaped), or involute .... (13)
12b. Leaf-blades terete (round in cross-section) or somewhat flattened. .... (15)

13a. Leaf-blades involute, mostly basal. *Juncus castaneus* Smith (chestnut-colored). Subalpine and alpine bogs and run-off streams.
13b. Leaf-blades equitant (overlapping in two ranks, like leaves of *Iris*) .... (14)

14a. Heads hemispheric, dark purple-black; styles exserted; seeds prominently tailed. *Juncus tracyi* Rydb. Wet places, especially roadsides, subalpine and montane.
14b. Heads more nearly spherical, brown; styles not prominent; seeds not tailed. *Juncus saximontanus* Nels. Swampy places, piedmont valleys to subalpine. Often growing with the last at higher altitudes.

15a. Capsules subulate (very narrow and sharp-pointed); flower clusters spherical .... (16)
15b. Capsules oblong with pointed tip, or abruptly narrowed to a beak from a rounded apex .... (17)

16a. Leaf-blade divergent from the stem; inner perianth whorl shorter than the outer; plants usually very robust; flower clusters usually over 1 cm in diameter. *Juncus torreyi* Cov. (for John Torrey). Common in sloughs and ditches, plains and piedmont valleys.
16b. Leaf-blade erect; inner perianth whorl longer than the outer; plants usually slender; flower clusters usually less than 1 cm in diameter. *Juncus nodosus* L. (knotted; from the rhizomes, which are thickened at intervals). Similar habitats.

17a. Head solitary, purplish-black, rarely more than one; each flower head usually exceeded by its lowest bract. *Juncus mertensianus* Bong. (for F. C. Mertens), SUBALPINE RUSH, Fig. 286. Subalpine and alpine, in swampy woodlands, bogs, and pond shores.
17b. Heads not solitary, nor purplish black, nor exceeded by the lowest bract; at least a few heads pedunculate .... (18)

18a. Flower clusters few (1 to 3), close together, dark, the perianth segments about as dark as the capsule; capsule abruptly mucronate from a rounded or flattened tip. *Juncus mertensianus* ssp. *gracilis* (Engelm.) F. J. Hermann. Infrequent, subalpine (*J. badius* Suksdorf).
18b. Flower clusters numerous, on stiffly divergent peduncles, the light-colored bracts contrasting with the darker perianth segments and capsules .... (19)

19a. Seeds with definite caudate tips ("tails") ....(20)
19b. Seeds merely dark-pointed or blunt, not caudate ....(21)

20a. Sepals and the acute petals firm, often rather rigid; seeds spindle-shaped, with conspicuous tails half as long as the body. ***Juncus brevicaudatus*** (Engelm.) Fern. Rare, in sloughs, Black Forest.
20b. Sepals and the blunt petals soft and thin-margined; seeds ellipsoid, with short tails 1/10 the length of the body. ***Juncus brachycephalus*** (Engelm.) Buch. Rare, with the preceding.

21a. Stamens 3 (this may be determined by dissection even in the fruiting condition, since the filaments are persistent). ***Juncus acuminatus*** Michx. Rare, on drying mudflats of the ponds in the piedmont valleys.
21b. Stamens 6 ....(22)

22a. Perianth segments acuminate; branches of the inflorescence divergent; plants often strongly stoloniferous. ***Juncus articulatus*** L. Introduced and established along streams in the piedmont valleys.
22b. Perianth segments blunt; branches of the inflorescence erect or ascending; rhizomes present, but plant not stoloniferous. ***Juncus alpinus*** Vill. Infrequent, in often alkaline mud, montane and subalpine.

Fig. 285. ***Juncus drummondii***   Fig. 286. ***Juncus mertensianus***

23a. Each flower subtended by a single bract; flowers grouped in heads.
....(24)
23b. Flowers each subtended by two small bracts; flowers scattered along the branches (if the inflorescence is condensed, the short branchlets are still discernible) ....(25)

24a. Bracts broad and papery; capsule twice to three times as long as wide; perianth 4-6 mm long. *Juncus longistylis* Torr. Swamps and ponds, montane and subalpine.
24b. Bracts subulate, green; capsule as wide as long; perianth 2-3 mm long. *Juncus marginatus* Rostk. Rare, in swampy places on the plains and piedmont valleys.

25a. Plants with long creeping rhizomes; sepals with incurved tips, clasping the capsule ....(26)
25b. Plants in tufts, without rhizomes; sepals with straight or spreading tips, standing away from the capsule ....(27)

26a. Culms and leaves green, not flattened; anthers about three times the length of the filaments; capsule ellipsoid-ovoid, equalling or only slightly exceeding the perianth. *Juncus gerardii* Loisel (for Louis Gérard), BLACK-GRASS. A salt-marsh species of the Atlantic coast, locally established around ponds in the piedmont valleys (introduced by waterfowl?).
26b. Culms and leaves glaucous, flattened; anthers only slightly longer than the filaments; capsule globose-obovoid, distinctly longer than the perianth. *Juncus compressus* L. Similar sites.

27a. Capsule completely separated internally into three locules. *Juncus confusus* Cov., COLORADO RUSH. Around springs, and in swampy meadows, plains to subalpine. The flower-cluster in this species is characteristically rather compact, without branches of varying lengths, as opposed to the next two species, which typically have rather open clusters. See Addenda.
27b. Capsule incompletely 3-loculed, the septa never meeting ..... (28)

28a. Leaf-auricles cartilaginous and yellowish; perianth spreading; capsule ovate. *Juncus dudleyi* Wieg. (for W. R. Dudley). Swampy places on the plains and mesas.
28b. Leaf-auricles membranous, thin at the margins; perianth appressed or directed forward; capsule oblong ....(29)

29a. Auricles of uninjured leaf-sheath prolonged or tongue-like; plants dwarf, up to 20 cm high, the short tuft of basal leaves with reddish sheaths. *Juncus platyphyllus* (Wieg.) Fern. Rare, found occasionally on drying pond margins, piedmont valleys.
29b. Auricles of uninjured leaf-sheath gradually rounded, following the curve of the sheath-summit, scarcely prolonged; plants usually tall, 3-6 dm high, the leaves elongate with brownish or reddish sheaths. *Juncus interior* Wieg. Common on the mesas and lower foothills.

LUZULA. Wood-rush

1a. Flowers on slender pedicels in a loose, drooping, many-flowered panicle; foliage glabrous except for a few long hairs near the throat of the leaf-sheath; perianth about 2 mm long, shorter than or barely equalling the capsule. *Luzula parviflora* (Ehrh.) Desv. (small-flowered), Wood-rush. Common in moist or swampy montane and subalpine woodlands.

1b. Flowers crowded, subsessile, in a few heads or spikes; foliage sparsely villous with long, loose hairs; perianth longer than the capsule ... (2)

2a. Leaves 1-4 mm wide, with subulate (often involute) tips; bracts at bases of flowers ciliate-fimbriate; mostly alpine; spikes usually nodding. *Luzula spicata* (L.) DC., Spike Wood-rush, Fig. 287. Very common on tundra and higher subalpine slopes.

2b. Leaves usually broader, flat, with blunt callous tips; bracts at bases of flowers entire or merely lacerate .... (3)

3a. Spikes short-cylindric, short-peduncled, the bracts and perianth segments pale brownish or straw-colored, the capsules darker brown; leaf-blades less than 5 mm wide. *Luzula multiflora* (Retz) Lejeune. Subalpine streamsides and pond margins.

3b. Spikes capitate, sessile or a few long-peduncled, the perianth segments almost as dark as the deep brown capsules; leaf-blades 5-8 mm wide. *Luzula subcapitata* (Rydb.) Harrington. Subalpine and alpine bogs.

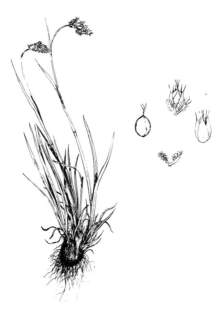

Fig. 287. *Luzula spicata*

JUNCAGINACEAE—ARROW-GRASS FAMILY

This is a very small family with about 16 species world-wide of which all but one belong to *Triglochin*. The genus is marked by its grass-like habit and slender racemes of greenish, inconspicuous flowers.

1a. Plants stout, from thick creeping rhizomes; carpels usually 6; fruit about twice as long as thick. ***Triglochin maritimum*** L., ARROW-GRASS, Fig. 288. Alkaline flats on the plains. The flower spikes resemble those of the common plantain, but the leaves are grass-like.

1b. Plants very slender, from slender rhizomes; carpels 3; fruit linear, much longer than thick. ***Triglochin palustre*** L. (of marshes), ARROW-GRASS, Fig. 288. Bogs and pond shores, subalpine and montane.

LEMNACEAE—DUCKWEED FAMILY

The duckweeds are the world's smallest flowering plants. The shoots are reduced to little floating or submerged disks or paddles with slotted sides from which new shoots and flowers arise. The flowers are very rarely produced and consist of a single stamen or carpel. Discovery of fruiting duckweed is an event worth celebrating. Duckweeds thrive under eutrophic conditions, hence can become real pests in waterways with too much nutritive material.

Fig. 288. ***Triglochin maritimum*** (left); ***T. palustre*** (right)

1a. Rootlets several; plant body prominently several-nerved, usually purple underneath. ***Spirodela polyrhiza*** (L.) Schleiden (many-rooted), Fig. 289. Ponds and sluggish streams on the plains and piedmont valleys.

1b. Rootlet solitary; plant body few-nerved, usually obscurely so, not purple underneath .... (2)

2a. Plant submerged; segments oblong, 6-10 mm long, stalked at the base, remaining connected in short chains. ***Lemna trisulca*** L. (three-furrowed), STAR DUCKWEED, Fig. 289.

2b. Plant floating; segments sessile or nearly so, soon separating, not more than 5 mm long .... (3)

3a. Lower surface strongly gibbous (swollen) and much paler than the upper; segments asymmetric, suborbicular or obovate. ***Lemna gibba*** L. (swollen). Forming floating masses on ponds and slow streams, mostly on the plains.

3b. Lower surface flat or nearly so; segments oblong-obovate or suborbicular, symmetrical or nearly so. ***Lemna minor*** L. (smaller), Fig. 289. In similar habitats and much more abundant.

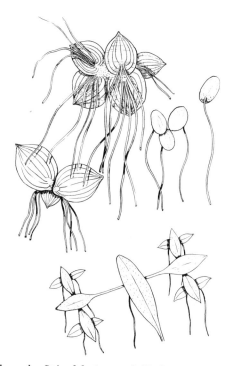

Fig. 289. Duckweeds: ***Spirodela*** (upper left), ***Lemna minor*** (upper right), ***Lemna trisulca*** (below)

LILIACEAE—LILY FAMILY

The lily flower is the model of the monocots, perfect in its symmetry with the parts all alternating in threes. It probably has received more study from beginning botany students than any other single flower and is a good place to learn the basic flower structure. Unfortunately, the uniformity of the flowers in a number of closely related families tended to result in their placement in this family. Recent research shows that the onions, yuccas, smilax, and asparagus deserve to be separated off into their own families.

1a. Leaves appearing basal, the cauline ones, when present, much reduced; leaves narrowly linear or grasslike, or, if broader, then definitely basal . . . . (2)
1b. Leaves arising at nodes on the main stem, and not reduced. (7)

2a. Flowers solitary or few . . . . (3)
2b. Flowers in racemes or panicles . . . . (6)

3a. Leaves linear, grass-like; flowers white; perianth segments erect or at most spreading . . . . (4)
3b. Leaves elliptic, not grass-like; flowers yellow with recurved perianth segments. **Erythronium grandiflorum** Pursh, AVALANCHE LILY, Fig. 297. Locally abundant on subalpine slopes, particularly near melting snowbanks. Most plants have yellow anthers, but some populations have a small percentage with red anthers.

4a. Inner perianth segments petal-like, much larger and broader than the outer, and with a conspicuous glandular pad on the inner face. **Calochortus gunnisonii** Wats. (for J. W. Gunnison), MARIPOSA or SEGO LILY, Fig. 298. Common on meadow slopes from the mesas to the lower alpine. Very dwarf at high elevations.
4b. Inner perianth segments similar to the outer, all petal-like; gland lacking . . . . (5)

5a. Perianth united to form a long tube, the base buried among the basal leaves; plants of the plains and mesas. **Leucocrinum montanum** Nutt., SAND LILY, Plate 16, Fig. 299. One of the earliest and best-known spring flowers.
5b. Perianth segments separate; stems bearing a few reduced leaves; plants of alpine tundra. **Lloydia serotina** (L.) Sw. (late-ripening), ALP LILY, Fig. 300. Common on alpine and higher subalpine slopes. Flowers white or greenish-white. This species has one of the most remarkable disjunct distributions of alpine plants, occurring in the mountains of western United States, Siberia, the Alps and Caucasus and the Himalaya, but absent in the American Arctic and northern Europe except for a few localities in Great Britain. Probably a very ancient species.

6a. Perianth segments 7-11 mm long; stamens not distinctly longer than the perianth; flowers in racemes, rarely somewhat paniculate.

Zigadenus elegans Pursh, Death Camas, Fig. 301. Common in subalpine meadows and lower tundra. The bulbs are extremely poisonous.

6b. Perianth segments about 4 mm long; stamens distinctly longer than the perianth; flowers in racemes or panicles. **Zigadenus venenosus** Wats. var. **gramineus** (Rydb.) Walsh *ex* M. Peck, Death Camas. Common in meadows on the plains and mesas (*Zigadenus* is the original spelling).

7a. Flowers red or orange, with dark spots; leaves broadly linear, scattered or tending to be whorled. **Lilium philadelphicum** L., Wood Lily, Plate 8, Fig. 291. Rare in ravines, foothills and montane. This is a truly endangered species and should never be collected. It has never been common and evidently is fast disappearing where unprotected.

7b. Flowers white or yellowish; leaves ovate or elliptic, alternate in two ranks .... (8)

8a. Stems simple; flowers in terminal racemes or panicles .... (9)

8b. Stems branched; flowers solitary or in few-flowered clusters ... (11)

9a. Tall, rank plants up to 2-3 meters tall with strongly pleated leaves and pyramidal panicles of greenish-white flowers; forming dense clumps on overgrazed subalpine meadows. **Veratrum tenuipetalum** Heller, Corn Husk Lily, Plate 25, Fig. 292.

9b. Low herbs usually not over a meter tall, solitary or a few together in shaded places, the leaves not strongly plicate .... (10)

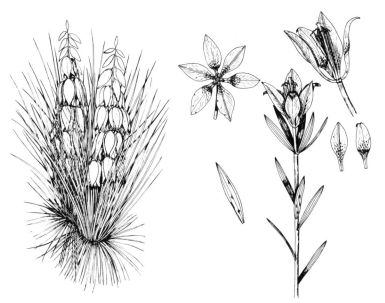

Fig. 290. *Yucca glauca*   Fig. 291. *Lilium philadelphicum*

10a. Flowers few, in a raceme. ***Smilacina stellata*** (L.) Desf. (starry), FEW-FLOWERED FALSE SOLOMON'S SEAL, Fig. 293. Cool, shaded ravines, from the plains to subalpine.

10b. Flowers numerous, in a panicle. ***Smilacina racemosa*** (L.) Desf. var. ***amplexicaulis*** Wats., FALSE SOLOMON'S SEAL, Fig. 294. In similar habitats.

11a. Flowers axillary, dangling at the ends of slender pedicels; perianth segments recurved; plant glabrous. ***Streptopus amplexifolius*** (L.) DC. (clasping-leaved), TWISTED-STALK, Fig. 295. Cool, shaded ravines, foothills to subalpine. Berry round, red.

11b. Flowers appearing terminal at the ends of the branches, on stout pedicels; perianth segments erect; plant pubescent. ***Disporum trachycarpum*** (Wats.) Britt. (rough-fruited). In similar habitats. Berry angular, orange.

NAJADACEAE—WATER-NYMPH FAMILY

One species, *Najas guadalupensis* (Spreng.) Magnus, Fig. 302. Frequent in ponds in the piedmont valleys.

Fig. 292. *Veratrum tenuipetalum*   Fig. 293. *Smilacina stellata*

ORCHIDACEAE—ORCHID FAMILY

Paradoxically, the orchid family is the second largest family of flowering plants considering numbers of species, and probably contains more rare and endangered species than any other large family. Their delicately tuned pollination mechanisms, symbiotic relationships with fungi, narrow ecological amplitudes and extremely specialized structure make it difficult for many species to survive in large numbers. In Colorado the species growing in very wet places tend to be in little danger of extinction, while those that grow on dry or only seasonally moist forest floors are very rare and endangered. John Long wrote a beautifully illustrated booklet on the Colorado Orchids in the Denver Natural History Museum's Pictorial series, which every orchid-lover should have as a supplement to this book.

1a. Plants without green leaves, saprophytic or parasitic .... (2)
1b. Plants with green leaves .... (5)

2a. Lip streaked, not spotted, with purple. ***Corallorhiza striata*** Lindl., STRIPED CORAL-ROOT. Infrequent in foothills and subalpine forests.
2b. Lip plain or spotted with purple .... (3)

3a. Lip white, not spotted; sepals and petals 1-nerved; plants usually yellowish. ***Corallorhiza trifida*** Chat. (3-cleft), LITTLE YELLOW CORAL-ROOT. Frequent in subalpine forests.
3b. Lip usually spotted with purple; sepals and petals 3-nerved; plants usually tinged with purple (except for rare albinos that are yellow). (4)

Fig. 294. ***Smilacina racemosa***   Fig. 295. ***Streptopus amplexifolius***

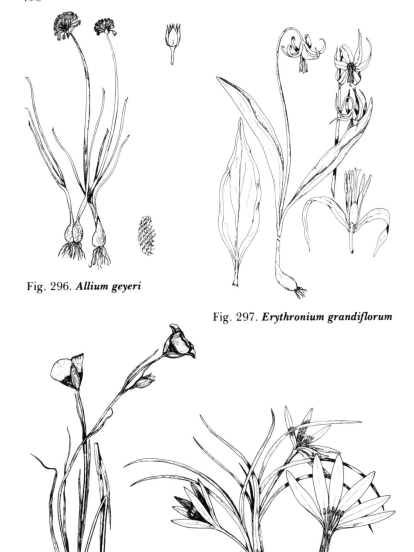

Fig. 296. *Allium geyeri*

Fig. 297. *Erythronium grandiflorum*

Fig. 298. *Calochortus gunnisonii*

Fig. 299. *Leucocrinum montanum*

4a. Lip unequally three-lobed, the two side lobes near the base of the lip. **Corallorhiza maculata** Raf., SPOTTED CORAL-ROOT. The most common species, found in dry woodlands from foothills to subalpine, flowering in summer.

4b. Lip narrowed at the base but not lobed. **Corallorhiza wisteriana** Conrad (for C. J. Wister), SPRING CORAL-ROOT. Smaller and more slender than the last, flowering earlier in the spring, foothills and montane.

5a. Lip of corolla a large, conspicuous slipper-shaped inflated sac. (6)

5b. Lip of corolla not as above . . . . (8)

6a. Flowers yellow or purple; leaves 2 or more; slipper rounded . . . (7)

6b. Flowers pink; leaf solitary, basal; slipper pointed. **Calypso bulbosa** (L.) Oakes, FAIRY SLIPPER, Plate 18, Fig. 303. Locally abundant in deep moist forests, foothills to subalpine. Endangered.

7a. Flowers yellow. **Cypripedium calceolus** L. ssp. **parviflorum** (Salisb.) Hultén (a small shoe; small-flowered), YELLOW LADY'S SLIPPER. Rare and almost exterminated by wild flower "lovers," foothills to subalpine. Endangered.

7b. Flowers purple or dull brown-purple. **Cypripedium fasciculatum** Kellogg *ex* Wats. (clustered), PURPLE LADY'S SLIPPER, Plate 20. Very rare, subalpine slopes, usually in the shelter of small firs. Endangered.

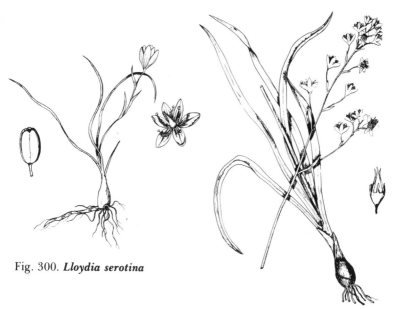

Fig. 300. **Lloydia serotina**

Fig. 301. **Zigadenus elegans**

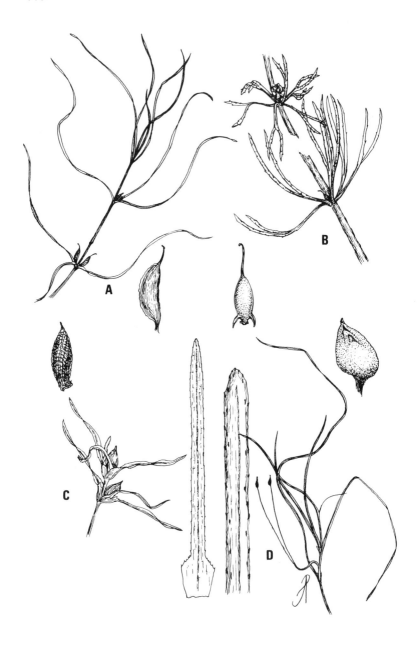

Fig. 302. A, *Zannichellia*; B, *Ceratophyllum*; C, *Najas*; D, *Ruppia*

8a. Flowers with definite spurs .... (9)
8b. Flowers lacking spurs, the lip sometimes saccate at the base .... (14)

9a. Bracts leaflike, several times longer than the flowers; lip of corolla 2-3-lobed at the apex. ***Coeloglossum viride*** (L.) Hartm. ssp. ***bracteatum*** (Muehl.) Hultén, GREEN BOG-ORCHID. Cool montane and subalpine forests (*Habenaria* of Ed. 4).
9b. Bracts not leaflike, shorter; lip of corolla entire .... (10)

10a. Leaf solitary, basal. ***Lysiella obtusata*** (Banks *ex* Pursh) Britt. & Rydb. Mossy streamsides, montane and subalpine.
10b. Leaves several, usually cauline but sometimes almost basal .... (11)

11a. Flowers white; lip rhombic-lanceolate, dilated at the base. ***Limnorchis dilatata*** (Pursh) Rydb. ssp. ***albiflora*** (Cham.) Löve & Simon, WHITE BOG-ORCHID, Fig. 304. Wet meadows and shores of subalpine ponds (*Habenaria* of Ed. 4).
11b. Flowers greenish; lip lanceolate to linear, not dilated at the base. (12)

12a. Inflorescence slender; flowers remote from each other (the spur may or may not be saccate) .... (13)
12b. Inflorescence stout; flowers crowded; spur never saccate. ***Limnorchis hyperborea*** (L.) Rydb. (far-northern), NORTHERN BOG-ORCHID. Moist streamsides, foothills to subalpine (*Habenaria* of Ed. 4).

Fig. 303. *Calypso bulbosa*    Fig. 304. *Limnorchis dilatata*

13a. Leaves grouped near the base of the stem; inflorescence very slender, up to 30 cm long; floral bracts ovate, shorter than the ovary; perianth small. *Piperia unalascensis* (Spreng.) Rydb. (of Unalaska), ALASKAN ORCHIS. Very rare, in cool foothills ravines. Endangered.

13b. Leaves distributed the length of the stem; inflorescence usually stouter, less than 20 cm long; floral bracts linear or lanceolate, equalling or exceeding the ovary. *Limnorchis saccata* (Greene) Löve & Simons. Swampy subalpine forests. Very closely related to *L. hyperborea* and possibly a race of it.

14a. Blade-bearing leaf solitary. *Malaxis monophylla* (L.) Sw. ssp. *brachypoda* (Gray) Löve & Löve, WHITE ADDERS-MOUTH. Extremely rare and endangered, foothills near Boulder.

14b. Blade-bearing leaves more than one .... (15)

15a. Stem leaves present .... (16)

15b. Stem leaves absent, or the leaves at least appearing to be basal, usually white along veins .... (17)

16a. Leaves 2, opposite, near the middle of the stem; inflorescence not spiral-twisted .... (18)

16b. Leaves more than 2, alternate; inflorescence conspicuously spiral-twisted. *Spiranthes romanzoffiana* Cham. & Schl. (for Count Romanzoff), LADY'S TRESSES. Common in subalpine bogs.

17a. Leaves 1-3 cm long; raceme rather loosely-flowered; lip saccate, with a flaring or recurved margin. *Goodyera repens* (L.) R. Br. (creeping), SMALL RATTLESNAKE-PLANTAIN. Very rare and endangered, in foothills and montane forests.

17b. Leaves 5-10 cm long; raceme rather densely-flowered; lip scarcely saccate, with an involute margin. *Goodyera oblongifolia* Raf., COMMON RATTLESNAKE-PLANTAIN. Frequent in cool ravines in the foothills and subalpine, threatened or endangered.

18a. Corolla lip oblong or linear, 2-cleft for half its length. *Listera cordata* (L.) R. Br. ssp. *nephrophylla* (Rydb.) Löve & Löve, TWAYBLADE. Frequent, moist subalpine forests and cool foothills ravines.

18b. Lip broader, not 2-cleft for half its length .... (19)

19a. Lip oblong, sagittate and broadest at the base, without lateral teeth and with a fleshy ridge in the center near the base. *Listera borealis* Morong, NORTHERN TWAYBLADE. Very rare, one record from Silver Plume. Endangered.

19b. Lip cuneate to obovate, not auriculate, broadest at the apex, with lateral teeth, without a fleshy ridge. *Listera convallarioides* (Sw.) Nutt. (with the leaves of *Convallaria*, Lily-of-the-valley), BROAD-LIPPED TWAYBLADE. Rare, in cool ravines in the foothills, also in subalpine forests. Endangered.

PONTEDERIACEAE—PICKEREL-WEED FAMILY

The most well-known species of this family is *Eichhornia crassipes*, the Water-hyacinth, a plant with strange balloon-like inflated petioles enabling the plant with its fleshy leaves, beautiful purplish flowers and masses of elongate floating roots to form huge floating rafts on the surfaces of streams and canals in the southern U.S. and tropical regions. Its ability to rapidly colonize and clog waterways makes it a major pest.

One genus and species, ***Heteranthera limosa*** (Sw.) Willd. (of mud), MUD PLANTAIN. This used to occur on muddy pond margins in the city of Denver but probably has long since disappeared. Perhaps it still occurs somewhere, but many years have passed since the last collection. The flowers are white or purplish.

POTAMOGETONACEAE—PONDWEED FAMILY

The pondweeds are found in midsummer in almost every pond of any size. Their presence is marked by the spikes of dull greenish flowers emerging from the water, and by floating lily-pad leaves. Some are completely submerged and found by dredging with a rake. The floating leaves of *Potamogeton* are very similar to those of *Persicaria*, but the latter has pinnately veined leaves and spikes of bright pink flowers. Potamogetons are important waterfowl food plants.

1a. Leaves all narrowly linear (1-3 mm wide) or bristle-like . . . . (2)
1b. Some or all leaves broader or with definitely expanded blades . . (5)

2a. Stipules united with the base of the leaf for a distance of 7 mm or more. ***Potamogeton pectinatus*** L. (comb-like). Common in ponds on the plains and piedmont valleys.
2b. Stipules free from the leaf or united for less than 6 mm . . . . . . (3)

3a. Fruits with dorsal keel prominent, thin, wing-like and undulate or toothed. ***Potamogeton foliosus*** Raf., LEAFY PONDWEED. Ponds and streams in the foothills to subalpine.
3b. Fruits with dorsal keel rounded or acute but never thin and wing-like . . . . (4)

4a. Stipules connate (united along their sides) when young; peduncles up to 8 cm long; spikes 6-12 mm long of 3 to 5 separated clusters. ***Potamogeton pusillus*** L. Similar habitats.
4b. Stipules free, not connate; peduncles rarely more than 3 cm long; spikes 2-8 mm long, 1 to 3 adjacent clusters. ***Potamogeton berchtoldii*** Fieber (for Friedrich, Graf von Berchtold). Similar habitats. The three above are a technical group and identification is difficult without mature fruit and an understanding of the stipules.

5a. Submerged leaves linear, or petioled and tapering to a sessile base, not clasping the stem; floating leaves present or absent . . . . (8)

5b. Leaves all submerged, oblong, cordate or rounded at the base, clasping ½ to ¾ the circumference of the stem .... (6)

6a. Blade 5 to 30 cm long, with a cucullate apex (like the prow of a rowboat); stem whitish; fruits 4-5 mm long, sharply 3-keeled. *Potamogeton praelongus* Wulf. (elongate), WHITE-STEMMED PONDWEED. Lakes and ponds at fairly high altitudes in the mountains.

6b. Blade 1-12 cm long, apex not cucullate but margins wavy; stem green; fruit 2-4 mm long, faintly 3-keeled .... (7)

7a. Leaf blades entire; plants not producing hard winter buds. *Potamogeton perfoliatus* L. ssp. *richardsonii* (Bennett) Hultén (clasping-leaved; for Sir John Richardson). Montane and subalpine, in rather still water.

7b. Leaf blades distinctly serrulate; plants producing hard winter buds with small, rigid, serrate, spreading leaf-blades. *Potamogeton crispus* L. A European introduction known from Evergreen Lake.

8a. Submerged leaves sessile; floating leaves (usually absent) delicate, translucent, tapering without sharp distinction into the petiole; fruits with hard, smooth rind. *Potamogeton alpinus* Balbis, NORTHERN PONDWEED. Subalpine ponds.

8b. Submerged leaves sessile or petioled; floating leaves leathery, opaque, the blade distinct from the petiole; rind soft and porous. (9)

9a. Submerged leaves lanceolate to elliptical, more than 5 mm wide. (10)

Fig. 305. *Potamogeton gramineus*   Fig. 306. *Sparganium eurycarpum*

9b. Submerged leaves ribbon-like, linear, or thread-like, not more than 4 mm wide .... (11)

10a. Mature spikes 4-6 cm long; floating leaves cuneate at the base, the narrowly lanceolate submerged leaves tapering gradually to each end. ***Potamogeton nodosus*** Poir. (knotty). Lakes and reservoirs on the plains.

10b. Mature spikes 1-2 cm long; stem usually with many lateral branches bearing numerous small leaves. ***Potamogeton gramineus*** L. (grass-like), Fig. 305. Lakes and reservoirs, plains and mountains.

11a. Submerged leaves ribbon-like, linear, 2-5 mm wide, with a prominent translucent netted band along the midvein. ***Potamogeton epihydrus*** Raf. (on the water). Common in swamps and pools, montane and subalpine.

11b. Submerged leaves filiform, 1-2 mm wide .... (12)

12a. Spikes of two kinds, the one above the water surface cylindric, many-flowered, the other submerged, globose, few-flowered; floating leaves small, 2-5 cm long. ***Potamogeton diversifolius*** Raf. (various-leaved). Lakes and reservoirs on the plains.

12b. Spikes all alike, cylindric; floating leaves large, 5-10 cm long. ***Potamogeton natans*** L. (swimming). Ponds and ditches, mostly on the plains.

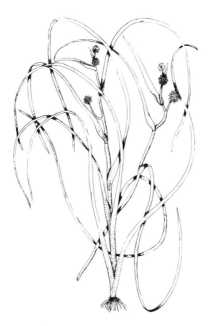

Fig. 307. ***Sparganium angustifolium***

RUPPIACEAE—DITCH-GRASS FAMILY

A very small family consisting of a single genus, *Ruppia*, and containing either one extremely polymorphic species or about seven poorly-delimited ones. **Ruppia maritima** L. occurs on the eastern edge of the piedmont valley area in seasonally flooded alkaline roadside ditches. When these places dry out in late summer, the *Ruppia* plants form a tangled mass of hairlike stems and leaves, with here and there a few long-stalked minute black fruits (Fig. 302).

SMILACACEAE—SMILAX FAMILY

One species, *Smilax lasioneuron* Hook. (hairy-nerved), CARRION FLOWER. Infrequent in gulches of the mesas and outer foothills. Although this plant is related closely to the eastern North American *S. herbacea*, our species, in my experience at least, does not have the odor of putrefying flesh of that species. Also, while it has strongly developed tendrils, it stands erect at least in early stages of development. The plants are dioecious, and eventually produce an umbel of large blue-black berries.

SPARGANIACEAE—BUR-REED FAMILY

The bur-reeds inhabit the margins of ponds. With their balls of flowers, the lower clusters carpellate and the upper staminate, sessile on a zigzag rachis, they are unmistakeable. When they get out into deep water, however, they do not flower, and their leaves become extremely long and the ribbon-like blades float on the water. Identification of *Sparganium* species requires material with mature fruits.

1a. Carpellate heads about 1 cm diam; plants small, with leaves 1 cm or less wide. ***Sparganium minimum*** Fries, ARCTIC BUR-REED, Fig. 308. Rare in subalpine bogs.
1b. Carpellate heads over 1 cm diam; plants usually robust, with broader leaves . . . . (2)

2a. Stigmas mostly 2; achenes sessile, obovoid to obpyramidal, distinctly flattened on top; sepals nearly as long as the achene. ***Sparganium eurycarpum*** Engelm. (broad-fruited), BUR-REED, Fig. 306. Formerly found along the Platte River near Denver, possibly extinct here.
2b. Stigma one; achenes mostly stalked, tapering at each end; sepals much shorter than the achene. ***Sparganium angustifolium*** Michx. (narrow-leaved), BUR-REED, Fig. 307.

TYPHACEAE—CAT-TAIL FAMILY

The flat leaves of cat-tails seem to be too weak to stand up to the high winds in the Front Range valleys, but note that the leaves of cat-tails are spirally twisted so that the whole leaf surface is never presented to the wind. Cat-tail marshes are important nesting grounds for sora rails, blackbirds and marsh wrens and should be preserved and encouraged for their miniature wildlife sanctuaries.

1a. Staminate and carpellate portions of the spike separated by a length of naked axis, the carpellate portion less than 2 cm in diameter; leaves convex on one side. ***Typha angustifolia*** L., Narrow-leaved Cat-tail, Fig. 309. In sloughs and along irrigation ditches in the piedmont valleys. Not as common as the next.
1b. Staminate and carpellate portions of the spike not separated, the carpellate portion more than 2 cm in diameter; leaves flat. ***Typha latifolia*** L., Broad-leaved Cat-tail, Fig. 309. Habitat similar to that of the preceding, very common.

Zannichelliaceae— Horned Pondweed Family

One species, ***Zannichellia palustris*** L. (of marshes), Fig. 302. Common in slow streams from the plains to the subalpine. The identification of the linear-leaved aquatics is difficult, but fortunately fruits are usually present in this species.

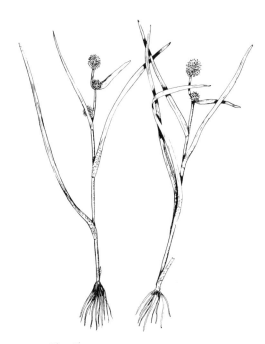

Fig. 308. ***Sparganium minimum***

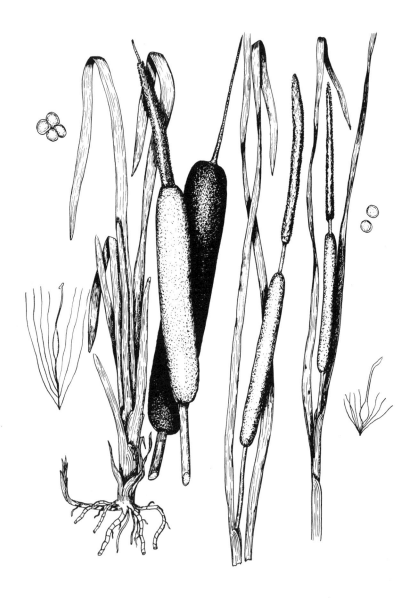

Fig. 309. Cat-tails: ***Typha latifolia*** (left), ***T. angustifolia*** (right)

Plate 17. **Stanleya pinnata**
PRINCES PLUME

Weber

Plate 18. **Calypso bulbosa**
FAIRY SLIPPER

Roberts

Plate 19. *Aquilegia caerulea* f. *daileyae*   Roberts
SPURLESS COLUMBINE

Plate 20. *Cypripedium fasciculatum*   Roberts
PURPLE LADY'S SLIPPER

Plate 22. *Eriogonum umbellatum*
SULPHUR-FLOWER

Roberts

Plate 21. *Abronia fragrans*
SAND-VERBENA

Roberts

Plate 23. *Mirabilis multiflora*
WILD FOUR-O'CLOCK

Roberts

Plate 24. *Drymocallis fissa*
CINQUEFOIL

Roberts

Plate 25. *Veratrum tenuipetalum*   Weber
CORN HUSK LILY

Plate 26. *Polemonium viscosum*   Weber
SKY PILOT

Plate 27. *Polanisia dodecandra*   Weber
Clammy-weed

Plate 28. *Telesonix jamesii*   Roberts
Telesonix

Plate 29. *Cirsium scopulorum*   Weber
ALPINE THISTLE

Plate 30. *Penstemon harbourii*   Weber
SCREE PENSTEMON

Plate 31. *Argemone polyanthemos*   Roberts
PRICKLY POPPY

Plate 32. *Clematis columbiana*   Weber
ROCKY MOUNTAIN CLEMATIS

Illustrated Glossary

Achene—a small, dry indehiscent, one-loculed, one-seeded fruit consisting usually of a single carpel.

Actinomorphic—having a radial symmetry.

Acuminate—drawn out at the apex into a gradually tapering point (Fig. 310).

Acute—terminating in a sharp or well-defined point (Fig. 311).

Adnate—attached or fused to.

Alternate—(leaves) having one leaf arising at each node (Fig. 312); (floral parts) having the members of one whorl attached between the members of the next outer or inner whorl (Fig. 313).

Ament—same as catkin.

Androecium—collective name for the stamens. The total set of stamens is called the androecium.

Androgynous—in *Carex*, having the staminate flowers above the carpellate ones, and in the same spike.

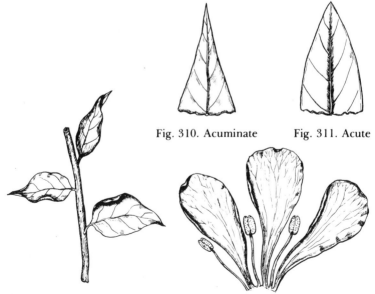

Fig. 310. Acuminate   Fig. 311. Acute

Fig. 312. Alternate leaves   Fig. 313. Stamens alternate to the petals

Angiosperms—seed plants in which the ovules are enclosed in carpels; flowering plants.

Annual—living through one season only.

Anterior—(in flowers) the side of the flower facing away from the axis of the inflorescence.

Anther—the pollen-bearing organ of the flower. See *Stamen.*

Anthesis—flowering time.

Aphyllopodic—having only bladeless leaf sheaths at the base of the flowering culm.

Appressed—lying close to or flat against.

Aril—a fleshy, usually colored appendage or covering on a seed.

Articulate—jointed.

Articulation—in grasses, the point at which organs (glumes or lemmas) break away from the stem. In a grass spikelet, if, at maturity, the florets fall from the plant and leave the glumes attached, we say the spikelet disarticulates above the glumes and between the florets. If the spikelet falls completely without leaving the glumes attached to the plant, we say the spikelet disarticulates below the glumes. Manipulating the spikelet with one's fingers or with a tweezers helps to determine the type of articulation.

Ascending—growing obliquely upward or curving upward during growth.

Attenuate—drawn out into a long, slender tip (extremely acuminate).

Auricle—(in milkweeds) an ear or flap-like appendage at the base of the hood; (in grasses) a similar appendage at the summit of the leaf sheath.

Awn—a stiff, bristle-like appendage.

Axil—the angle formed by a leaf with the stem to which it is attached, Buds, for example, are found in the *axils* of leaves, that is, at the place where the leaf joins the stem.

Axile—a type of placentation in which the ovules are attached to the ventral suture of the carpel. Peas and beans, for example, show axile placentation involving only one carpel. Tomato or apple shows axile placentation involving up to five carpels (Fig. 314).

Axillary—situated in, or arising from, the axil of a leaf. Usually opposed to *terminal.*

Axis—an imaginary line running lengthwise through the center of an organ such as a flower or stem.

Banner—the broad, erect, upper petal of the flower of legumes, as in sweet-peas.

Fig. 314. Axile placentation

Fig. 315. Barbellate

Fig. 316 Basal placentation

Barbellate—having minute prongs. Commonly refers to the pappus of Compositae, in which each bristle has very short barbs, as seen with a hand lens (Fig 315).

Basal—(leaves) produced at ground level; (placentation) having the ovules attached at the base of the ovary only (Fig. 316). In many cases the ovary contains only one seed, which is attached at the base of the ovary and fills the locule.

Beak—a prominent, firm, slender tip (Fig. 317). In some legumes the keel petals are abruptly narrowed at the tip to form a beak; in mustards the tip of the fruit is something abruptly narrowed with the non-ovule-bearing portions forming a beak.

Bearded—having a tuft of long hairs.

Bidentate—two-toothed. In *Carex*, this is an important characteristic in some species in which the tip of the perigynium is bidentate (Fig. 318). *Biennial*—of two years duration. A biennial plant produces a rosette of basal leaves the first year, sends up a flower stalk the second year, produces seeds, and dies.

Bifid—cleft in two.

Bilabiate—two-lipped, referring especially to the corolla in such groups as mints and figworts.

Bipinnate—twice pinnately compound (Fig. 319).

Bipinnatifid—twice pinnatifid (Fig. 320).

Bisexual—(in flowers) having both stamens and carpels; same as *Perfect*.

Blade—the flat, expanded portion of a leaf or petal.

Bloom—a whitish waxy or powdery (glaucous) covering on leaves or twigs, easily rubbed off.

Bract—a much-reduced leaf, usually subtending a flower (Fig. 321).

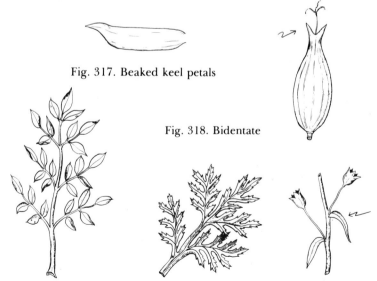

Fig. 317. Beaked keel petals

Fig. 318. Bidentate

Fig. 319. Bipinnate leaf   Fig. 320. Bipinnatifid leaf   Fig. 321. Bract

Bulb—a spherical underground bud or stem with fleshy scales or coats, as in onions. In a bulb the spherical structure consists mostly of scales, whereas in a corm the scales are minute and the round mass consists of the fleshy stem.

Caespitose—growing in clumps.

Callus—hardened base of the lemma in grasses. In *Stipa* (needle-grass) the callus is very hard and sharp-pointed, like a needle.

Calyx—the outer set of perianth segments, usually green; collective name for the sepals.

Campanulate—bell-shaped (Fig. 322).

Canescent—having a hoary, grayish pubescence of short hairs.

Capillary—hair-like or thread-like.

Capitate—head-like; collected into a dense, short cluster.

Capsule—a dry, dehiscent fruit composed of more than one carpel. *Yucca* is a good example (Fig. 323).

Carpel—the basic unit of a gynoecium, a single "in-rolled spore-bearing leaf" (stigma, style, and ovary). A good example of a typical carpel is the pod of a pea, or a peanut-shell. See also *Gynoecium*.

Carpellate—having carpels; also, lacking stamens. Same as *pistillate*.

Caryopsis—the grain (fruit) of grasses.

Catkin—a spike of inconspicuous and usually unisexual flowers, as in willows and birches.

Caudex—the persistent woody, underground base of an otherwise herbaceous stem; an erect or ascending underground stem.

Cauline—borne on the stem, above ground. Refers to leaves, opposed to *basal*.

Centimeter—ten millimeters (2.54 cm = 1 inch).

Ciliate—marginally fringed with hairs (Fig. 324).

Circumscissile—dehiscent by a transverse circular line, as the capsule of plantains. (Fig. 325).

Circumpolar—distributed around the world in the Northern Hemisphere.

Claw—the narrow stalk of som petals (particularly mustards) Fig. 326).

Cleft—deeply cut.

cm—centimeter.

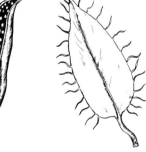

Fig. 322. Campanulate corolla

Fig. 323. Capsule of *Yucca*

Fig. 324. Ciliate

Collar—a horizontal line crossing the outside of a grass leaf where the blade joins the sheath. The collar is often thickened or covered with hairs.

Coma—a tuft of hair, as on the seeds of *Epilobium*.

Compound—composed of from two to many similar united parts, as carpels in a *compound* ovary (a tomato fruit is a compound ovary, consisting of four or five united carpels), or, divided into a number of similar parts, as the leaflets of *compound* leaves.

Compressed—flattened. In a *laterally* compressed grass spikelet the flattening involves the side of the spikelets, so that the individual florets are folded in half. In a dorsally compressed spikelet the florets on opposite sides of the axis are pressed *towards* each other, and the individual florets are flattened out rather than folded.

Connate—united, either by fusion or pressure.

Cordate—heart-shaped, referring to the outline or the base of a leaf (Fig. 327).

Coriaceous—leathery in texture.

Corm—the enlarged fleshy base of a stem, bulb-like but solid. Example: gladiolus, spring beauty.

Corolla—collective name for the petals, the inner whorl of perianth segments.

Corona—a crown or collar attached to the inside of the corolla, as in daffodils and milkweeds.

Cotyledons—the first, or seed-leaves of a plant; the two halves of a peanut "kernel" are its cotyledons. The two great groups of flowering plants, Monocots and Dicots, are so called because of the difference in number of cotyledons in the seeds.

Crenate—with rounded marginal teeth (Fig. 328).

Crenulate—finely crenate.

Culm—the "stem" of grasses and sedges, consisting principally of overlapping leaf-sheaths.

Cuneate—wedge-shaped, usually referring to the base of a leaf (Fig. 329).

Fig. 325. Circumscissile   Fig. 326. Claw   Fig. 327. Cordate leaf

Fig. 328. Crenate   Fig. 329. Cuneate

Cuspidate—tipped with a sharp, firm point.

Cyme—a flower-cluster, usually opposite-branched, with the terminal or central flowers blooming earliest (Fig. 330).

Deciduous—falling off at the end of a growing season; not persistent or evergreen.

Decimeter—ten centimeters.

Declined—directed downward toward the base (not as sharply so as *reflexed*).

Decumbent—prostrate except for the ascending tips of the branches.

Decurrent—referring to the bases of leaves, which sometimes continue down the stem beyond the point of attachment (Fig. 331).

Dehiscent—splitting open at maturity.

Deltoid—triangular, shaped like the Greek letter *delta*.

Dentate—toothed, with the teeth directed outward (Fig. 332).

Denticulate—minutely dentate.

Diadelphous—(stamens) united into two sets. In some legumes, nine of the ten stamens in a flower are united by the filaments, the tenth is separate.

Dichotomous—equal forked branches, most commonly occurring in ferns (Fig. 333).

Digitate—compounded or veined in such a way as to suggest the fingers of a hand (Fig. 334).

Dioecious—bearing the staminate flowers on one individual and the carpellate flowers on another of the same species (*plants* may be *dioecious*; their *flowers* are then *imperfect* or *unisexual*; *flowers* are never dioecious).

Fig. 330. Cyme

Fig. 331. Decurrent

Fig. 332. Dentate

Fig. 333. Dichotomous branching

Fig. 334. Digitate

Disarticulating—breaking off from the main axis, as spikelets of grasses. See *articulation*.

Disjunct—occurring in two widely separated geographic areas.

Disk-flowers—the central regular or tubular flowers of Compositae. In the sunflower or daisy, for example, the central part of the "flower" is composed of a great number of these "disk-flowers," while the "petals" are in reality complete flowers also (ray-flowers). A daisy or sunflower is really a cluster of a great many tiny flowers, resembling a single flower.

Dissected—cut into numerous narrow segments.

Distinct—separate, not united.

Divergent—spreading apart, curving away from the main axis (Fig. 335).

Divided—cut to the base into lobes or segments.

dm—decimeter.

Dorsal—pertaining to the part of an organ facing *away* from the axis, as the *underside* of a leaf; abaxial. This is a usage quite different from that of zoology.

Drupe—the fruit of cherry or plum, a fleshy one-seeded fruit in which the seed is enclosed in a hard "stone."

Elliptical—having the shape of an ellipse (Fig. 336).

Emarginate—having a shallow notch at the tip (Fig. 337).

Endemic—confined to a given region.

Entire—without marginal teeth.

Epigynous—borne on top of the ovary (flowers are epigynous if they have an inferior ovary). See Introduction.

Equitant—folded over, as if astride, as the leaves of *Iris*.

Even-pinnate—pinnately compound, with the terminal leaflet missing.

Exserted—projecting beyond the enveloping organs (Fig. 338).

Farinose—with a mealy or powdery covering.

Fascicle—bundle, cluster.

Fertile—having a gynoecium; producing seed; in ferns, bearing sporangia.

Fibrillose—shredding into fine fibres.

Filament—the stalk supporting an anther.

Fig. 335. Divergent awns   Fig. 336. Elliptic

Fig. 337. Emarginate   Fig. 338. Flower with exserted stamens

Filiform—thread-like.

Flexuous—curved, wavy.

Floccose—having loose tufts of soft, cottony hair.

Floret—a small flower, specifically applied to the flowers of grasses and composites.

Foliaceous—leaf-like, either in texture or in shape, or both.

Foliolate—referring to leaflets in a compound leaf (a clover leaf is *trifoliolate*).

Follicle—a fruit formed from a single carpel, dehiscing along one edge only. Example: Delphinium, Columbine (Fig. 339).

Free—not united; separate.

Free-central—a type of placentation in which the ovules are attached to a central stalk within the ovary and are not connected to the carpel margins by partitions (Fig. 340).

Fruit—the part of a plant which bears the seeds; usually an ovary, its contents, and any floral parts which may be associated with it at maturity. The term is also loosely used to refer to cones of gymnosperms, and to spore-bearing structures of ferns, mosses, and the lower plants.

Fruticose—shrubby.

Galea—a hood- or helmet-shaped sepal or petal or the upper lip of some zygomorphic corollas (Fig. 341).

Geniculate—bent abruptly, like a knee. Most commonly refers to the bent awns of some grasses.

Gibbous—swollen on one side.

Glabrate—almost glabrous.

Glabrous—smooth, without hairs.

Gladiate—sword-shaped, like the leaves of Iris.

Gland—an organ of secretion; also commonly used to refer to any structure in flowers whose function is unknown.

Glandular—having glands; sticky. Glandular hairs are often ball-tipped, and stems bearing these hairs usually collect dirt and trash, are sticky to the touch, or stain the pressing-papers.

Glaucous—having a bloom or whitish covering on the stem or leaf.

Globose—spherical.

Glomerate—crowded into a compact, spherical cluster.

Glume—one of the two empty bracts forming the base of the grass spikelet.

Glutinous—sticky.

Fig. 339. Follicle   Fig. 340. Free-central placentation   Fig. 341. Galea

Graduate—(in Compositae) having the inner phyllaries longer than the outer.

Gynaecandrous—(in *Carex*) having the carpellate flowers above the staminate ones in the same spike.

Gynoecium—a carpel or an aggregation of carpels, either separate or united; collective name for all the carpels in a single flower.

Habitat—the kind of locality in which a plant usually grows.

Hastate—like an arrowhead but with the basal lobes pointing outward (Fig. 342).

Head—a compact, usually hemispherical flower-cluster.

Herbaceous—not woody.

Herbage—the vegetative portion of the plant.

Hirsute—clothed with coarse, stiff hairs.

Hispid—clothed with stiff, bristle-like hairs.

Hyaline—transparent or translucent.

Hypanthium—a cup or tube bearing on its rim the stamens, petals, and sepals. See Introduction.

Hypogynous—refers to flowers in which the stamens, petals, and sepals are attached below the ovary; flowers with superior ovaries are hypogynous. See Introduction.

Imbricate—overlapping like shingles.

Imperfect—having only stamens or carpels, not both.

Incised—cut sharply, deeply, and irregularly into lobes or segments.

Included—not protruding beyond the enveloping organs (opposite of *exserted*).

Indehiscent—not splitting open at maturity.

Indurate—hardened.

Indusium—a membranous flap or "umbrella" covering the sorus of ferns; usually withers and disappears as the sporangia ripen.

Inferior—refers to ovaries which are either imbedded in the receptacle or fused with the surrounding floral parts. The ovary of apple is inferior, i.e., it is imbedded in the fused floral parts, which form a fleshy covering. See Introduction.

Inflorescence—flower-cluster.

Internerves—in grasses, the portion of a lemma, palea, or glume situated between the nerves or veins.

Internode—the portion of a stem between two nodes (Fig. 343).

Fig. 342. Hastate leaf   Fig. 343. Internode

Interrupted—broken up into several units and not in a continuous spike (referring to flower clusters) (Fig. 344).

Involucre—a circle or cluster of bracts at the base of a flower-cluster, sometimes fused into a cup.

Involute—having the edges rolled inward.

Irregular—showing inequality in the size, shape or arrangement of the parts, often loosely used as synonym for zygomorphic.

Keel—a prominent dorsal rib, ridge, or crease (or in the legumes, the two fused petals enclosing the stamens).

Labiate—lipped, as the corolla of mints.

Lanceolate—lance-shaped, long and narrow but broadest at the base (Fig. 345).

Lateral—referring to the side, as opposed to dorsal or ventral. Sometimes the opposite of terminal.

Leaflet—a segment of a compound leaf.

Legume—the fruit (pod) of plants belonging to the pea family; also, any member of the pea family.

Lemma—the outer bract of the grass floret.

Lenticels—wart-like, usually light-colored, spots on the bark of twigs.

Lenticular—disk-shaped, with two convex sides, lentil-shaped.

Ligule—in grasses, the flap of tissue on the ventral (adaxial) side of a leaf at the place where the blade joins the sheath, i.e., the ligule is between the blade and the culm; in Compositae, a ray-flower or strap-shaped corolla.

Linear—long and narrow, with parallel margins (Fig. 346).

Lobe—a division or segment of an organ.

Locule—one of the cavities or chambers in an ovary or anther (commonly called a "cell").

Loment—a legume which is constricted between the seeds, breaking up into several indehiscent, one-seeded segments (Fig. 347).

m—meter (39.36 inches or approx. 3 feet).

Merous—refers to the number of segments in a whorl of floral parts (a flower having 3 sepals, 3 petals, 3 stamens, and 3 carpels is 3-merous).

Fig. 344. Interrupted spike   Fig. 345. Lanceolate   Fig. 346. Linear leaf

Fig. 347. Loment

Fig. 348. Mucronate

Mesophytes—plants adapted to medium conditions as to moisture and light.

Meter—10 decimeters; 39.36 inches.

Millimeter—one-tenth of a centimeter.

mm—millimeter.

Monadelphous—united into a single group, as stamens. In some legumes, and in mallows, the stamens are all united by their filaments, thus monadelphous.

Monoecious—having the stamens and carpels in different flowers on the same plant (a *plant* may be monoecious; its *flowers* are unisexual or imperfect).

Monotypic—having only one species (or other taxon).

Mucronate—having a minute and abrupt point (mucro) at the apex (Fig. 348).

Murications—(in dandelions) the minute sharp points covering the fruit.

Nerve—vein.

Nodal Spines—thorns situated at the nodes.

Node—a point on the stem where one or more leaves are attached.

Ob—a prefix implying "the reverse." For example, an obovate leaf is ovate with the widest part near the apex rather than the base (Fig. 349).

Oblong—rectangular in general outline but with corners rounded (Fig. 350).

Obsolete—vestigial or almost completely lacking.

Obtuse—blunt or rounded at the end.

Odd-pinnate—pinnately compound, with the terminal leaflet present (having an odd number of leaflets) (Fig. 351).

Opposite—(leaves) originating in pairs on the stem, i.e., with two leaves at a node (Fig. 352); (stamens) attached directly in front of a petal, instead of between petals (Fig. 353).

Orbicular—round, circular.

Ovary—the part of the gynoecium or carpel which contains the seeds.

Ovate—egg-shaped and broadest at the base (Fig. 354).

Ovule—the seed, before fertilization.

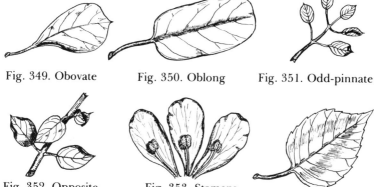

Fig. 349. Obovate   Fig. 350. Oblong   Fig. 351. Odd-pinnate

Fig. 352. Opposite leaves   Fig. 353. Stamens opposite the petals   Fig. 354. Ovate

Palate—the projecting part of the lower lip of a two-lipped corolla, which closes the throat (as in snapdragon) (Fig. 355).

Palea—the ventral, or inner, of the two bracts of the floret of grasses; the bract opposite, and enfolded by, the lemma.

Palmate—having veins, lobes, or segments which radiate from a single point, as maple leaves. See also *Digitate*.

Panicle—a repeatedly branched inflorescence with pedicelled flowers (Fig. 356).

Paniculate—arranged in a panicle.

Papillose—minutely warty or pimply.

Pappus—the modified calyx of Compositae, usually composed of bristles or awns. The "parachute" of a dandelion flower, and the barbs of a beggar's-tick, are examples.

Parasitic—depending on living tissue of other organisms for a source of food.

Parietal—a type of placentation in which the ovules are attached to the side of the ovary (Fig. 357). This term only applies to ovaries which consist of more than one carpel.

Pedicel—the stalk of a single flower (Fig. 358).

Pedicellate—having a pedicel.

Peduncle—the common stalk of a flower cluster (Fig. 358).

Perennial—living year after year.

Perfect—having all the essential organs (stamens and carpels); bisexual.

Perianth—collective name for the sepals and petals; commonly used for the accessory organs when sepals are not easily distinguished from petals, as in tulip.

Pericarp—the ovary wall.

Perigynium—the inflated sac enclosing the ovary in *Carex*, represented in *Kobresia* by an open sheath.

Persistent—lasting, not deciduous, remaining attached to the stem.

Petal—one of the white or colored inner perianth segments.

Petaloid—resembling a petal.

Petiolate—having a petiole.

Petiole—leaf stalk.

Phyllaries—the bracts of the involucre in Compositae. In dandelion, for

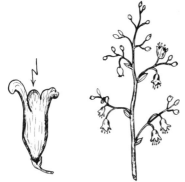

Fig. 357. Parietal placentation

Fig. 355. Palate   Fig. 356. Panicle   Fig. 358. Pedicel and peduncle

example, each of the green bracts surrounding the head is one phyllary.

Phyllopodic—in *Carex*, having leaves with blades at the base of the flowering culm.

Pilose—having long soft hairs (more sparsely so than villous).

Pinna—a primary division of a fern frond (the whole fern leaf is called a *frond*. Fronds are divided into main branches, or pinnae; pinnae may be divided further into *pinnules*).

Pinnate—having veins, lobes, or divisions in the form of a feather, i.e., with one main axis having lateral offshoots (Fig. 359).

Pinnatifid—pinnately cleft into narrow segments, but the segments not stalked (Fig. 360).

Pinnatisect—pinnately dissected.

Pinnule—a secondary division of a fern frond (a division of a pinna).

Placenta—the part of the ovary to which the ovules are attached. This term does not apply to the stalk of the ovule, but merely to the point of attachment.

Placentation—the mode of attachment of the ovules to the ovary (axile, parietal, basal, or free-central).

Plumose—feathery (usually refers to a style, bristle, or awn having delicate side-branches) (Fig. 361).

Pome—the fruit of apples and their relatives.

Posterior—the side of the flower facing the axis of the inflorescence (in flowers such as *Castilleja*, the upper side).

Prostrate—lying flat on the ground.

Puberulent—very minutely pubescent.

Pubescent—hairy.

Raceme—an elongated inflorescence with a single main axis along which single, stalked flowers are arranged (Fig. 362). Compare with panicle, spike, and cyme.

Rachilla—the axis within the spikelet in grasses; the stalk of the individual floret.

Rachis—the axis of the inflorescence or of a compound leaf.

Fig. 360. Pinnatifid

Fig. 359. Pinnate

Fig. 361. Plumose bristle   Fig. 362. Raceme

Ray-flowers—the strap-shaped marginal flowers of Compositae (the "petals" of daisies). Although they resemble petals, each ray-flower is complete with corolla and, usually, essential organs.

Receptacle—the tip of the floral axis, to which the sepals, petals, stamens, and carpels are attached.

Reflexed—bent abruptly downward.

Regular—radially symmetrical (Fig. 363).

Regularly—evenly, uniformly.

Remote—widely separated, as flowers on a spike.

Replum—the partition between the two locules in the fruits of mustards.

Retrorse—directed backwards or downwards.

Revolute—having the margins rolled back or under; opposite of *Involute*.

Rhizome—a prostrate underground stem or branch, rooting at the nodes; differs from a root in possessing nodes and internodes, and usually scale leaves.

Rib—a prominent vein or ridge, particularly on carpel walls.

Rootstock—strictly, a rhizome; often loosely applied to either a rhizome or a caudex.

Rosette—a cluster of closely crowded radiating leaves at ground level.

Rotate—wheel-shaped, flat and circular in outline; term applied to very open corollas.

Ruderal—growing in waste places or among rubbish.

Saccate—bag-shaped.

Sagittate—arrow-shaped, with the basal lobes directed downward (Fig. 364).

Salient—projecting, protruding.

Samara—an indehiscent winged fruit, such as that of maple (Fig. 365).

Saprophytic—depending on dead organic materials for a source of food.

Scabrous—rough to the touch.

Scape—a leafless flower stalk arising from the ground or from a cluster of basal leaves.

Scapose—bearing a scape.

Scarious—dry, thin, scale-like, not green.

Secund—one-sided.

Seed—a ripened ovule.

Sepal—one of the outer perianth segments; a segment of the calyx.

Septate-nodulose—(in sedges) having minute knob-like partitions crossing between the veins. These can usually be seen without splitting the leaf.

Serrate—having sharp teeth pointing forward (Fig. 366).

Serrulate—minutely serrate.

Sessile—lacking a stalk.

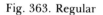
Fig. 363. Regular   Fig. 364. Sagittate   Fig. 365. Maple samara

Sheath—the basal portion of a leaf of a grass-like plant, the part which surrounds the stem.

Silicle—a short silique.

Silique—the fruit of mustards. A silique consists of two carpel walls, called *valves*, separated by a partition, the *replum*. The seeds are attached to the rim of the replum. At maturity, the valves fall away from the fruit, leaving the replum as a very thin, papery partition. If the silique is flattened parallel to the replum, the valves are flattened against the face of the replum, and the replum is roughly the same shape as the valve. If the silique is flattened perpendicular to the replum, the valves are folded and the replum bisects the face of the silique.

Simple—not branched (stems); not compound (leaves).

Sinuate—wavy-margined.

Sinus—the cleft or indentation between lobes.

Sorus (plural, sori)—a cluster of sporangia. The sori are the dark dots found on the undersides of fruiting fern fronds.

Spatulate—oblong, but narrowed at the base (Fig. 367).

Spicate—arranged in or resembling a spike.

Spike—an elongated inflorescence bearing sessile flowers (Fig. 368).

Spikelet—(in grasses and sedges) the smallest flower cluster in an inflorescence, usually forming a distinct and compact unit.

Spinulose—having minute spines.

Sporangium—structure containing spores.

Spp.—species, plural.

Spur—a hollow projection of a petal or sepal, as in columbine and violet.

Squamiform—scale-like.

Squarrose—spreading or recurved at the tip.

Ssp.—subspecies.

Stamen—the pollen-producing organ of a flower, situated between the petals and the carpels (Fig. 369).

Staminate—having stamens but not carpels.

Staminodia—non-functional stamens, usually lacking well-developed anthers.

Stellate—star-shaped.

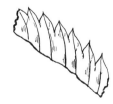

Fig. 366. Serrate

Fig. 367. Spatulate

Fig. 368. Spike

Fig. 369. Stamen

Sterile—not producing seed; lacking a gynoecium, or (in stamens) lacking anthers.

Stigma—that part of the style which is receptive to pollen, usually recognized by its sticky-glandular, pollen-covered surface.

Stipe—a stalk, as of a gynoecium (Fig. 370).

Stipitate—having a stipe.

Stipule—an appendage, sometimes leaf-like, sometimes papery, at the base of the petiole of a leaf. Stipules usually occur in pairs (Fig. 371).

Stolon—a slender, modified stem running along the ground, usually above the surface of the soil, as in strawberry.

Strap-shaped—oblong, as the ray-corollas of a daisy.

Striate—marked with fine longitudinal lines or furrows.

Style—the slender upper part of the carpel or gynoecium. A style is not necessarily present on a gynoecium.

Sub—prefix meaning almost, as in *subequal*.

Subspecies—a subdivision of a species, usually having a distinct geographic range as well as morphological differences. The term *variety*, although denoting a lower category, is often synonymous with *subspecies*.

Subtend—to occur below, as, a bract *subtends* a flower.

Subulate—awl-shaped.

Superior—referring to the gynoecium, when it is attached only at its base and is not fused to the surrounding parts. The ovary is superior even if surrounded by a floral tube, as long as its wall is not fused to the surrounding parts. See *Hypogynous*.

Suture—a junction or seam of union; also, the line of dehiscence. In the pea, the pod splits along the dorsal and ventral *sutures*. The ovules are attached along the ventral *suture*.

Syncarpous—having united carpels.

Taproot—a primary, often fleshy, vertical root.

Tawny—tan or brownish.

Taxon—any named taxonomic entity, such as a genus, family, or species (plural taxa).

Tendril—a slender clasping or twining outgrowth of stems or leaves (Fig. 372).

Terete—cylindrical; circular in cross-section.

Ternate—compounded into divisions or groups of three.

Fig. 370. Stipe   Fig. 371. Stipules   Fig. 372. Tendril

Thallus—a relatively undifferentiated plant body, without stems or leaves, as in liverworts.

Thyrse—a compact cylindrical or conical panicle.

Tomentose—densely clothed with woolly or cottony hairs.

Tomentum—a cottony or woolly pubescence.

Torulose—constricted at intervals along its length, in extreme instances resembling a string of beads (Fig. 373).

Trifoliolate—having three leaflets.

Trigonous—three-angled, three-sided.

Truncate—abruptly cut off at the end.

Tubercle—a small, expanded structure, such as the base of the style in some sedges (*Eleocharis*).

Tubinate—top-shaped; inversely conical (Fig. 374).

Umbel—an inflorescence in which the pedicels radiate from a single point, like the spokes of an umbrella (Fig. 375).

Unisexual—having only stamens or carpels, never both.

Utricle—an inflated achene-like fruit in which the carpel wall loosely invests the single seed.

Valve—one of the pieces into which a capsule splits.

Var.—variety. See *Subspecies*.

Ventral—on the side facing the axis (the upper side of a leaf is its ventral side); adaxial.

Villous—clothed with long, soft hairs.

Viscid—sticky.

Whorl—a circle or ring of organs. When more than two leaves are found at a node, the leaves are *whorled*.

Winter Annual—a plant which begins growth in the fall, then flowers, sets seed and dies the following season, as winter wheat.

Xerophytes—plants adapted to very dry conditions.

Zygomorphic—bilaterally symmetrical. A zygomorphic flower can be divided only one way to produce mirror images. Snapdragon is a good example of a zygomorphic flower.

Fig. 373. A torulose pod   Fig. 374. Turbinate   Fig. 375. Umbel

USEFUL REFERENCES

ANDERSON, EDGAR. 1949. Introgressive Hybridization. John Wiley & Sons, Inc., New York.

BENSON, LYMAN. 1957. Plant Classification. D. C. Heath and Company, Boston.

————. 1962. Plant Taxonomy, Methods and Principles. Ronald Press Company, New York.

BOISSEVAIN, CHARLES H., and CAROL DAVIDSON. 1940. Colorado Cacti, an Illustrated Guide Describing All of the Native Colorado Cacti. Abbey Garden Press, Pasadena.

CHASE, AGNES. 1959. First Book of Grasses. Smithsonian Institution, Washington, D. C.

CLEMENTS, F. E., and E. S. CLEMENTS. 1920. Flowers of Mountain and Plain. H. W. Wilson Co., New York.

CORRELL, DONOVAN S. and HELEN B. 1975. Aquatic and Wetland Plants of Southwestern United States. 2 vols. Stanford University Press, California.

DANIELS, FRANCIS POTTER. 1911. The Flora of Boulder, Colorado, and Vicinity. University of Missouri Studies, Science Ser., 2 (2): 1-311.

EASTWOOD, ALICE. 1898. A Popular Flora of Denver, Colorado. Zoë Publishing Co., San Francisco.

EWAN, JOSEPH A. 1950. Rocky Mountain Naturalists. University of Denver Press.

GLEASON, H. A. 1952. The New Britton and Brown Illustrated Flora of the Northeastern United States and Adjacent Canada. Vol. I-III. New York Botanical Garden.

GOULD, FRANK W. 1968. Grass Systematics. McGraw Hill Book Co., New York.

HARRINGTON, H. D. 1954. Manual of the Plants of Colorado. Sage Books, Denver.

HARRINGTON, H. D., and L. W. DURRELL. 1950. Colorado Ferns. Colorado State University, Fort Collins.

HEISER, CHARLES B., Jr. 1973. Seed to Civilization, the Story of Man's Food. W. H. Freeman & Co., San Francisco.

HERMANN, FREDERICK J. 1970. Manual of the Carices of the Rocky Mountains and Colorado Basin. Agric. Handbook No. 374. U.S. Govt. Printing Office.

————. 1975. Manual of the Rushes (*Juncus* spp.) of the Rocky Mountains and Colorado Basin. U.S.D.A. For. Serv. Gen. Tech. Rep. RM-18, 107 pp. Fort Collins.

HITCHCOCK, A. S. 1951. Manual of Grasses of the U. S. [Ed. 2, revised by Agnes Chase]. U.S.D.A. Misc. Publ. 200 (reprinted by Dover Publications, Inc., New York).

IVES, JACK D. & ROGER G. BARRY, eds. 1974. Arctic and Alpine Environments. Methuen & Co., Ltd., London.

KELLY, GEORGE W. 1970. A Guide to the Woody Plants of Colorado. Pruitt Publishing Co., Boulder.

KINGSBURY, JOHN M. 1964. Poisonous Plants of the United States and Canada. 626 pages. Prentice Hall, Inc., Engelwood Cliffs, N. J.

LINNÉ, CARL VON. 1737. Critica Botanica. Leiden (reprinted in translation by the Ray Society, 1938).

LONG, JOHN C. 1965. Native Orchids of Colorado. Denver Museum of Natural History, Pictorial No. 16.

MACKENZIE, K. K. 1940. North American Cariceae [species of *Carex*]. 2 vols. New York Botanical Garden. These two books of illustrations are indispensable for the serious student of the sedges.

MARR, JOHN W. 1961. Ecosystems of the East Slope of the Front Range in Colorado. University of Colorado Studies, Series in Biology, No. 8: 1-134.

MATSUMURA, YOSHIHARU, and H. D. HARRINGTON. 1955. The True Aquatic Vascular Plants of Colorado. Colorado State University, Fort Collins, Tech. Bull. 57.

McKEAN, WILLIAM T. (ed.). 1956. Winter Guide to Native Shrubs of the Central Rocky Mountains, with summer key. State of Colorado Dept. of Game and Fish, Denver.

McKELVEY, SUSAN DELANO. 1955. Botanical Exploration of the Trans-Mississippi West, 1790-1850. Arnold Arboretum, Jamaica Plain, Mass.

MORE, ROBERT E. 1949. Colorado Evergreens. Denver Museum of Natural History & University of Denver. Has excellent photographs of our native conifers.

NELSON, RUTH ASHTON. 1961. Plants of Rocky Mountain National Park. U. S. Gov't. Printing Office, Washington.

PESMAN, M. WALTER. 1952. Meet the Natives. 5th ed., revised, published privately.

PRESTON, RICHARD J. 1940. Rocky Mountain Trees. Iowa State University Press, Ames.

RAMALEY, FRANCIS. 1927. Colorado Plant Life. University of Colorado Press, Boulder.

RICKETT, HAROLD WILLIAM. 1974. Wild Flowers of the United States. Volume Six, The Central Mountains and Plains. McGraw Hill Book Co., New York.

ROBERTS, HAROLD and RHODA. 1953. Some Common Colorado Wild Flowers. Denver Museum of Natural History Pictorial No. 8.

————. 1957. Mountain Wild Flowers of Colorado. Denver Museum of Natural History Pictorial No. 13.

SAVILE, D. B. O. 1962. Collection and Care of Botanical Specimens. Canada Dept. Agr., Research Branch, Publ. 1113. Ottawa.

SMITH, E. C., and L. W. DURRELL. 1944. Sedges and Rushes of Colorado. Colorado State University, Fort Collins, Bull. 32.

STEARN, WILLIAM T. 1966. Botanical Latin: History, Grammar, Syntax, Terminology and Vocabulary. Hafner Publ. Co., New York. Indispensable to the student interested in the international language of botany.

WEBER, WILLIAM A. 1965. Plant Geography in the Southern Rocky Mountains. Pp. 453-468 in *The Quaternary of the United States* (H. E. Wright, Jr., and David G. Frey, eds.). Princeton University Press.

WILLARD, BETTIE E., and C. H. HARRIS. 1963. Alpine Wildflowers of Rocky Mountain National Park. Rocky Mountain Nature Assoc., Estes Park.

Index

Italicized names are synonyms

Addenda

Page 99. **Drymaria effusa** Gray var. **depressa** (Greene) Duke has been found by Fred J. Hermann on the margin of a drying pond in aspen groves in Rocky Mountain National Park. Unlike **Spergularia**, the plant is never glandular; it is hardly over 1 cm tall and consists of a dense cluster of inconspicuous flowers arising out of a small cluster of fleshly linear leaves; the stipules are extremely small and the petals linear and bifid, just equalling the sepals.

Page 122. **Echinacea angustifolia** DC., Purple Coneflower, was recently found in a moist meadow near Boulder. In Key B one would take choice 3a, but no choice in 4 would fit. This is a tall unbranched plant with narrow, alternate, stiff-hairy leaves. The single head terminating each stem is large, with long narrow pale violet ray-flowers and a conical disk with very stiff inner bracts exceeding the ray-flowers, presenting a teasel-like texture.

Page 123. **Matricaria perforata** Merat (**M. inodora** L.), an annual weed closely resembling **Anthemis cotula** but lacking any receptacular chaff, would, except for the leaf form, key out at 12b. It has been a common weed in the Blue River Valley of Middle Park for many years and recently has become established and rampant along roadsides and meadows near Evergreen. **Anthemis** has a strong odor; **Matricaria** virtually is odorless.

Page 142. **Centaurea maculosa** Lam. now occurs as a rampant weed near Evergreen. It is a biennial with pinnatifid leaves and purple or white flowers. The phyllaries are fringed, dark-tipped, with a short terminal spine.

Page 235. A close relative, **Mentzelia sinuata** (Rydb.) Hill, first described from the Boulder area, has been found to be distinctly different from **M. speciosa** by having broader (1-3 cm wide) sinuate-margined leaves (in **M. speciosa** up to 1 cm wide and pinnatifid-dentate). **M. sinuata** has nine pairs of chromosomes compared with ten in **M. speciosa**.

Page 269. The European **Lysimachia vulgaris** L.., formerly cultivated in North Boulder, is now well-established on the floodplain of Boulder Creek. It differs from **L. ciliata** by having the flowers in open terminal cymes.

Page 303. **Galium verum** L., Yellow Bedstraw, is an introduced European weedy perennial now established near Boulder. It is a tall plant with masses of bright yellow flowers and narrowly linear leaves usually six at a node.

Page 357. The mistletoe on Pinyon Pine (stems olive-green to brownish), according to Hawksworth and Wiens, is **A. divaricatum** Engelm., that on Limber and Bristlecone Pine (stems yellowish green) is **A. cyanocarpum** Coulter & Nelson. **A. campylopodum** is a species of the far west and does not occur in Colorado.

Page 430. **Juncus vaseyi** Engelm. has been collected near Eldora, Boulder County. It differs from **J. confusus** by having the seeds provided with long tails and by having terete leaves with just a shallow groove on the upper side. It is probably generally distributed but overlooked in the subalpine.

METRIC CONVERSION TABLE
FOR COLORADO ALTITUDES

COLORADO ALTITUDES

feet	=	meters
3000		914
3100		944
3300		1006
3500		1067
3700		1128
3900		1189
4000		1219
4100		1250
4300		1311
4500		1372
4700		1433
4900		1494
5000		1524
5100		1554
5300		1615
5500		1676
5700		1737
5900		1798
6000		1829
6100		1859
6300		1920
6500		1981
6700		2042
6900		2103
7000		2134
7100		2164
7300		2225
7500		2286
7700		2347
7900		2408
8000		2438
8100		2469
8300		2530
8500		2591
8700		2652
8900		2713
9000		2743
9100		2774
9300		2835
9500		2896
9700		2957
9900		3018
10000		3048
10100		3078
10300		3139
10500		3200
10700		3261
10900		3322
11000		3353
11100		3383
11300		3444
11500		3505
11700		3566
11900		3627
12000		3658
12100		3688
12300		3749
12500		3810
12700		3871
12900		3932
13000		3962
13100		3993
13300		4054
13500		4115
13700		4176
13900		4237
14000		4267
14100		4298
14300		4350
14500		4420

To convert feet to
meters, multiply by
.3048

ALTITUDES OF COLORADO TOWNS IN METERS

Alamosa	2300
Aspen	2411
Boulder	1631
Buena Vista	2377
Castle Rock	1885
Cheyenne Wells	1258
Colorado Springs	1798
Cortez	1889
Craig	1882
Delta	1518
Denver	1609
Durango	1983
Fairplay	2916
Fort Collins	1554
Glenwood Springs	1752
Grand Junction	1398
Gunnison	2348
Hot Sulphur Springs	2336
Julesburg	1057
Kremmling	2232
Leadville	3109
La Junta	1250
Lamar	1102
Limon	1609
Meeker	1902
Montrose	1774
Ouray	2353
Pagosa Springs	2166
Pueblo	1423
Rangely	1585
Rifle	1622
Saguache	2377
Salida	2149
Silverton	2835
Steamboat Springs	2037
Trinidad	1828
Walden	2469
Walsenburg	1886
Wray	1072
Yuma	1258

ALTITUDES OF MOUNTAIN PASSES IN METERS

Apishapa	3354
Berthoud	3448
Cochetopa	3058
Cottonwood	3696
Cucharas	3046
Cumbres	3055
Douglas	2520
Fremont	3450
Gore	2903
Hoosier	3518
Independence	3687
Kenosha	3048
La Manga	3118
La Veta	2860
Lizard Head	3116
Loveland	3655
McClure	2896
Milner	3279
Molas	3325
Monarch	3448
Rabbit Ears	2950
Raton	2388
Red Mountain	3358
Slumgullion	3463
Trail Ridge	3713
Trout Creek	2849
Vail	3232
Wilkerson	2934
Wolf Creek	3307
Yellow Jacket	2347

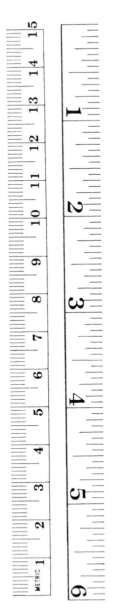

METRIC SYSTEM TABLE
1 mm. = approx. 1/25 of an inch
10 mm. = 1 cm. (approx. 2/5 of an inch)
10 cm. = 1 dm. (approx. 4 inches)
10 dm. = 1 m. (approx. 40 inches)

Cover Photo by Roberts
Primula parryi, PARRY PRIMROSE